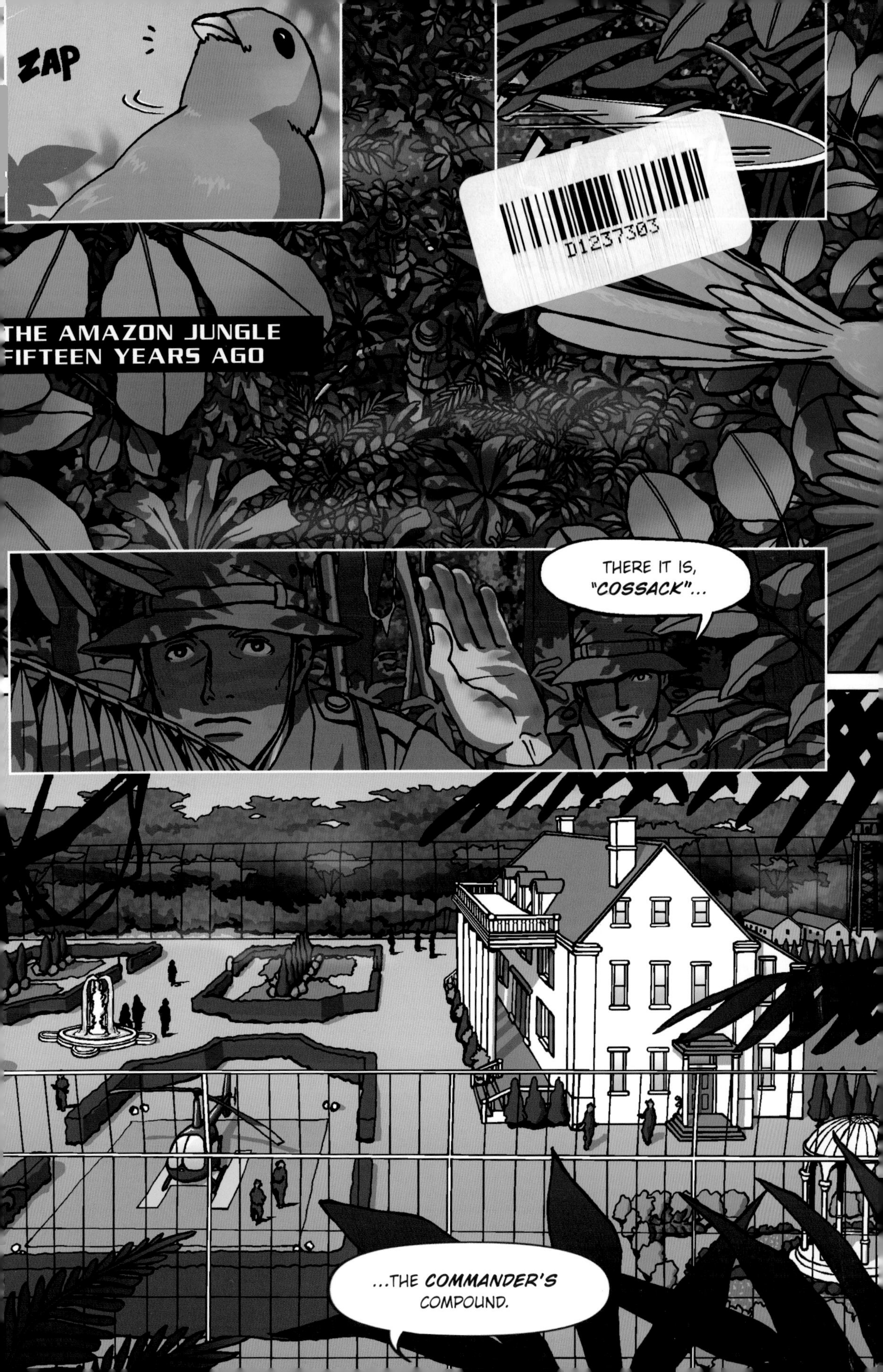
ZAP
THE AMAZON JUNGLE
FIFTEEN YEARS AGO
THERE IT IS, "COSSACK"...
...THE COMMANDER'S COMPOUND.

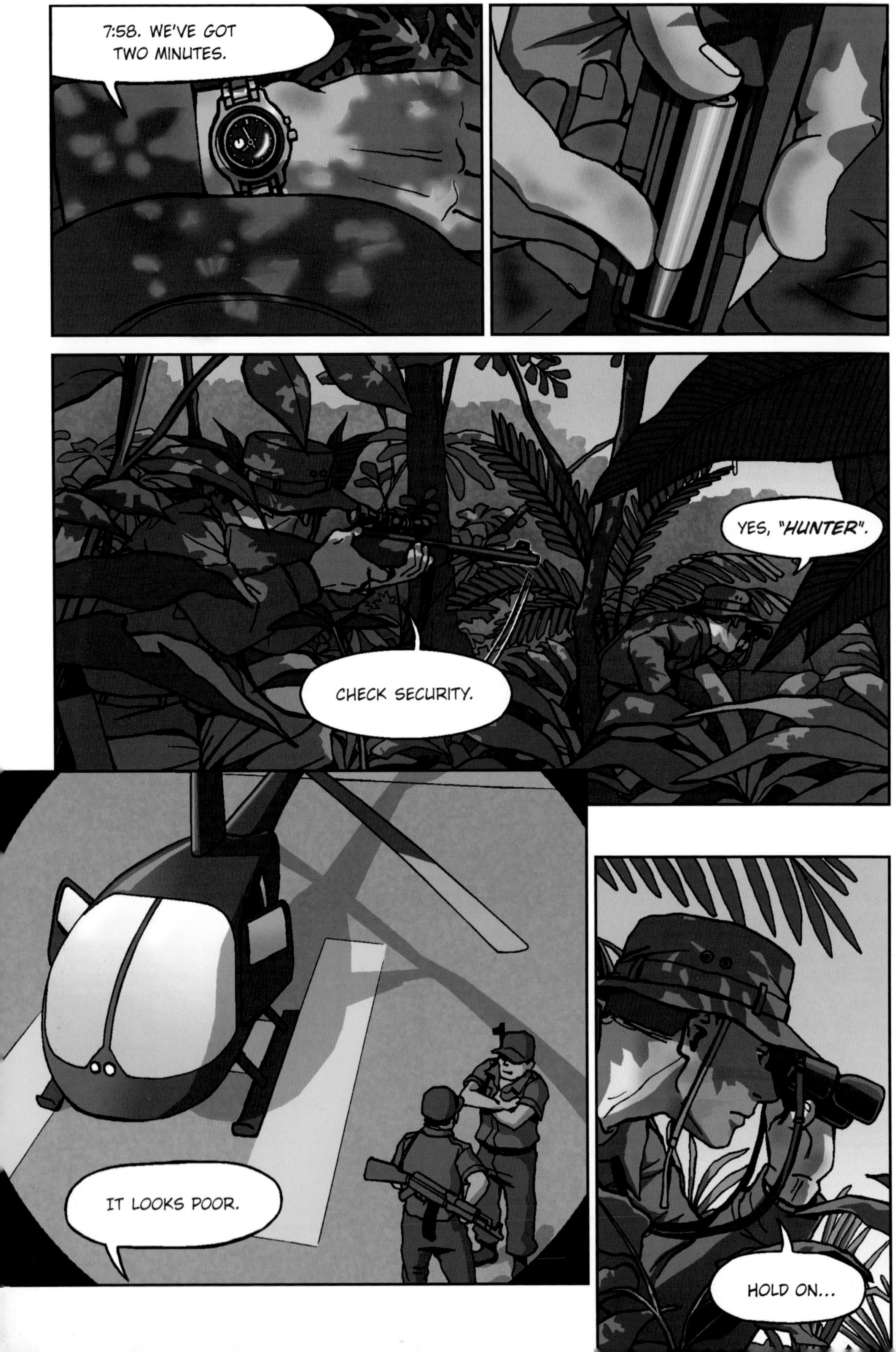
7:58. WE'VE GOT TWO MINUTES.
YES, "HUNTER".
CHECK SECURITY.
IT LOOKS POOR.
HOLD ON...

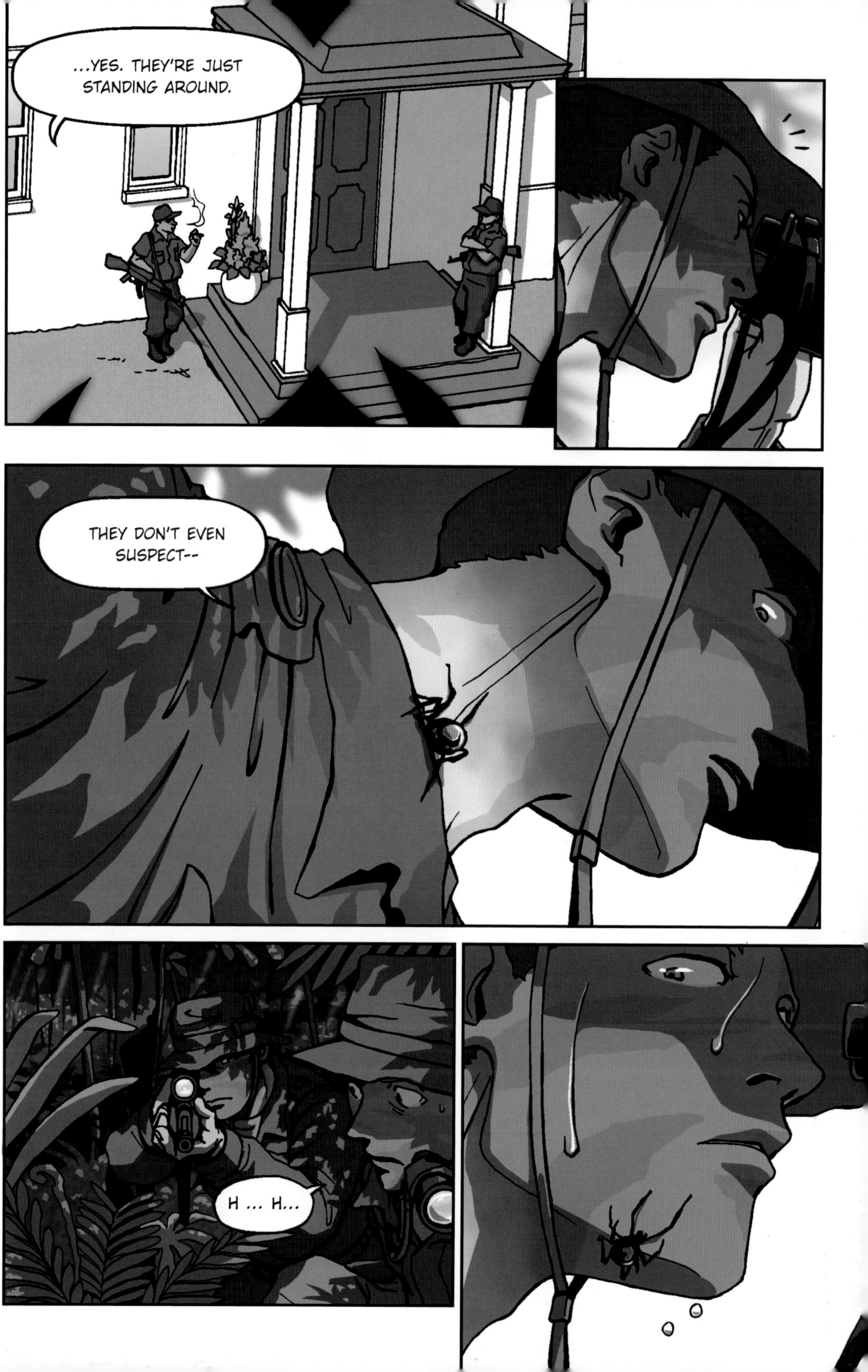
...YES. THEY'RE JUST STANDING AROUND.
THEY DON'T EVEN SUSPECT--
H ... H...

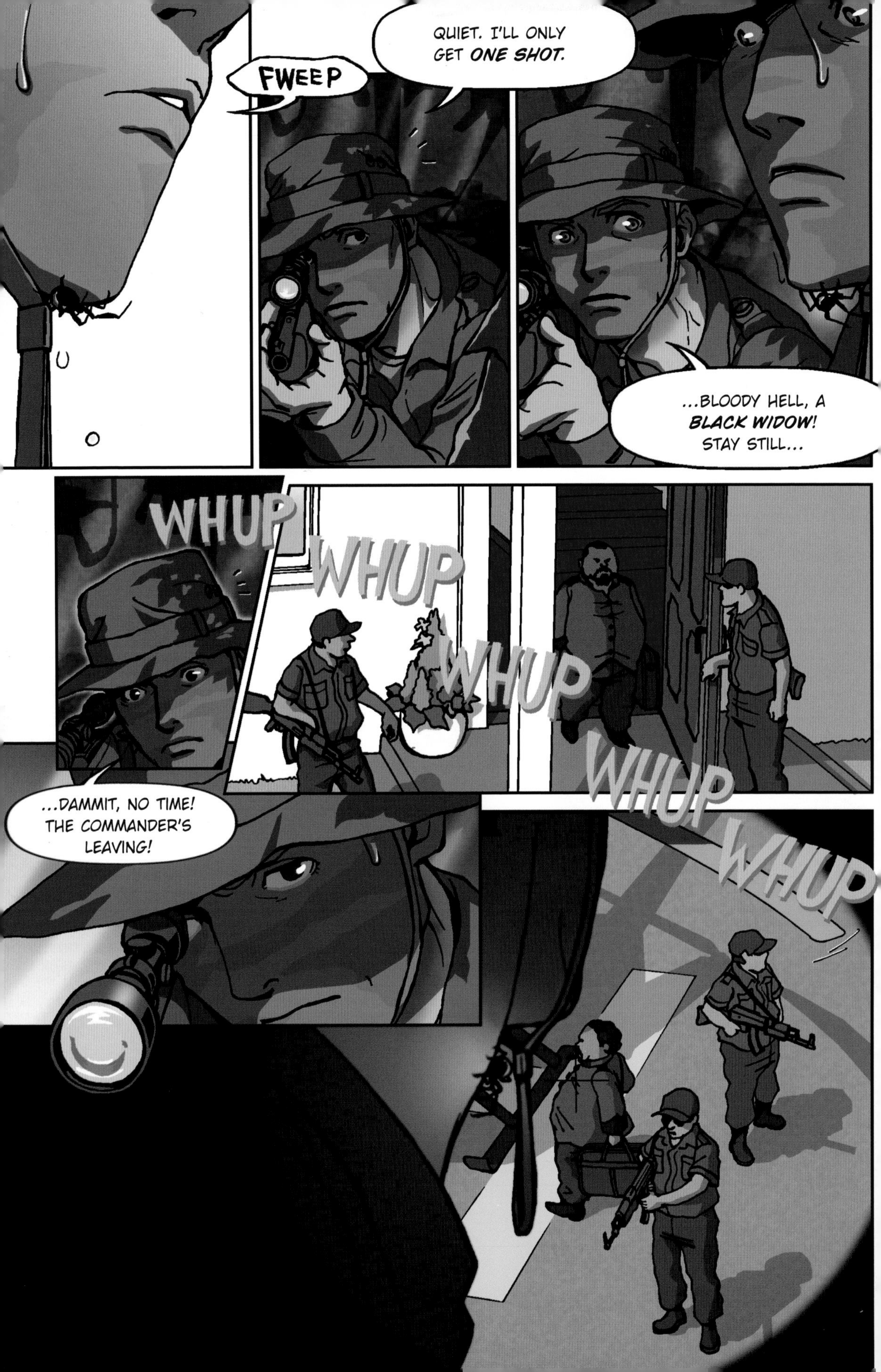

FWEEP
QUIET. I'LL ONLY GET ONE SHOT.
...BLOODY HELL, A BLACK WIDOW! STAY STILL...
WHUP
WHUP
WHUP
WHUP
...DAMMIT, NO TIME! THE COMMANDER'S LEAVING!
WHUP

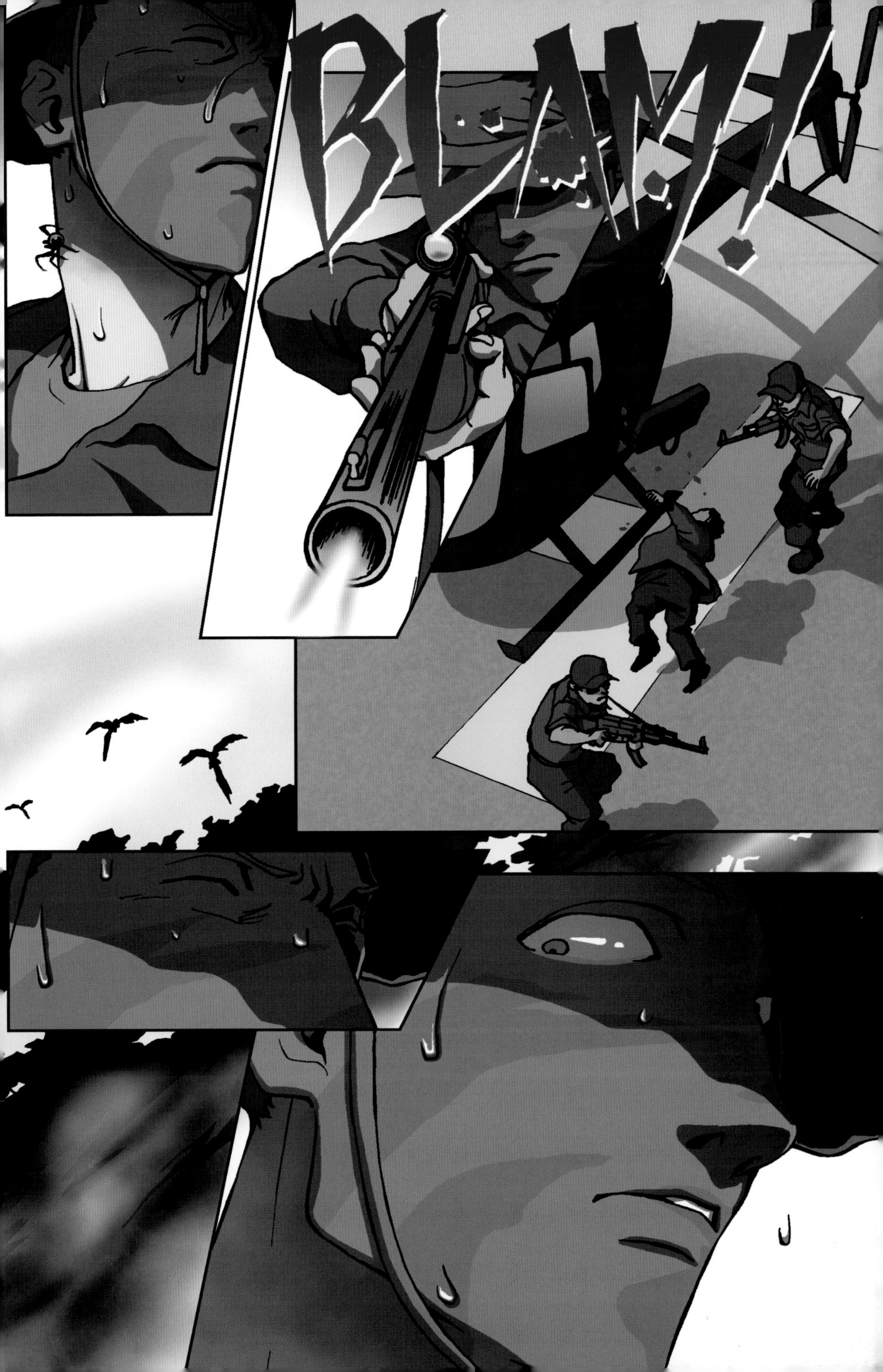
BLAM!

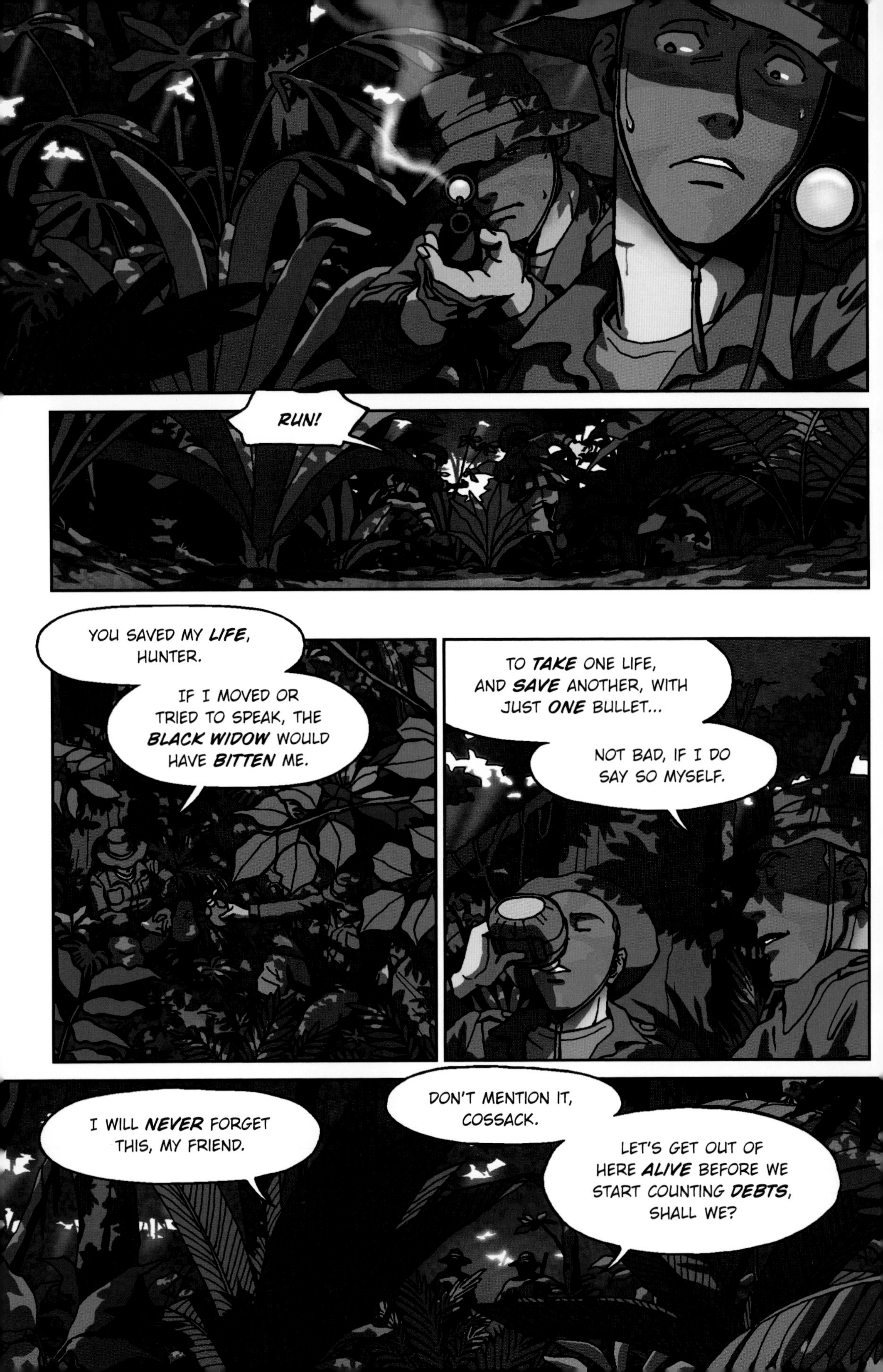
RUN!
YOU SAVED MY LIFE, HUNTER.
IF I MOVED OR TRIED TO SPEAK, THE BLACK WIDOW WOULD HAVE BITTEN ME.
TO TAKE ONE LIFE, AND SAVE ANOTHER, WITH JUST ONE BULLET...
NOT BAD, IF I DO SAY SO MYSELF.
I WILL NEVER FORGET THIS, MY FRIEND.
DON'T MENTION IT, COSSACK.
LET'S GET OUT OF HERE ALIVE BEFORE WE START COUNTING DEBTS, SHALL WE?

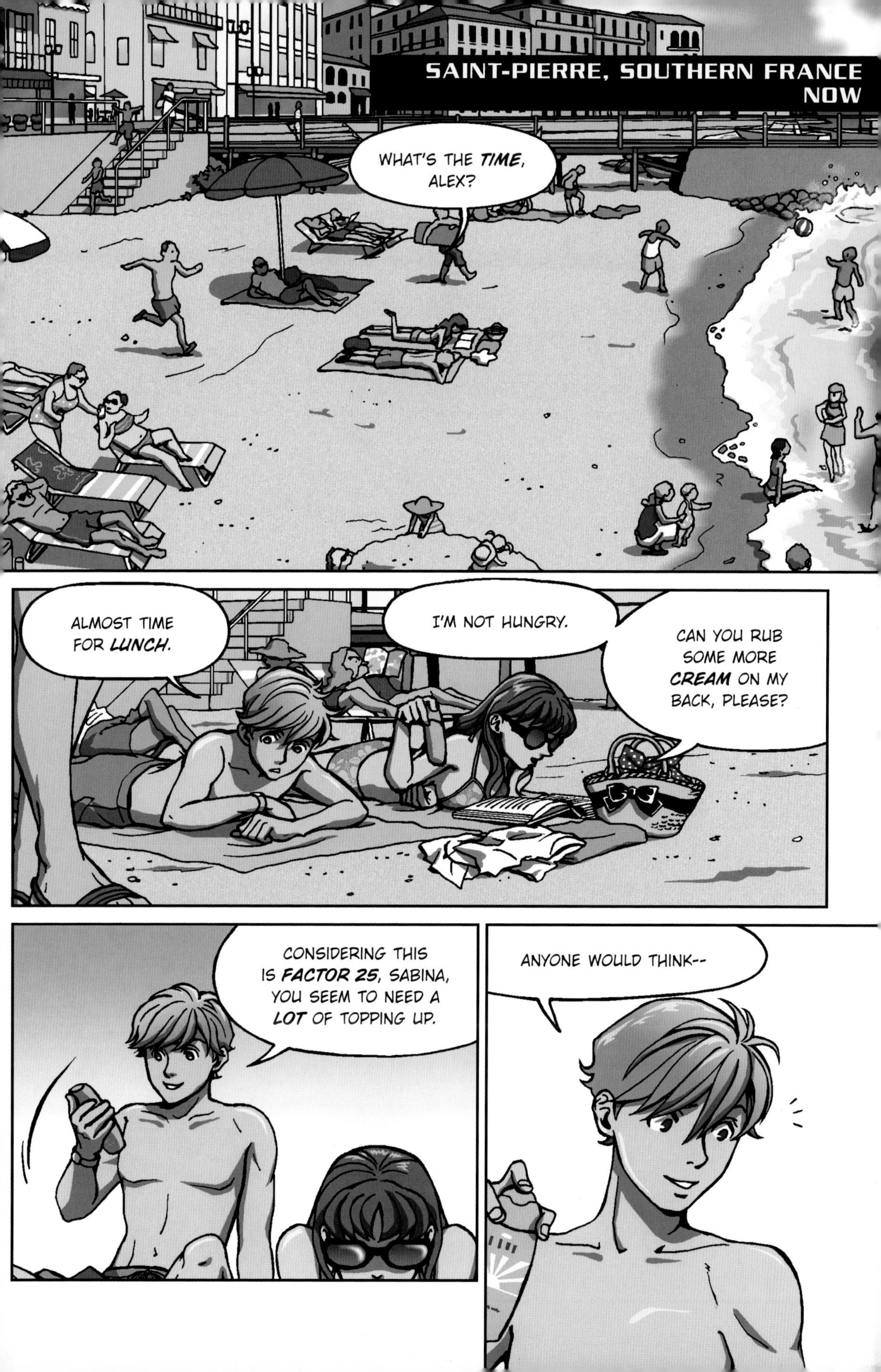
SAINT-PIERRE, SOUTHERN FRANCE
NOW
WHAT'S THE *TIME*, ALEX?
ALMOST TIME FOR *LUNCH*.
I'M NOT HUNGRY.
CAN YOU RUB SOME MORE *CREAM* ON MY BACK, PLEASE?
CONSIDERING THIS IS *FACTOR 25*, SABINA, YOU SEEM TO NEED A *LOT* OF TOPPING UP.
ANYONE WOULD THINK--

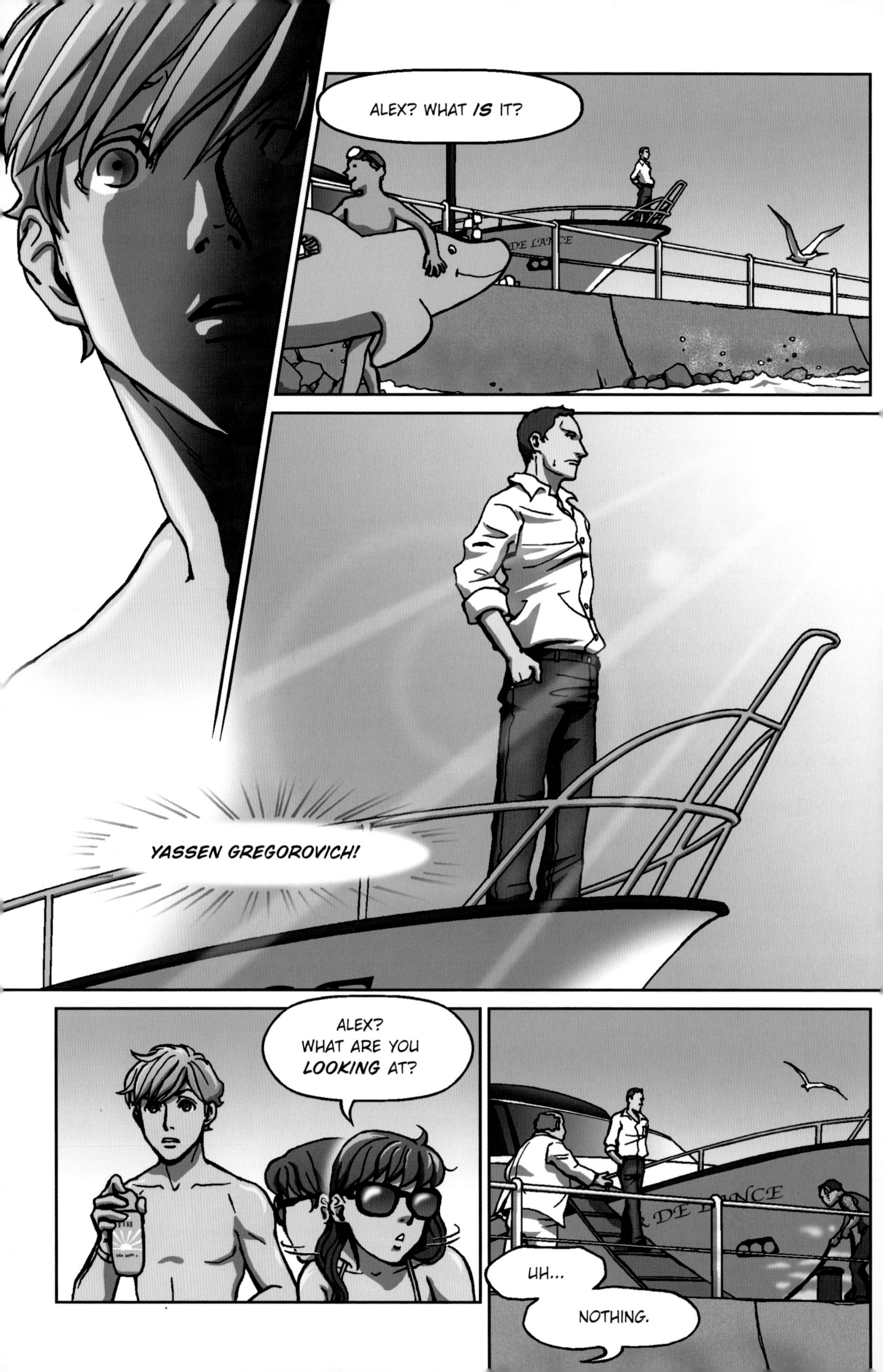
ALEX? WHAT IS IT?
DE LANCE
YASSEN GREGOROVICH!
ALEX? WHAT ARE YOU LOOKING AT?
DE LANCE
UH...
NOTHING.

JUST WAIT THERE, SAB. I NEED A *DRINK*.

I'VE GOT *WATER* RIGHT HERE.

NO, I ... I WANT A *COKE*.

I'LL ONLY BE A MINUTE.

HMPH. *BOYS!*

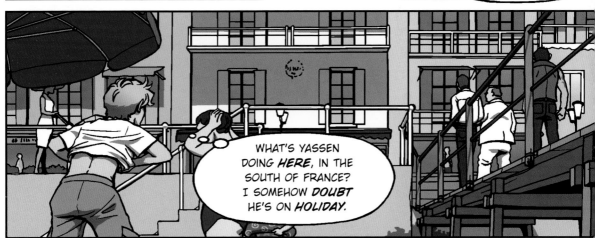

WHAT'S YASSEN DOING *HERE*, IN THE SOUTH OF FRANCE? I SOMEHOW *DOUBT* HE'S ON *HOLIDAY*.

THEY'RE HEADING INTO TOWN. I SHOULD *FOLLOW* THEM...

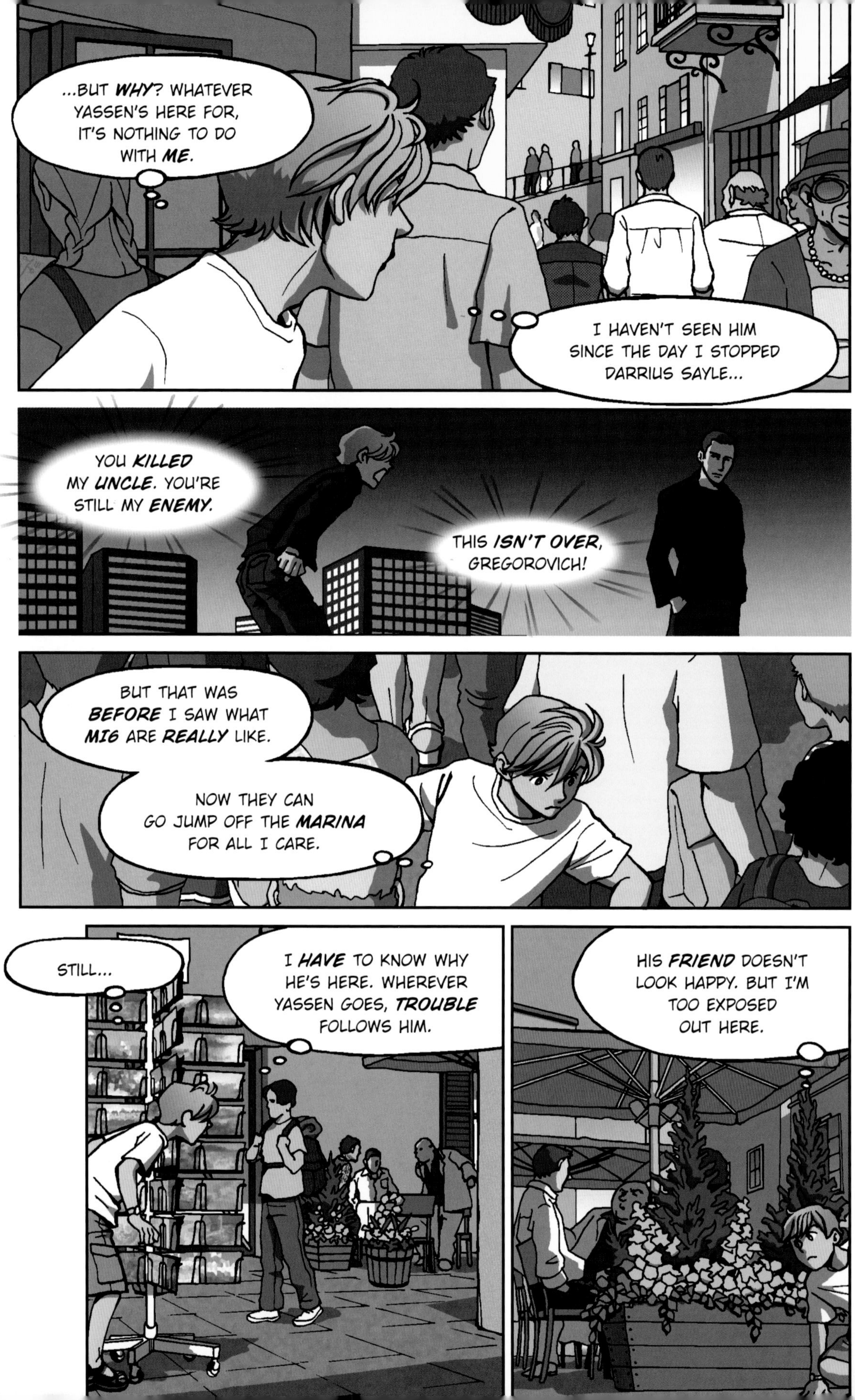
...BUT WHY? WHATEVER YASSEN'S HERE FOR, IT'S NOTHING TO DO WITH ME.
I HAVEN'T SEEN HIM SINCE THE DAY I STOPPED DARRIUS SAYLE...
YOU KILLED MY UNCLE. YOU'RE STILL MY ENEMY.
THIS ISN'T OVER, GREGOROVICH!
BUT THAT WAS BEFORE I SAW WHAT MI6 ARE REALLY LIKE.
NOW THEY CAN GO JUMP OFF THE MARINA FOR ALL I CARE.
STILL...
I HAVE TO KNOW WHY HE'S HERE. WHEREVER YASSEN GOES, TROUBLE FOLLOWS HIM.
HIS FRIEND DOESN'T LOOK HAPPY. BUT I'M TOO EXPOSED OUT HERE.

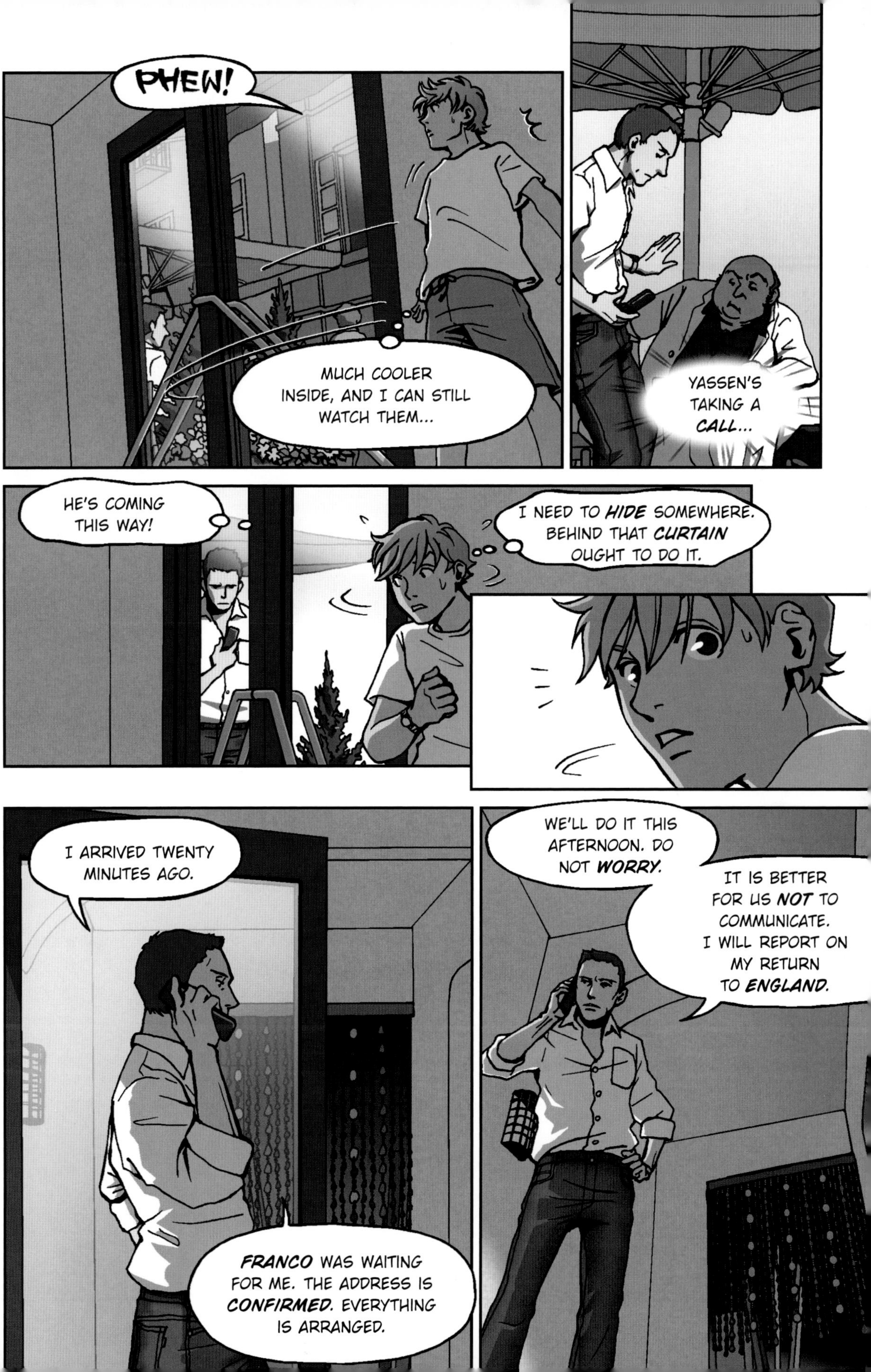
PHEW!
MUCH COOLER INSIDE, AND I CAN STILL WATCH THEM...
YASSEN'S TAKING A *CALL*...
HE'S COMING THIS WAY!
I NEED TO *HIDE* SOMEWHERE. BEHIND THAT *CURTAIN* OUGHT TO DO IT.
I ARRIVED TWENTY MINUTES AGO.
FRANCO WAS WAITING FOR ME. THE ADDRESS IS *CONFIRMED*. EVERYTHING IS ARRANGED.
WE'LL DO IT THIS AFTERNOON. DO NOT *WORRY*.
IT IS BETTER FOR US *NOT* TO COMMUNICATE. I WILL REPORT ON MY RETURN TO *ENGLAND*.

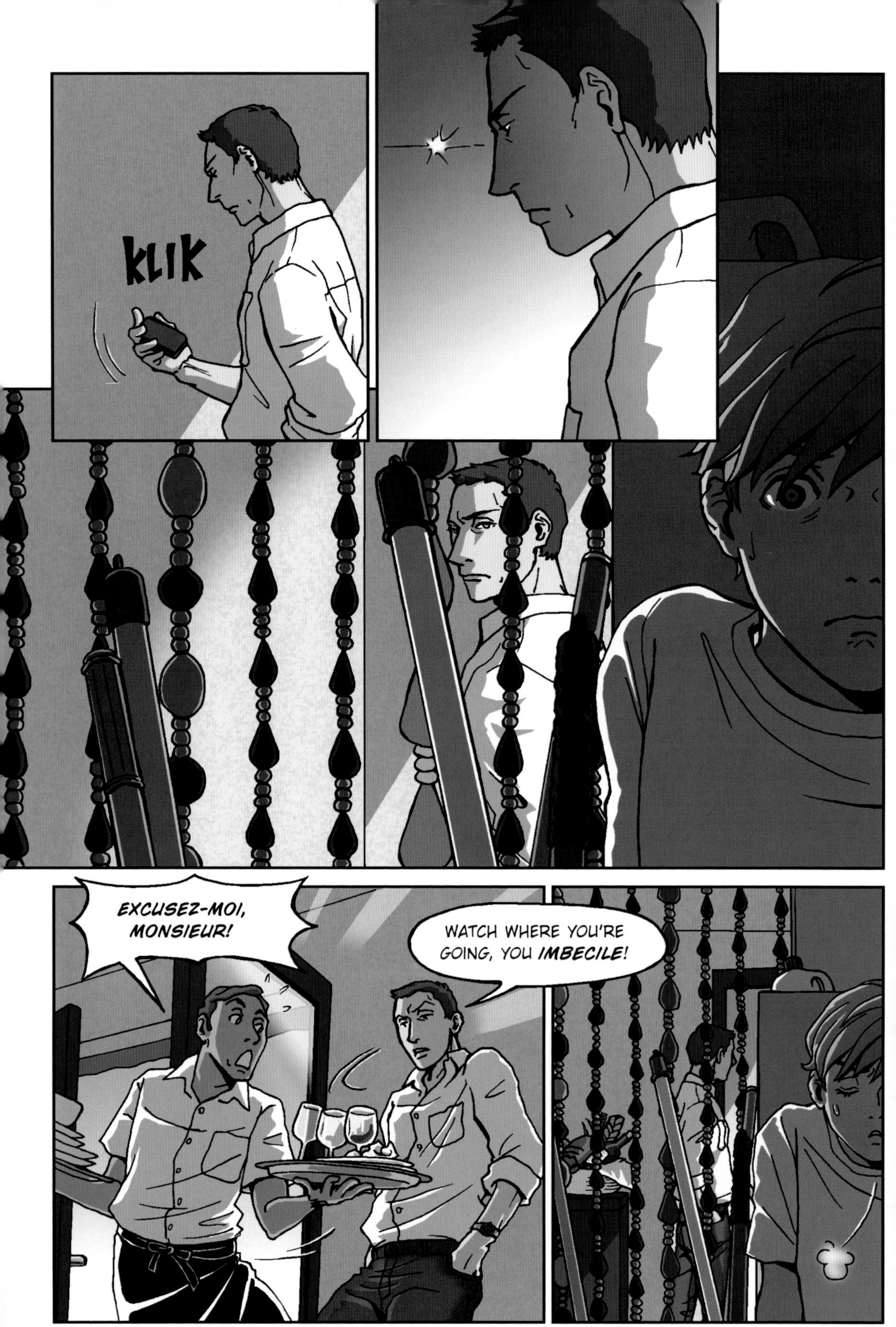
KLIK
EXCUSEZ-MOI, MONSIEUR!
WATCH WHERE YOU'RE GOING, YOU *IMBECILE*!

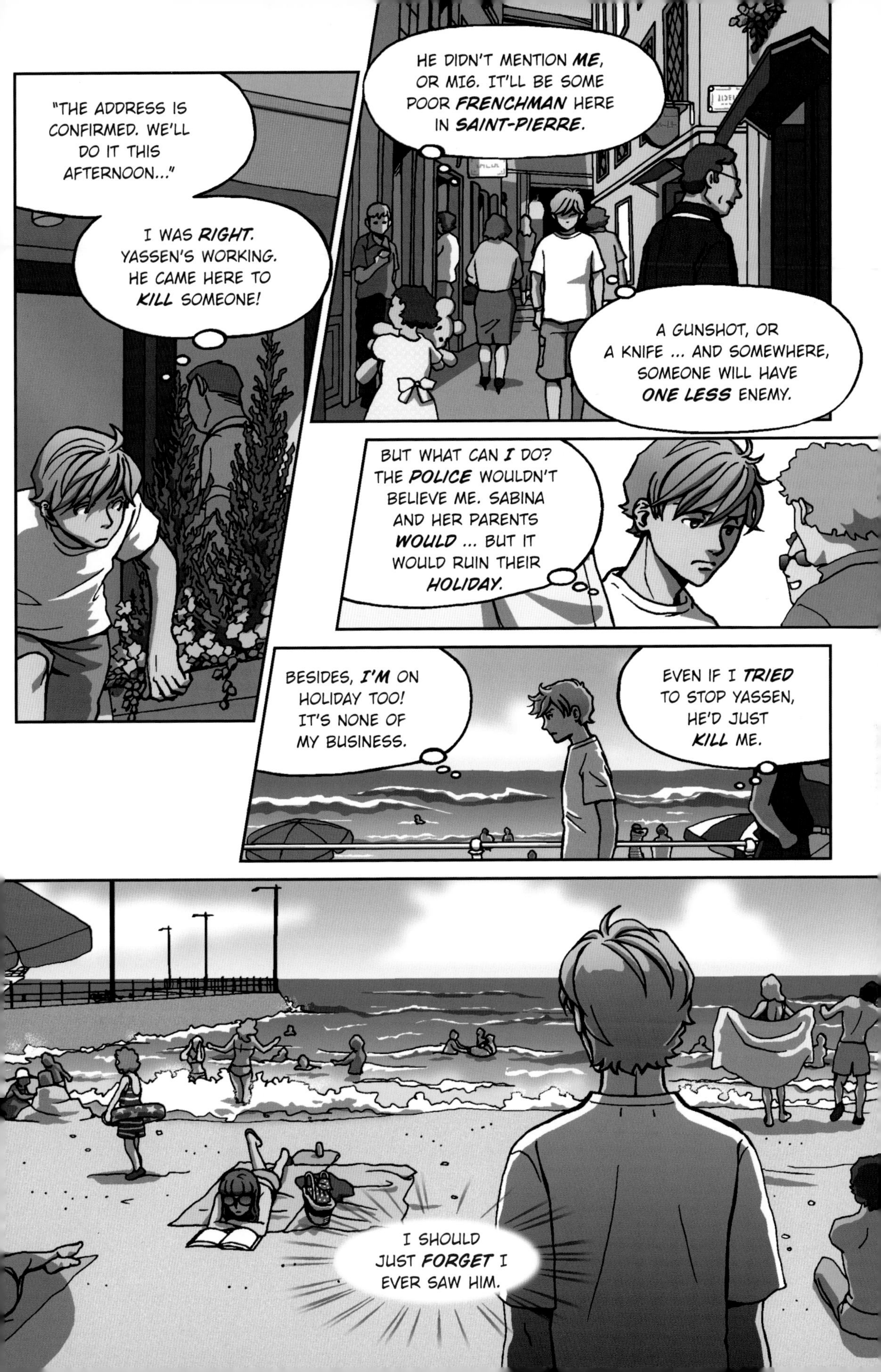
"THE ADDRESS IS CONFIRMED. WE'LL DO IT THIS AFTERNOON..."
I WAS RIGHT. YASSEN'S WORKING. HE CAME HERE TO KILL SOMEONE!
HE DIDN'T MENTION ME, OR MI6. IT'LL BE SOME POOR FRENCHMAN HERE IN SAINT-PIERRE.
A GUNSHOT, OR A KNIFE ... AND SOMEWHERE, SOMEONE WILL HAVE ONE LESS ENEMY.
BUT WHAT CAN I DO? THE POLICE WOULDN'T BELIEVE ME. SABINA AND HER PARENTS WOULD ... BUT IT WOULD RUIN THEIR HOLIDAY.
BESIDES, I'M ON HOLIDAY TOO! IT'S NONE OF MY BUSINESS.
EVEN IF I TRIED TO STOP YASSEN, HE'D JUST KILL ME.
I SHOULD JUST FORGET I EVER SAW HIM.

OH, GOD, LOOK AT *THAT* ONE!

FOUR OUT OF TWENTY, *MAX.*

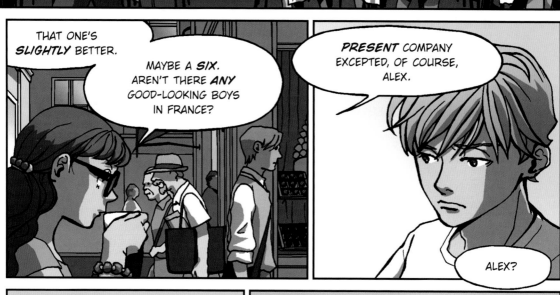

THAT ONE'S *SLIGHTLY* BETTER.

MAYBE A *SIX.* AREN'T THERE *ANY* GOOD-LOOKING BOYS IN FRANCE?

PRESENT COMPANY EXCEPTED, OF COURSE, ALEX.

ALEX?

SORRY, I WAS *MILES* AWAY.

SO WHAT DO *I* SCORE ON YOUR FAMOUS *BOY SCALE*, THEN?

TWELVE AND A HALF. BUT *DON'T* WORRY. ANOTHER TEN YEARS AND YOU'LL BE *PERFECT.*

COME ON, LET'S GET *OUT* OF HERE.

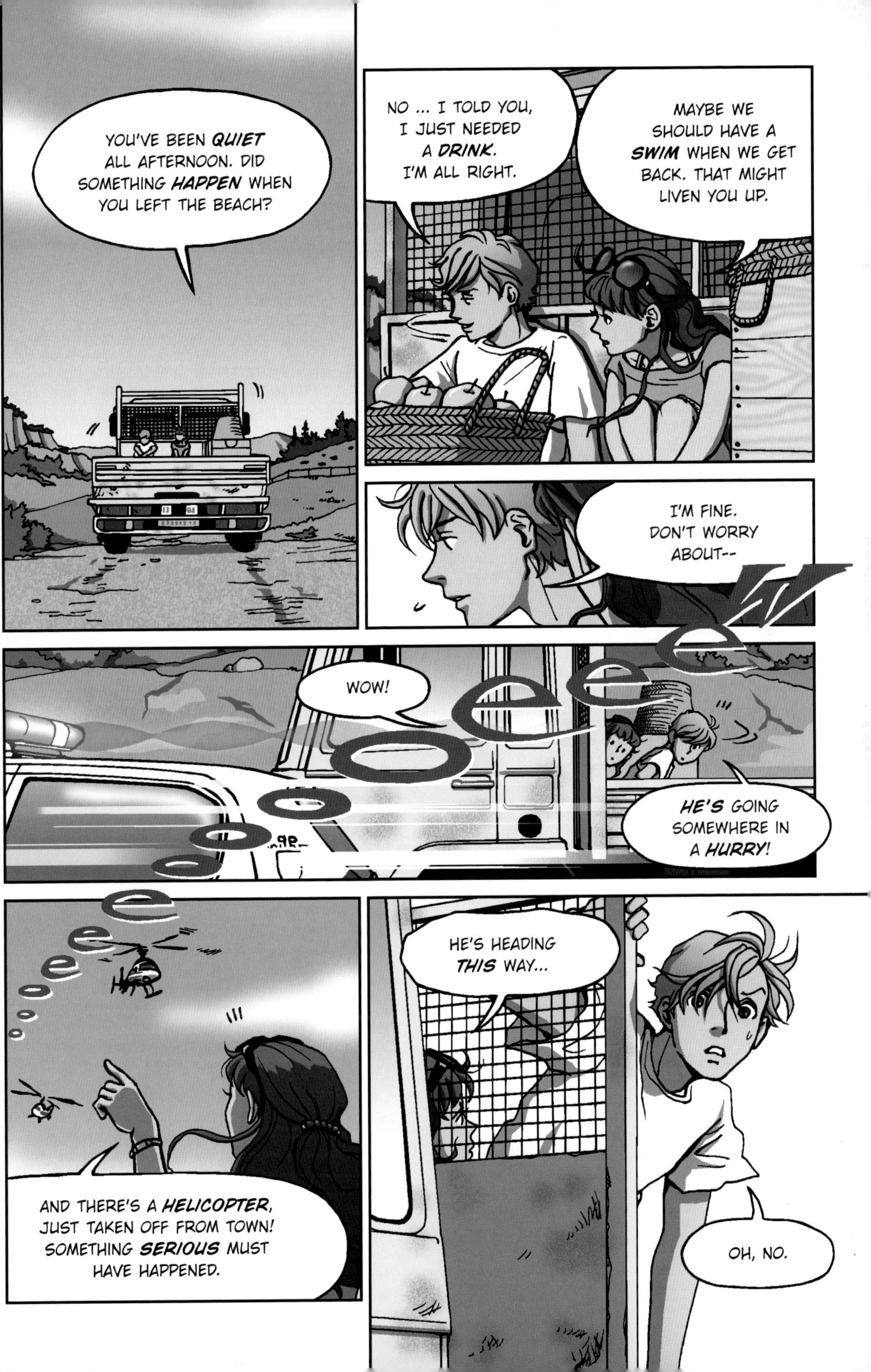
YOU'VE BEEN QUIET ALL AFTERNOON. DID SOMETHING HAPPEN WHEN YOU LEFT THE BEACH?
NO ... I TOLD YOU, I JUST NEEDED A DRINK. I'M ALL RIGHT.
MAYBE WE SHOULD HAVE A SWIM WHEN WE GET BACK. THAT MIGHT LIVEN YOU UP.
I'M FINE. DON'T WORRY ABOUT--
WOW!
HE'S GOING SOMEWHERE IN A HURRY!
HE'S HEADING THIS WAY...
AND THERE'S A HELICOPTER, JUST TAKEN OFF FROM TOWN! SOMETHING SERIOUS MUST HAVE HAPPENED.
OH, NO.

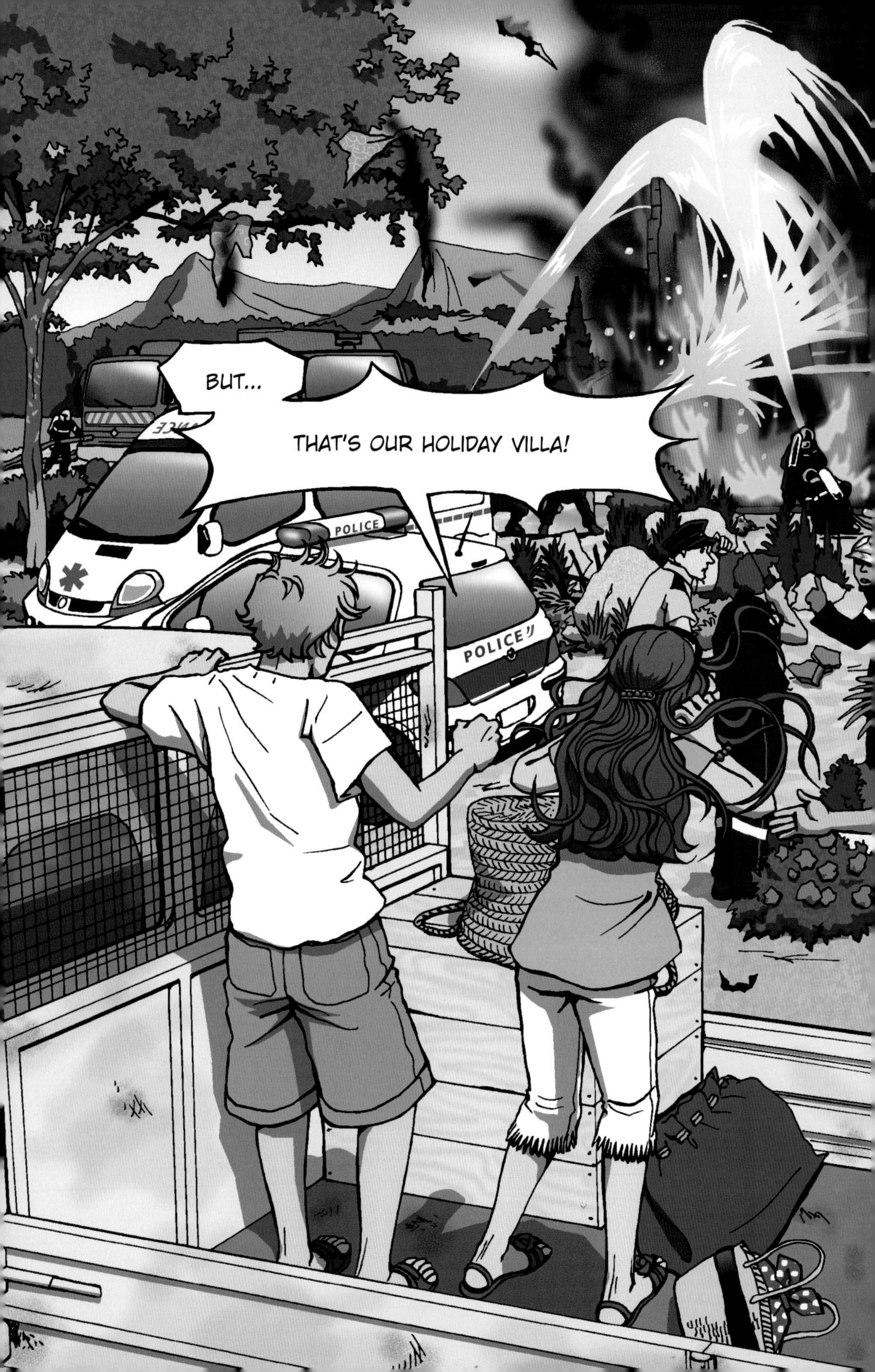
BUT...
THAT'S OUR HOLIDAY VILLA!
POLICE
POLICE

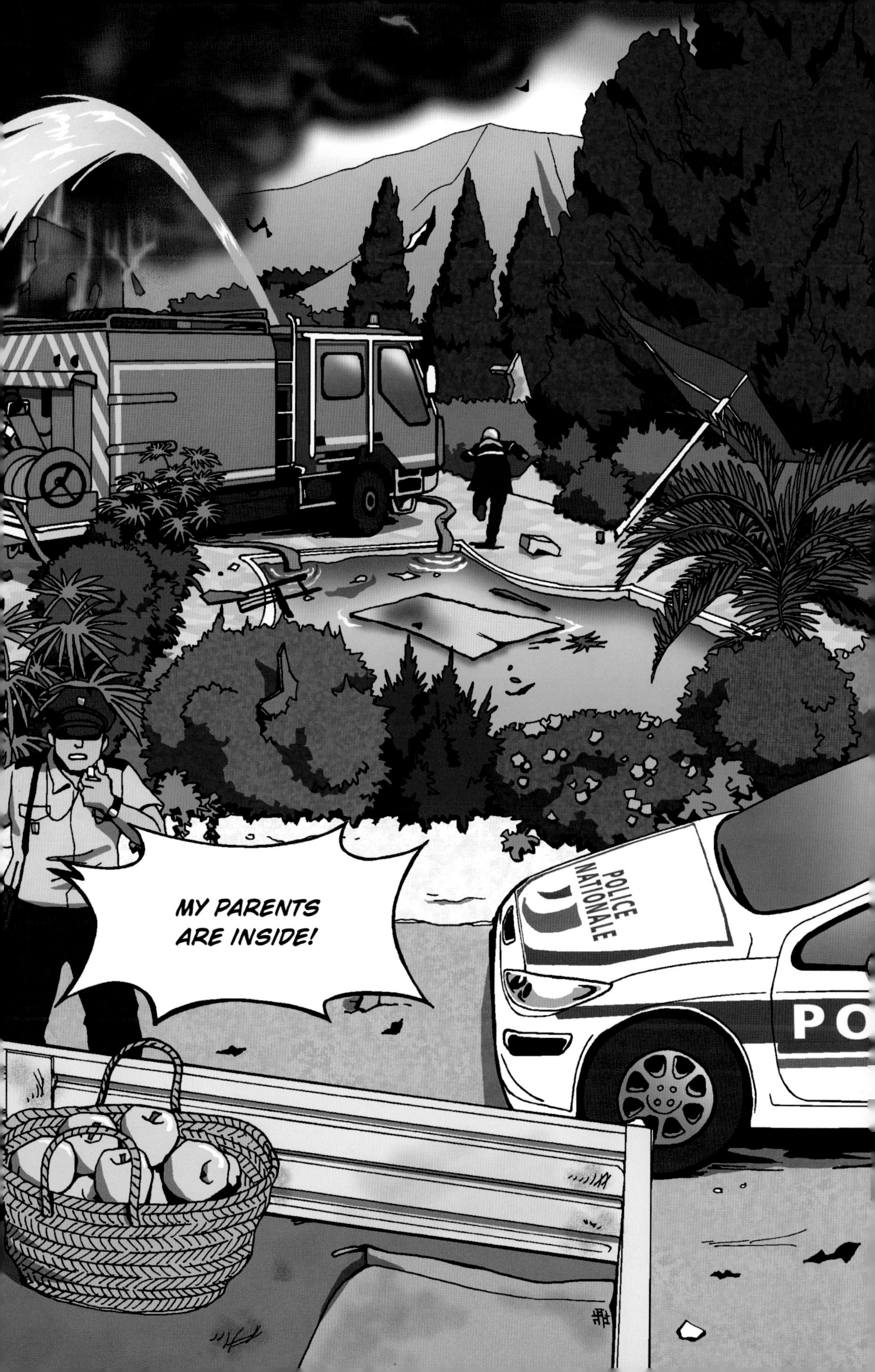
MY PARENTS ARE INSIDE!
POLICE NATIONALE
PO

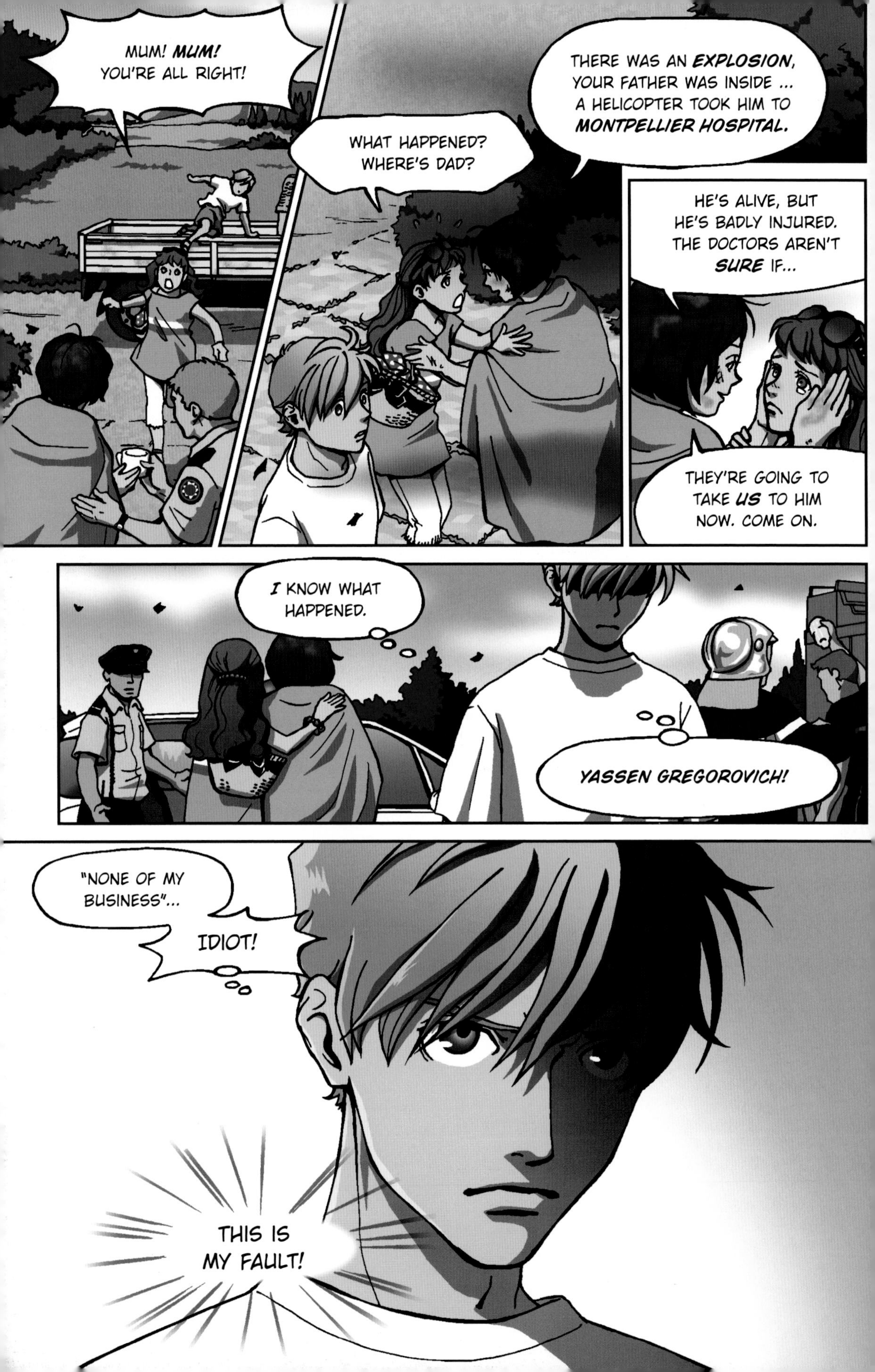
MUM! MUM! YOU'RE ALL RIGHT!
WHAT HAPPENED? WHERE'S DAD?
THERE WAS AN EXPLOSION, YOUR FATHER WAS INSIDE ... A HELICOPTER TOOK HIM TO MONTPELLIER HOSPITAL.
HE'S ALIVE, BUT HE'S BADLY INJURED. THE DOCTORS AREN'T SURE IF...
THEY'RE GOING TO TAKE US TO HIM NOW. COME ON.
I KNOW WHAT HAPPENED.
YASSEN GREGOROVICH!
"NONE OF MY BUSINESS"...
IDIOT!
THIS IS MY FAULT!

First published 2012 by Walker Books Ltd
87 Vauxhall Walk, London SE11 5HJ

4 6 8 10 9 7 5

Text and illustrations © 2012 Walker Books Ltd
Based on the original novel *Eagle Strike* © 2003 Stormbreaker Productions Ltd

Anthony Horowitz has asserted his moral rights.

Trademarks © 2003 Stormbreaker Productions Ltd
Alex Rider™, Boy with Torch Logo™, AR Logo™

This book has been typeset in Wild Words and Serpentine Bold

Printed in China

British Library Cataloguing in Publication Data:
a catalogue record for this book is available
from the British Library

ISBN 978-1-4063-1877-7

www.walker.co.uk

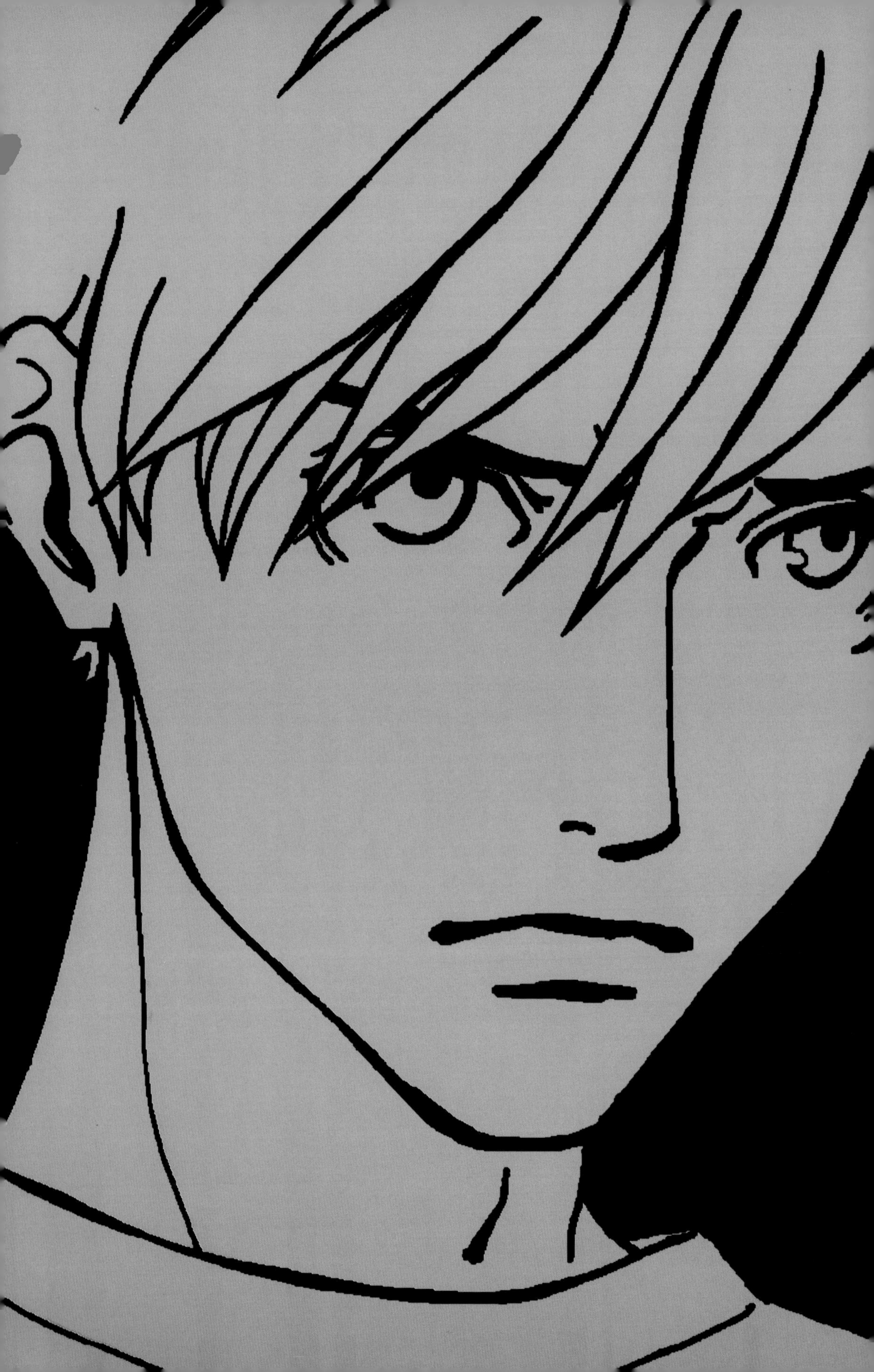

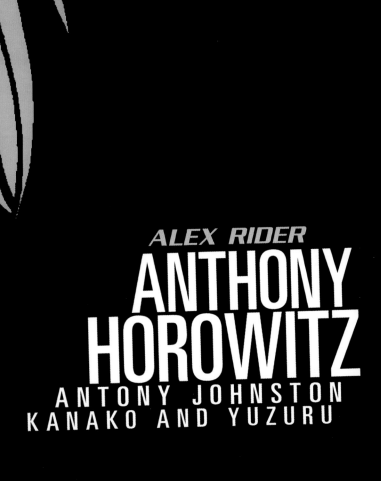

ALEX RIDER

ANTHONY HOROWITZ

ANTONY JOHNSTON
KANAKO AND YUZURU

THE GRAPHIC NOVEL

WALKER

EAGLE STRIKE

EXCUSEZ-MOI.
I **KNOW** WHO
DID THIS.

COMMENT?

THERE'S A BIG WHITE
YACHT AT THE JETTY
IN TOWN. YOU CAN'T
MISS IT.

ON BOARD IS A
MAN CALLED **YASSEN
GREGOROVICH.** YOU MUST
ARREST HIM BEFORE
HE CAN **ESCAPE.**

AH...

WAIT HERE,
PLEASE.

THEY **HAVE** TO
BELIEVE ME. ALL THEY
NEED TO **DO** IS CHECK OUT
THE YACHT.

HELLO,

WHAT'S THAT?

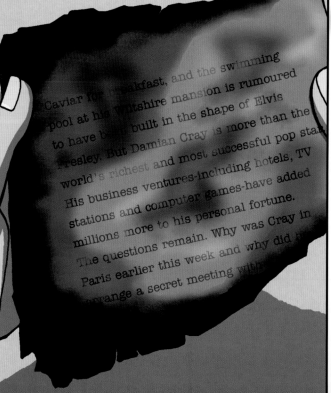

Caviar for breakfast, and the swimming
pool at his Wiltshire mansion is rumoured
to have been built in the shape of Elvis
Presley. But Damian Cray is more than the
world's richest and most successful pop star.
His business ventures-including hotels, TV
stations and computer games-have added
millions more to his personal fortune.
The questions remain. Why was Cray in
Paris earlier this week and why did he
arrange a secret meeting with

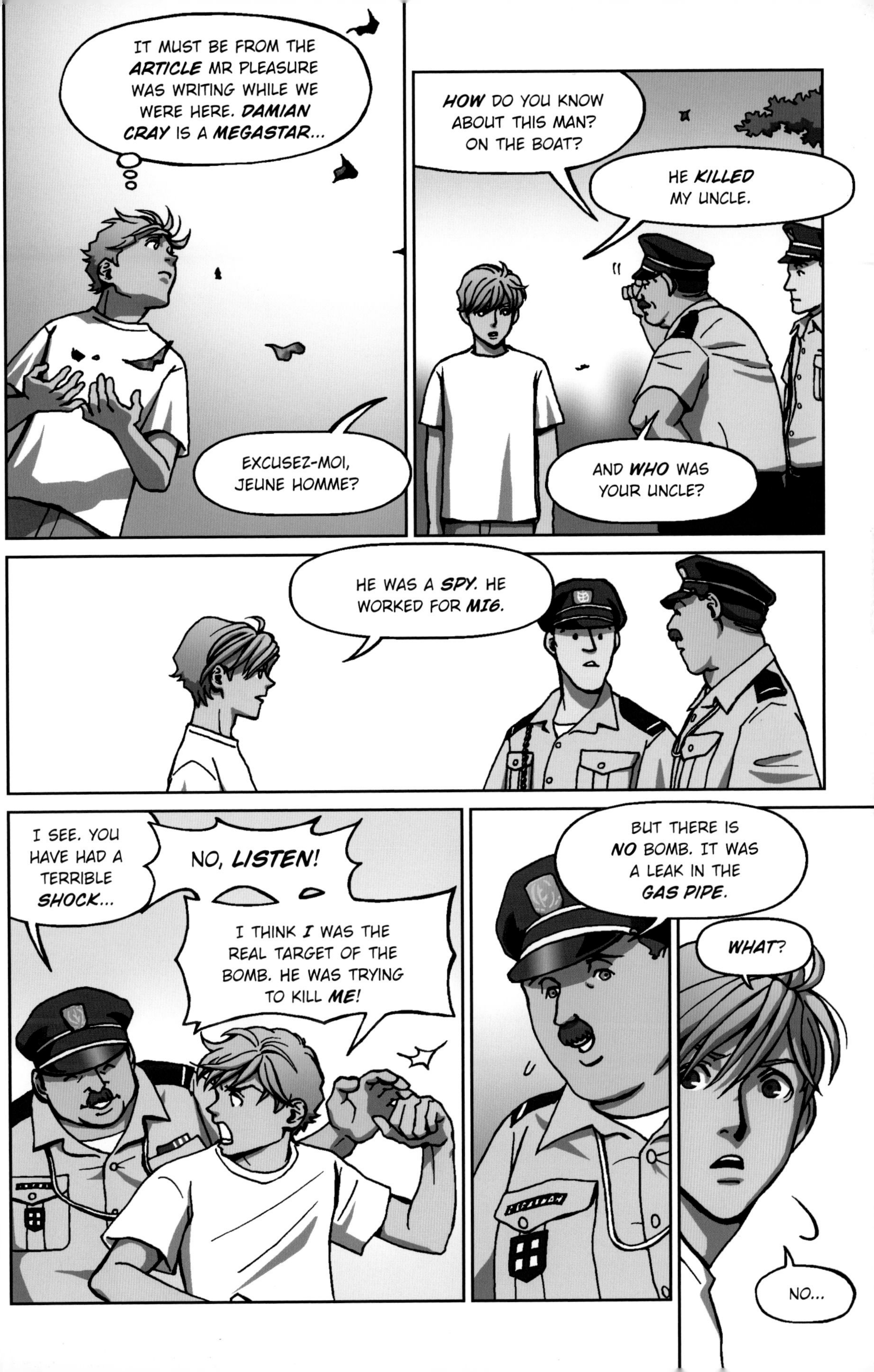
IT MUST BE FROM THE ARTICLE MR PLEASURE WAS WRITING WHILE WE WERE HERE. DAMIAN CRAY IS A MEGASTAR...
EXCUSEZ-MOI, JEUNE HOMME?
HOW DO YOU KNOW ABOUT THIS MAN? ON THE BOAT?
HE KILLED MY UNCLE.
AND WHO WAS YOUR UNCLE?
HE WAS A SPY. HE WORKED FOR MI6.
I SEE. YOU HAVE HAD A TERRIBLE SHOCK...
NO, LISTEN!
I THINK I WAS THE REAL TARGET OF THE BOMB. HE WAS TRYING TO KILL ME!
BUT THERE IS NO BOMB. IT WAS A LEAK IN THE GAS PIPE.
WHAT?
NO...

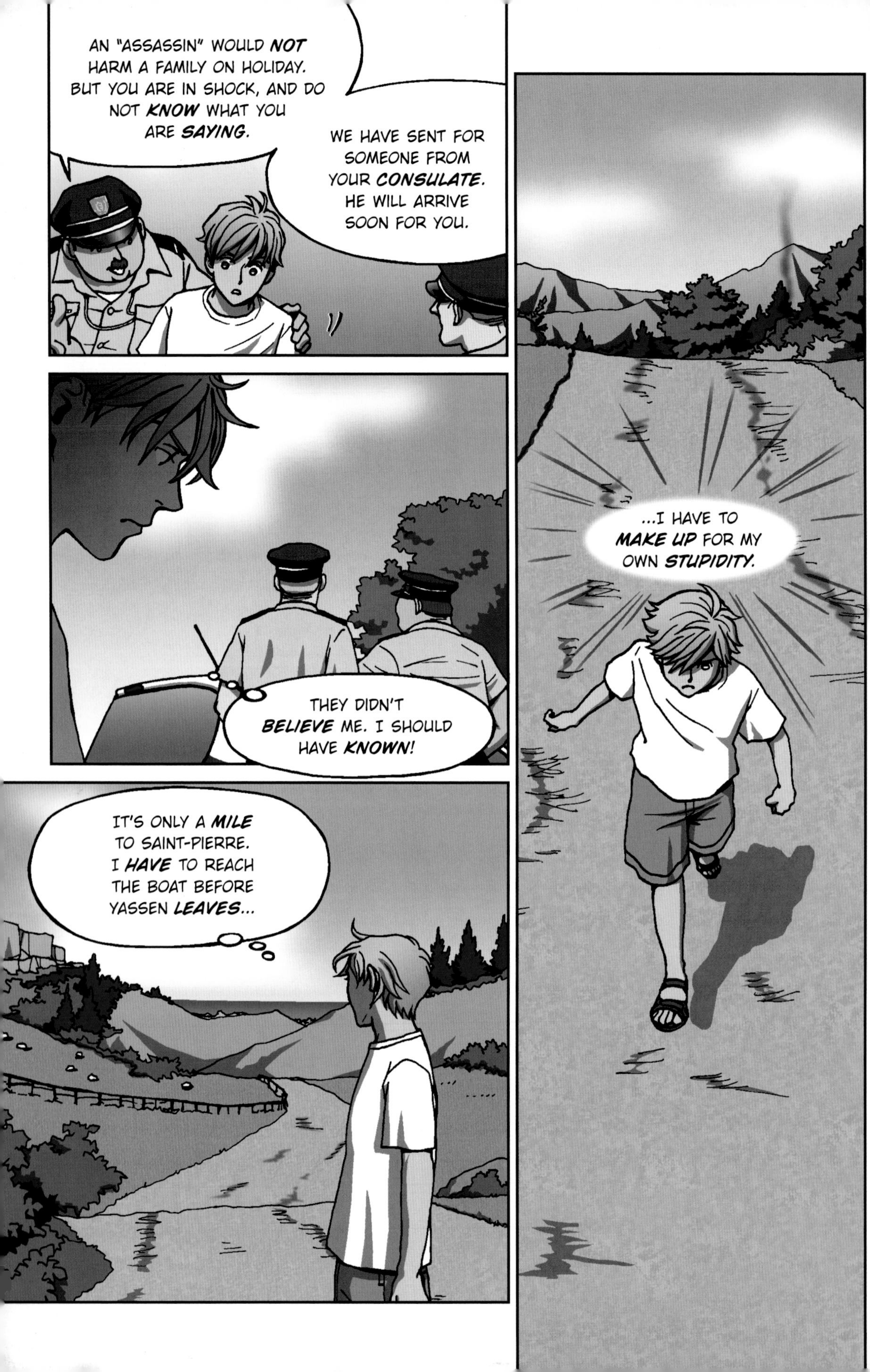
AN "ASSASSIN" WOULD NOT HARM A FAMILY ON HOLIDAY. BUT YOU ARE IN SHOCK, AND DO NOT KNOW WHAT YOU ARE SAYING.
WE HAVE SENT FOR SOMEONE FROM YOUR CONSULATE. HE WILL ARRIVE SOON FOR YOU.
THEY DIDN'T BELIEVE ME. I SHOULD HAVE KNOWN!
IT'S ONLY A MILE TO SAINT-PIERRE. I HAVE TO REACH THE BOAT BEFORE YASSEN LEAVES...
...I HAVE TO MAKE UP FOR MY OWN STUPIDITY.

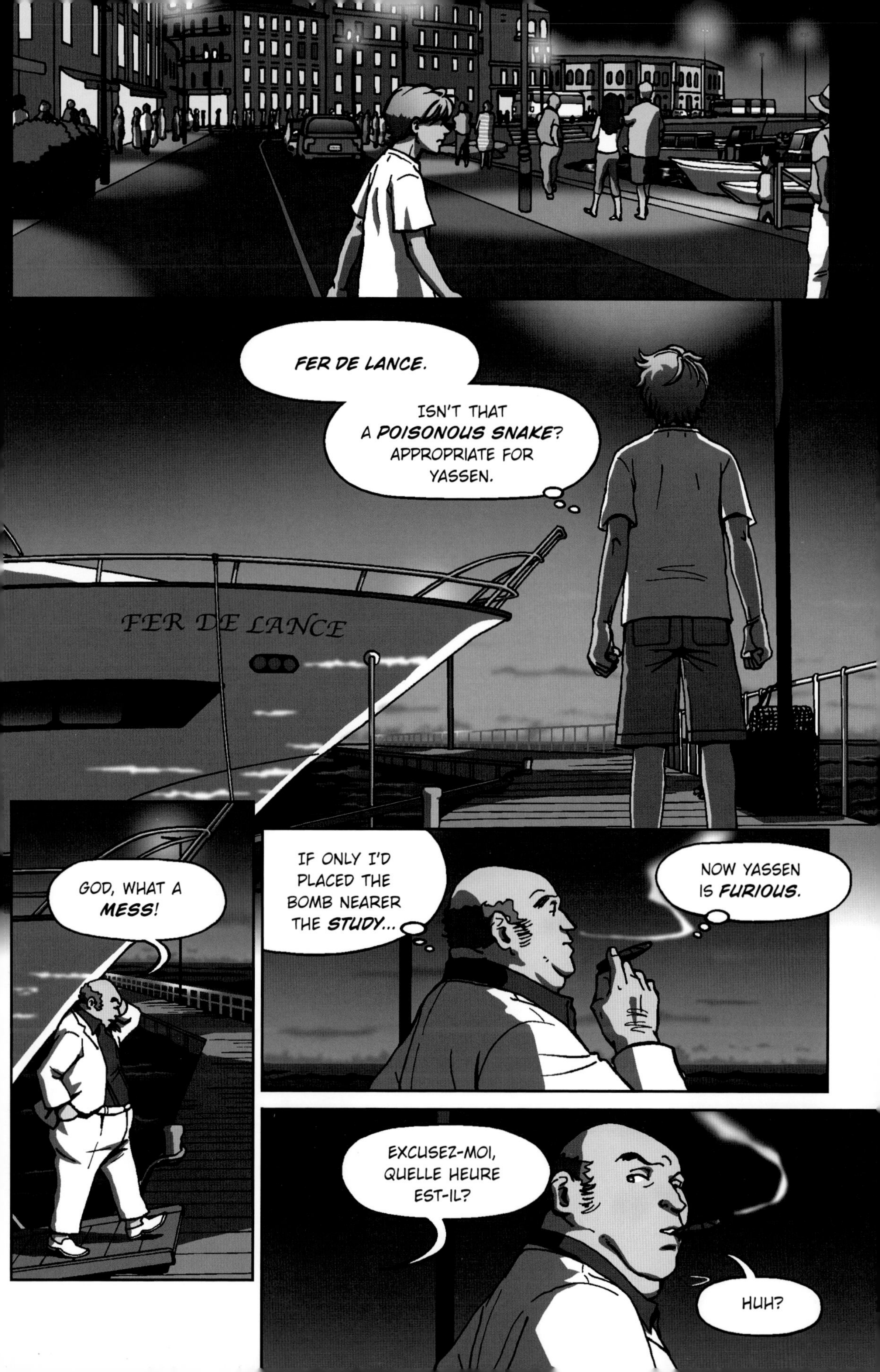
FER DE LANCE.
ISN'T THAT A POISONOUS SNAKE? APPROPRIATE FOR YASSEN.
FER DE LANCE
GOD, WHAT A MESS!
IF ONLY I'D PLACED THE BOMB NEARER THE STUDY...
NOW YASSEN IS FURIOUS.
EXCUSEZ-MOI, QUELLE HEURE EST-IL?
HUH?

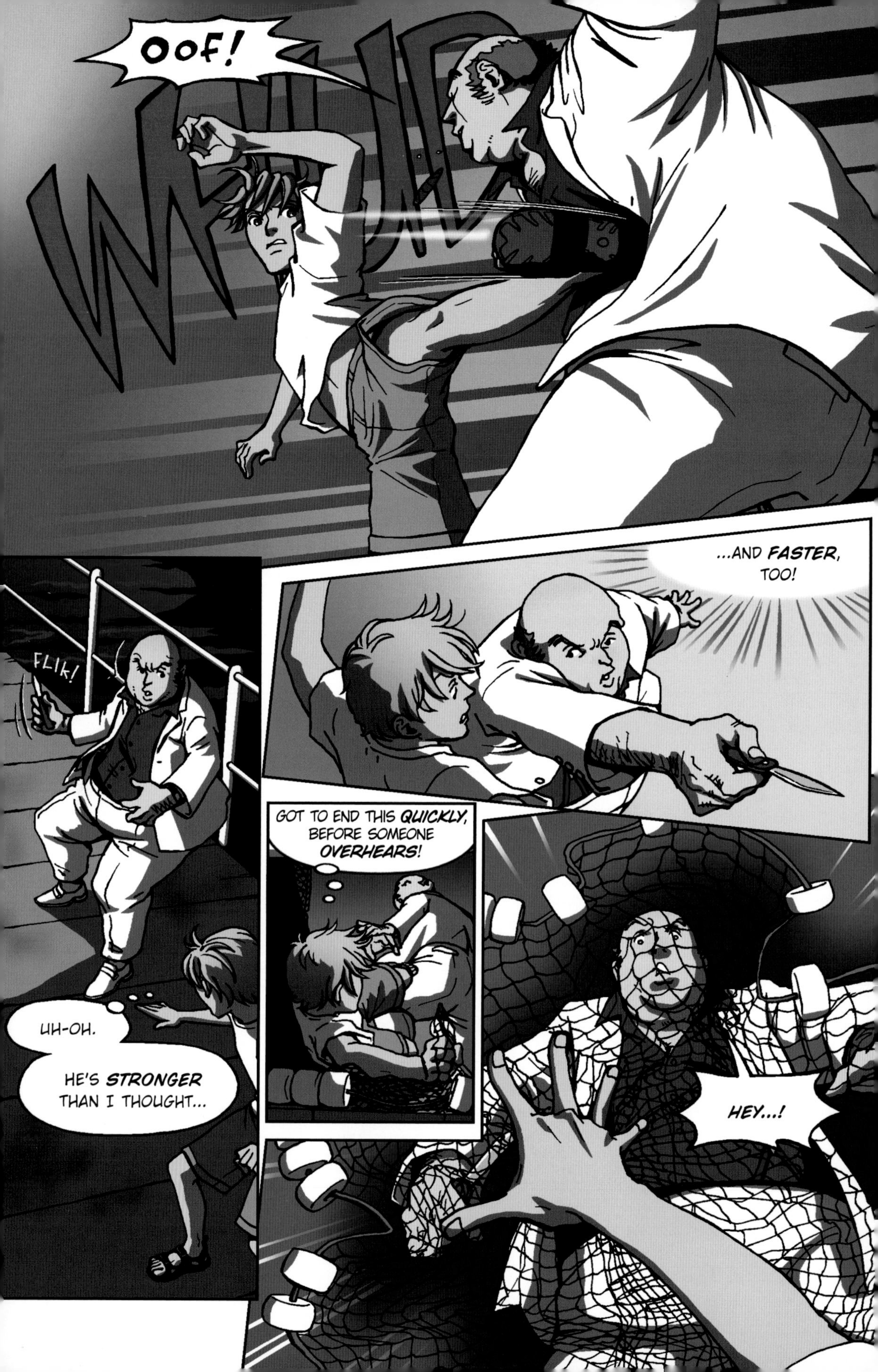
OOF!
WHUMP
...AND FASTER, TOO!
FLIK!
UH-OH.
HE'S STRONGER THAN I THOUGHT...
GOT TO END THIS QUICKLY, BEFORE SOMEONE OVERHEARS!
HEY...!

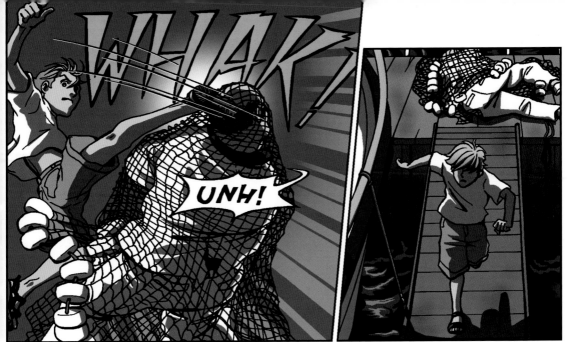

UNH!

HE MUST HAVE BEEN SITTING *HERE* BEFORE HE WENT OUT ON THE JETTY.

THAT *PHONE* LOOKS FAMILIAR.

IT'S THE ONE *YASSEN* USED IN THE RESTAURANT. LET'S SEE *WHO* HE WAS CALLING...

12:53
44-207-79460909

44 IS THE CODE FOR ENGLAND. AND *207* IS LONDON.

THIS IS THE NUMBER OF WHOEVER GAVE THE *ORDER!*

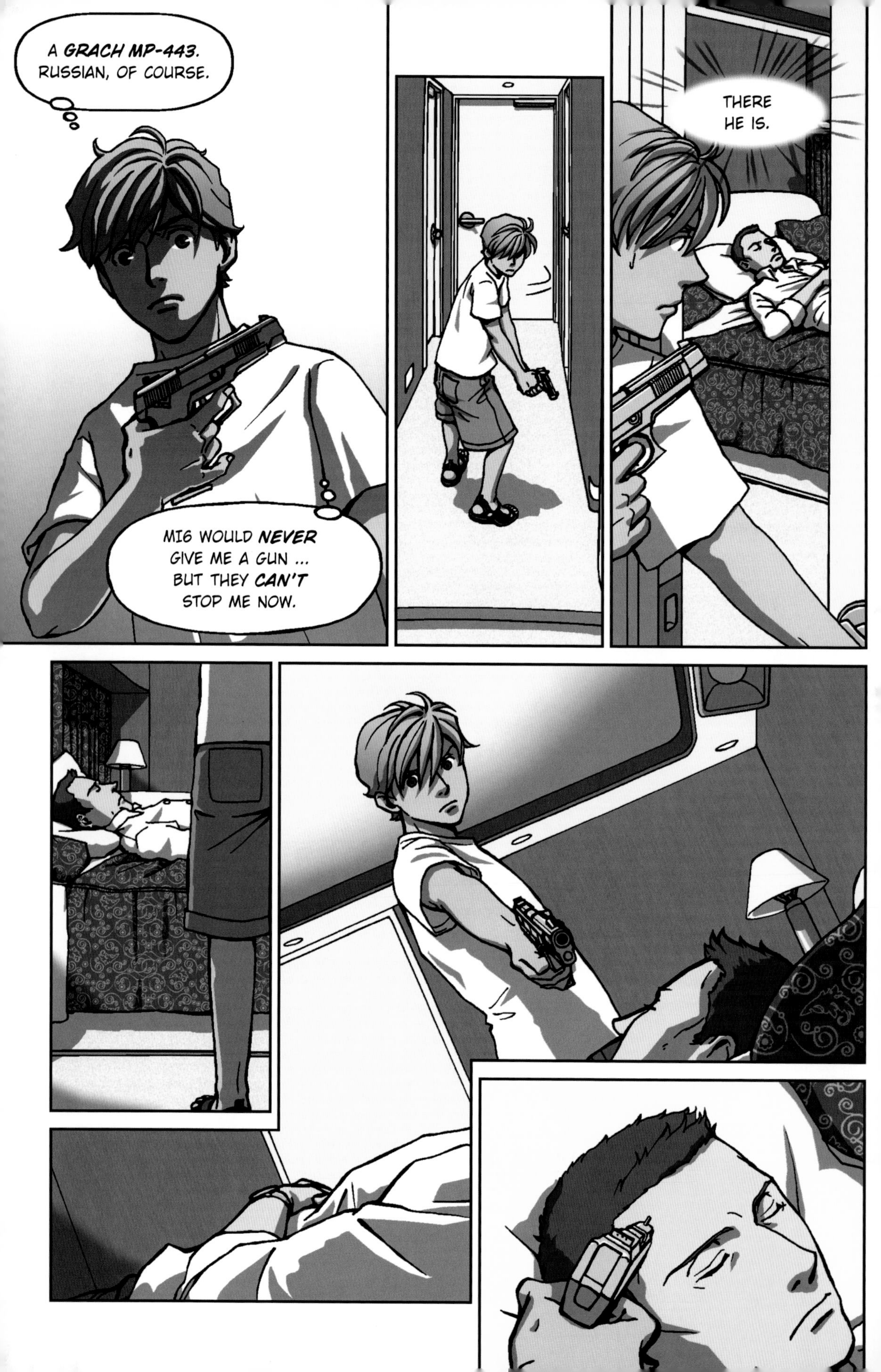
A GRACH MP-443. RUSSIAN, OF COURSE.
MI6 WOULD NEVER GIVE ME A GUN ... BUT THEY CAN'T STOP ME NOW.
THERE HE IS.

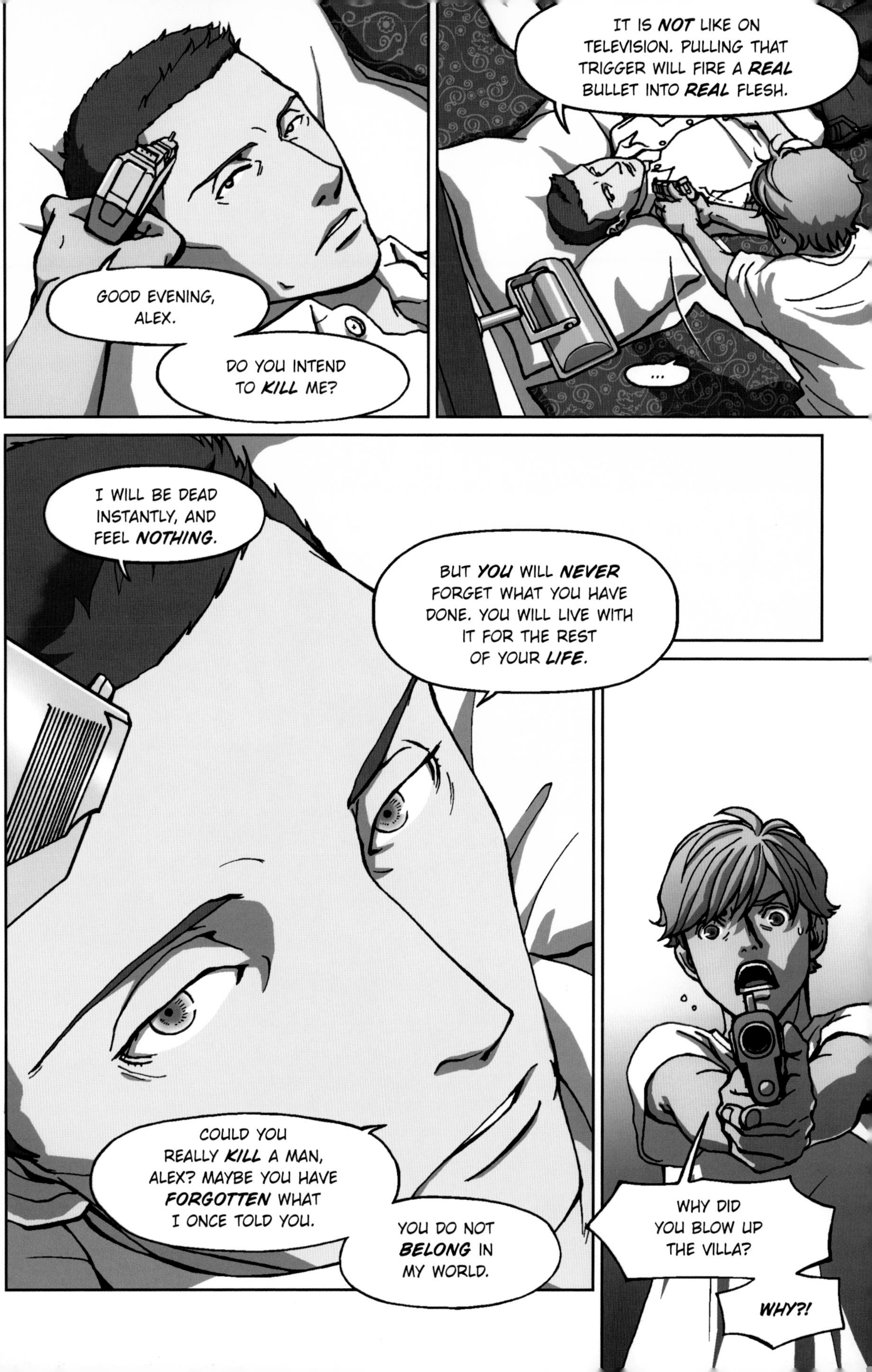
GOOD EVENING, ALEX.
DO YOU INTEND TO KILL ME?
IT IS NOT LIKE ON TELEVISION. PULLING THAT TRIGGER WILL FIRE A REAL BULLET INTO REAL FLESH.
...
I WILL BE DEAD INSTANTLY, AND FEEL NOTHING.
BUT YOU WILL NEVER FORGET WHAT YOU HAVE DONE. YOU WILL LIVE WITH IT FOR THE REST OF YOUR LIFE.
COULD YOU REALLY KILL A MAN, ALEX? MAYBE YOU HAVE FORGOTTEN WHAT I ONCE TOLD YOU.
YOU DO NOT BELONG IN MY WORLD.
WHY DID YOU BLOW UP THE VILLA?
WHY?!

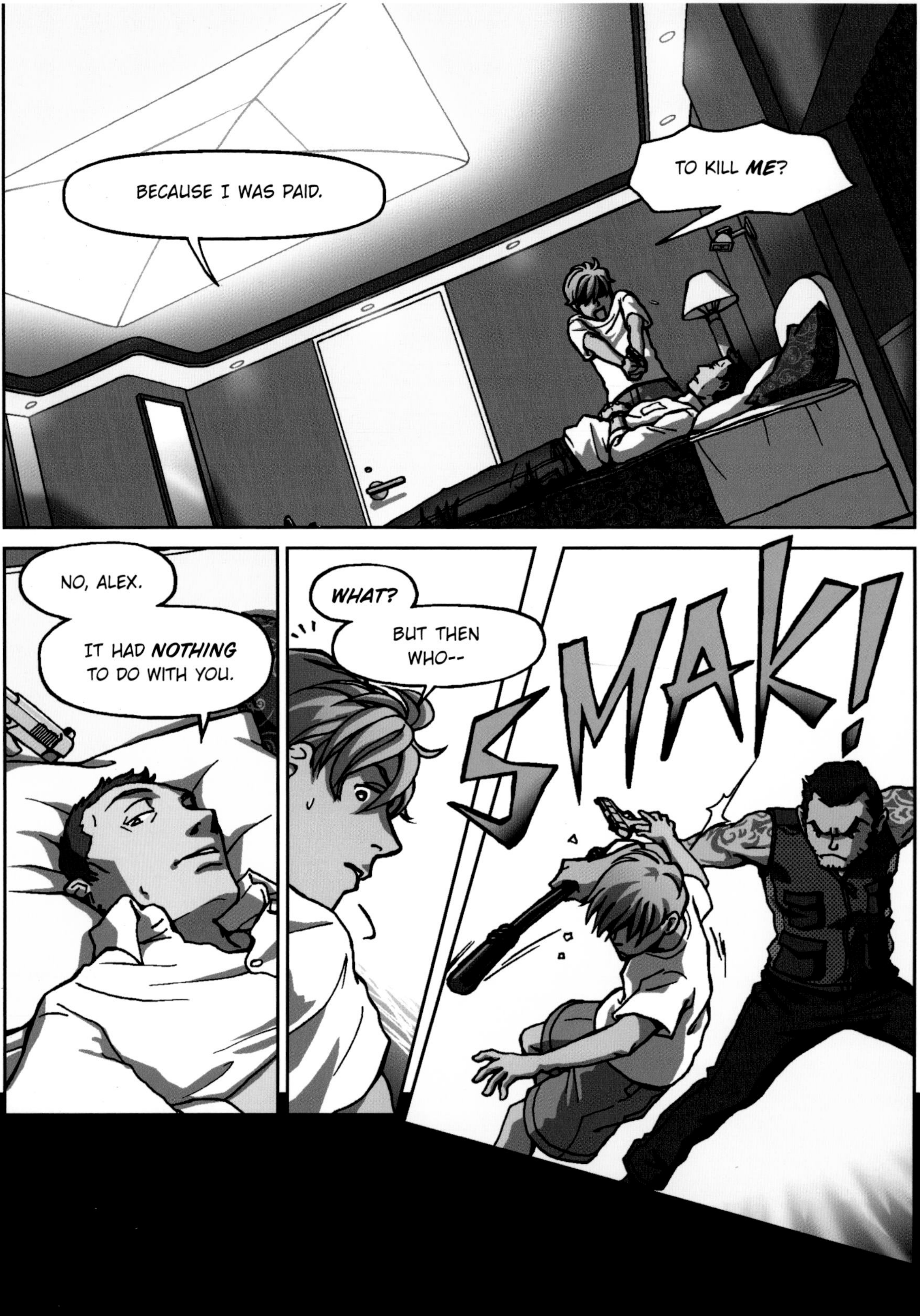
BECAUSE I WAS PAID.
TO KILL ME?
NO, ALEX.
IT HAD NOTHING TO DO WITH YOU.
WHAT?
BUT THEN WHO--
SMAK!

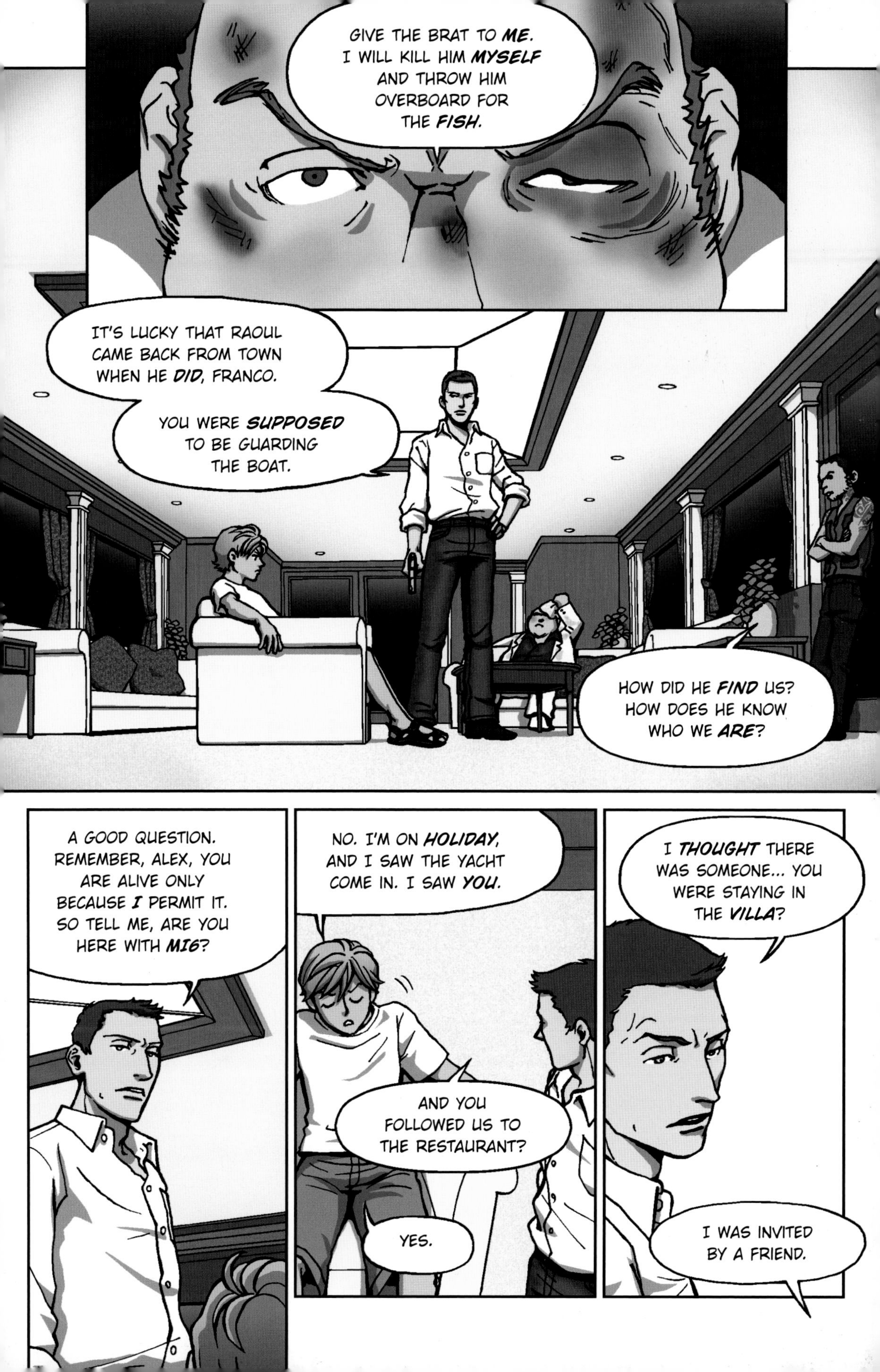
GIVE THE BRAT TO ME. I WILL KILL HIM MYSELF AND THROW HIM OVERBOARD FOR THE FISH.
IT'S LUCKY THAT RAOUL CAME BACK FROM TOWN WHEN HE DID, FRANCO.
YOU WERE SUPPOSED TO BE GUARDING THE BOAT.
HOW DID HE FIND US? HOW DOES HE KNOW WHO WE ARE?
A GOOD QUESTION. REMEMBER, ALEX, YOU ARE ALIVE ONLY BECAUSE I PERMIT IT. SO TELL ME, ARE YOU HERE WITH MI6?
NO. I'M ON HOLIDAY, AND I SAW THE YACHT COME IN. I SAW YOU.
AND YOU FOLLOWED US TO THE RESTAURANT?
YES.
I THOUGHT THERE WAS SOMEONE... YOU WERE STAYING IN THE VILLA?
I WAS INVITED BY A FRIEND.

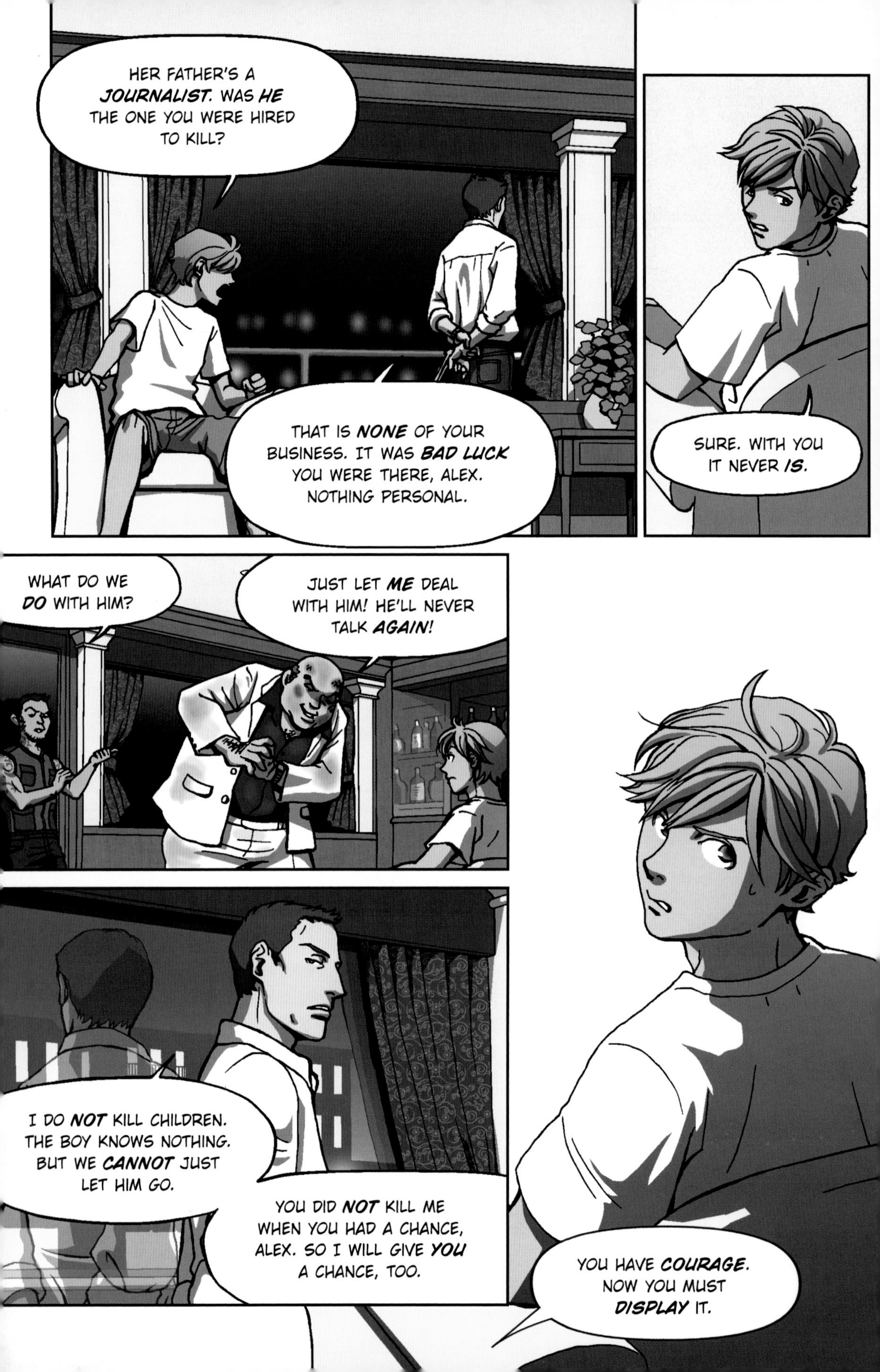
HER FATHER'S A JOURNALIST. WAS HE THE ONE YOU WERE HIRED TO KILL?
THAT IS NONE OF YOUR BUSINESS. IT WAS BAD LUCK YOU WERE THERE, ALEX. NOTHING PERSONAL.
SURE. WITH YOU IT NEVER IS.
WHAT DO WE DO WITH HIM?
JUST LET ME DEAL WITH HIM! HE'LL NEVER TALK AGAIN!
I DO NOT KILL CHILDREN. THE BOY KNOWS NOTHING. BUT WE CANNOT JUST LET HIM GO.
YOU DID NOT KILL ME WHEN YOU HAD A CHANCE, ALEX. SO I WILL GIVE YOU A CHANCE, TOO.
YOU HAVE COURAGE. NOW YOU MUST DISPLAY IT.

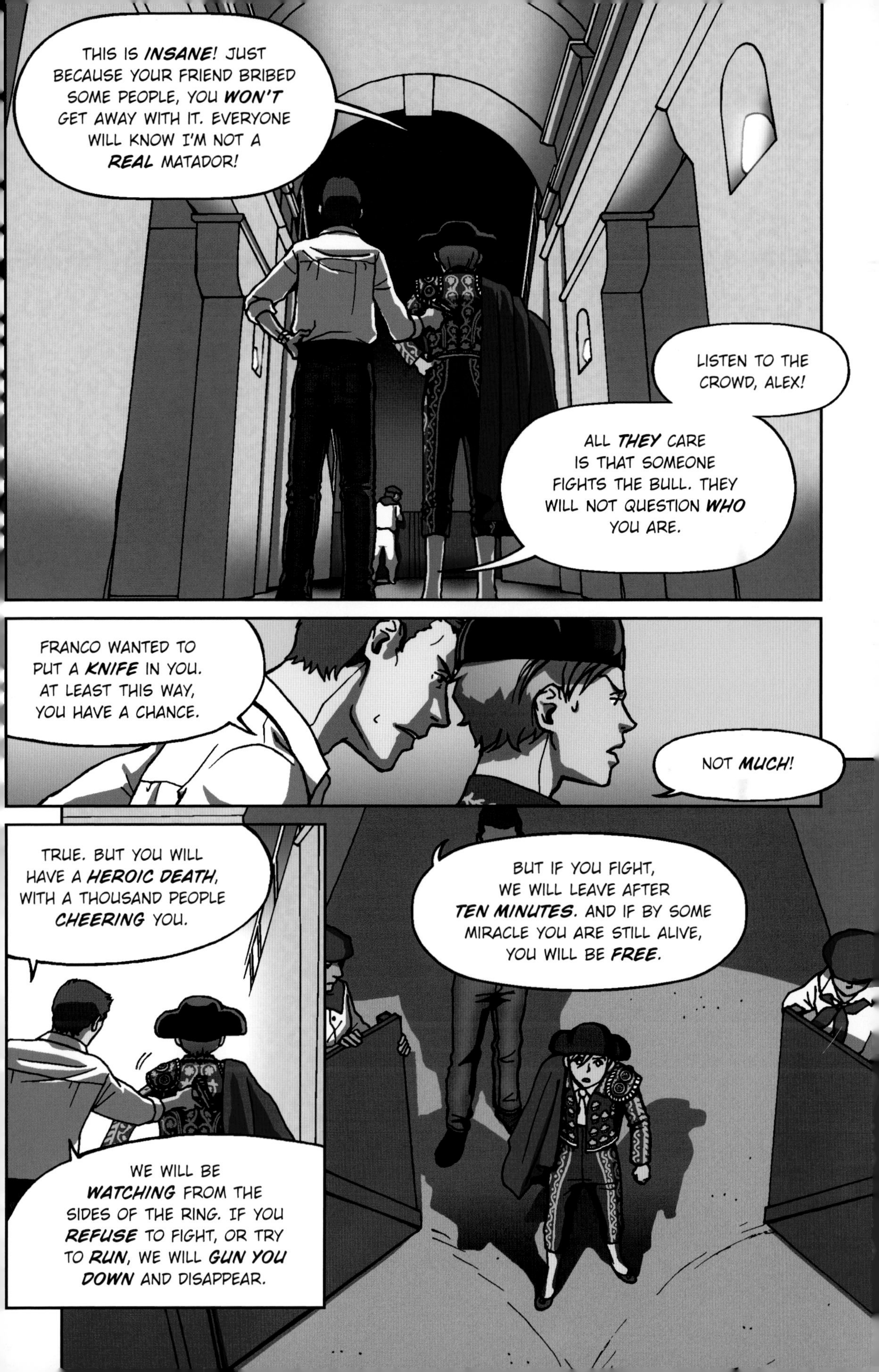
THIS IS INSANE! JUST BECAUSE YOUR FRIEND BRIBED SOME PEOPLE, YOU WON'T GET AWAY WITH IT. EVERYONE WILL KNOW I'M NOT A REAL MATADOR!
LISTEN TO THE CROWD, ALEX!
ALL THEY CARE IS THAT SOMEONE FIGHTS THE BULL. THEY WILL NOT QUESTION WHO YOU ARE.
FRANCO WANTED TO PUT A KNIFE IN YOU. AT LEAST THIS WAY, YOU HAVE A CHANCE.
NOT MUCH!
TRUE. BUT YOU WILL HAVE A HEROIC DEATH, WITH A THOUSAND PEOPLE CHEERING YOU.
BUT IF YOU FIGHT, WE WILL LEAVE AFTER TEN MINUTES. AND IF BY SOME MIRACLE YOU ARE STILL ALIVE, YOU WILL BE FREE.
WE WILL BE WATCHING FROM THE SIDES OF THE RING. IF YOU REFUSE TO FIGHT, OR TRY TO RUN, WE WILL GUN YOU DOWN AND DISAPPEAR.

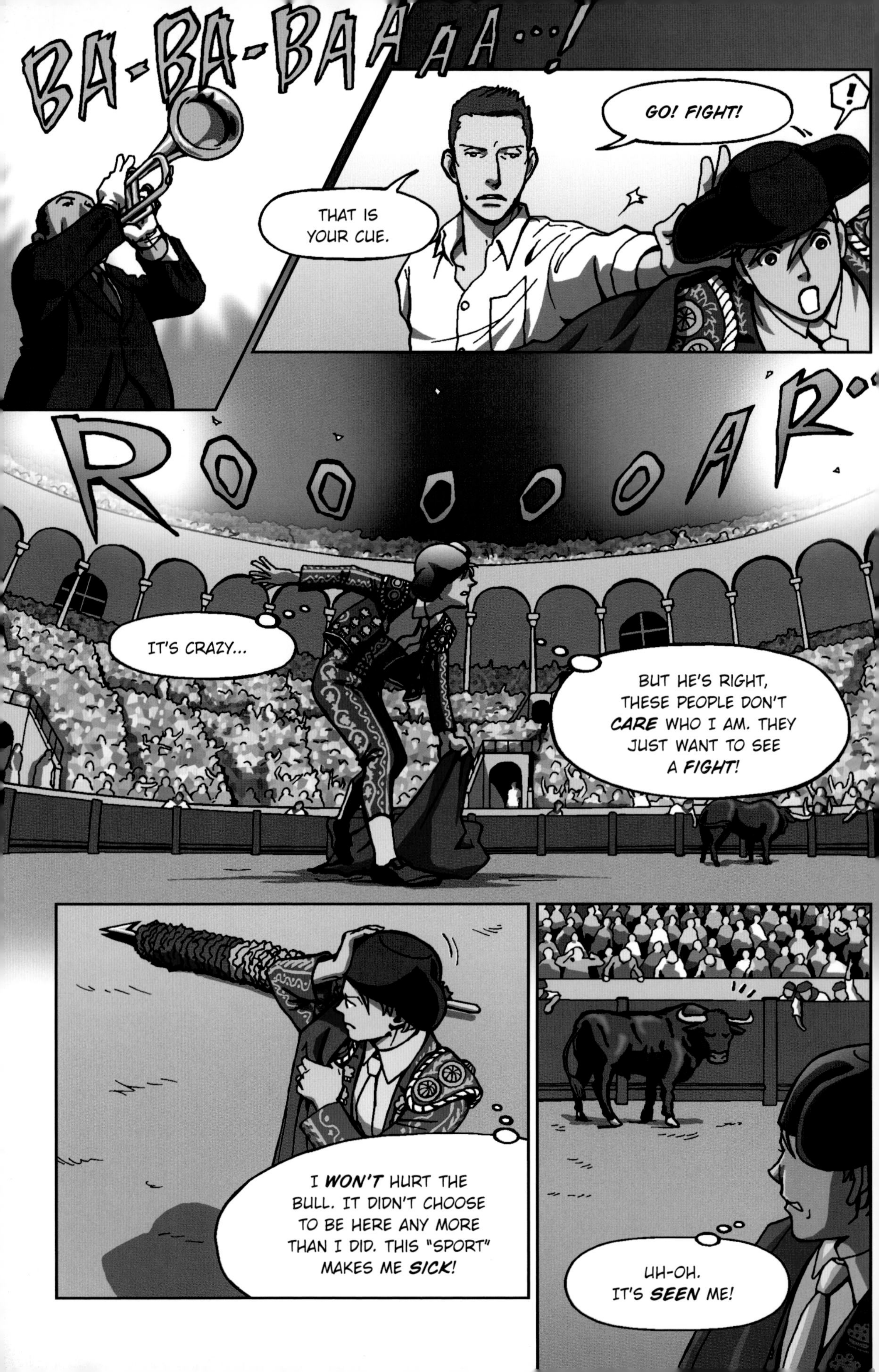
BA-BA-BAAAAA...!
THAT IS YOUR CUE.
GO! FIGHT!
!
ROOOOOAR...
IT'S CRAZY...
BUT HE'S RIGHT, THESE PEOPLE DON'T CARE WHO I AM. THEY JUST WANT TO SEE A FIGHT!
I WON'T HURT THE BULL. IT DIDN'T CHOOSE TO BE HERE ANY MORE THAN I DID. THIS "SPORT" MAKES ME SICK!
UH-OH. IT'S SEEN ME!

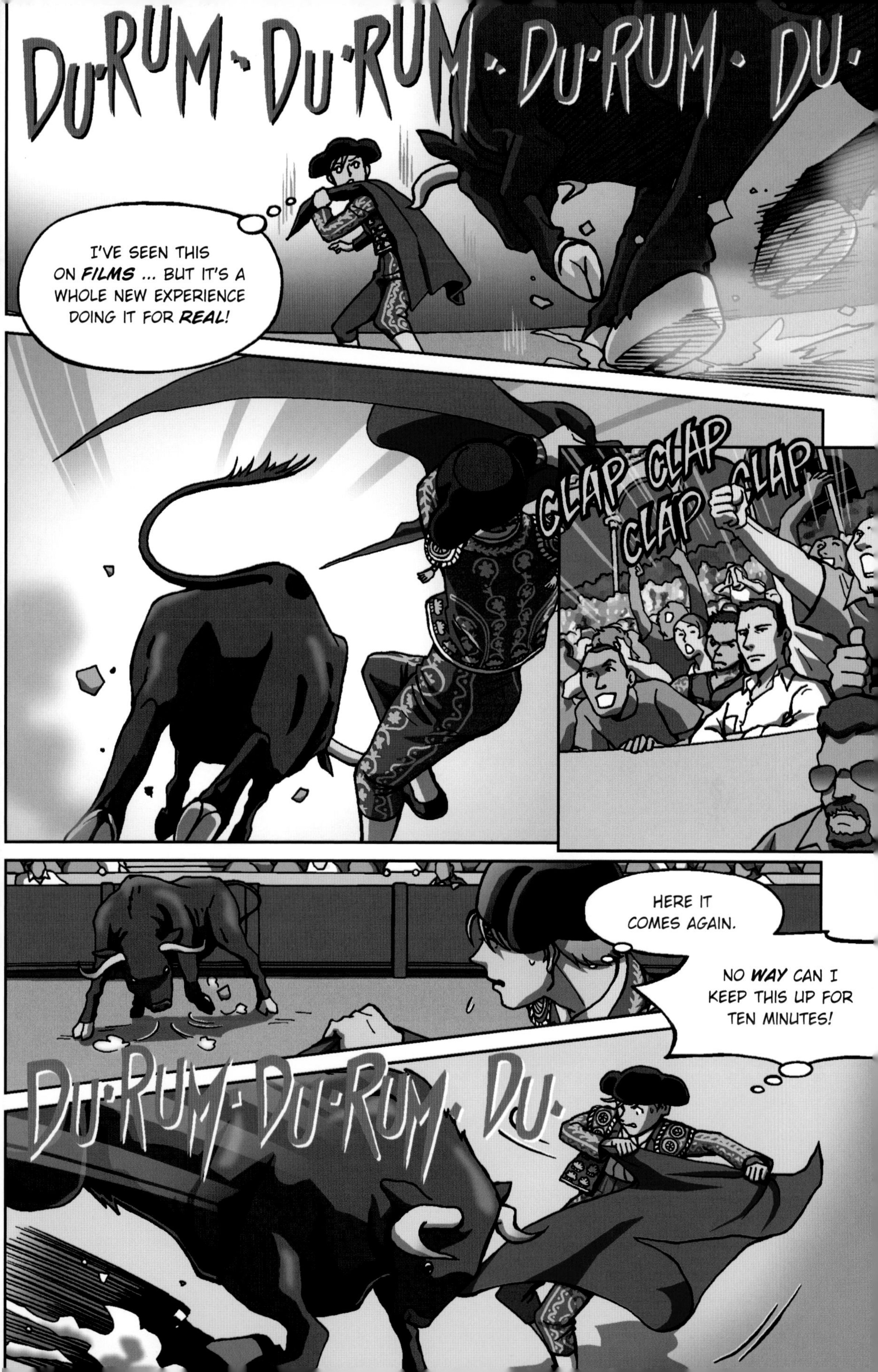
DU-RUM-DU-RUM-DU-RUM-DU-
I'VE SEEN THIS ON *FILMS* ... BUT IT'S A WHOLE NEW EXPERIENCE DOING IT FOR *REAL*!
CLAP CLAP CLAP CLAP
HERE IT COMES AGAIN.
NO *WAY* CAN I KEEP THIS UP FOR TEN MINUTES!
DU-RUM-DU-RUM-DU-

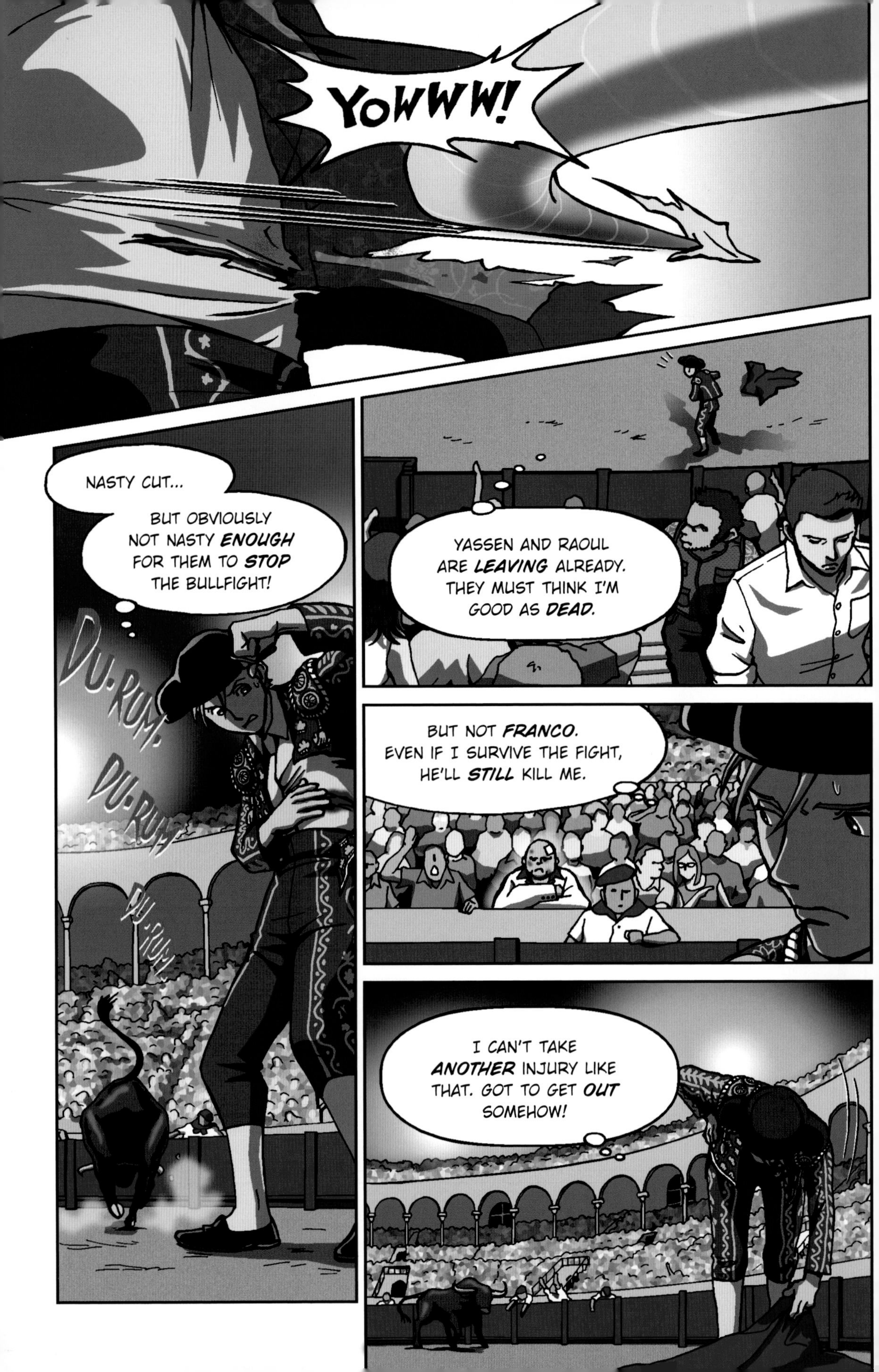
YOWWW!
NASTY CUT...
BUT OBVIOUSLY NOT NASTY ENOUGH FOR THEM TO STOP THE BULLFIGHT!
DU-RUM. DU-RUM. DU-RUM.
YASSEN AND RAOUL ARE LEAVING ALREADY. THEY MUST THINK I'M GOOD AS DEAD.
BUT NOT FRANCO. EVEN IF I SURVIVE THE FIGHT, HE'LL STILL KILL ME.
I CAN'T TAKE ANOTHER INJURY LIKE THAT. GOT TO GET OUT SOMEHOW!

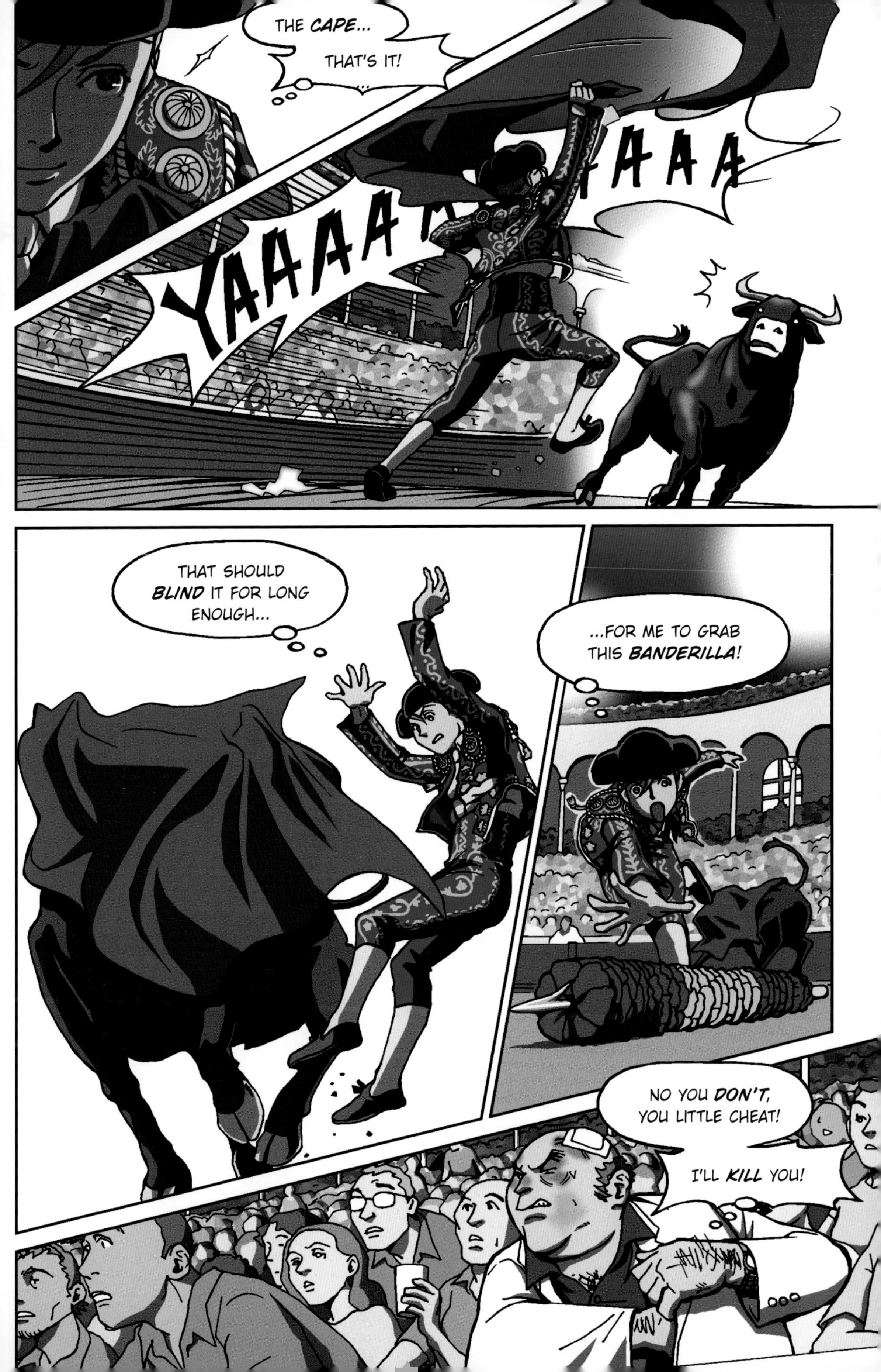
THE CAPE... THAT'S IT!
YAAAAAAAAAA
THAT SHOULD BLIND IT FOR LONG ENOUGH...
...FOR ME TO GRAB THIS BANDERILLA!
NO YOU DON'T, YOU LITTLE CHEAT!
I'LL KILL YOU!

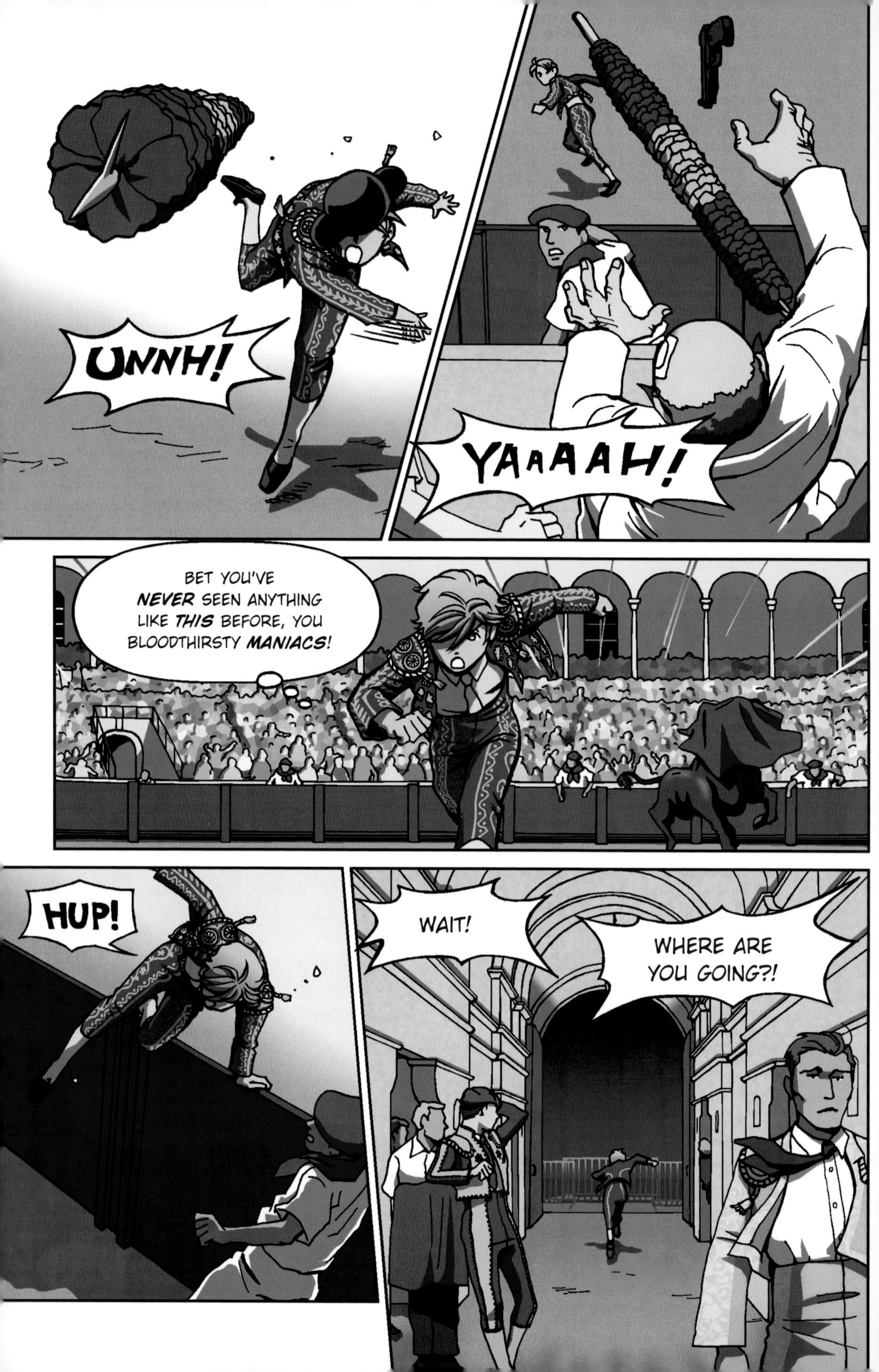
UNNH!
YAAAAH!
BET YOU'VE *NEVER* SEEN ANYTHING LIKE *THIS* BEFORE, YOU BLOODTHIRSTY *MANIACS*!
HUP!
WAIT!
WHERE ARE YOU GOING?!

KRAKA-THOOM!

HMMM. THAT NUMBER I FOUND ON YASSEN'S MOBILE...

OPERATOR?

A REVERSE CHARGE CALL TO *ENGLAND*, PLEASE. THE NUMBER IS *4420779460909*.

YASSEN WILL BE LONG GONE. SO *NOW* WHAT?

MY NAME?

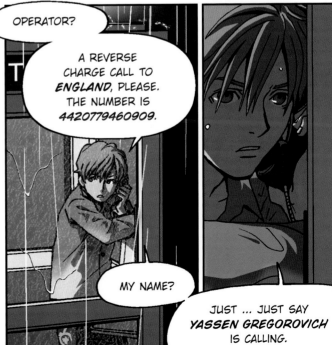

JUST ... JUST SAY *YASSEN GREGOROVICH* IS CALLING.

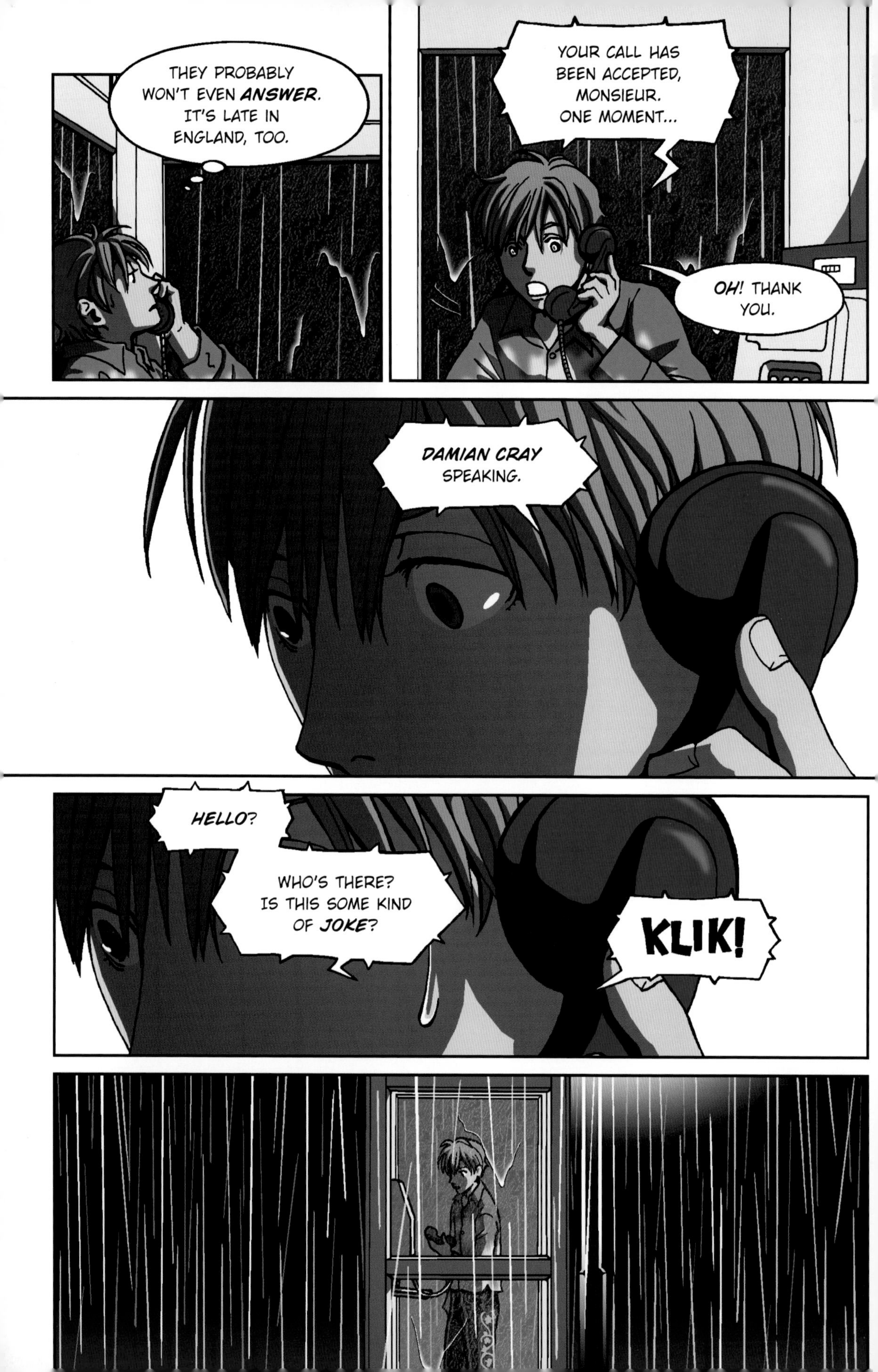
THEY PROBABLY WON'T EVEN ANSWER. IT'S LATE IN ENGLAND, TOO.
YOUR CALL HAS BEEN ACCEPTED, MONSIEUR. ONE MOMENT...
OH! THANK YOU.
DAMIAN CRAY SPEAKING.
HELLO?
WHO'S THERE? IS THIS SOME KIND OF JOKE?
KLIK!

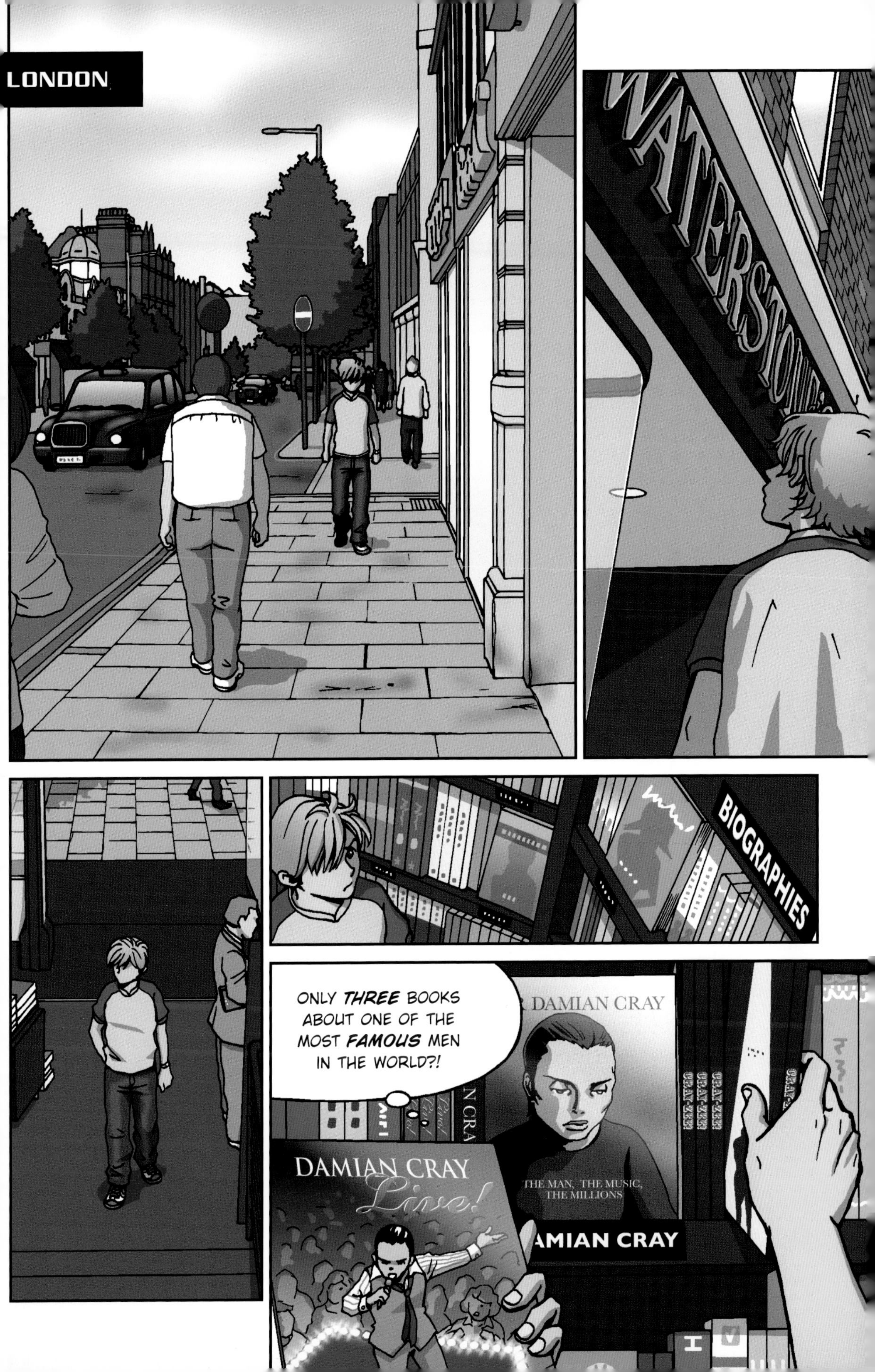
LONDON
WATERSTONE'S
BIOGRAPHIES
ONLY THREE BOOKS ABOUT ONE OF THE MOST FAMOUS MEN IN THE WORLD?!
DAMIAN CRAY
THE MAN, THE MUSIC, THE MILLIONS
AMIAN CRAY
DAMIAN CRAY
Live!

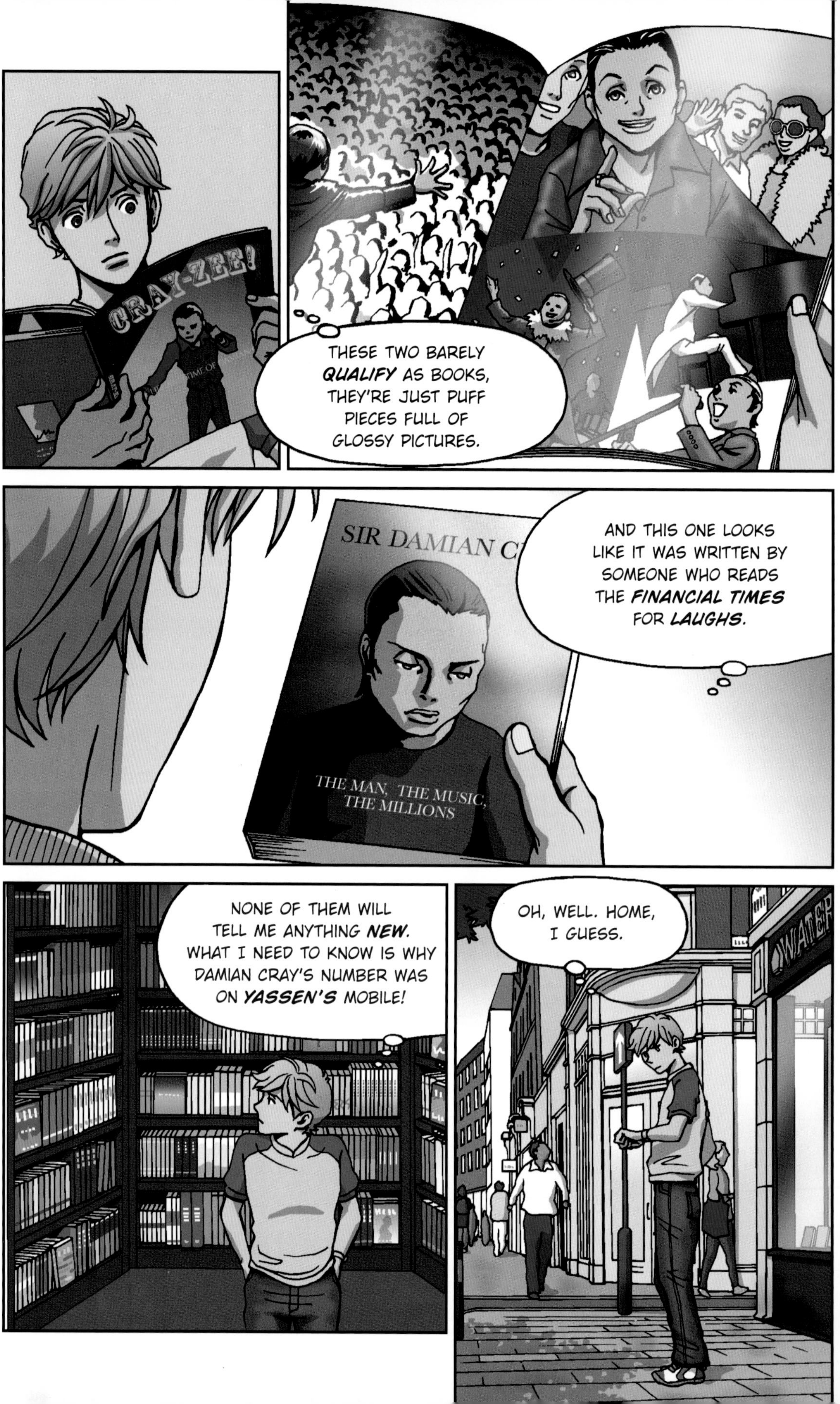
CRAY-ZEE!
THESE TWO BARELY **QUALIFY** AS BOOKS, THEY'RE JUST PUFF PIECES FULL OF GLOSSY PICTURES.
SIR DAMIAN
AND THIS ONE LOOKS LIKE IT WAS WRITTEN BY SOMEONE WHO READS THE ***FINANCIAL TIMES*** FOR ***LAUGHS.***
THE MAN, THE MUSIC, THE MILLIONS
NONE OF THEM WILL TELL ME ANYTHING ***NEW.*** WHAT I NEED TO KNOW IS WHY DAMIAN CRAY'S NUMBER WAS ON ***YASSEN'S*** MOBILE!
OH, WELL. HOME, I GUESS.

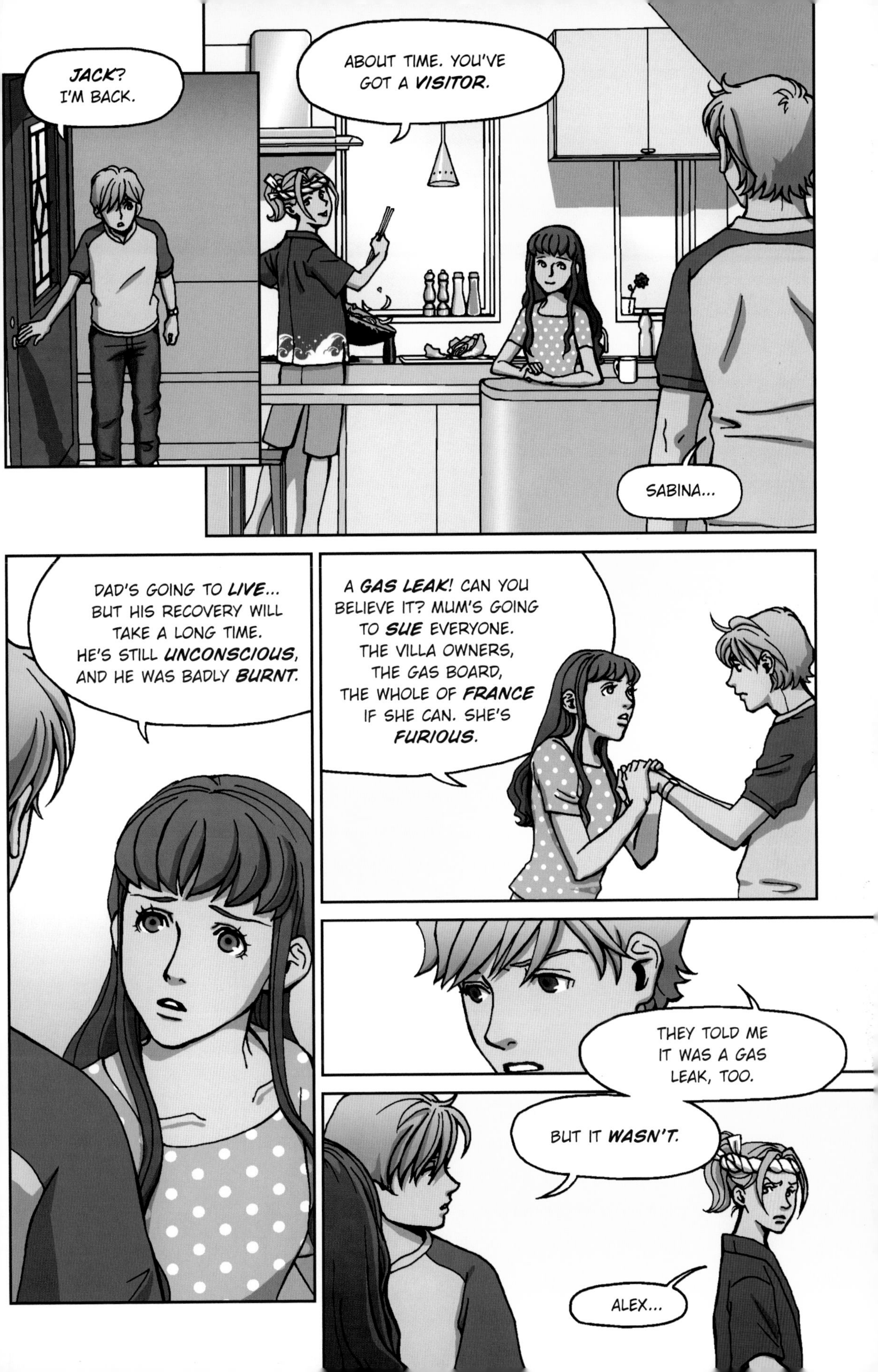
JACK? I'M BACK.
ABOUT TIME. YOU'VE GOT A VISITOR.
SABINA...
DAD'S GOING TO LIVE... BUT HIS RECOVERY WILL TAKE A LONG TIME. HE'S STILL UNCONSCIOUS, AND HE WAS BADLY BURNT.
A GAS LEAK! CAN YOU BELIEVE IT? MUM'S GOING TO SUE EVERYONE. THE VILLA OWNERS, THE GAS BOARD, THE WHOLE OF FRANCE IF SHE CAN. SHE'S FURIOUS.
THEY TOLD ME IT WAS A GAS LEAK, TOO.
BUT IT WASN'T.
ALEX...

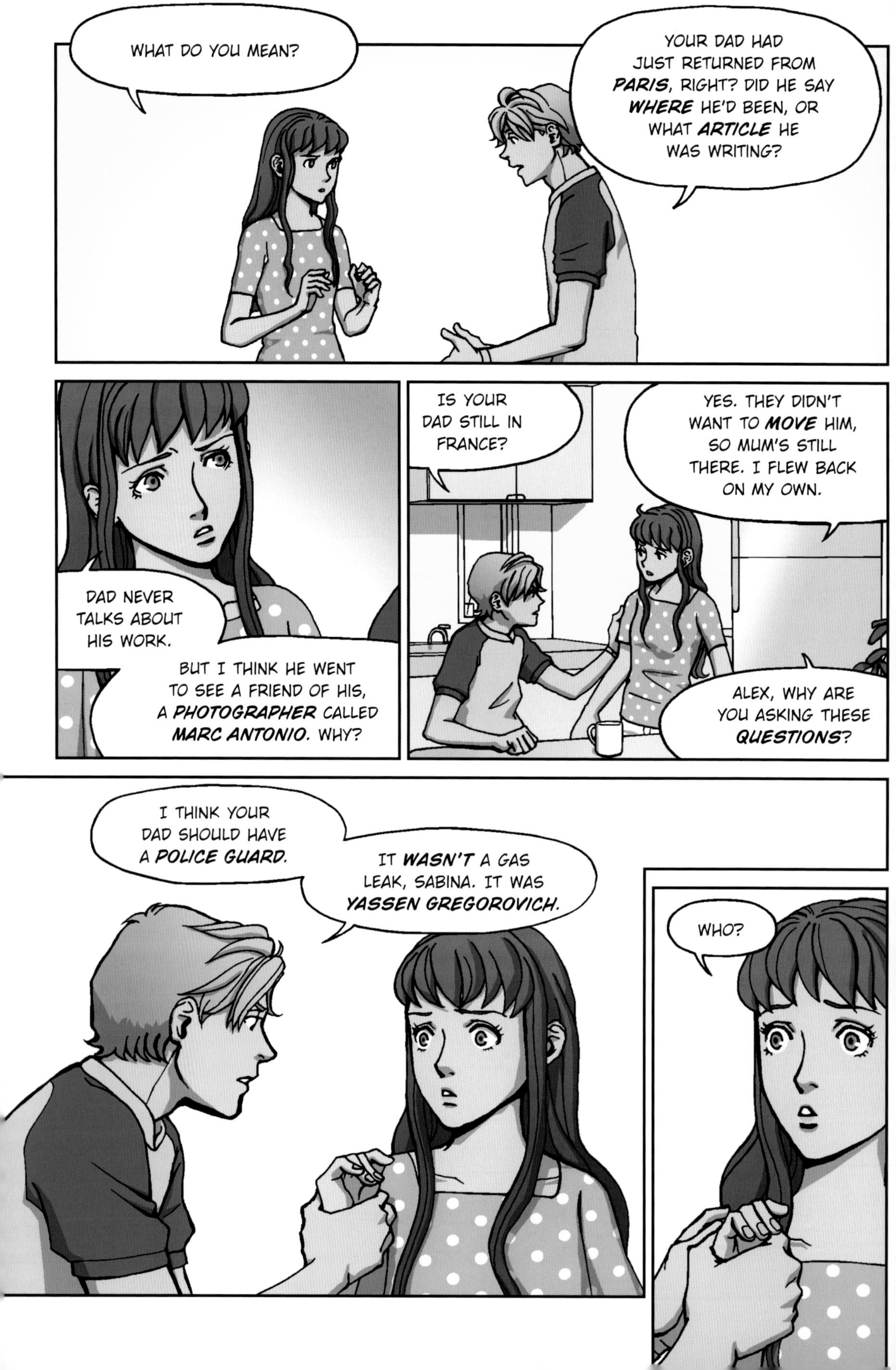
WHAT DO YOU MEAN?
YOUR DAD HAD JUST RETURNED FROM PARIS, RIGHT? DID HE SAY WHERE HE'D BEEN, OR WHAT ARTICLE HE WAS WRITING?
DAD NEVER TALKS ABOUT HIS WORK.
BUT I THINK HE WENT TO SEE A FRIEND OF HIS, A PHOTOGRAPHER CALLED MARC ANTONIO. WHY?
IS YOUR DAD STILL IN FRANCE?
YES. THEY DIDN'T WANT TO MOVE HIM, SO MUM'S STILL THERE. I FLEW BACK ON MY OWN.
ALEX, WHY ARE YOU ASKING THESE QUESTIONS?
I THINK YOUR DAD SHOULD HAVE A POLICE GUARD.
IT WASN'T A GAS LEAK, SABINA. IT WAS YASSEN GREGOROVICH.
WHO?

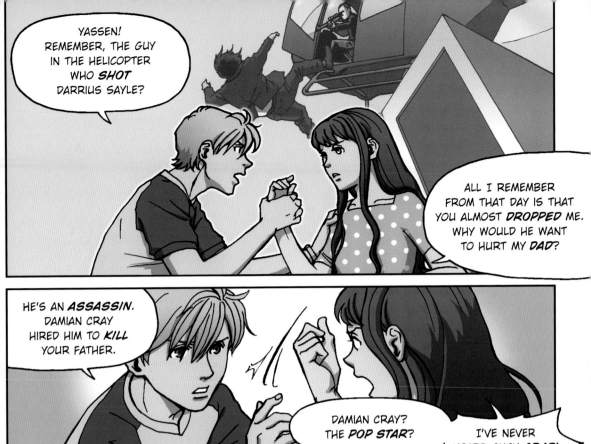

YASSEN! REMEMBER, THE GUY IN THE HELICOPTER WHO **SHOT** DARRIUS SAYLE?

ALL I REMEMBER FROM THAT DAY IS THAT YOU ALMOST **DROPPED** ME. WHY WOULD HE WANT TO HURT MY **DAD**?

HE'S AN **ASSASSIN**. DAMIAN CRAY HIRED HIM TO **KILL** YOUR FATHER.

DAMIAN CRAY? THE **POP STAR**?

I'VE NEVER HEARD SUCH **CRAP**!

YOUR DAD WAS WRITING AN **ARTICLE** ABOUT CRAY. AND I FOUND CRAY'S **NUMBER** ON YASSEN'S MOBILE.

YOU HAVE TO **TRUST** ME. I'VE SEEN THIS SORT OF THING BEFORE, REMEMBER?

ALEX, THIS IS **TOO MUCH**!

YOU'RE ALL "OH, I'M **NOT** A SPY, I'M NOT A SPY", UNTIL YOU WANT ME TO BELIEVE SOME **COCK-AND-BULL STORY**, AND THEN SUDDENLY YOU'RE AN **EXPERT**!

I **FOLLOWED** HIM FROM THE BEACH! I **KNEW** HE WAS PLANNING SOMETHING! I SHOULD HAVE **STOPPED** HIM, BUT I DIDN'T KNOW WHAT HE WAS GOING TO DO...

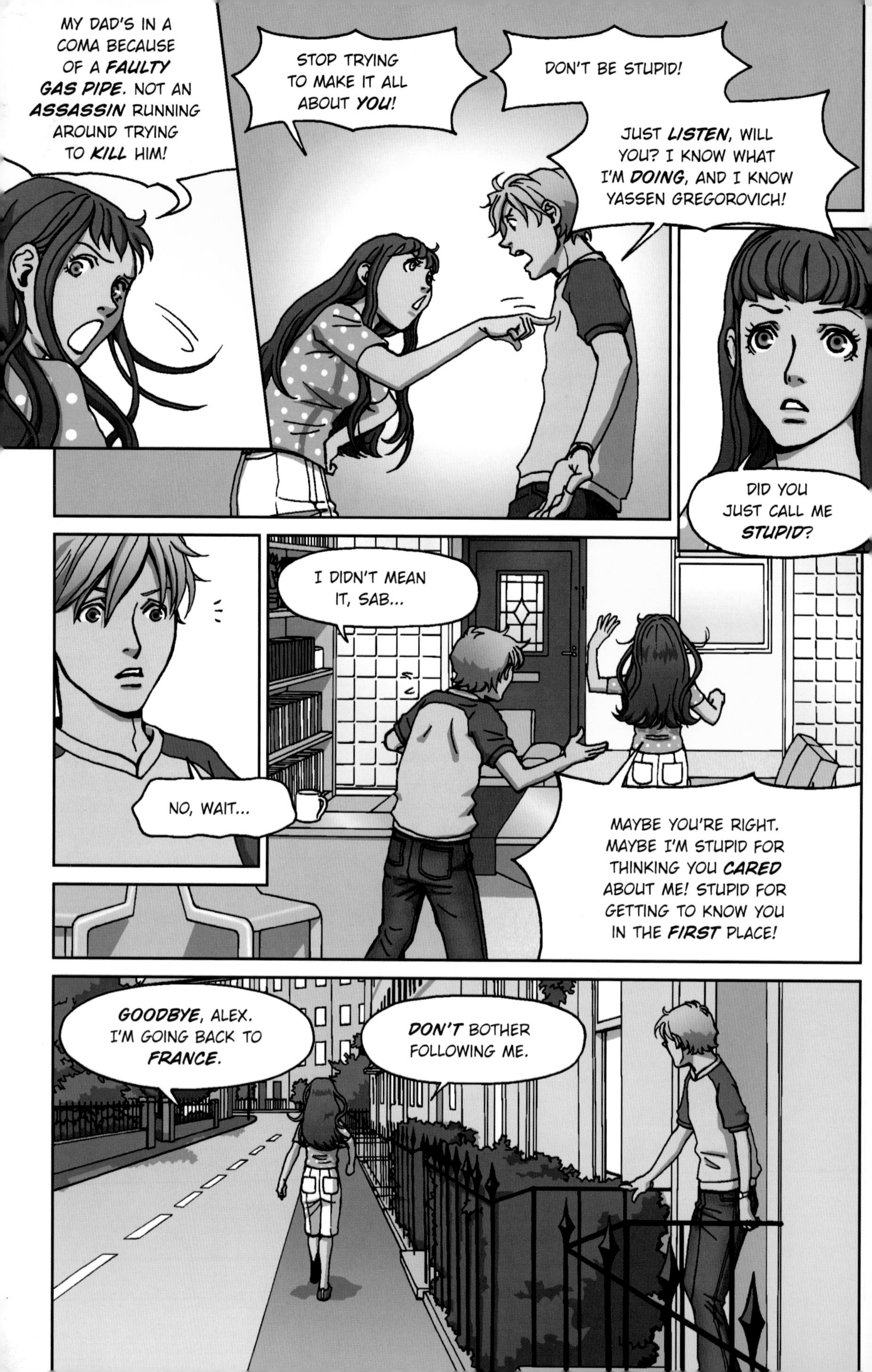
MY DAD'S IN A COMA BECAUSE OF A FAULTY GAS PIPE. NOT AN ASSASSIN RUNNING AROUND TRYING TO KILL HIM!
STOP TRYING TO MAKE IT ALL ABOUT YOU!
DON'T BE STUPID!
JUST LISTEN, WILL YOU? I KNOW WHAT I'M DOING, AND I KNOW YASSEN GREGOROVICH!
DID YOU JUST CALL ME STUPID?
NO, WAIT...
I DIDN'T MEAN IT, SAB...
MAYBE YOU'RE RIGHT. MAYBE I'M STUPID FOR THINKING YOU CARED ABOUT ME! STUPID FOR GETTING TO KNOW YOU IN THE FIRST PLACE!
GOODBYE, ALEX. I'M GOING BACK TO FRANCE.
DON'T BOTHER FOLLOWING ME.

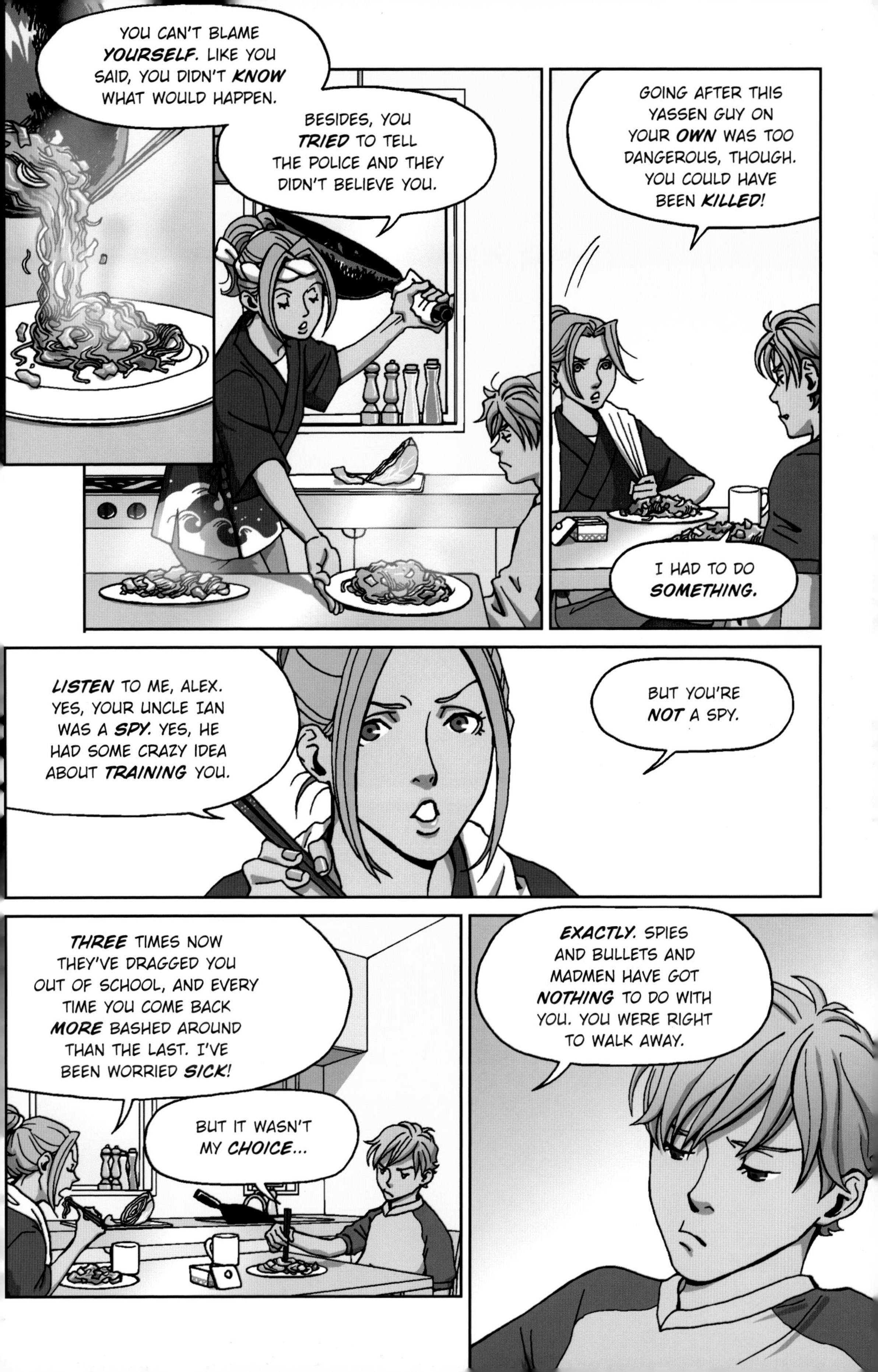
YOU CAN'T BLAME YOURSELF. LIKE YOU SAID, YOU DIDN'T KNOW WHAT WOULD HAPPEN.
BESIDES, YOU TRIED TO TELL THE POLICE AND THEY DIDN'T BELIEVE YOU.
GOING AFTER THIS YASSEN GUY ON YOUR OWN WAS TOO DANGEROUS, THOUGH. YOU COULD HAVE BEEN KILLED!
I HAD TO DO SOMETHING.
LISTEN TO ME, ALEX. YES, YOUR UNCLE IAN WAS A SPY. YES, HE HAD SOME CRAZY IDEA ABOUT TRAINING YOU.
BUT YOU'RE NOT A SPY.
THREE TIMES NOW THEY'VE DRAGGED YOU OUT OF SCHOOL, AND EVERY TIME YOU COME BACK MORE BASHED AROUND THAN THE LAST. I'VE BEEN WORRIED SICK!
BUT IT WASN'T MY CHOICE...
EXACTLY. SPIES AND BULLETS AND MADMEN HAVE GOT NOTHING TO DO WITH YOU. YOU WERE RIGHT TO WALK AWAY.

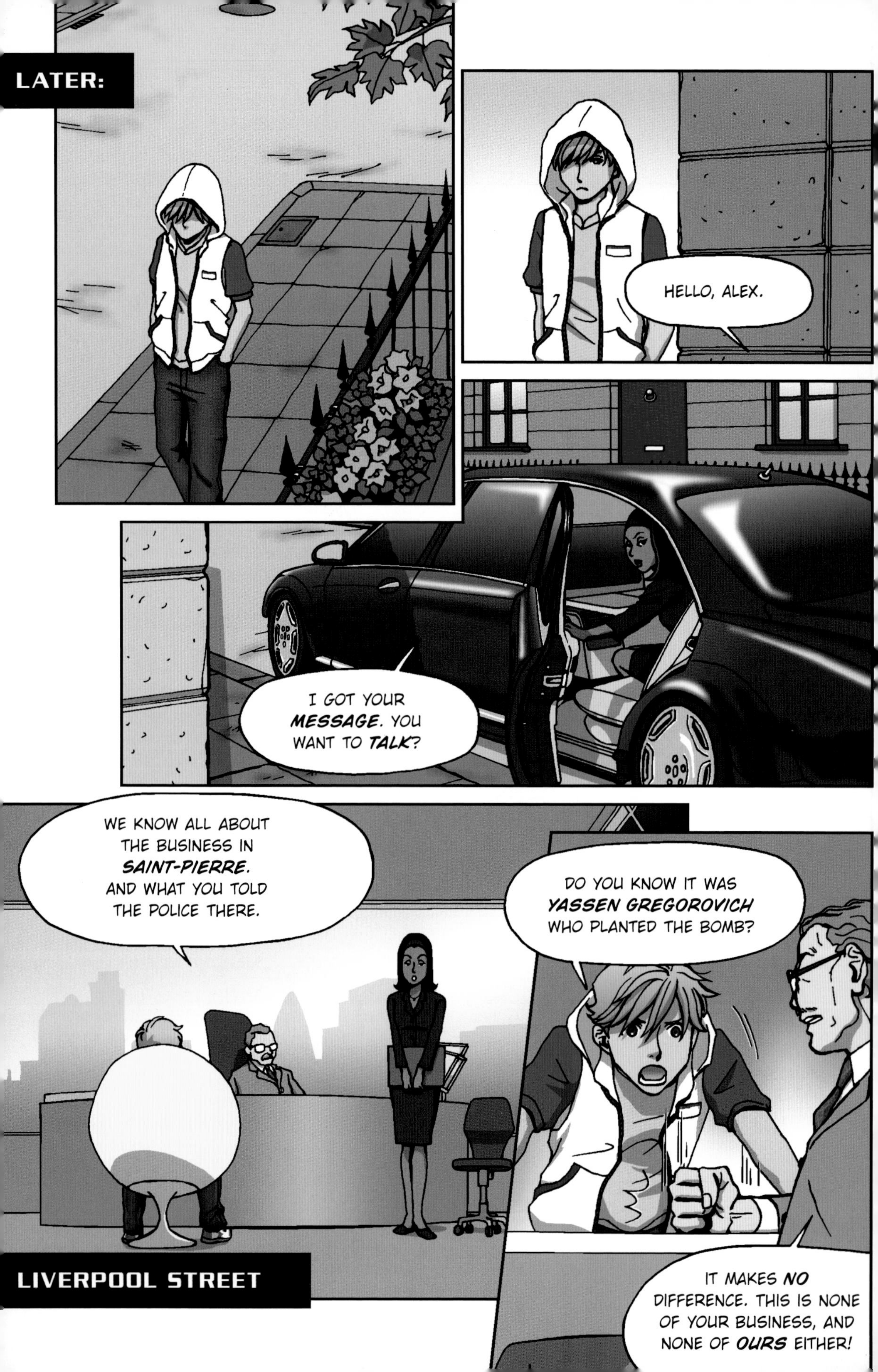
LATER:
HELLO, ALEX.
I GOT YOUR MESSAGE. YOU WANT TO TALK?
LIVERPOOL STREET
WE KNOW ALL ABOUT THE BUSINESS IN SAINT-PIERRE. AND WHAT YOU TOLD THE POLICE THERE.
DO YOU KNOW IT WAS YASSEN GREGOROVICH WHO PLANTED THE BOMB?
IT MAKES NO DIFFERENCE. THIS IS NONE OF YOUR BUSINESS, AND NONE OF OURS EITHER!

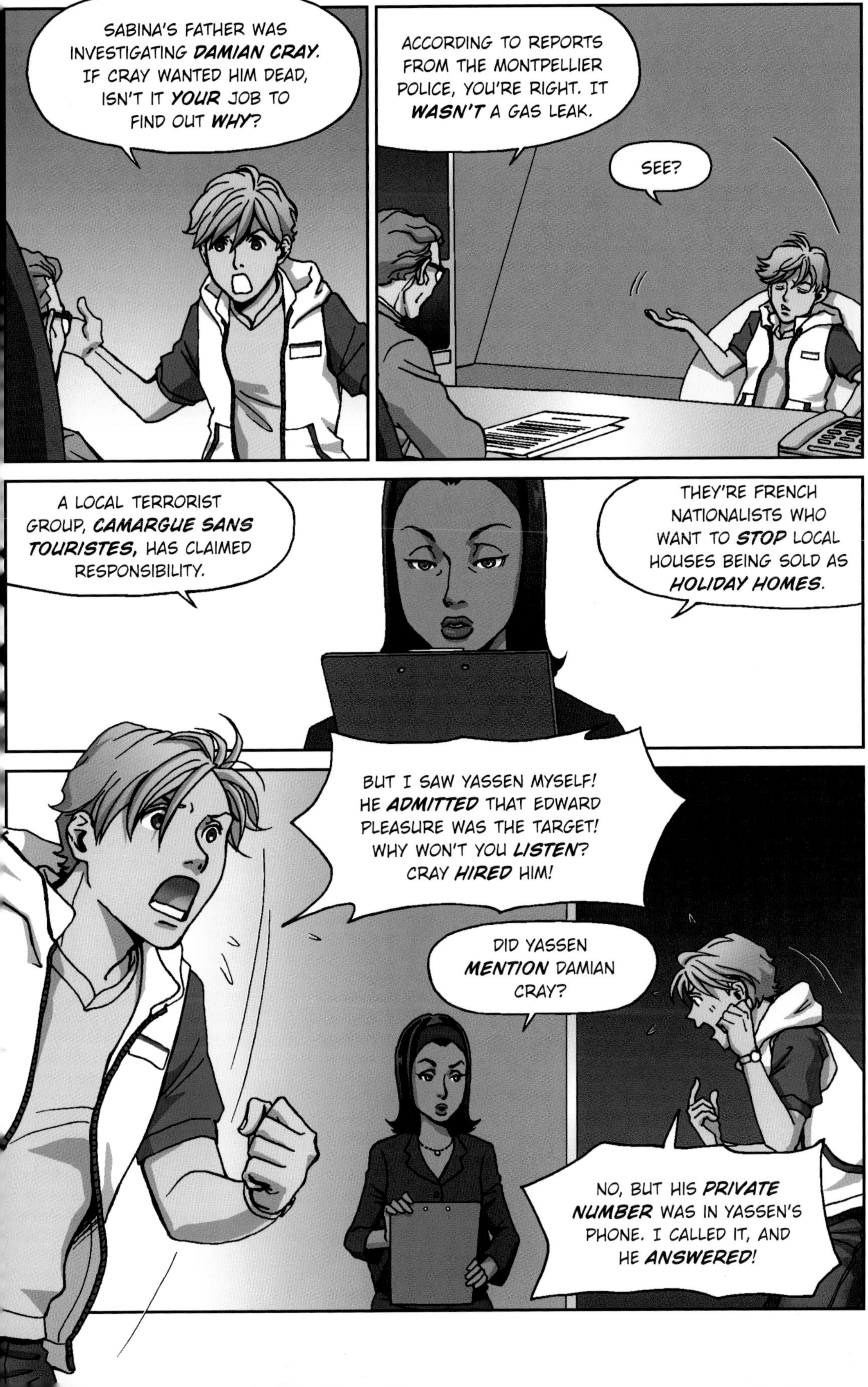
SABINA'S FATHER WAS INVESTIGATING DAMIAN CRAY. IF CRAY WANTED HIM DEAD, ISN'T IT YOUR JOB TO FIND OUT WHY?
ACCORDING TO REPORTS FROM THE MONTPELLIER POLICE, YOU'RE RIGHT. IT WASN'T A GAS LEAK.
SEE?
A LOCAL TERRORIST GROUP, CAMARGUE SANS TOURISTES, HAS CLAIMED RESPONSIBILITY.
THEY'RE FRENCH NATIONALISTS WHO WANT TO STOP LOCAL HOUSES BEING SOLD AS HOLIDAY HOMES.
BUT I SAW YASSEN MYSELF! HE ADMITTED THAT EDWARD PLEASURE WAS THE TARGET! WHY WON'T YOU LISTEN? CRAY HIRED HIM!
DID YASSEN MENTION DAMIAN CRAY?
NO, BUT HIS PRIVATE NUMBER WAS IN YASSEN'S PHONE. I CALLED IT, AND HE ANSWERED!

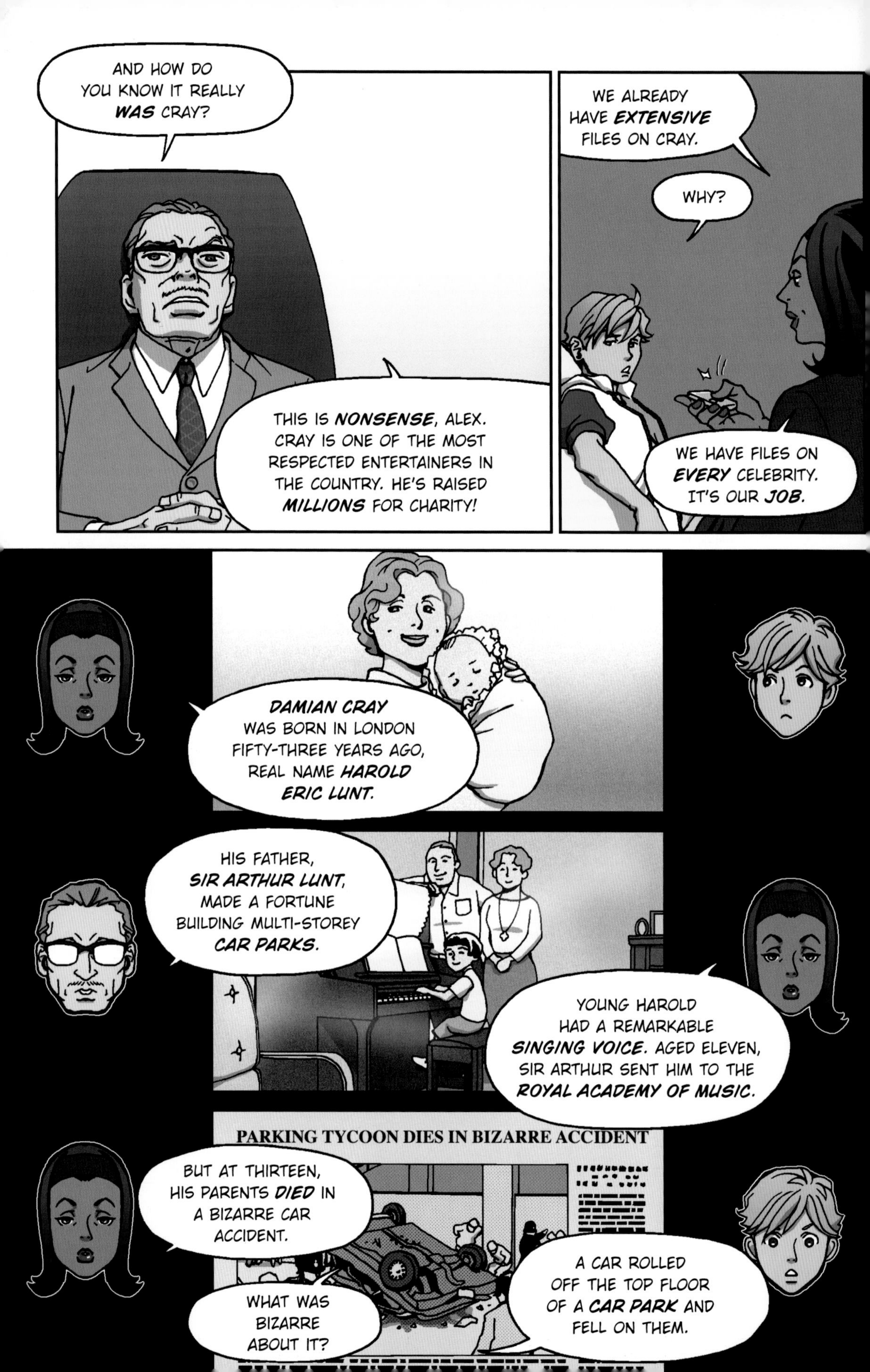
AND HOW DO YOU KNOW IT REALLY *WAS* CRAY?
THIS IS *NONSENSE*, ALEX. CRAY IS ONE OF THE MOST RESPECTED ENTERTAINERS IN THE COUNTRY. HE'S RAISED *MILLIONS* FOR CHARITY!
WE ALREADY HAVE *EXTENSIVE* FILES ON CRAY.
WHY?
WE HAVE FILES ON *EVERY* CELEBRITY. IT'S OUR *JOB*.
DAMIAN CRAY WAS BORN IN LONDON FIFTY-THREE YEARS AGO, REAL NAME *HAROLD ERIC LUNT*.
HIS FATHER, *SIR ARTHUR LUNT*, MADE A FORTUNE BUILDING MULTI-STOREY *CAR PARKS*.
YOUNG HAROLD HAD A REMARKABLE *SINGING VOICE*. AGED ELEVEN, SIR ARTHUR SENT HIM TO THE *ROYAL ACADEMY OF MUSIC*.
PARKING TYCOON DIES IN BIZARRE ACCIDENT
BUT AT THIRTEEN, HIS PARENTS *DIED* IN A BIZARRE CAR ACCIDENT.
WHAT WAS BIZARRE ABOUT IT?
A CAR ROLLED OFF THE TOP FLOOR OF A *CAR PARK* AND FELL ON THEM.

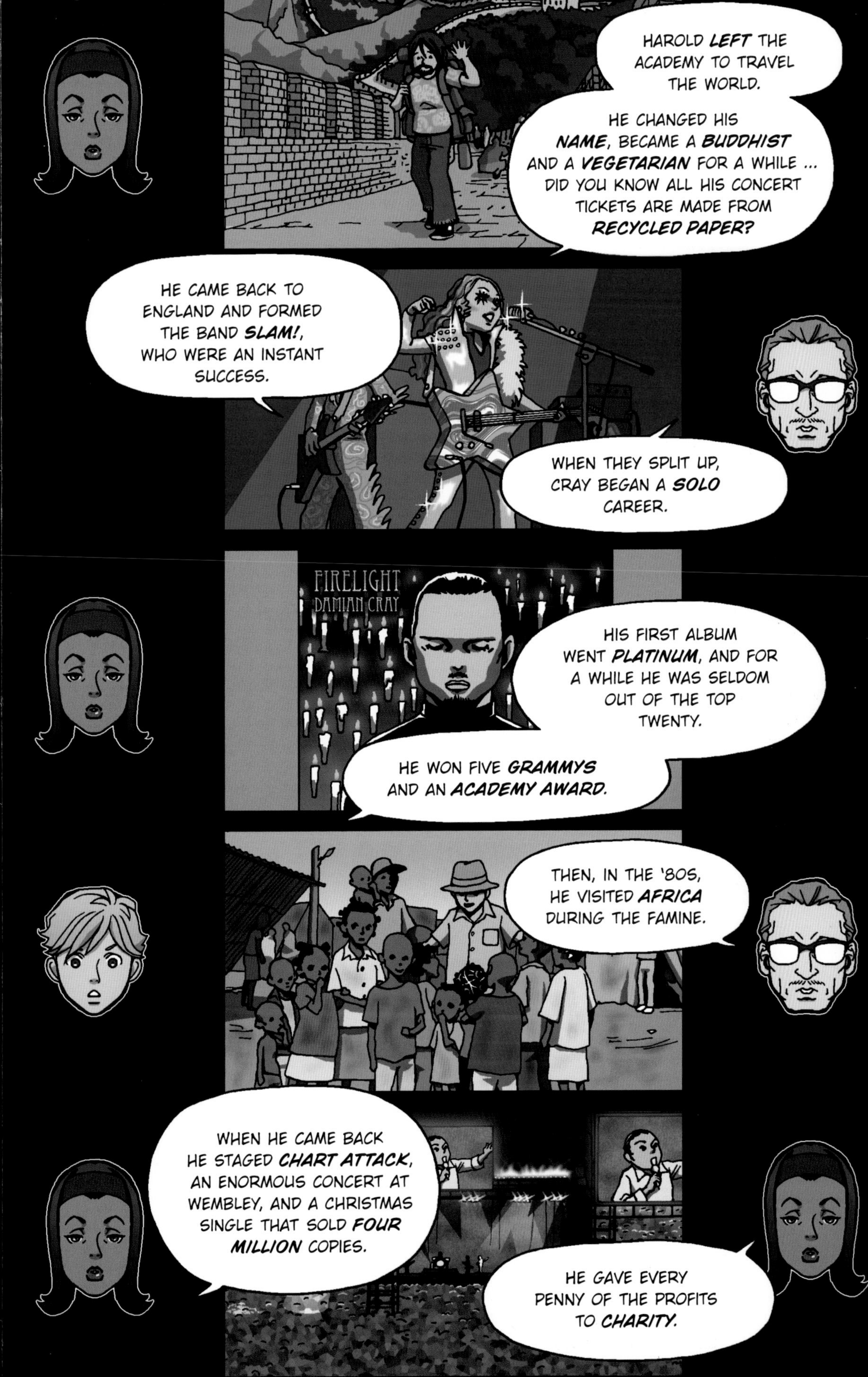
HAROLD LEFT THE ACADEMY TO TRAVEL THE WORLD.
HE CHANGED HIS NAME, BECAME A BUDDHIST AND A VEGETARIAN FOR A WHILE ... DID YOU KNOW ALL HIS CONCERT TICKETS ARE MADE FROM RECYCLED PAPER?
HE CAME BACK TO ENGLAND AND FORMED THE BAND SLAM!, WHO WERE AN INSTANT SUCCESS.
WHEN THEY SPLIT UP, CRAY BEGAN A SOLO CAREER.
FIRELIGHT
DAMIAN CRAY
HIS FIRST ALBUM WENT PLATINUM, AND FOR A WHILE HE WAS SELDOM OUT OF THE TOP TWENTY.
HE WON FIVE GRAMMYS AND AN ACADEMY AWARD.
THEN, IN THE '80S, HE VISITED AFRICA DURING THE FAMINE.
WHEN HE CAME BACK HE STAGED CHART ATTACK, AN ENORMOUS CONCERT AT WEMBLEY, AND A CHRISTMAS SINGLE THAT SOLD FOUR MILLION COPIES.
HE GAVE EVERY PENNY OF THE PROFITS TO CHARITY.

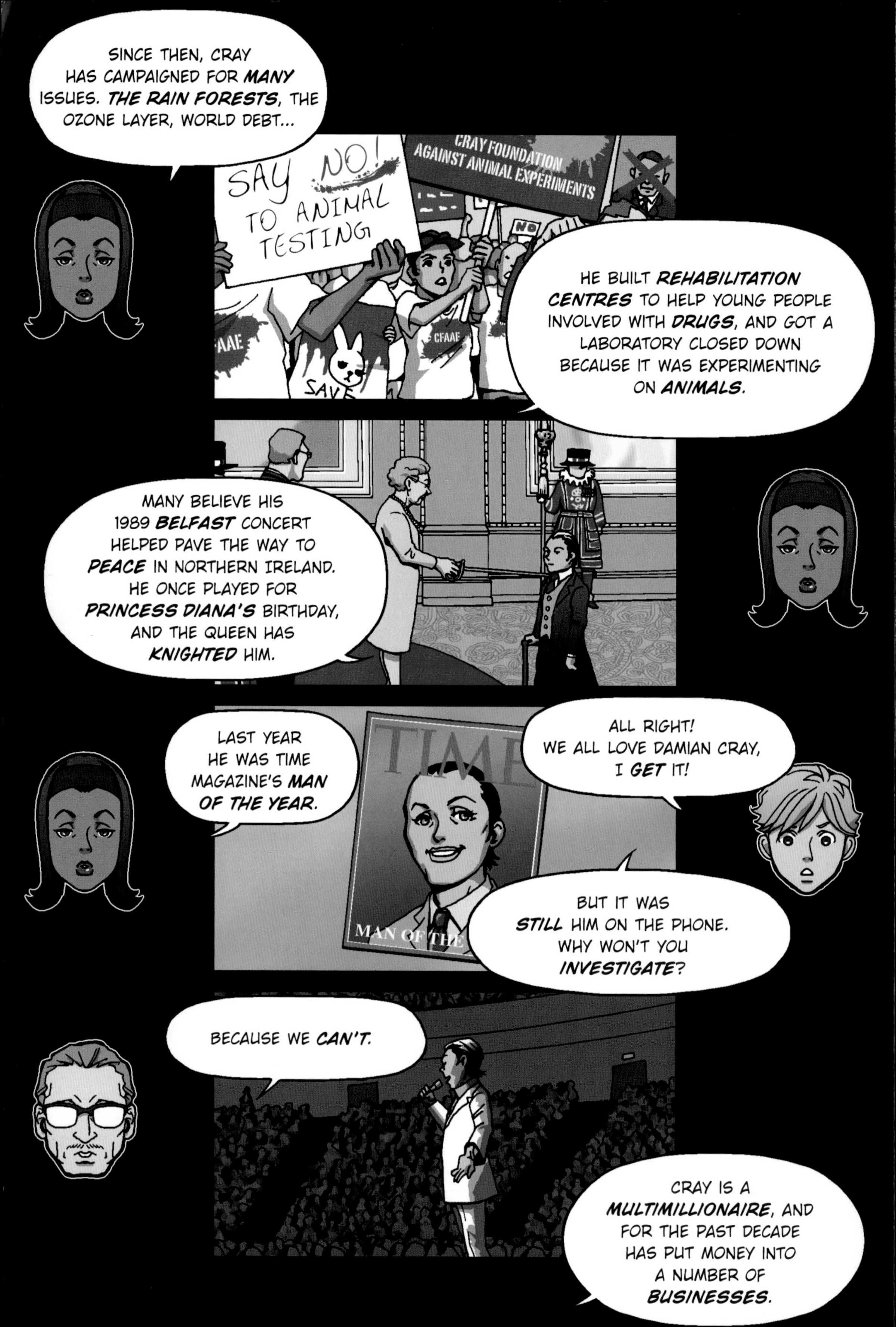
SINCE THEN, CRAY HAS CAMPAIGNED FOR *MANY* ISSUES. ***THE RAIN FORESTS***, THE OZONE LAYER, WORLD DEBT...
SAY NO! TO ANIMAL TESTING
CRAY FOUNDATION AGAINST ANIMAL EXPERIMENTS
CFAAE
HE BUILT ***REHABILITATION CENTRES*** TO HELP YOUNG PEOPLE INVOLVED WITH ***DRUGS***, AND GOT A LABORATORY CLOSED DOWN BECAUSE IT WAS EXPERIMENTING ON ***ANIMALS***.
MANY BELIEVE HIS 1989 ***BELFAST*** CONCERT HELPED PAVE THE WAY TO ***PEACE*** IN NORTHERN IRELAND. HE ONCE PLAYED FOR ***PRINCESS DIANA'S*** BIRTHDAY, AND THE QUEEN HAS ***KNIGHTED*** HIM.
LAST YEAR HE WAS TIME MAGAZINE'S ***MAN OF THE YEAR***.
TIME
ALL RIGHT! WE ALL LOVE DAMIAN CRAY, I ***GET*** IT!
BUT IT WAS ***STILL*** HIM ON THE PHONE. WHY WON'T YOU ***INVESTIGATE***?
BECAUSE WE ***CAN'T***.
CRAY IS A ***MULTIMILLIONAIRE***, AND FOR THE PAST DECADE HAS PUT MONEY INTO A NUMBER OF ***BUSINESSES***.

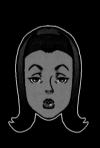

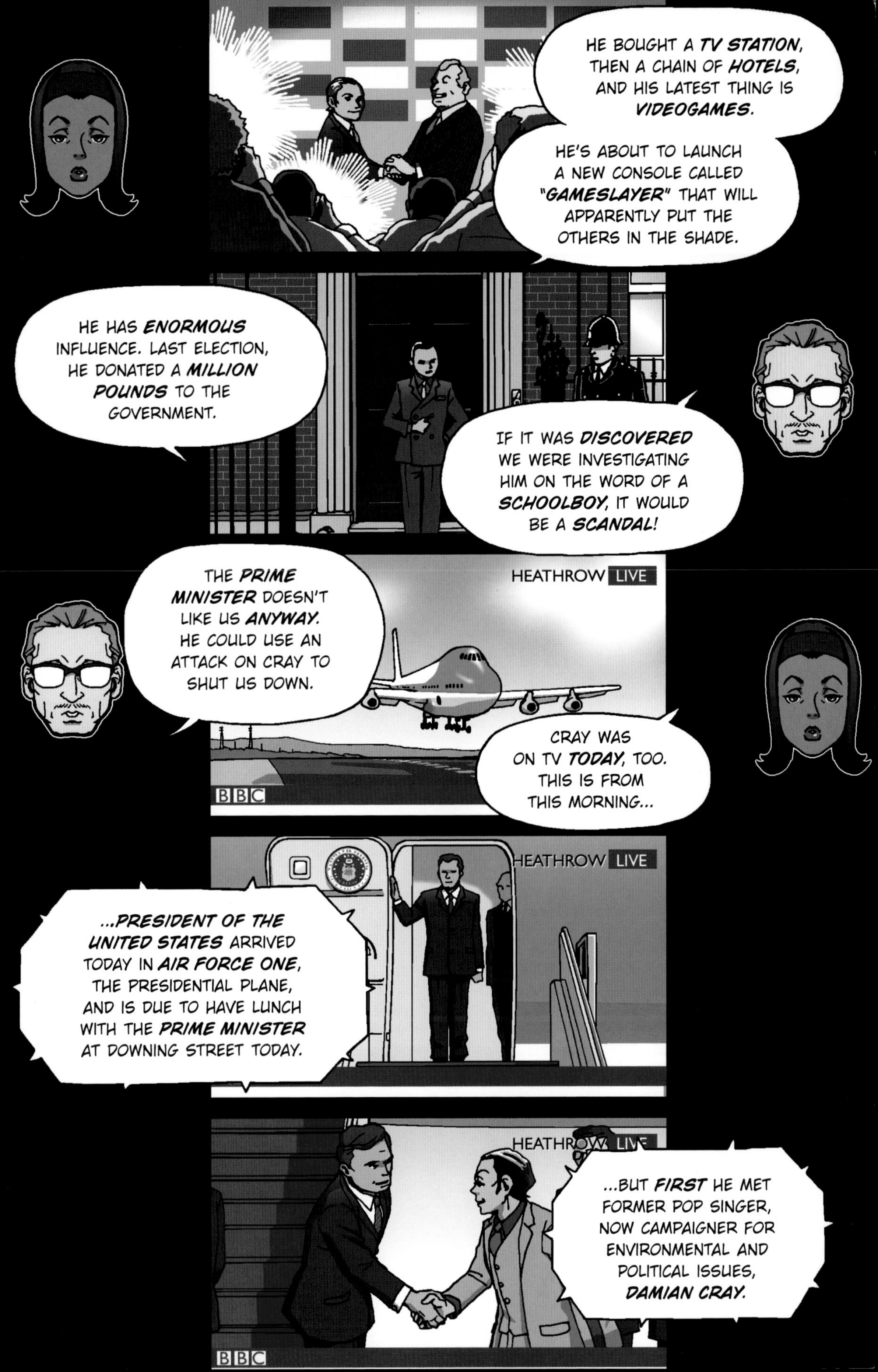
HE BOUGHT A TV STATION, THEN A CHAIN OF HOTELS, AND HIS LATEST THING IS VIDEOGAMES.
HE'S ABOUT TO LAUNCH A NEW CONSOLE CALLED "GAMESLAYER" THAT WILL APPARENTLY PUT THE OTHERS IN THE SHADE.
HE HAS ENORMOUS INFLUENCE. LAST ELECTION, HE DONATED A MILLION POUNDS TO THE GOVERNMENT.
IF IT WAS DISCOVERED WE WERE INVESTIGATING HIM ON THE WORD OF A SCHOOLBOY, IT WOULD BE A SCANDAL!
HEATHROW LIVE
THE PRIME MINISTER DOESN'T LIKE US ANYWAY. HE COULD USE AN ATTACK ON CRAY TO SHUT US DOWN.
CRAY WAS ON TV TODAY, TOO. THIS IS FROM THIS MORNING...
BBC
HEATHROW LIVE
...PRESIDENT OF THE UNITED STATES ARRIVED TODAY IN AIR FORCE ONE, THE PRESIDENTIAL PLANE, AND IS DUE TO HAVE LUNCH WITH THE PRIME MINISTER AT DOWNING STREET TODAY.
HEATHROW LIVE
...BUT FIRST HE MET FORMER POP SINGER, NOW CAMPAIGNER FOR ENVIRONMENTAL AND POLITICAL ISSUES, DAMIAN CRAY.
BBC

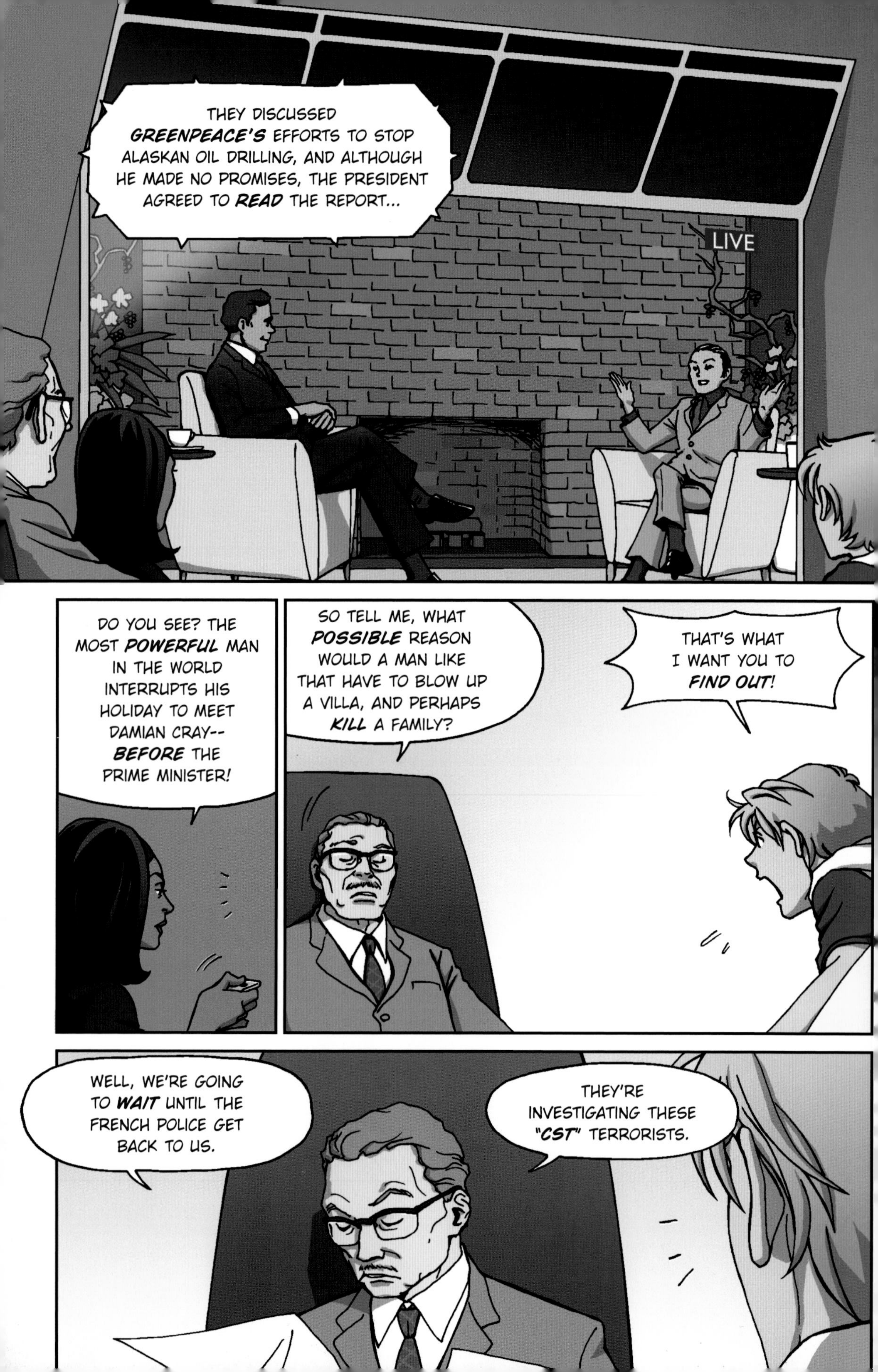
THEY DISCUSSED GREENPEACE'S EFFORTS TO STOP ALASKAN OIL DRILLING, AND ALTHOUGH HE MADE NO PROMISES, THE PRESIDENT AGREED TO READ THE REPORT...
LIVE
DO YOU SEE? THE MOST POWERFUL MAN IN THE WORLD INTERRUPTS HIS HOLIDAY TO MEET DAMIAN CRAY-- BEFORE THE PRIME MINISTER!
SO TELL ME, WHAT POSSIBLE REASON WOULD A MAN LIKE THAT HAVE TO BLOW UP A VILLA, AND PERHAPS KILL A FAMILY?
THAT'S WHAT I WANT YOU TO FIND OUT!
WELL, WE'RE GOING TO WAIT UNTIL THE FRENCH POLICE GET BACK TO US.
THEY'RE INVESTIGATING THESE "CST" TERRORISTS.

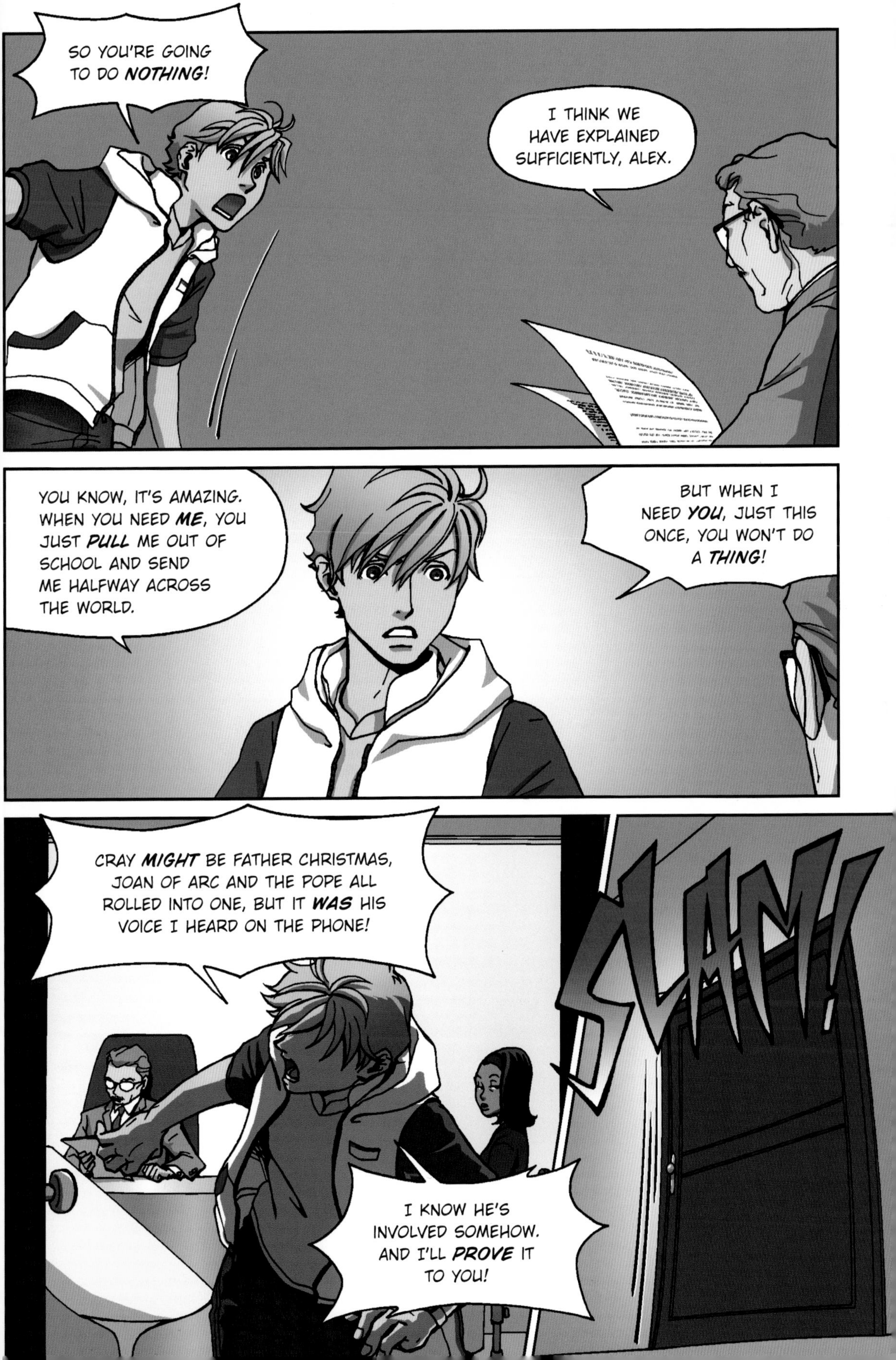
SO YOU'RE GOING TO DO NOTHING!
I THINK WE HAVE EXPLAINED SUFFICIENTLY, ALEX.
YOU KNOW, IT'S AMAZING. WHEN YOU NEED ME, YOU JUST PULL ME OUT OF SCHOOL AND SEND ME HALFWAY ACROSS THE WORLD.
BUT WHEN I NEED YOU, JUST THIS ONCE, YOU WON'T DO A THING!
CRAY MIGHT BE FATHER CHRISTMAS, JOAN OF ARC AND THE POPE ALL ROLLED INTO ONE, BUT IT WAS HIS VOICE I HEARD ON THE PHONE!
I KNOW HE'S INVOLVED SOMEHOW. AND I'LL PROVE IT TO YOU!
SLAM!

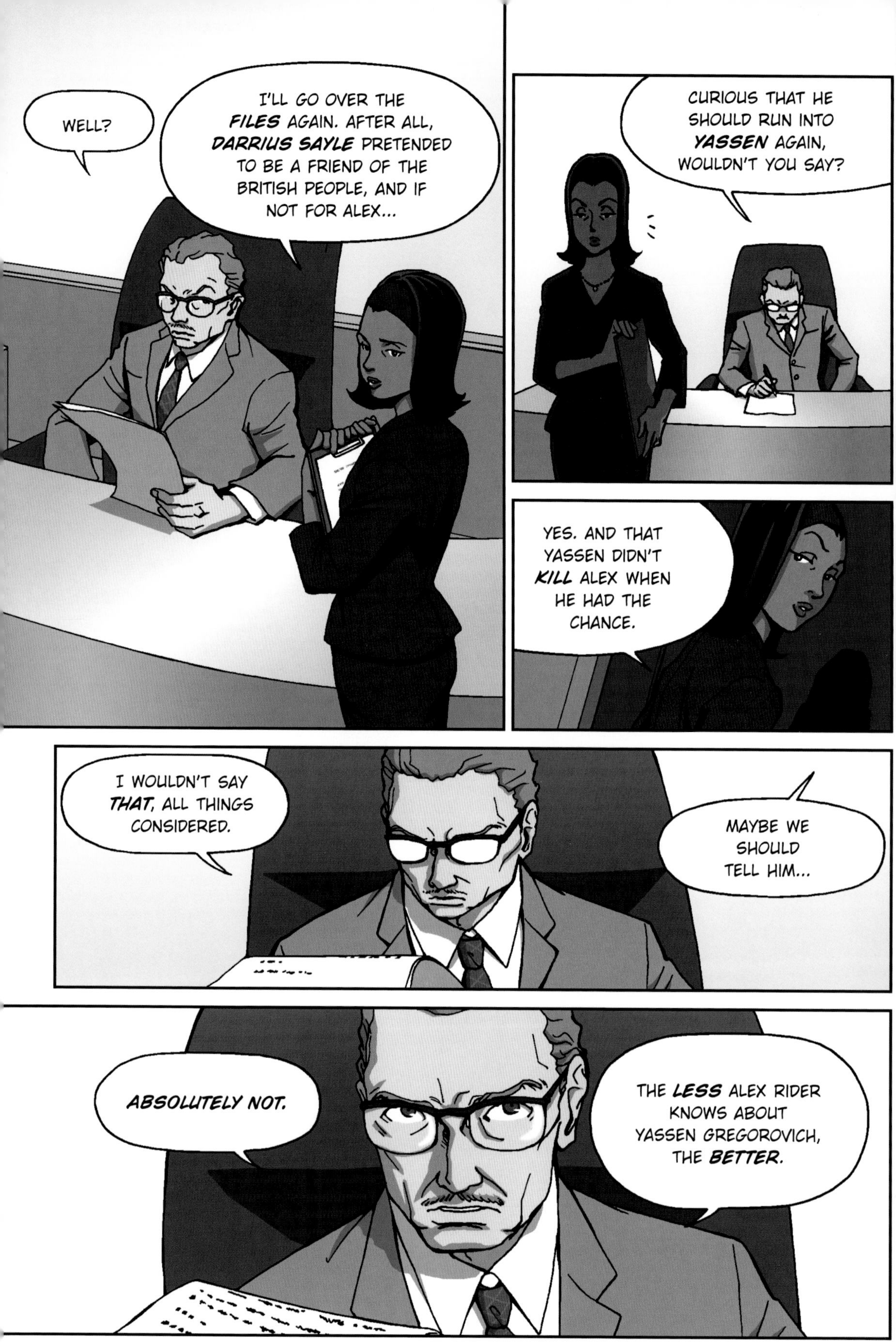
WELL?
I'LL GO OVER THE FILES AGAIN. AFTER ALL, DARRIUS SAYLE PRETENDED TO BE A FRIEND OF THE BRITISH PEOPLE, AND IF NOT FOR ALEX...
CURIOUS THAT HE SHOULD RUN INTO YASSEN AGAIN, WOULDN'T YOU SAY?
YES. AND THAT YASSEN DIDN'T KILL ALEX WHEN HE HAD THE CHANCE.
I WOULDN'T SAY THAT, ALL THINGS CONSIDERED.
MAYBE WE SHOULD TELL HIM...
ABSOLUTELY NOT.
THE LESS ALEX RIDER KNOWS ABOUT YASSEN GREGOROVICH, THE BETTER.

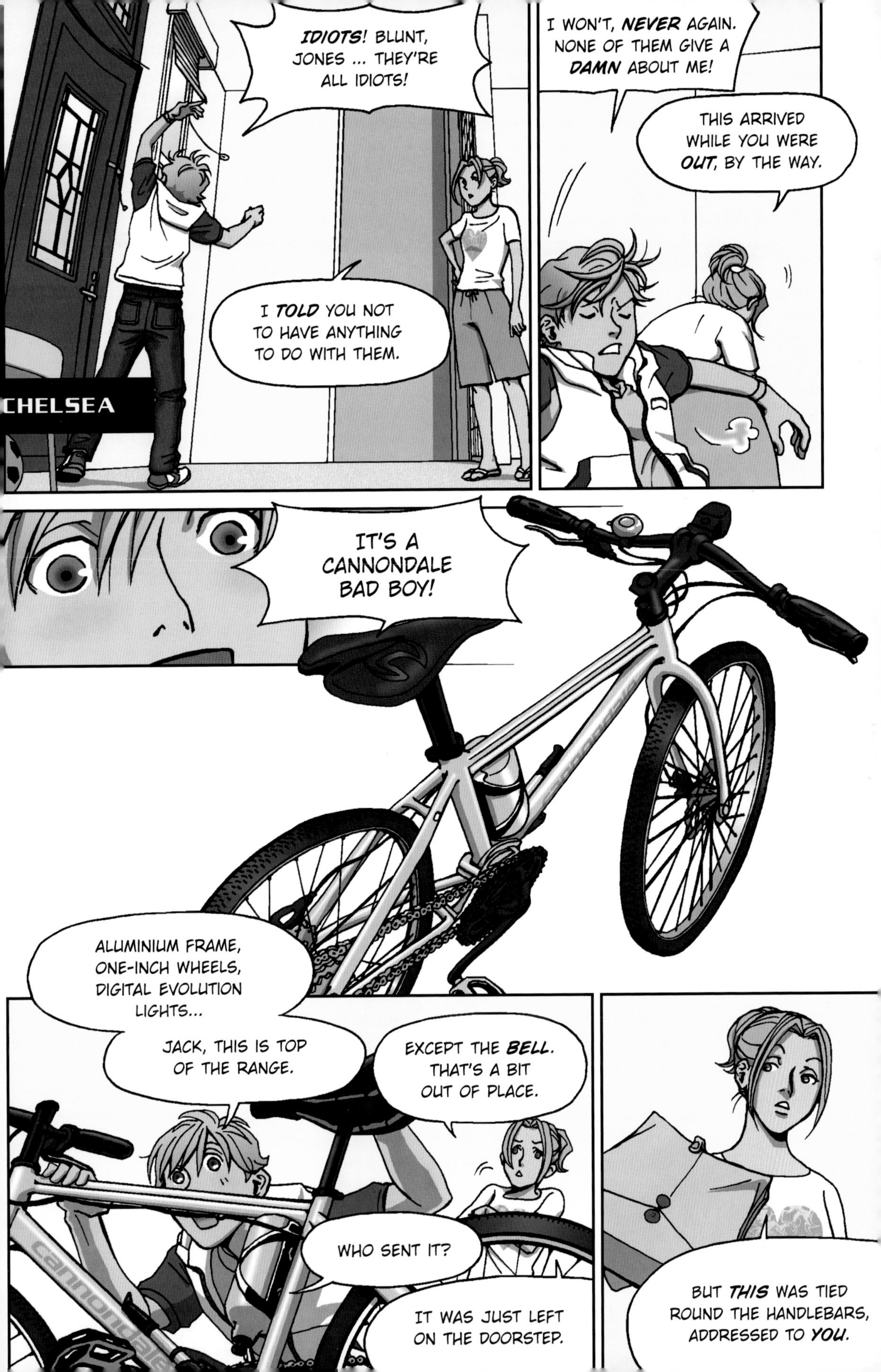
IDIOTS! BLUNT, JONES ... THEY'RE ALL IDIOTS!
I TOLD YOU NOT TO HAVE ANYTHING TO DO WITH THEM.
CHELSEA
I WON'T, NEVER AGAIN. NONE OF THEM GIVE A DAMN ABOUT ME!
THIS ARRIVED WHILE YOU WERE OUT, BY THE WAY.
IT'S A CANNONDALE BAD BOY!
ALUMINIUM FRAME, ONE-INCH WHEELS, DIGITAL EVOLUTION LIGHTS...
JACK, THIS IS TOP OF THE RANGE.
EXCEPT THE BELL. THAT'S A BIT OUT OF PLACE.
WHO SENT IT?
IT WAS JUST LEFT ON THE DOORSTEP.
BUT THIS WAS TIED ROUND THE HANDLEBARS, ADDRESSED TO YOU.

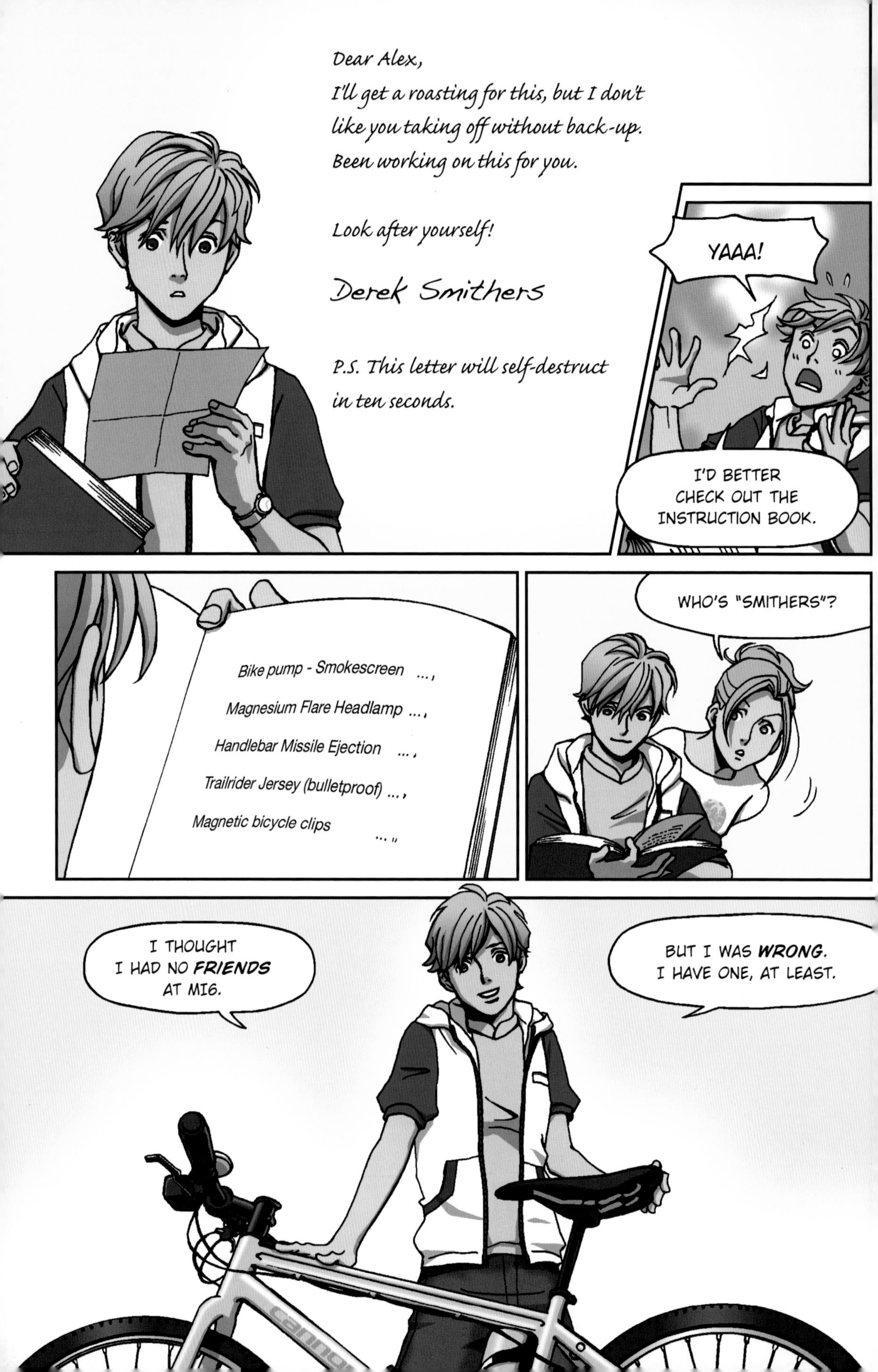
Dear Alex,
I'll get a roasting for this, but I don't like you taking off without back-up. Been working on this for you.
Look after yourself!
Derek Smithers
P.S. This letter will self-destruct in ten seconds.
YAAA!
I'D BETTER CHECK OUT THE INSTRUCTION BOOK.
Bike pump - Smokescreen ...,
Magnesium Flare Headlamp ...,
Handlebar Missile Ejection ...,
Trailrider Jersey (bulletproof) ...,
Magnetic bicycle clips ..."
WHO'S "SMITHERS"?
I THOUGHT I HAD NO FRIENDS AT MI6.
BUT I WAS WRONG. I HAVE ONE, AT LEAST.

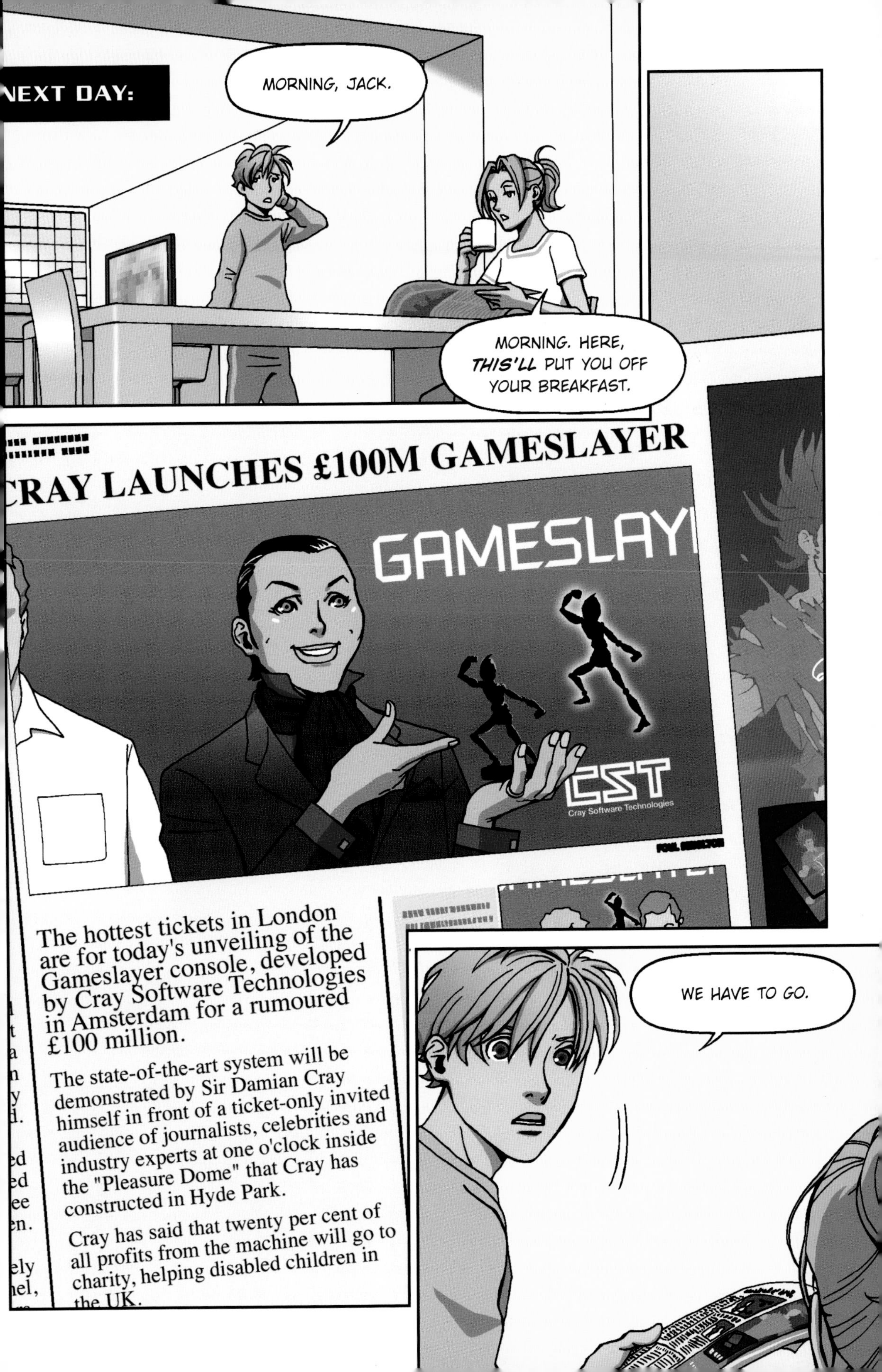
NEXT DAY:
MORNING, JACK.
MORNING. HERE, *THIS'LL* PUT YOU OFF YOUR BREAKFAST.
CRAY LAUNCHES £100M GAMESLAYER
GAMESLAY
CST
Cray Software Technologies
The hottest tickets in London are for today's unveiling of the Gameslayer console, developed by Cray Software Technologies in Amsterdam for a rumoured £100 million.
The state-of-the-art system will be demonstrated by Sir Damian Cray himself in front of a ticket-only invited audience of journalists, celebrities and industry experts at one o'clock inside the "Pleasure Dome" that Cray has constructed in Hyde Park.
Cray has said that twenty per cent of all profits from the machine will go to charity, helping disabled children in the UK.
WE HAVE TO GO.

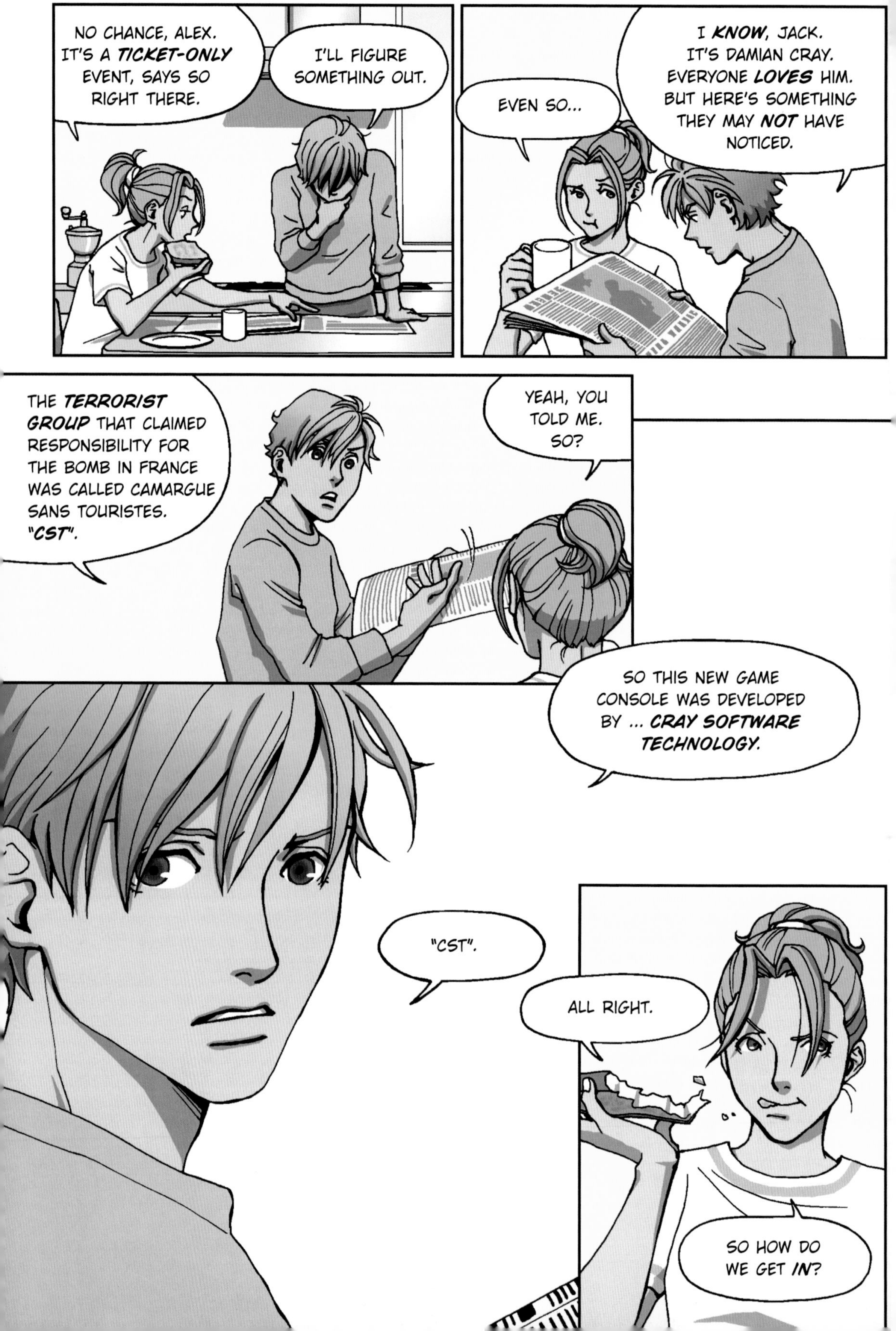
NO CHANCE, ALEX. IT'S A **TICKET-ONLY** EVENT, SAYS SO RIGHT THERE.
I'LL FIGURE SOMETHING OUT.
EVEN SO...
I **KNOW**, JACK. IT'S DAMIAN CRAY. EVERYONE **LOVES** HIM. BUT HERE'S SOMETHING THEY MAY **NOT** HAVE NOTICED.
THE **TERRORIST GROUP** THAT CLAIMED RESPONSIBILITY FOR THE BOMB IN FRANCE WAS CALLED CAMARGUE SANS TOURISTES. "**CST**".
YEAH, YOU TOLD ME. SO?
SO THIS NEW GAME CONSOLE WAS DEVELOPED BY ... **CRAY SOFTWARE TECHNOLOGY.**
"CST".
ALL RIGHT.
SO HOW DO WE GET **IN**?

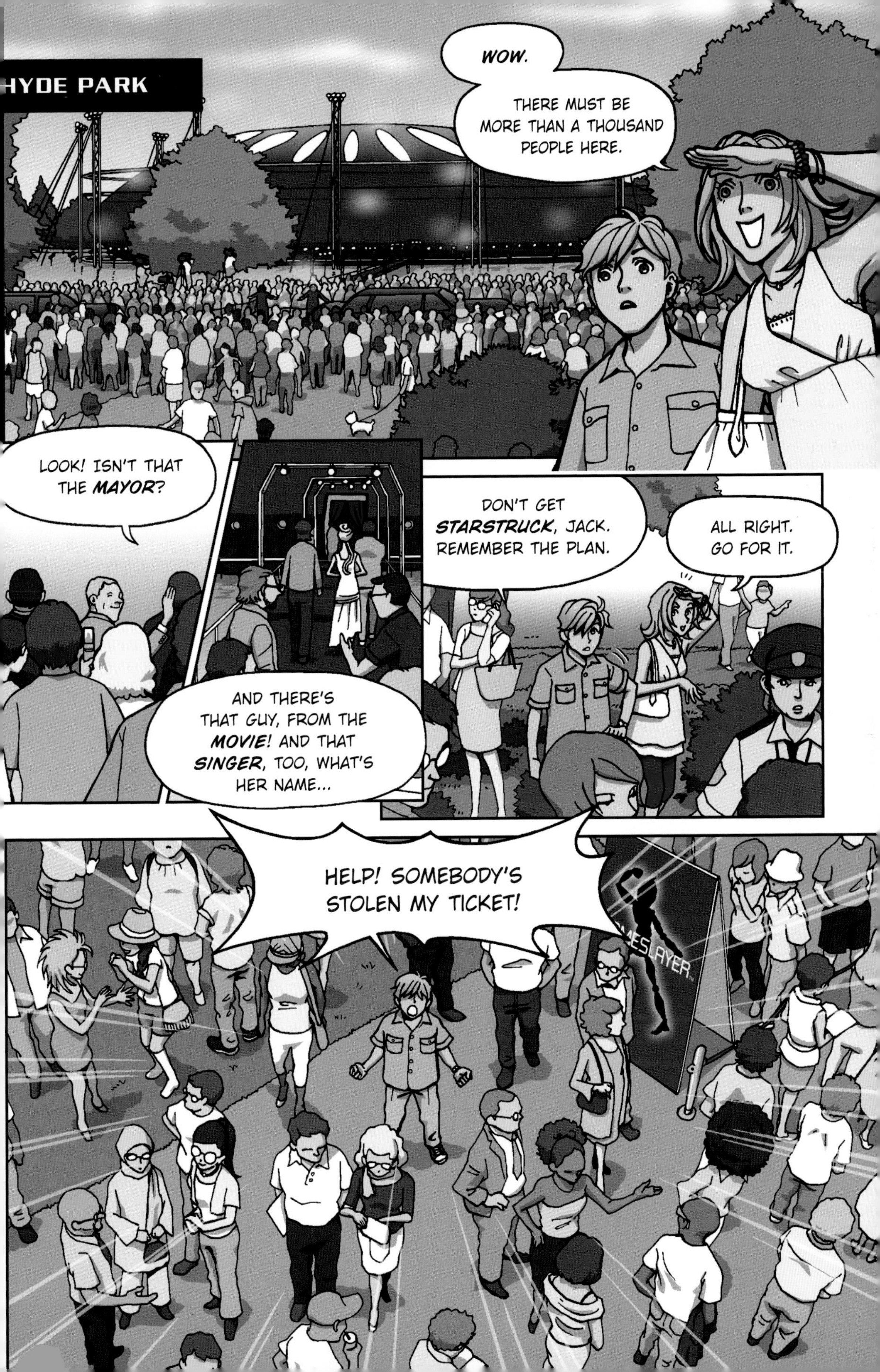
HYDE PARK
WOW.
THERE MUST BE MORE THAN A THOUSAND PEOPLE HERE.
LOOK! ISN'T THAT THE MAYOR?
DON'T GET STARSTRUCK, JACK. REMEMBER THE PLAN.
ALL RIGHT. GO FOR IT.
AND THERE'S THAT GUY, FROM THE MOVIE! AND THAT SINGER, TOO, WHAT'S HER NAME...
HELP! SOMEBODY'S STOLEN MY TICKET!

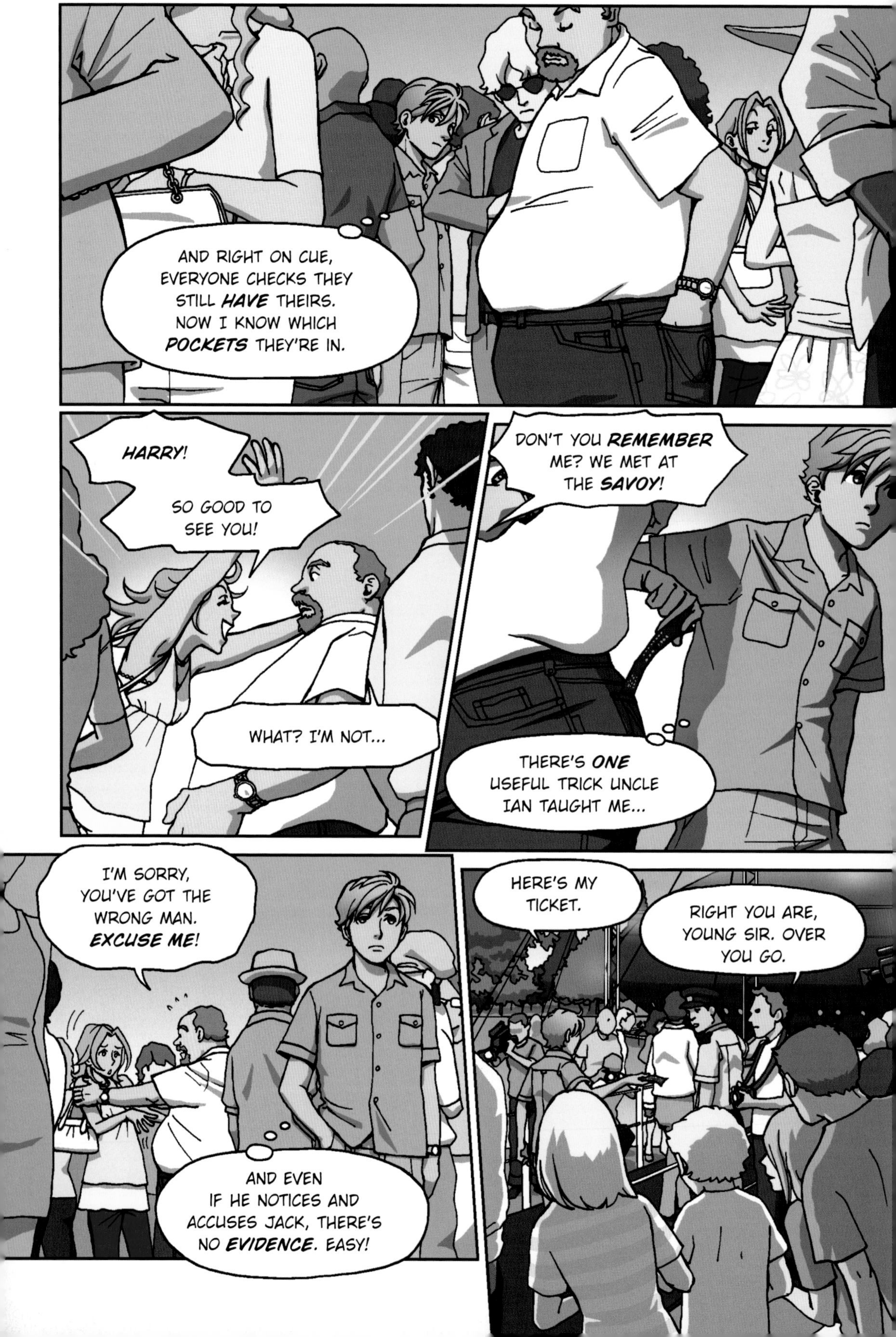
AND RIGHT ON CUE, EVERYONE CHECKS THEY STILL HAVE THEIRS. NOW I KNOW WHICH POCKETS THEY'RE IN.
HARRY!
SO GOOD TO SEE YOU!
WHAT? I'M NOT...
DON'T YOU REMEMBER ME? WE MET AT THE SAVOY!
THERE'S ONE USEFUL TRICK UNCLE IAN TAUGHT ME...
I'M SORRY, YOU'VE GOT THE WRONG MAN. EXCUSE ME!
AND EVEN IF HE NOTICES AND ACCUSES JACK, THERE'S NO EVIDENCE. EASY!
HERE'S MY TICKET.
RIGHT YOU ARE, YOUNG SIR. OVER YOU GO.

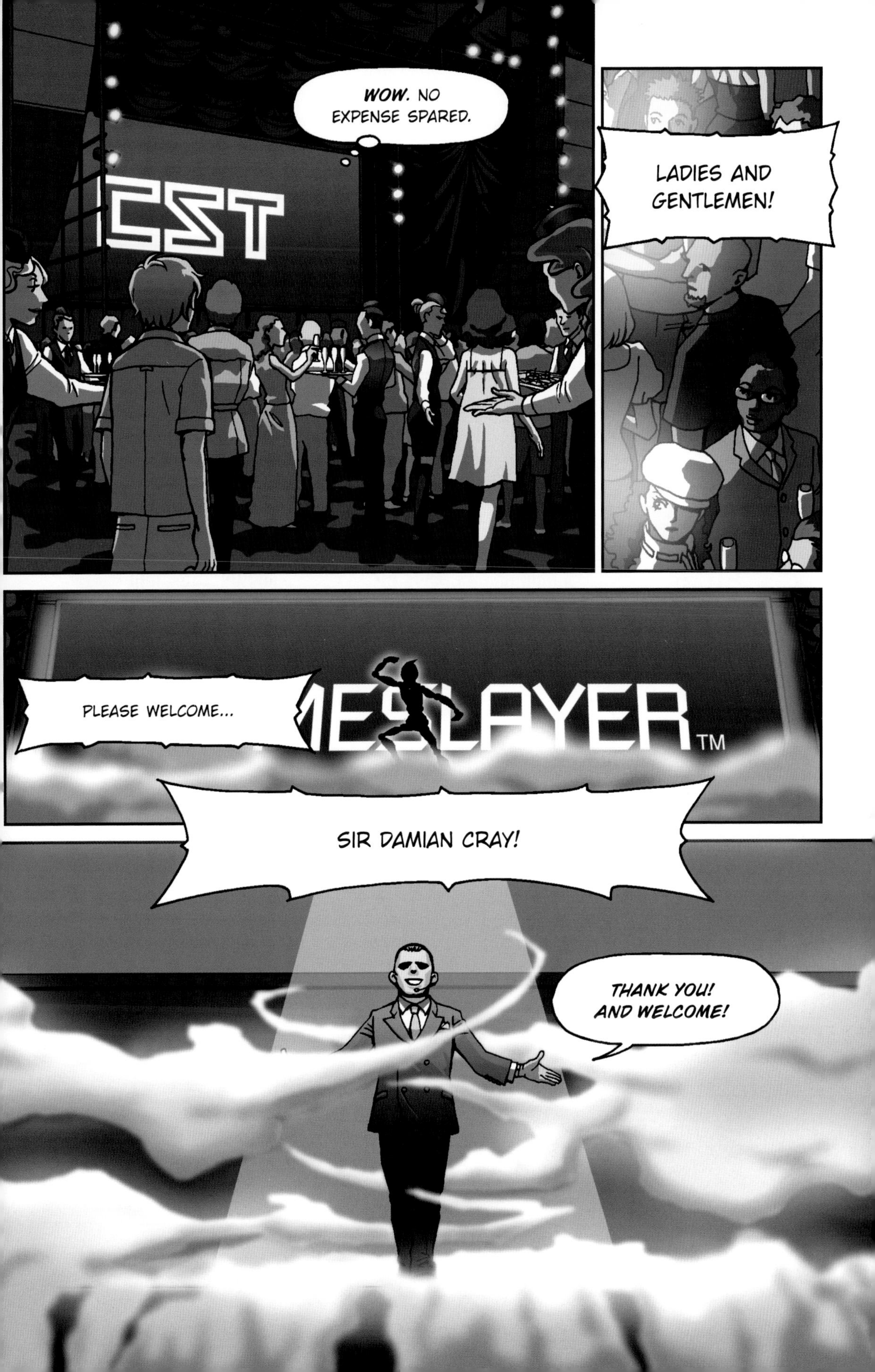
WOW. NO EXPENSE SPARED.
LADIES AND GENTLEMEN!
MESLAYER TM
PLEASE WELCOME...
SIR DAMIAN CRAY!
THANK YOU! AND WELCOME!

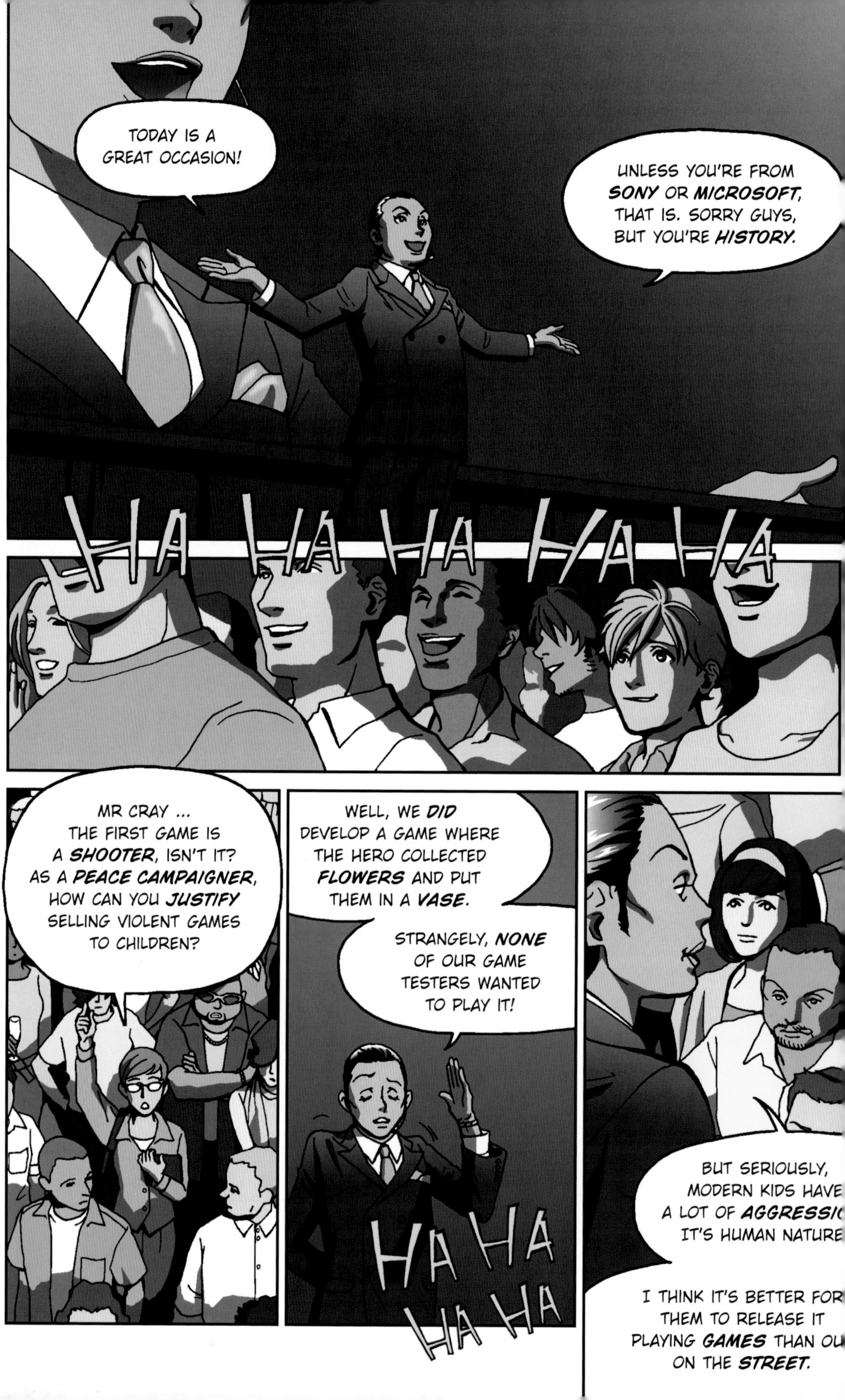
TODAY IS A GREAT OCCASION!
UNLESS YOU'RE FROM SONY OR MICROSOFT, THAT IS. SORRY GUYS, BUT YOU'RE HISTORY.
HA HA HA HA HA
MR CRAY ... THE FIRST GAME IS A SHOOTER, ISN'T IT? AS A PEACE CAMPAIGNER, HOW CAN YOU JUSTIFY SELLING VIOLENT GAMES TO CHILDREN?
WELL, WE DID DEVELOP A GAME WHERE THE HERO COLLECTED FLOWERS AND PUT THEM IN A VASE.
STRANGELY, NONE OF OUR GAME TESTERS WANTED TO PLAY IT!
HA HA HA HA
BUT SERIOUSLY, MODERN KIDS HAVE A LOT OF AGGRESSI
IT'S HUMAN NATURE
I THINK IT'S BETTER FOR THEM TO RELEASE IT PLAYING GAMES THAN OU ON THE STREET.

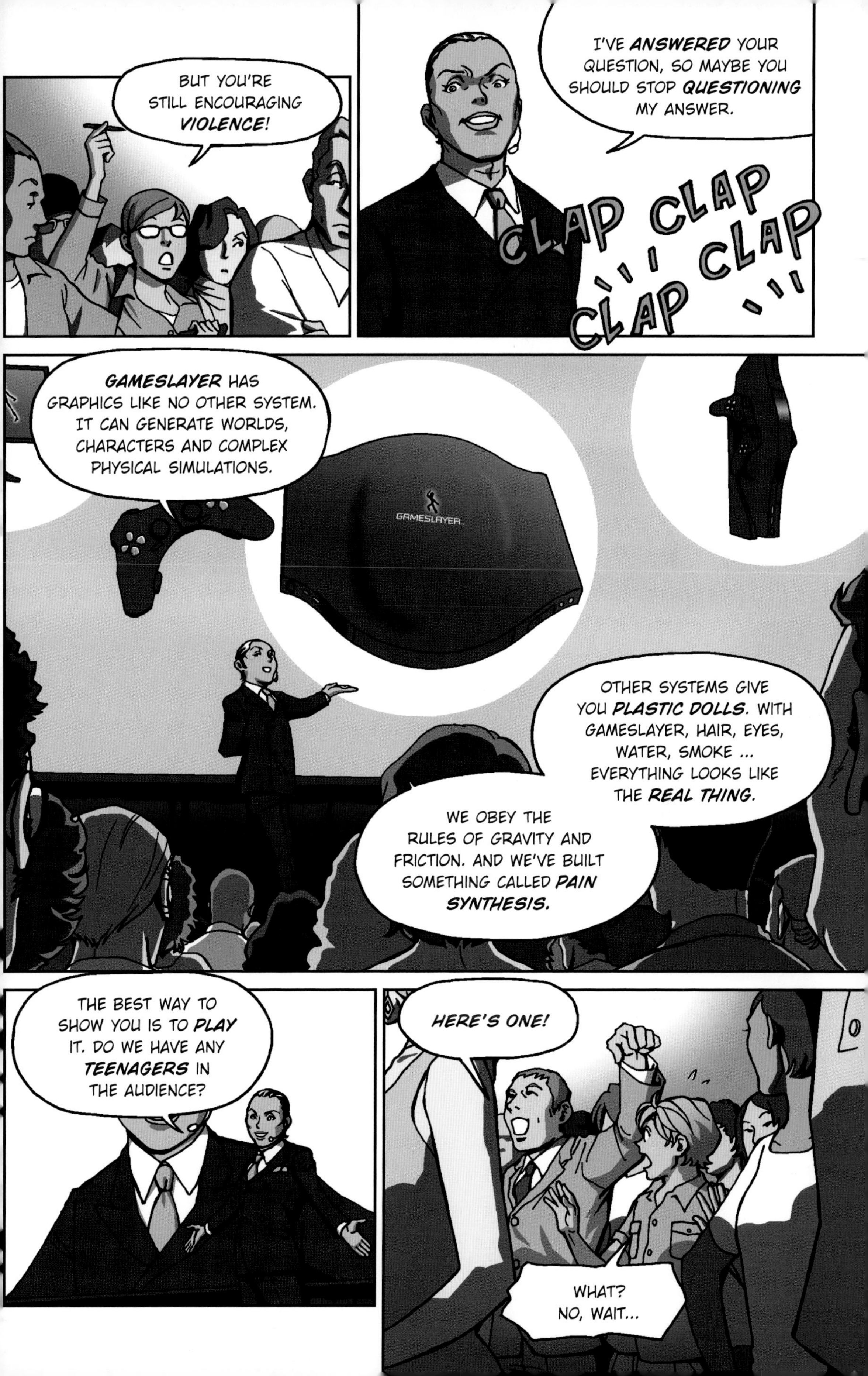
BUT YOU'RE STILL ENCOURAGING VIOLENCE!
I'VE ANSWERED YOUR QUESTION, SO MAYBE YOU SHOULD STOP QUESTIONING MY ANSWER.
CLAP CLAP CLAP CLAP
GAMESLAYER HAS GRAPHICS LIKE NO OTHER SYSTEM. IT CAN GENERATE WORLDS, CHARACTERS AND COMPLEX PHYSICAL SIMULATIONS.
GAMESLAYER
OTHER SYSTEMS GIVE YOU PLASTIC DOLLS. WITH GAMESLAYER, HAIR, EYES, WATER, SMOKE ... EVERYTHING LOOKS LIKE THE REAL THING.
WE OBEY THE RULES OF GRAVITY AND FRICTION. AND WE'VE BUILT SOMETHING CALLED PAIN SYNTHESIS.
THE BEST WAY TO SHOW YOU IS TO PLAY IT. DO WE HAVE ANY TEENAGERS IN THE AUDIENCE?
HERE'S ONE!
WHAT? NO, WAIT...

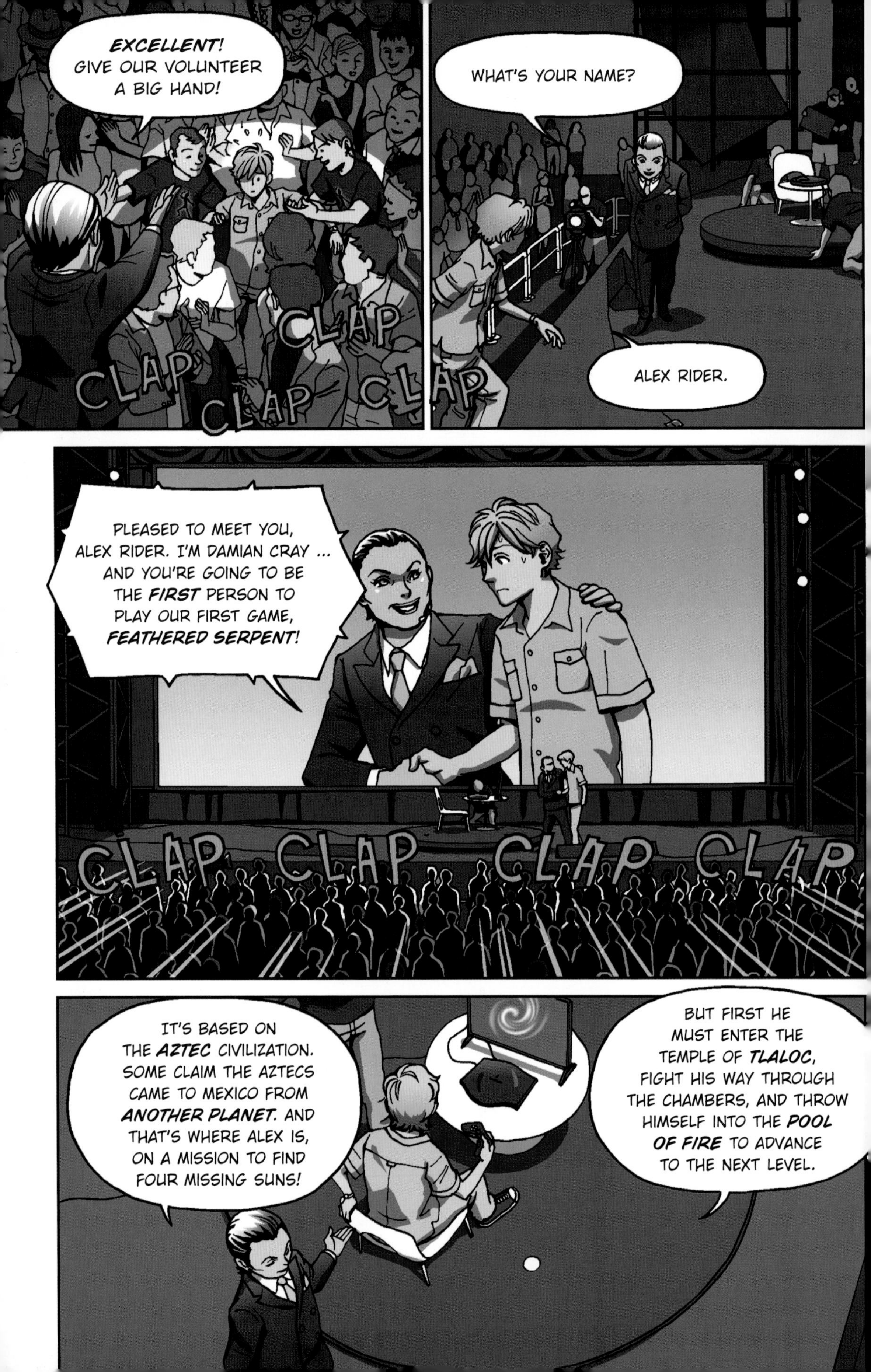

EXCELLENT! GIVE OUR VOLUNTEER A BIG HAND!
CLAP CLAP CLAP CLAP
WHAT'S YOUR NAME?
ALEX RIDER.
PLEASED TO MEET YOU, ALEX RIDER. I'M DAMIAN CRAY ... AND YOU'RE GOING TO BE THE FIRST PERSON TO PLAY OUR FIRST GAME, FEATHERED SERPENT!
CLAP CLAP CLAP CLAP
IT'S BASED ON THE AZTEC CIVILIZATION. SOME CLAIM THE AZTECS CAME TO MEXICO FROM ANOTHER PLANET. AND THAT'S WHERE ALEX IS, ON A MISSION TO FIND FOUR MISSING SUNS!
BUT FIRST HE MUST ENTER THE TEMPLE OF TLALOC, FIGHT HIS WAY THROUGH THE CHAMBERS, AND THROW HIMSELF INTO THE POOL OF FIRE TO ADVANCE TO THE NEXT LEVEL.

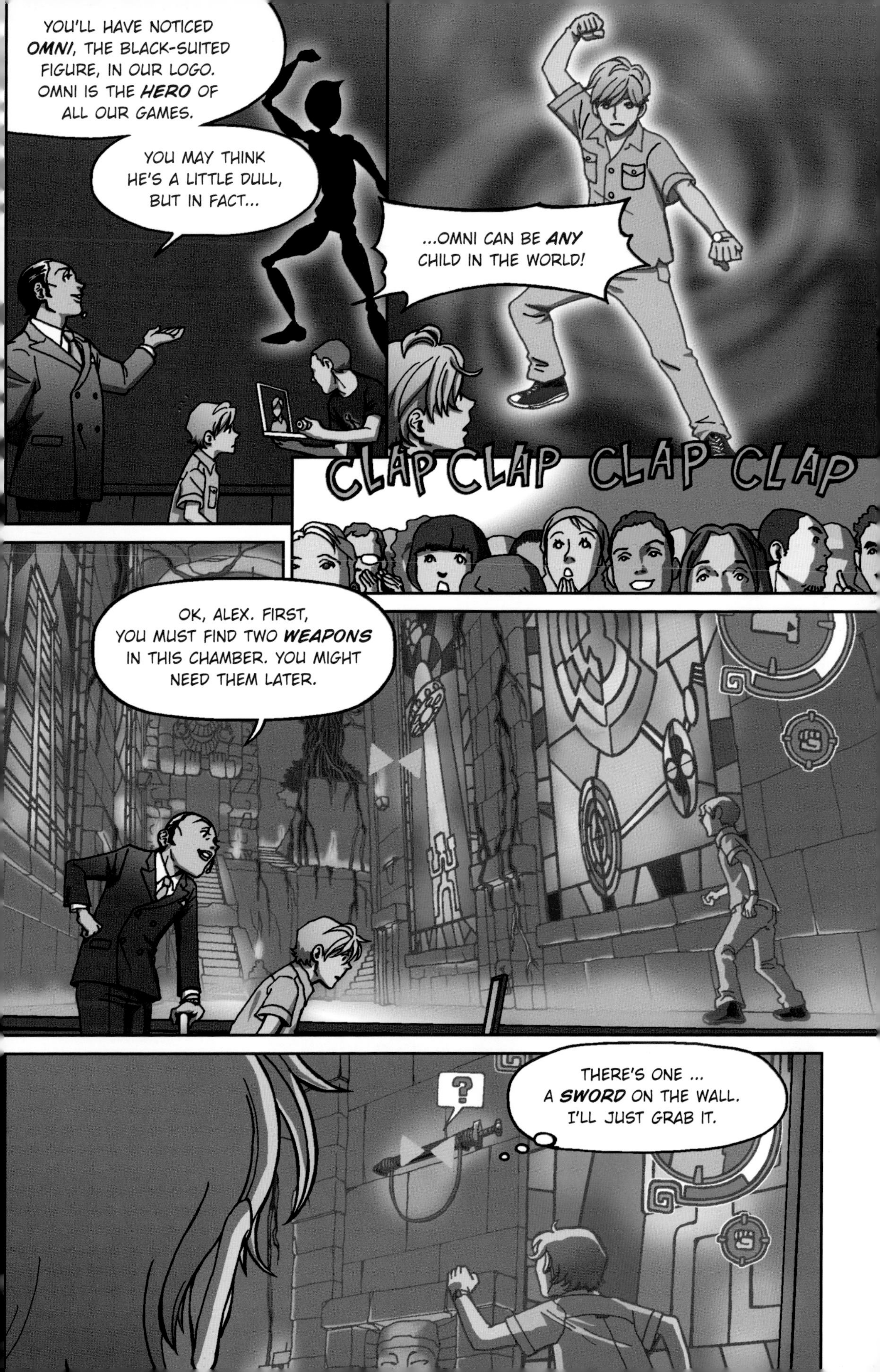
YOU'LL HAVE NOTICED OMNI, THE BLACK-SUITED FIGURE, IN OUR LOGO. OMNI IS THE HERO OF ALL OUR GAMES.
YOU MAY THINK HE'S A LITTLE DULL, BUT IN FACT...
...OMNI CAN BE ANY CHILD IN THE WORLD!
CLAP CLAP CLAP CLAP
OK, ALEX. FIRST, YOU MUST FIND TWO WEAPONS IN THIS CHAMBER. YOU MIGHT NEED THEM LATER.
?
THERE'S ONE ... A SWORD ON THE WALL. I'LL JUST GRAB IT.

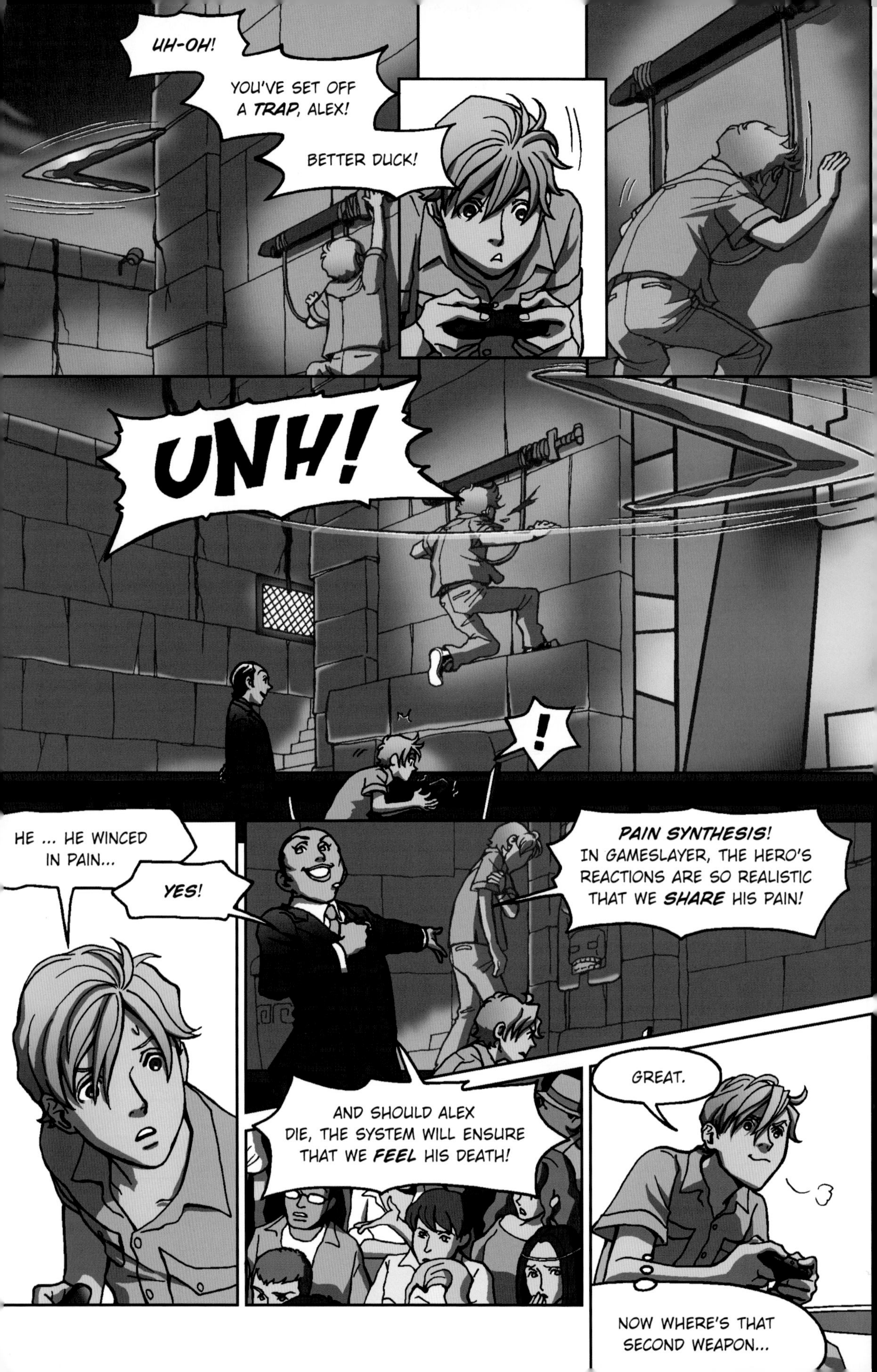
UH-OH!
YOU'VE SET OFF A TRAP, ALEX!
BETTER DUCK!
UNH!
!
HE ... HE WINCED IN PAIN...
YES!
PAIN SYNTHESIS! IN GAMESLAYER, THE HERO'S REACTIONS ARE SO REALISTIC THAT WE SHARE HIS PAIN!
AND SHOULD ALEX DIE, THE SYSTEM WILL ENSURE THAT WE FEEL HIS DEATH!
GREAT.
NOW WHERE'S THAT SECOND WEAPON...

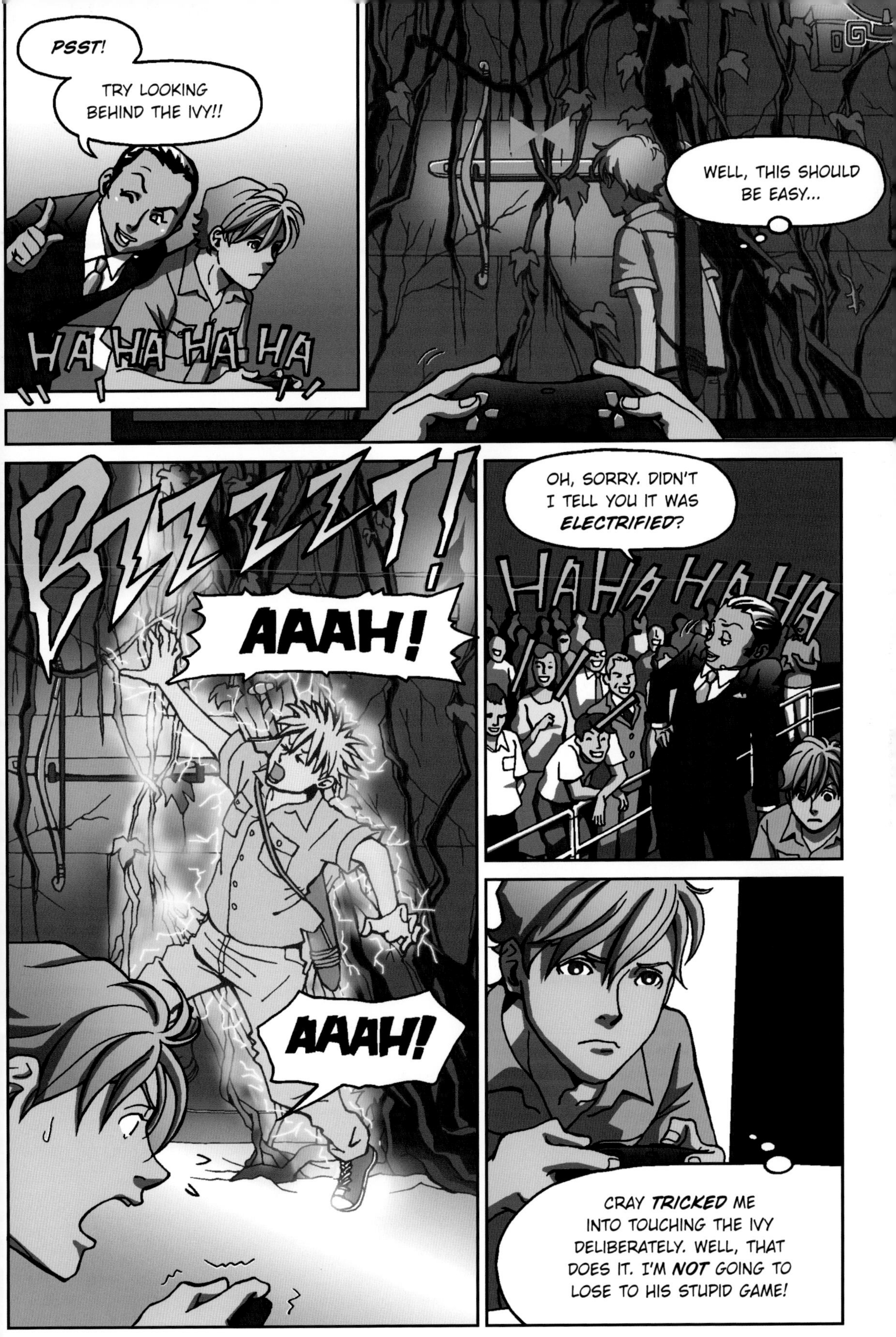
PSST!
TRY LOOKING BEHIND THE IVY!!
HA HA HA HA
WELL, THIS SHOULD BE EASY...
BZZZZT!
AAAH!
AAAH!
OH, SORRY. DIDN'T I TELL YOU IT WAS *ELECTRIFIED*?
HAHAHAHAHA
CRAY ***TRICKED*** ME INTO TOUCHING THE IVY DELIBERATELY. WELL, THAT DOES IT. I'M ***NOT*** GOING TO LOSE TO HIS STUPID GAME!

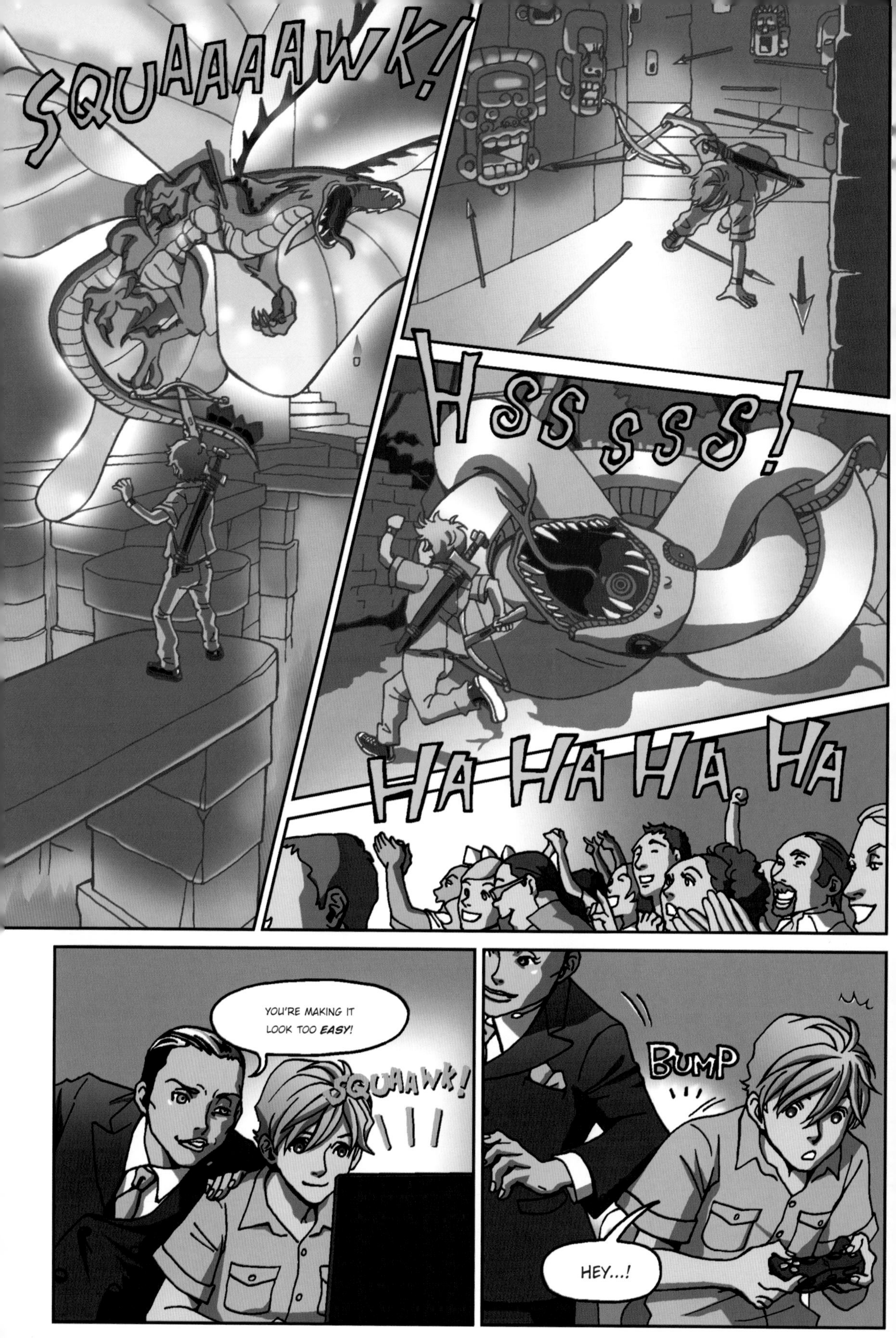
SQUAAAAAWK!
HSSSSS!
HA HA HA HA
YOU'RE MAKING IT LOOK TOO *EASY!*
SQUAWK!
BUMP
HEY...!

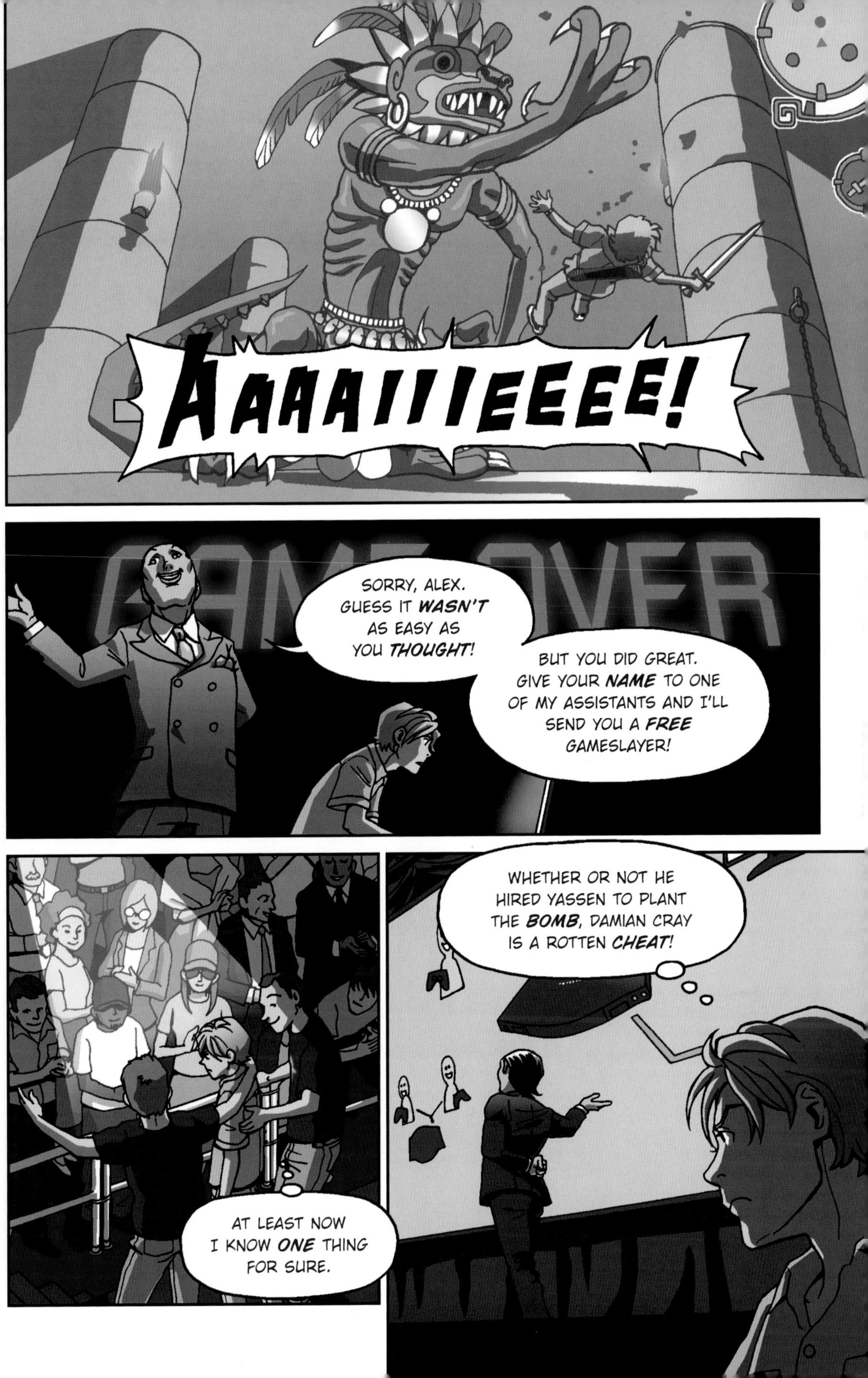
AAAAIIIEEEEE!
GAME OVER
SORRY, ALEX. GUESS IT WASN'T AS EASY AS YOU THOUGHT!
BUT YOU DID GREAT. GIVE YOUR NAME TO ONE OF MY ASSISTANTS AND I'LL SEND YOU A FREE GAMESLAYER!
AT LEAST NOW I KNOW ONE THING FOR SURE.
WHETHER OR NOT HE HIRED YASSEN TO PLANT THE BOMB, DAMIAN CRAY IS A ROTTEN CHEAT!

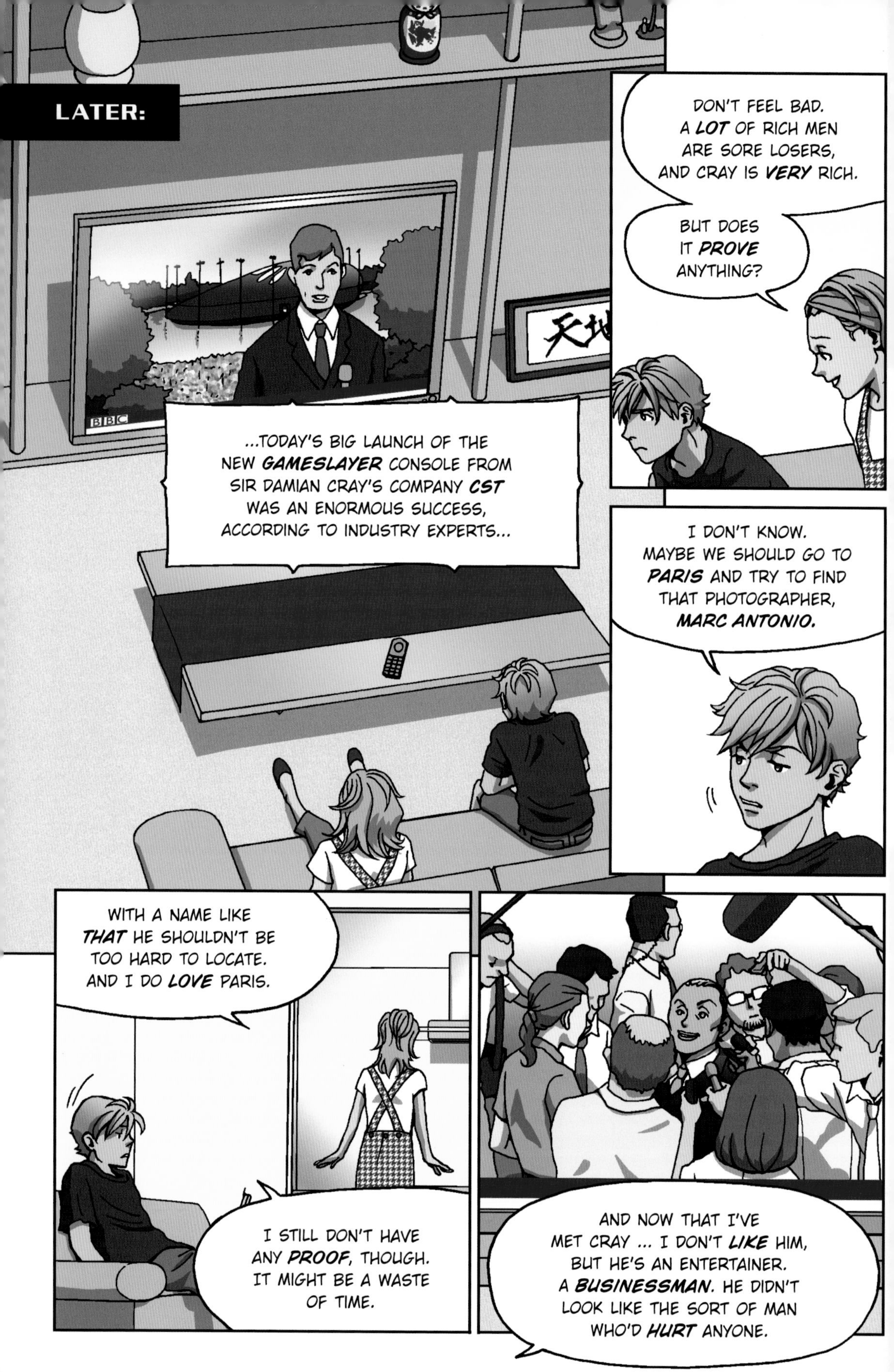
LATER:
...TODAY'S BIG LAUNCH OF THE NEW GAMESLAYER CONSOLE FROM SIR DAMIAN CRAY'S COMPANY CST WAS AN ENORMOUS SUCCESS, ACCORDING TO INDUSTRY EXPERTS...
BBC
DON'T FEEL BAD. A LOT OF RICH MEN ARE SORE LOSERS, AND CRAY IS VERY RICH.
BUT DOES IT PROVE ANYTHING?
I DON'T KNOW. MAYBE WE SHOULD GO TO PARIS AND TRY TO FIND THAT PHOTOGRAPHER, MARC ANTONIO.
WITH A NAME LIKE THAT HE SHOULDN'T BE TOO HARD TO LOCATE. AND I DO LOVE PARIS.
I STILL DON'T HAVE ANY PROOF, THOUGH. IT MIGHT BE A WASTE OF TIME.
AND NOW THAT I'VE MET CRAY ... I DON'T LIKE HIM, BUT HE'S AN ENTERTAINER. A BUSINESSMAN. HE DIDN'T LOOK LIKE THE SORT OF MAN WHO'D HURT ANYONE.

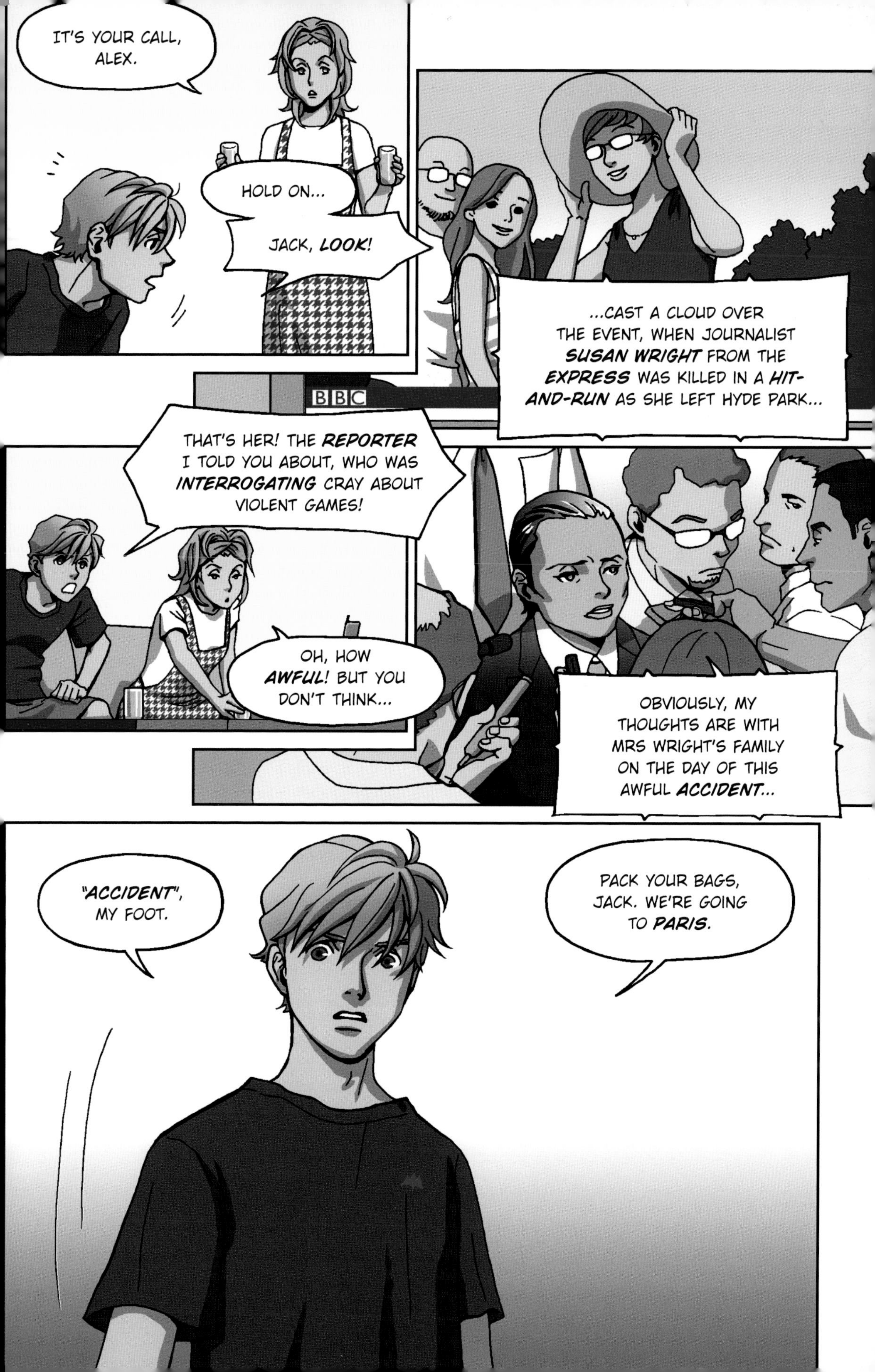
IT'S YOUR CALL, ALEX.
HOLD ON...
JACK, LOOK!
...CAST A CLOUD OVER THE EVENT, WHEN JOURNALIST SUSAN WRIGHT FROM THE EXPRESS WAS KILLED IN A HIT-AND-RUN AS SHE LEFT HYDE PARK...
BBC
THAT'S HER! THE REPORTER I TOLD YOU ABOUT, WHO WAS INTERROGATING CRAY ABOUT VIOLENT GAMES!
OH, HOW AWFUL! BUT YOU DON'T THINK...
OBVIOUSLY, MY THOUGHTS ARE WITH MRS WRIGHT'S FAMILY ON THE DAY OF THIS AWFUL ACCIDENT...
"ACCIDENT", MY FOOT.
PACK YOUR BAGS, JACK. WE'RE GOING TO PARIS.

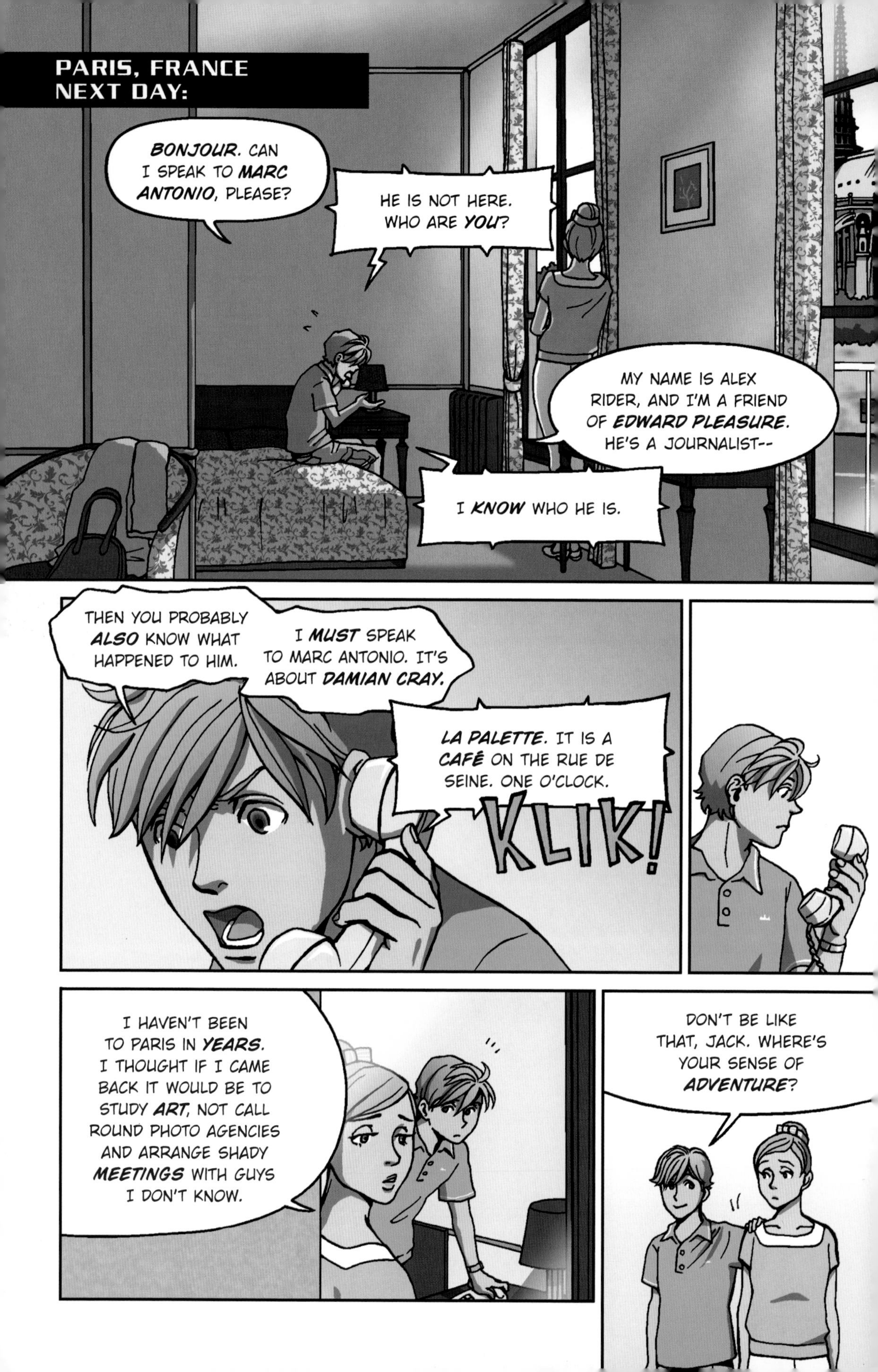
PARIS, FRANCE NEXT DAY:
BONJOUR. CAN I SPEAK TO MARC ANTONIO, PLEASE?
HE IS NOT HERE. WHO ARE YOU?
MY NAME IS ALEX RIDER, AND I'M A FRIEND OF EDWARD PLEASURE. HE'S A JOURNALIST--
I KNOW WHO HE IS.
THEN YOU PROBABLY ALSO KNOW WHAT HAPPENED TO HIM.
I MUST SPEAK TO MARC ANTONIO. IT'S ABOUT DAMIAN CRAY.
LA PALETTE. IT IS A CAFÉ ON THE RUE DE SEINE. ONE O'CLOCK.
KLIK!
I HAVEN'T BEEN TO PARIS IN YEARS. I THOUGHT IF I CAME BACK IT WOULD BE TO STUDY ART, NOT CALL ROUND PHOTO AGENCIES AND ARRANGE SHADY MEETINGS WITH GUYS I DON'T KNOW.
DON'T BE LIKE THAT, JACK. WHERE'S YOUR SENSE OF ADVENTURE?

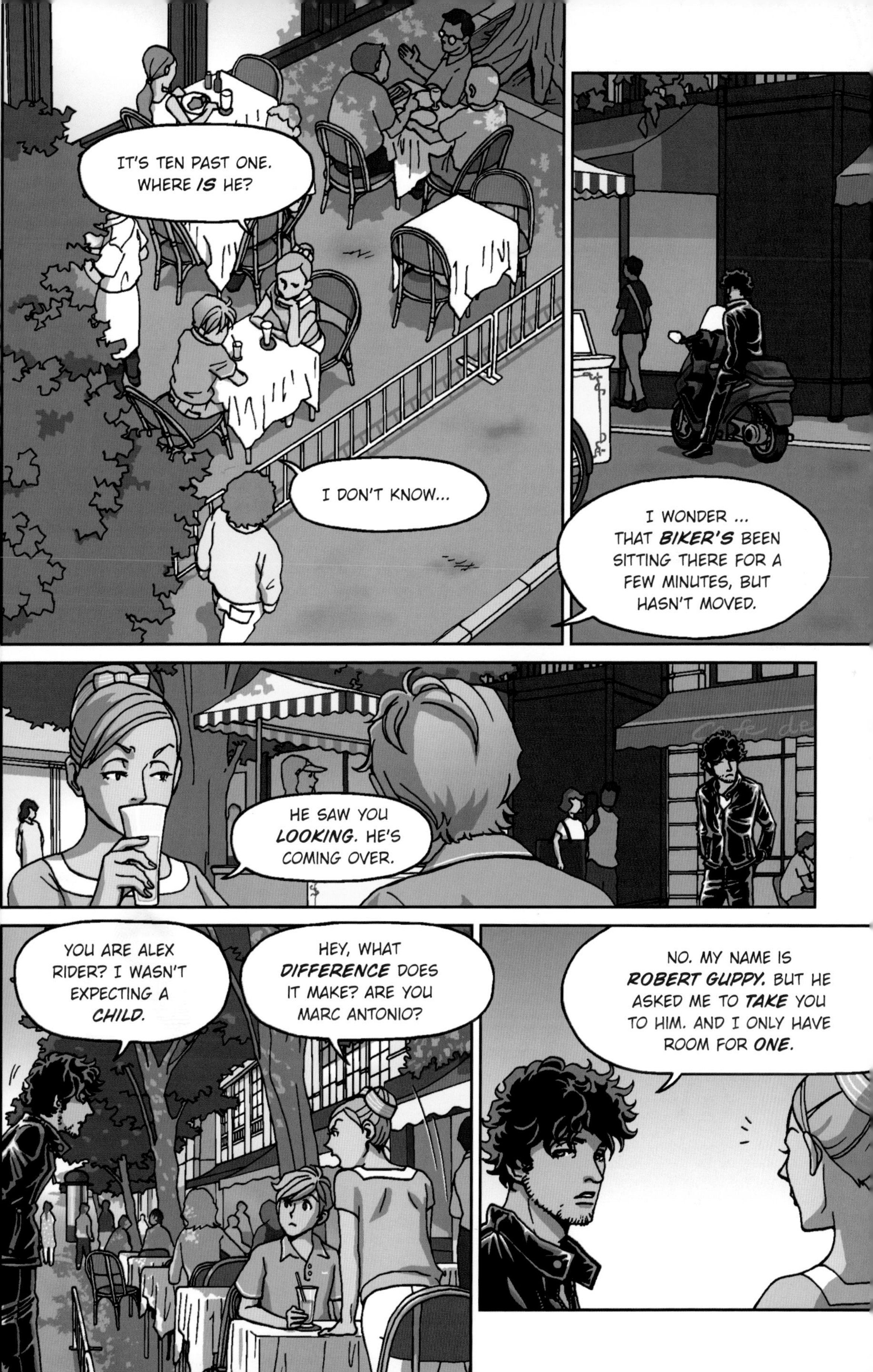
IT'S TEN PAST ONE. WHERE IS HE?
I DON'T KNOW...
I WONDER ... THAT BIKER'S BEEN SITTING THERE FOR A FEW MINUTES, BUT HASN'T MOVED.
HE SAW YOU LOOKING. HE'S COMING OVER.
YOU ARE ALEX RIDER? I WASN'T EXPECTING A CHILD.
HEY, WHAT DIFFERENCE DOES IT MAKE? ARE YOU MARC ANTONIO?
NO. MY NAME IS ROBERT GUPPY. BUT HE ASKED ME TO TAKE YOU TO HIM. AND I ONLY HAVE ROOM FOR ONE.

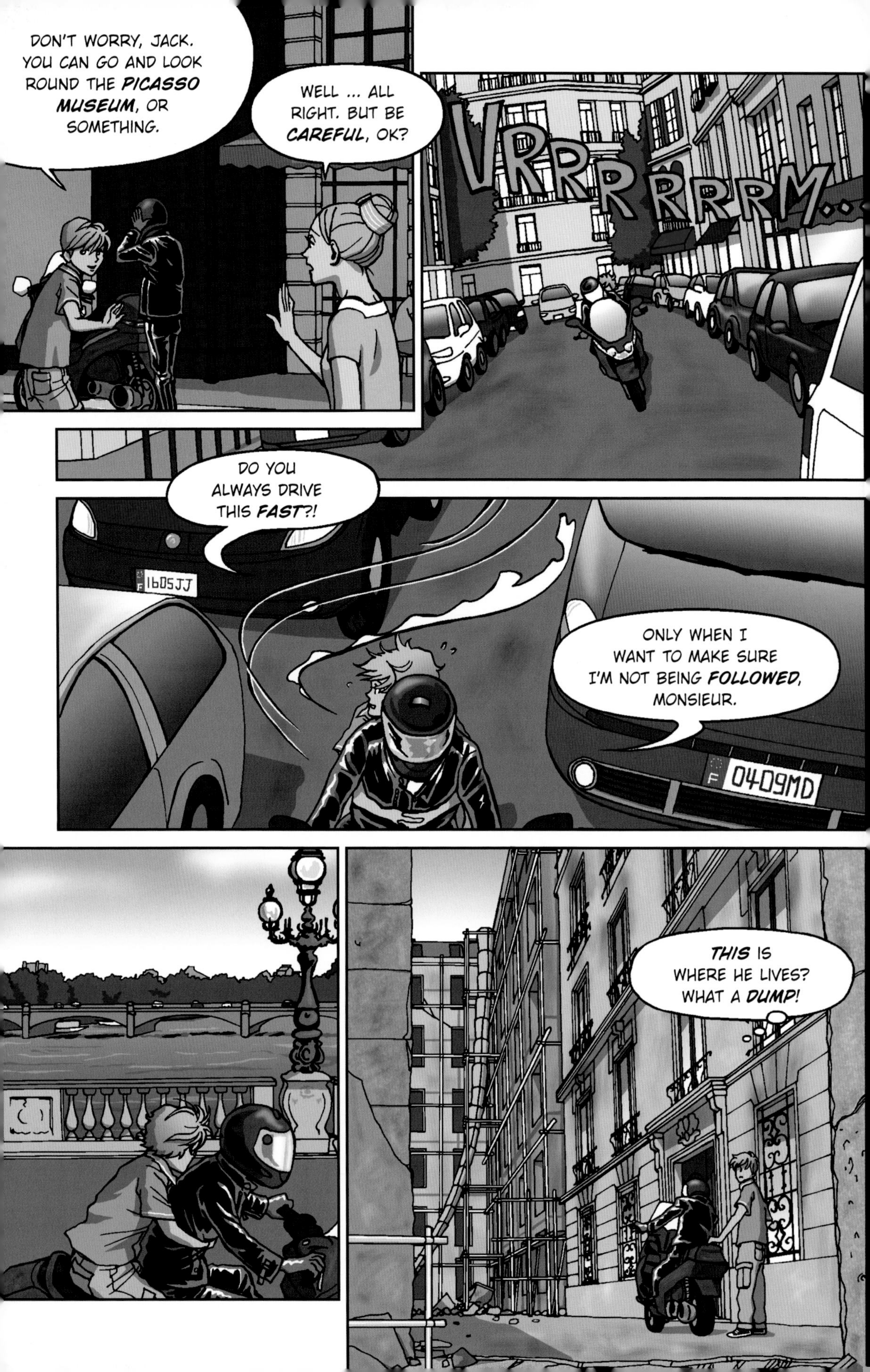
DON'T WORRY, JACK. YOU CAN GO AND LOOK ROUND THE **PICASSO MUSEUM**, OR SOMETHING.
WELL ... ALL RIGHT. BUT BE **CAREFUL**, OK?
VRRRRRRM...
DO YOU ALWAYS DRIVE THIS **FAST**?!
F 1605JJ
ONLY WHEN I WANT TO MAKE SURE I'M NOT BEING **FOLLOWED**, MONSIEUR.
F 0409MD
THIS IS WHERE HE LIVES? WHAT A **DUMP**!

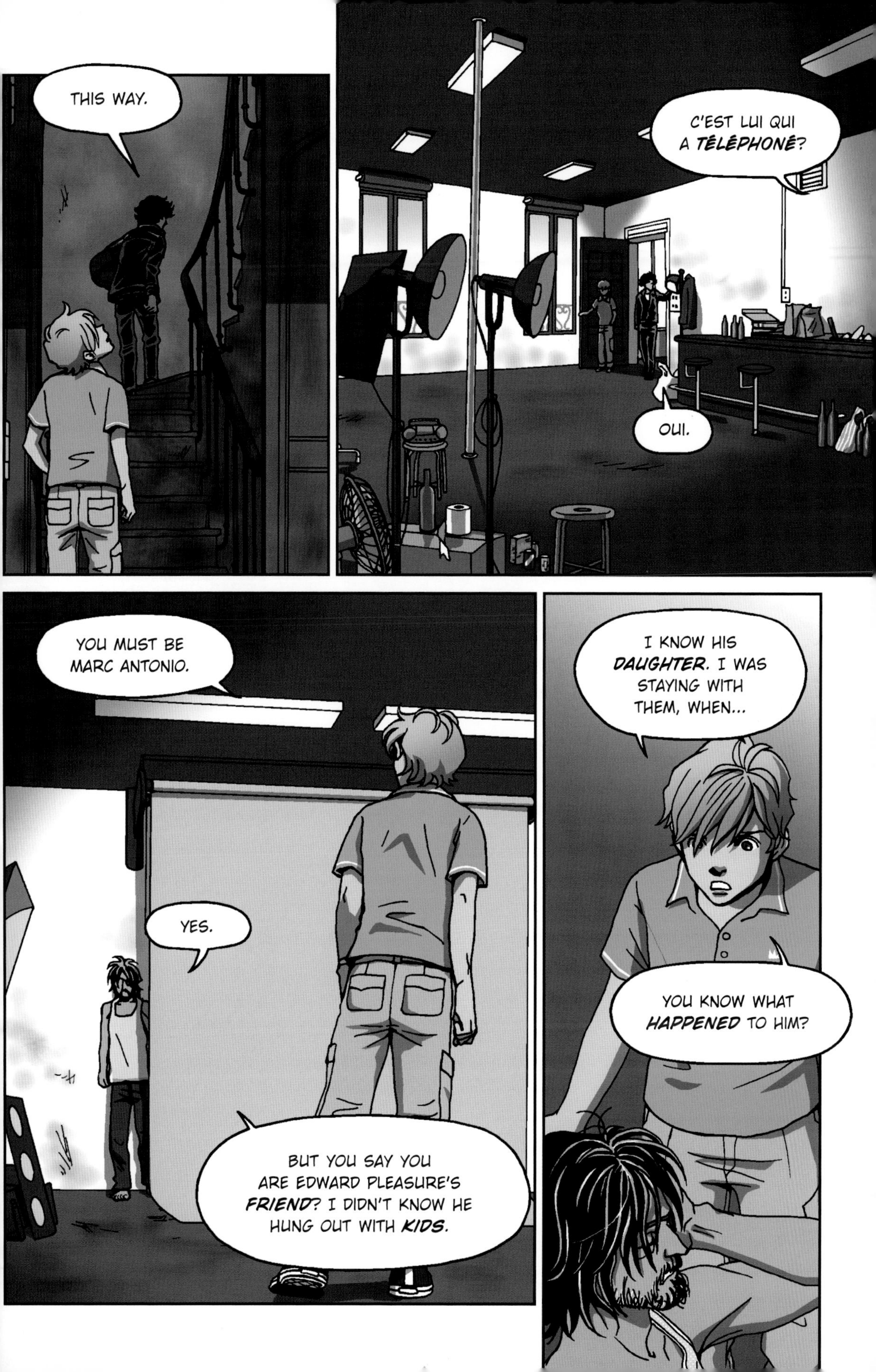
THIS WAY.
C'EST LUI QUI A TÉLÉPHONÉ?
OUI.
YOU MUST BE MARC ANTONIO.
YES.
BUT YOU SAY YOU ARE EDWARD PLEASURE'S FRIEND? I DIDN'T KNOW HE HUNG OUT WITH KIDS.
I KNOW HIS DAUGHTER. I WAS STAYING WITH THEM, WHEN...
YOU KNOW WHAT HAPPENED TO HIM?

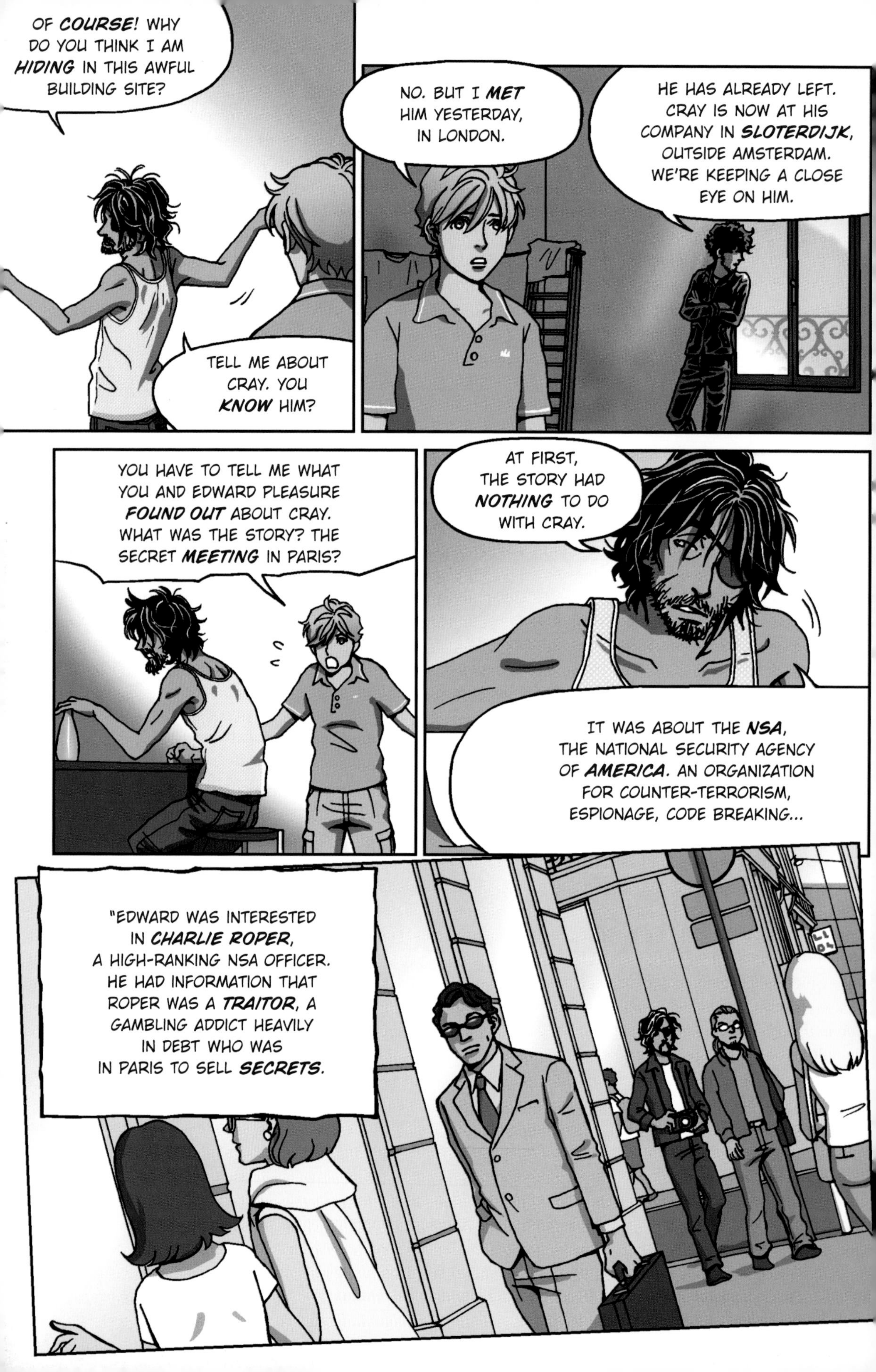
OF COURSE! WHY DO YOU THINK I AM HIDING IN THIS AWFUL BUILDING SITE?
TELL ME ABOUT CRAY. YOU KNOW HIM?
NO. BUT I MET HIM YESTERDAY, IN LONDON.
HE HAS ALREADY LEFT. CRAY IS NOW AT HIS COMPANY IN SLOTERDIJK, OUTSIDE AMSTERDAM. WE'RE KEEPING A CLOSE EYE ON HIM.
YOU HAVE TO TELL ME WHAT YOU AND EDWARD PLEASURE FOUND OUT ABOUT CRAY. WHAT WAS THE STORY? THE SECRET MEETING IN PARIS?
AT FIRST, THE STORY HAD NOTHING TO DO WITH CRAY.
IT WAS ABOUT THE NSA, THE NATIONAL SECURITY AGENCY OF AMERICA. AN ORGANIZATION FOR COUNTER-TERRORISM, ESPIONAGE, CODE BREAKING...
"EDWARD WAS INTERESTED IN CHARLIE ROPER, A HIGH-RANKING NSA OFFICER. HE HAD INFORMATION THAT ROPER WAS A TRAITOR, A GAMBLING ADDICT HEAVILY IN DEBT WHO WAS IN PARIS TO SELL SECRETS.

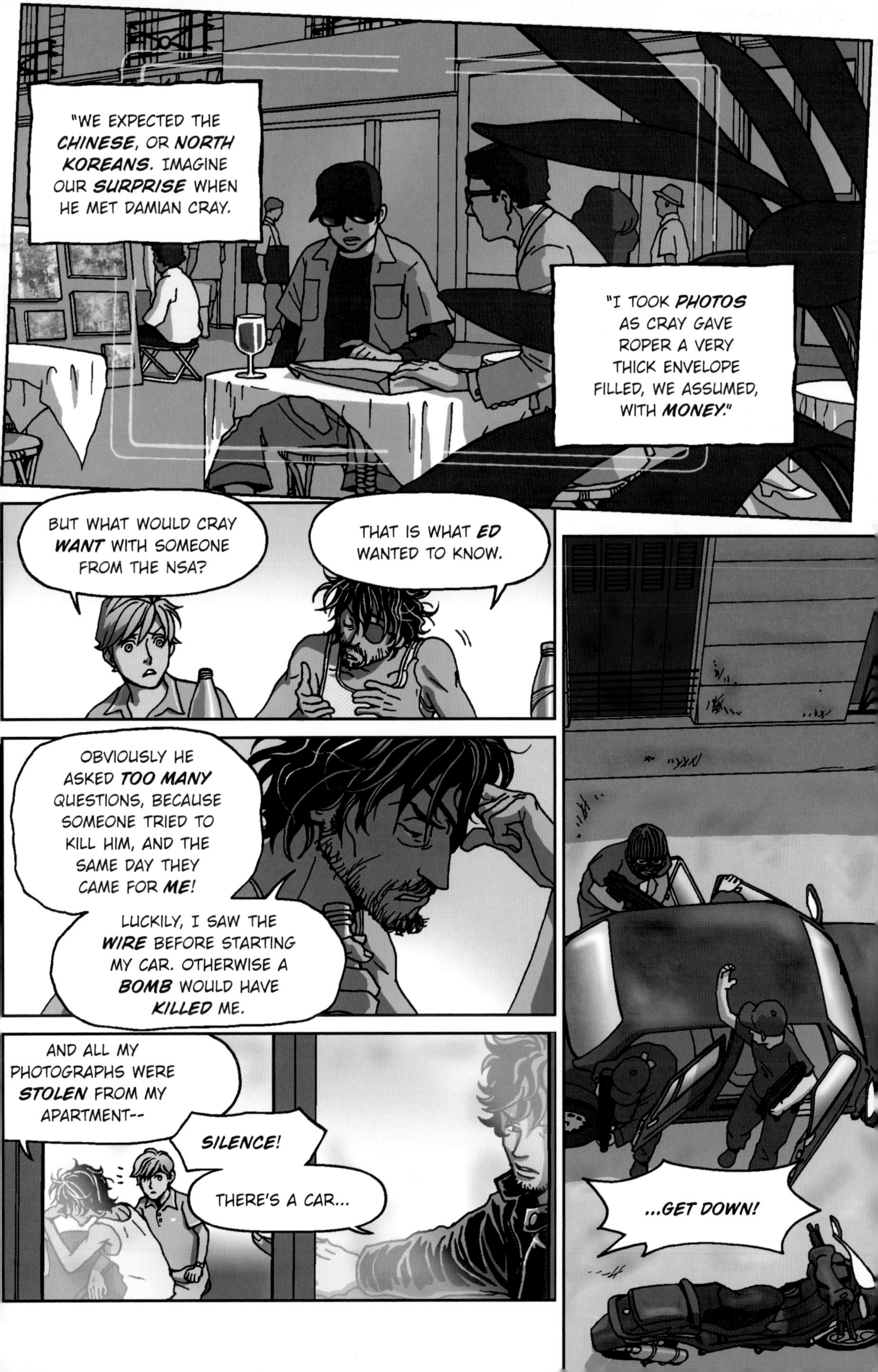
"WE EXPECTED THE CHINESE, OR NORTH KOREANS. IMAGINE OUR SURPRISE WHEN HE MET DAMIAN CRAY.
"I TOOK PHOTOS AS CRAY GAVE ROPER A VERY THICK ENVELOPE FILLED, WE ASSUMED, WITH MONEY."
BUT WHAT WOULD CRAY WANT WITH SOMEONE FROM THE NSA?
THAT IS WHAT ED WANTED TO KNOW.
OBVIOUSLY HE ASKED TOO MANY QUESTIONS, BECAUSE SOMEONE TRIED TO KILL HIM, AND THE SAME DAY THEY CAME FOR ME!
LUCKILY, I SAW THE WIRE BEFORE STARTING MY CAR. OTHERWISE A BOMB WOULD HAVE KILLED ME.
AND ALL MY PHOTOGRAPHS WERE STOLEN FROM MY APARTMENT--
SILENCE!
THERE'S A CAR...
...GET DOWN!

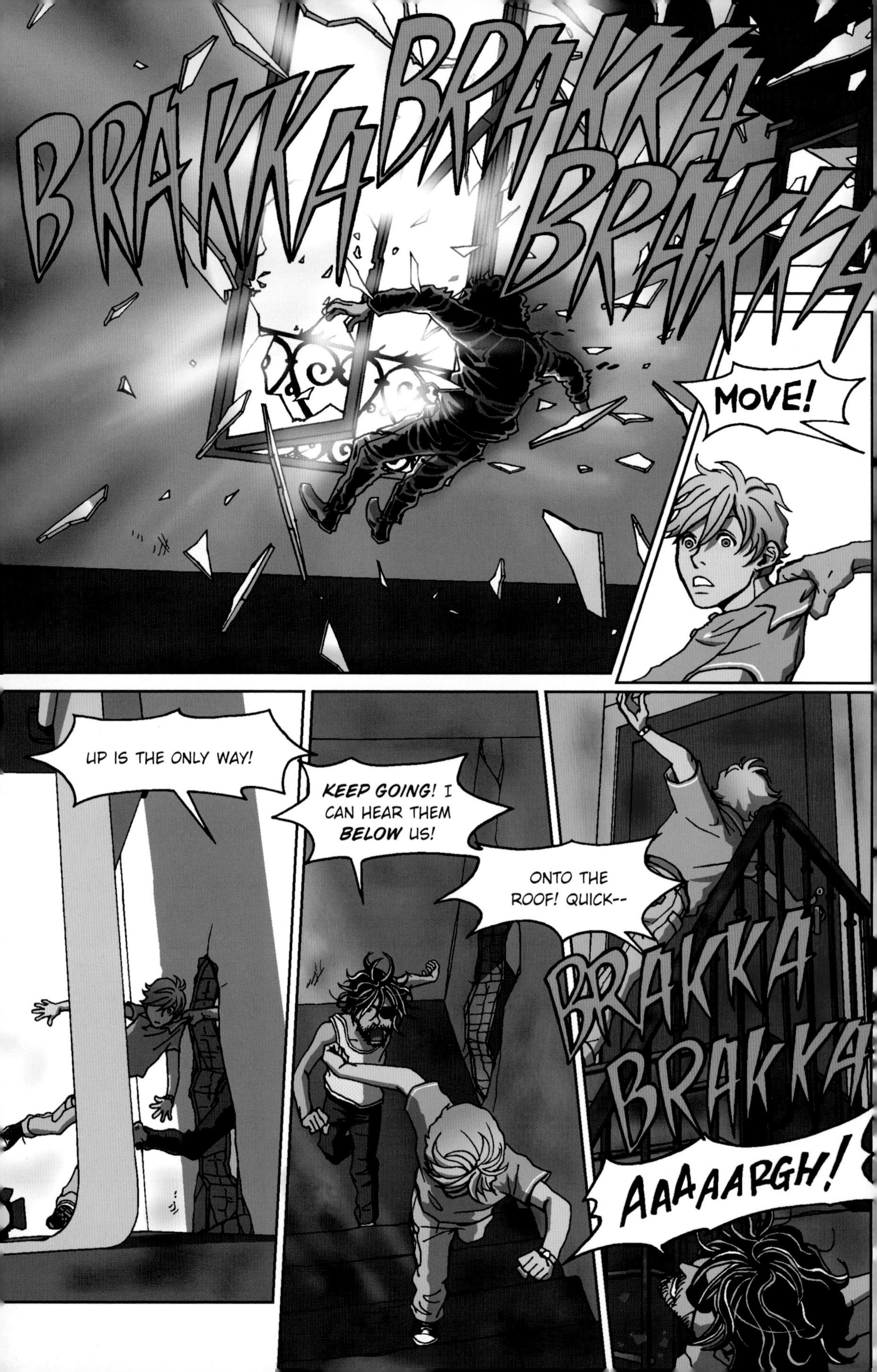
BRAKKA BRAKKA BRAKKA
MOVE!
UP IS THE ONLY WAY!
KEEP GOING! I CAN HEAR THEM BELOW US!
ONTO THE ROOF! QUICK--
BRAKKA BRAKKA
AAAAARGH!

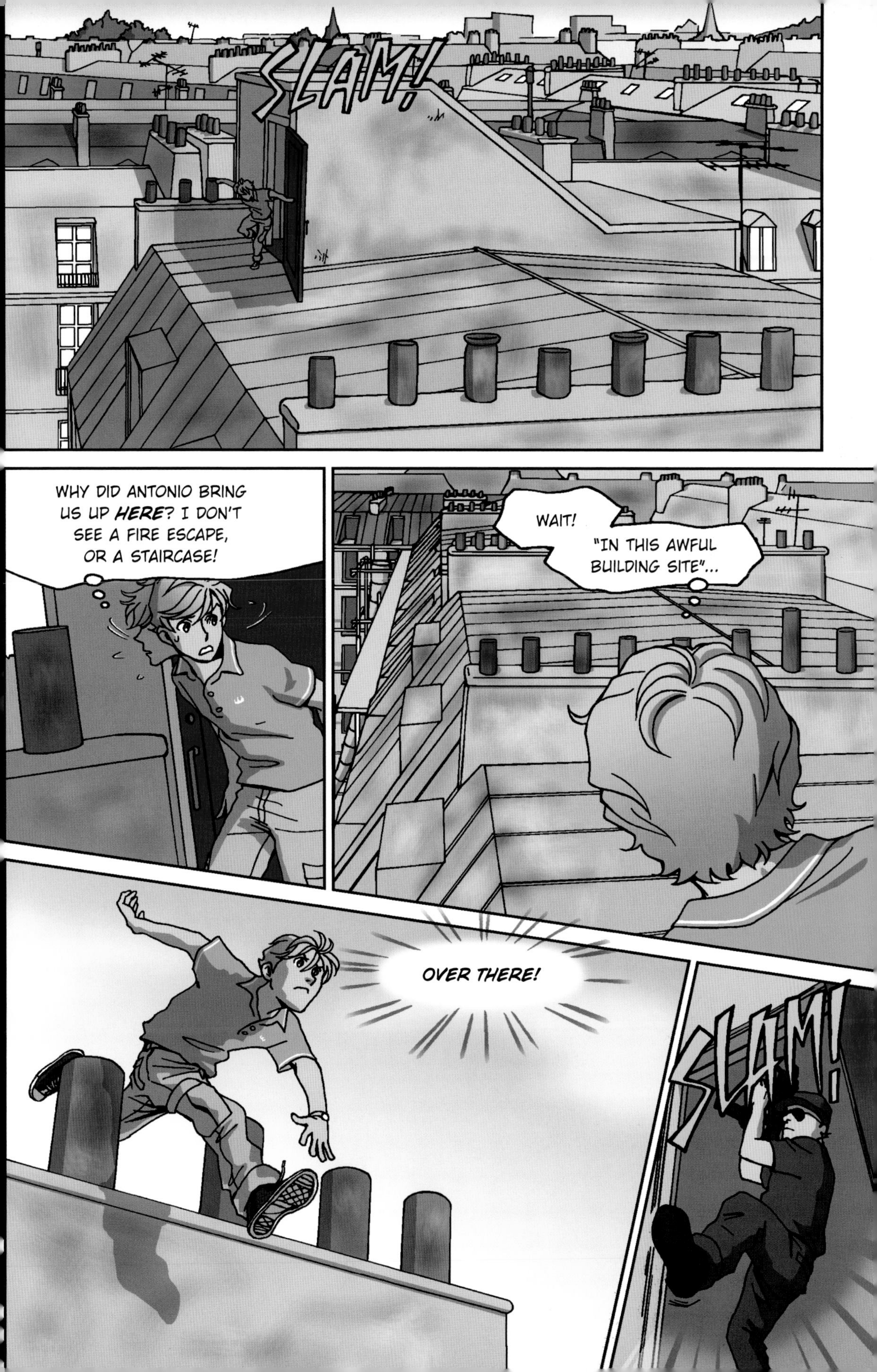
SLAM!
WHY DID ANTONIO BRING US UP *HERE*? I DON'T SEE A FIRE ESCAPE, OR A STAIRCASE!
WAIT!
"IN THIS AWFUL BUILDING SITE"...
OVER THERE!
SLAM!

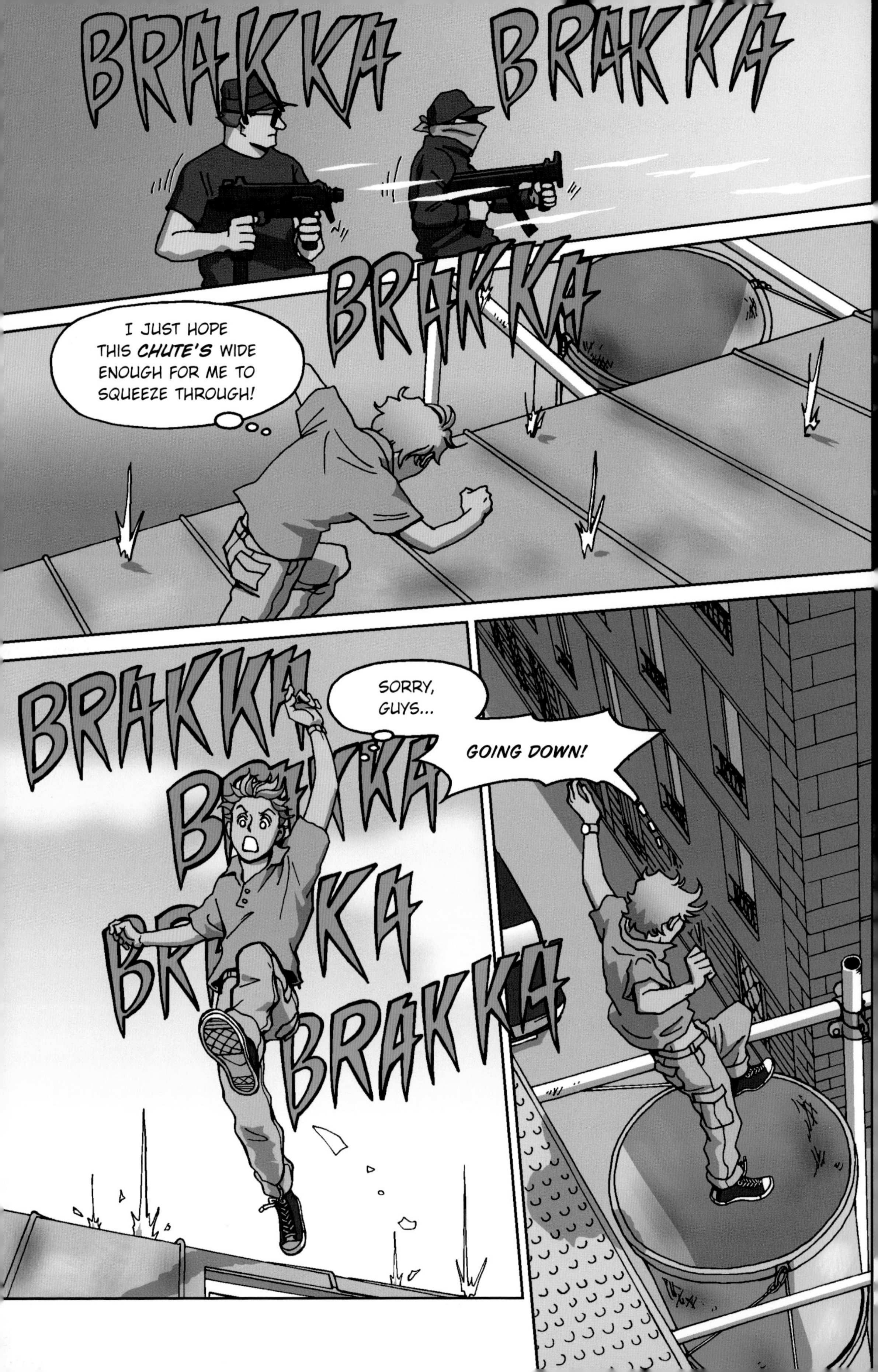
BRAKKA BRAKKA
BRAKKA
I JUST HOPE THIS CHUTE'S WIDE ENOUGH FOR ME TO SQUEEZE THROUGH!
BRAKKA
BRAKKA
BRAKKA
BRAKKA
SORRY, GUYS...
GOING DOWN!

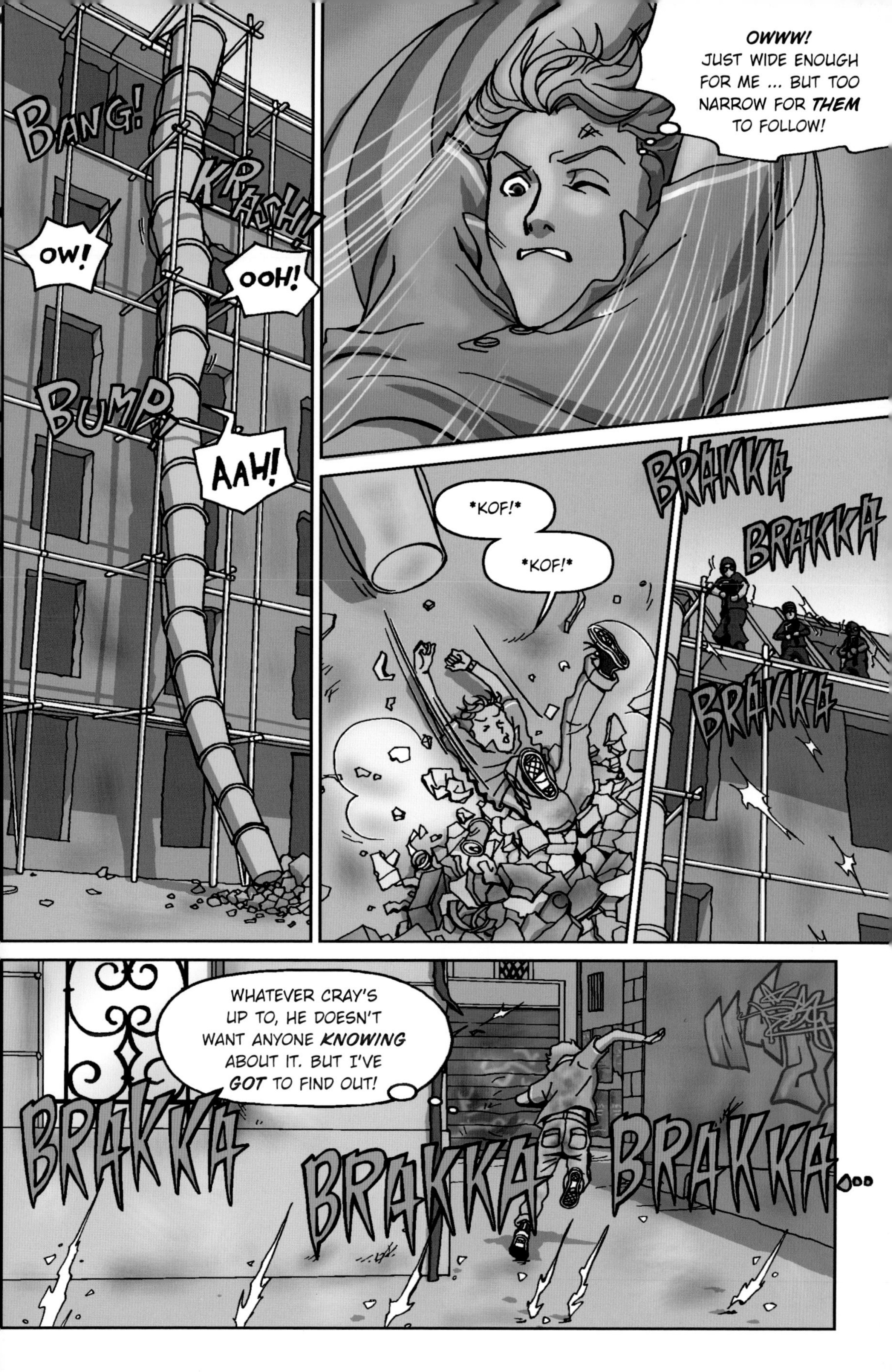
BANG!
KRASH!
OW!
OOH!
BUMP!
AAH!
OWWW!
JUST WIDE ENOUGH FOR ME ... BUT TOO NARROW FOR THEM TO FOLLOW!
KOF!
KOF!
BRAKKA
BRAKKA
BRAKKA
WHATEVER CRAY'S UP TO, HE DOESN'T WANT ANYONE KNOWING ABOUT IT. BUT I'VE GOT TO FIND OUT!
BRAKKA
BRAKKA
BRAKKA...

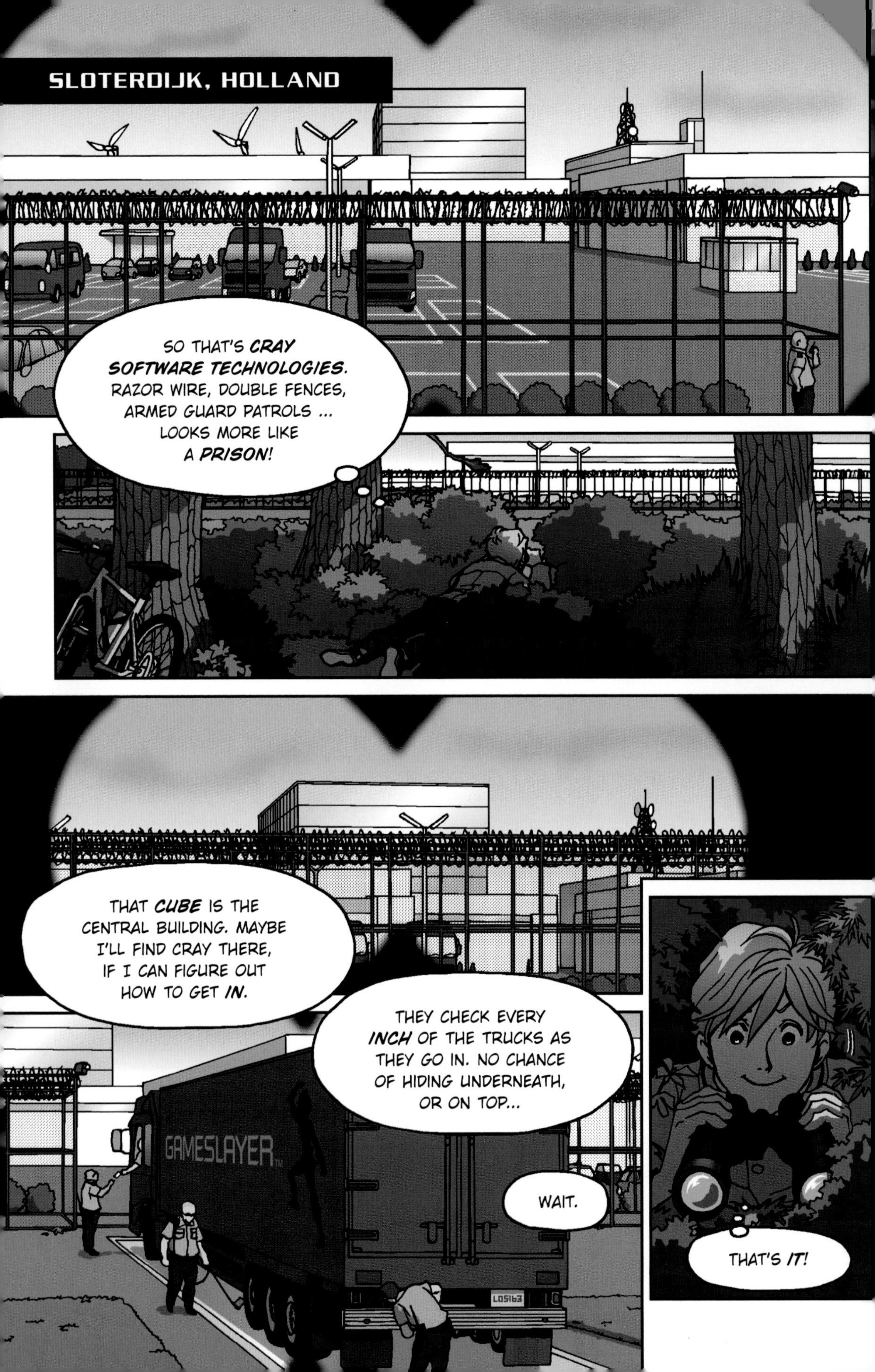
SLOTERDIJK, HOLLAND
SO THAT'S CRAY SOFTWARE TECHNOLOGIES. RAZOR WIRE, DOUBLE FENCES, ARMED GUARD PATROLS ... LOOKS MORE LIKE A PRISON!
THAT CUBE IS THE CENTRAL BUILDING. MAYBE I'LL FIND CRAY THERE, IF I CAN FIGURE OUT HOW TO GET IN.
THEY CHECK EVERY INCH OF THE TRUCKS AS THEY GO IN. NO CHANCE OF HIDING UNDERNEATH, OR ON TOP...
GAMESLAYER
WAIT.
THAT'S IT!

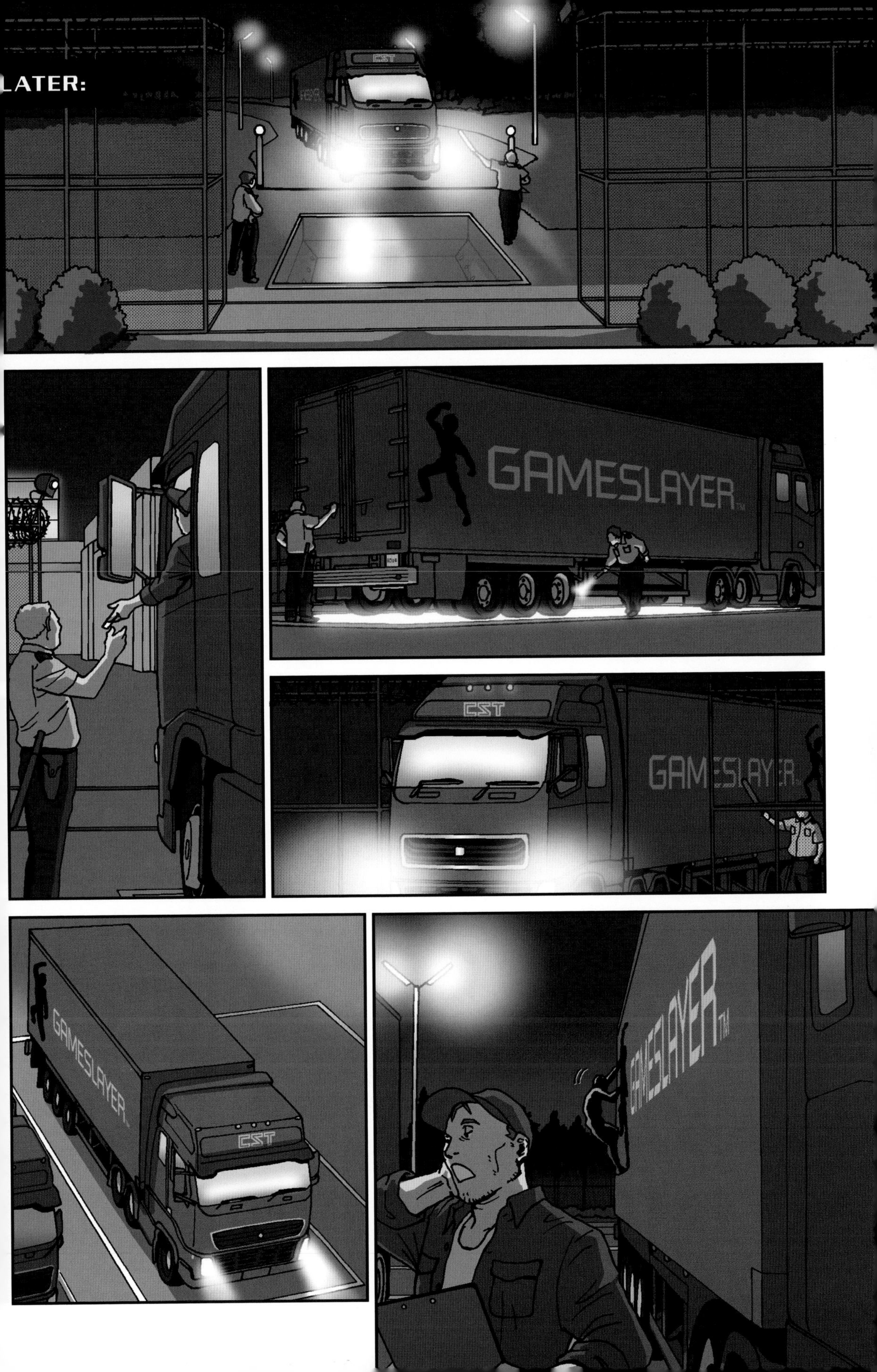

LATER:
CST
GAMESLAYER TM
CST
GAMESLAYER
GAMESLAYER
CST
GAMESLAYER TM

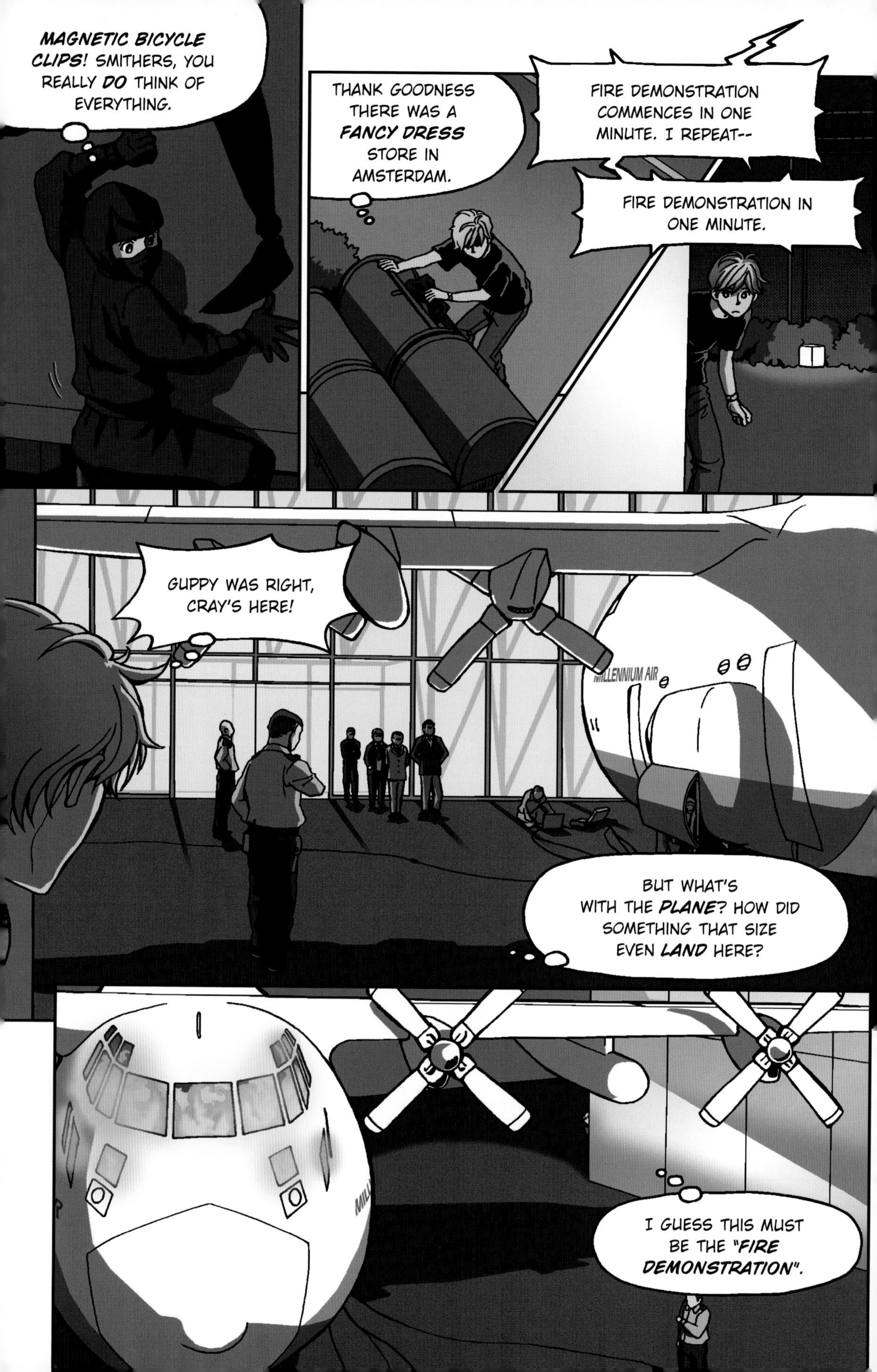
MAGNETIC BICYCLE CLIPS! SMITHERS, YOU REALLY DO THINK OF EVERYTHING.
THANK GOODNESS THERE WAS A FANCY DRESS STORE IN AMSTERDAM.
FIRE DEMONSTRATION COMMENCES IN ONE MINUTE. I REPEAT--
FIRE DEMONSTRATION IN ONE MINUTE.
GUPPY WAS RIGHT, CRAY'S HERE!
MILLENNIUM AIR
BUT WHAT'S WITH THE PLANE? HOW DID SOMETHING THAT SIZE EVEN LAND HERE?
I GUESS THIS MUST BE THE "FIRE DEMONSTRATION".

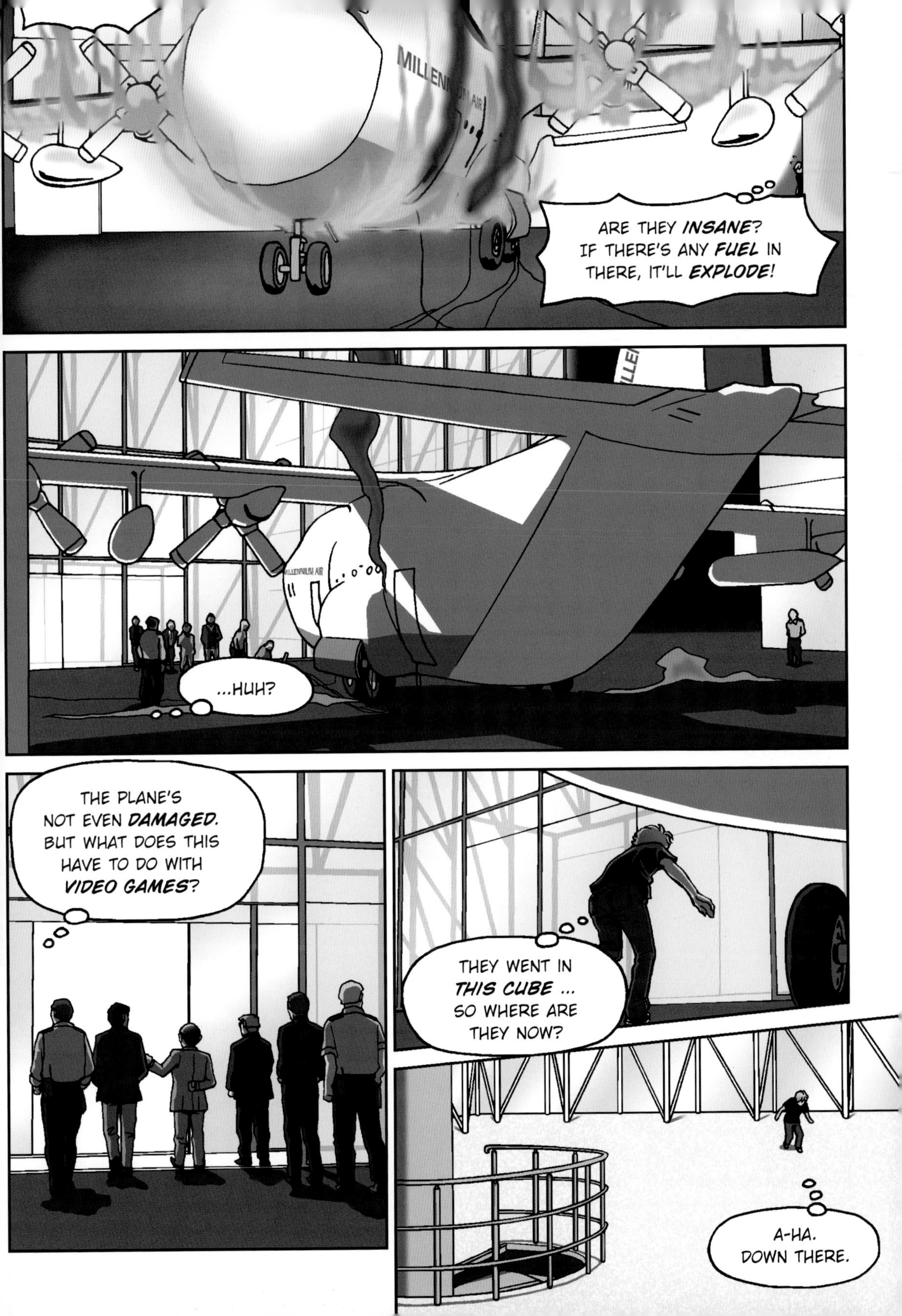
MILLENNIUM AIR
ARE THEY INSANE? IF THERE'S ANY FUEL IN THERE, IT'LL EXPLODE!
...HUH?
THE PLANE'S NOT EVEN DAMAGED. BUT WHAT DOES THIS HAVE TO DO WITH VIDEO GAMES?
THEY WENT IN THIS CUBE ... SO WHERE ARE THEY NOW?
A-HA. DOWN THERE.

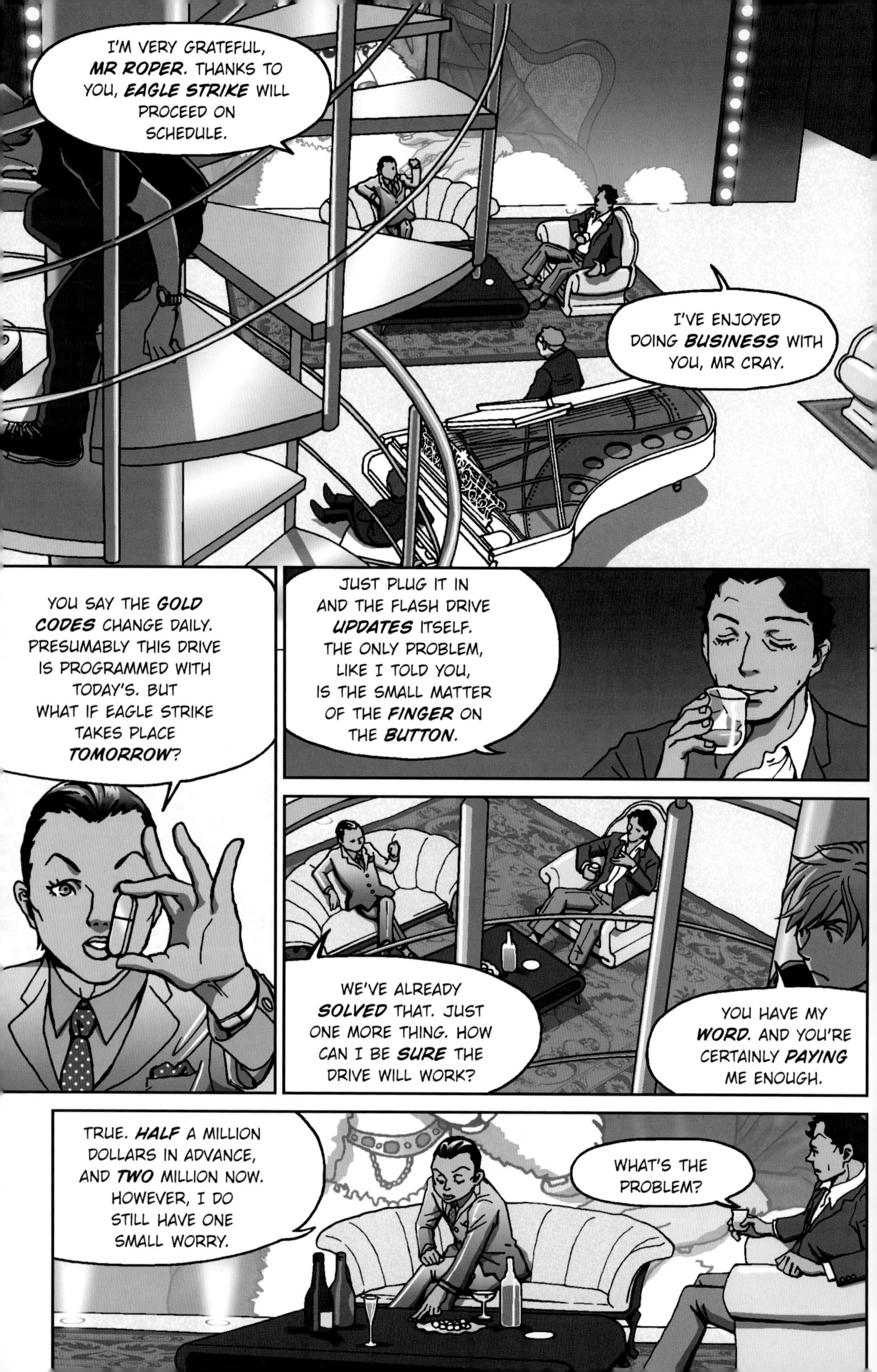

I'M VERY GRATEFUL, MR ROPER. THANKS TO YOU, EAGLE STRIKE WILL PROCEED ON SCHEDULE.
I'VE ENJOYED DOING BUSINESS WITH YOU, MR CRAY.
YOU SAY THE GOLD CODES CHANGE DAILY. PRESUMABLY THIS DRIVE IS PROGRAMMED WITH TODAY'S. BUT WHAT IF EAGLE STRIKE TAKES PLACE TOMORROW?
JUST PLUG IT IN AND THE FLASH DRIVE UPDATES ITSELF. THE ONLY PROBLEM, LIKE I TOLD YOU, IS THE SMALL MATTER OF THE FINGER ON THE BUTTON.
WE'VE ALREADY SOLVED THAT. JUST ONE MORE THING. HOW CAN I BE SURE THE DRIVE WILL WORK?
YOU HAVE MY WORD. AND YOU'RE CERTAINLY PAYING ME ENOUGH.
TRUE. HALF A MILLION DOLLARS IN ADVANCE, AND TWO MILLION NOW. HOWEVER, I DO STILL HAVE ONE SMALL WORRY.
WHAT'S THE PROBLEM?

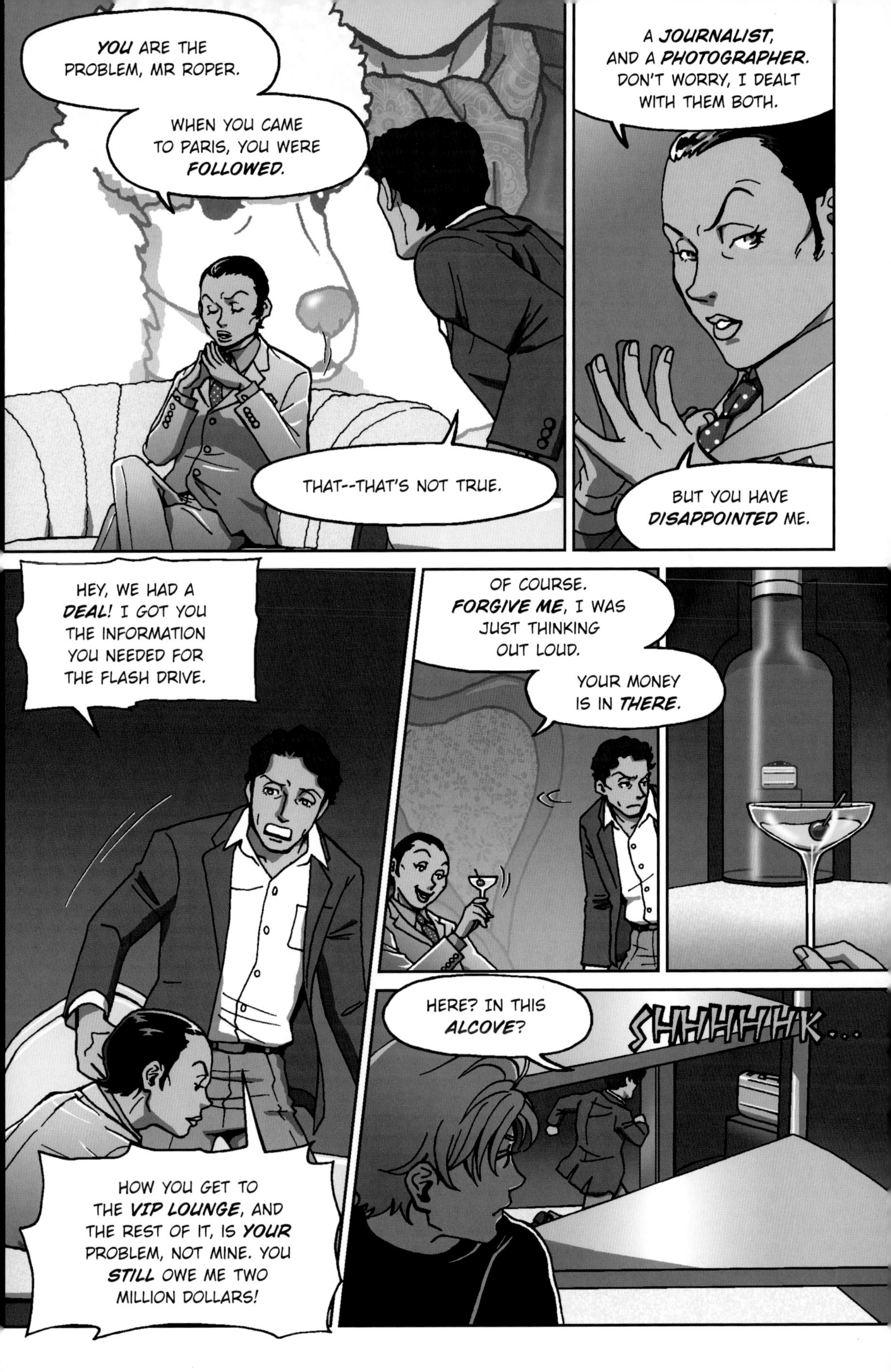

YOU ARE THE PROBLEM, MR ROPER.
WHEN YOU CAME TO PARIS, YOU WERE FOLLOWED.
THAT--THAT'S NOT TRUE.
A JOURNALIST, AND A PHOTOGRAPHER. DON'T WORRY, I DEALT WITH THEM BOTH.
BUT YOU HAVE DISAPPOINTED ME.
HEY, WE HAD A DEAL! I GOT YOU THE INFORMATION YOU NEEDED FOR THE FLASH DRIVE.
HOW YOU GET TO THE VIP LOUNGE, AND THE REST OF IT, IS YOUR PROBLEM, NOT MINE. YOU STILL OWE ME TWO MILLION DOLLARS!
OF COURSE. FORGIVE ME, I WAS JUST THINKING OUT LOUD.
YOUR MONEY IS IN THERE.
HERE? IN THIS ALCOVE?
SHHHHHHK...

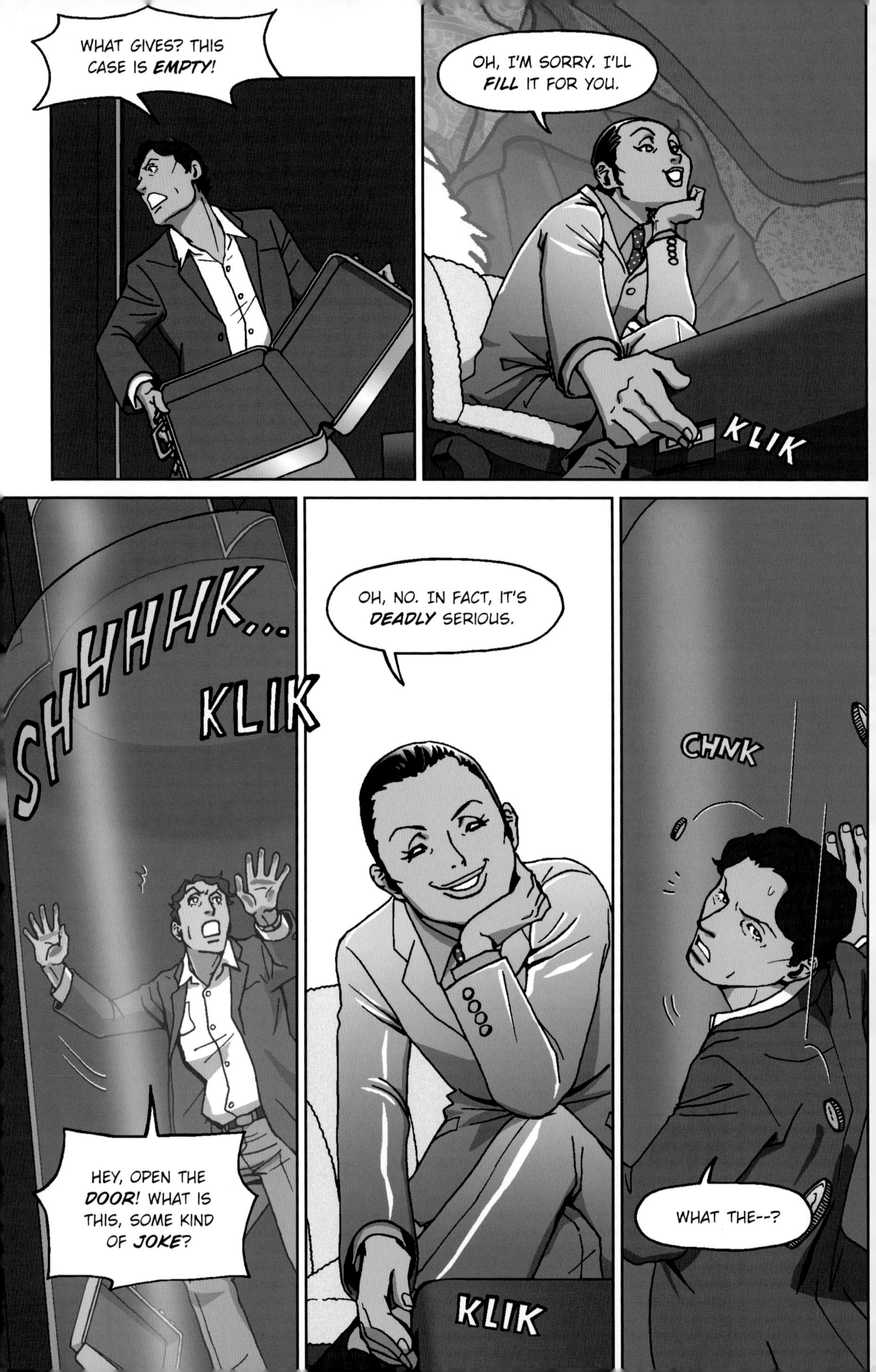
WHAT GIVES? THIS CASE IS EMPTY!
OH, I'M SORRY. I'LL FILL IT FOR YOU.
KLIK
SHHHHK...
KLIK
HEY, OPEN THE DOOR! WHAT IS THIS, SOME KIND OF JOKE?
OH, NO. IN FACT, IT'S DEADLY SERIOUS.
KLIK
CHNK
WHAT THE--?

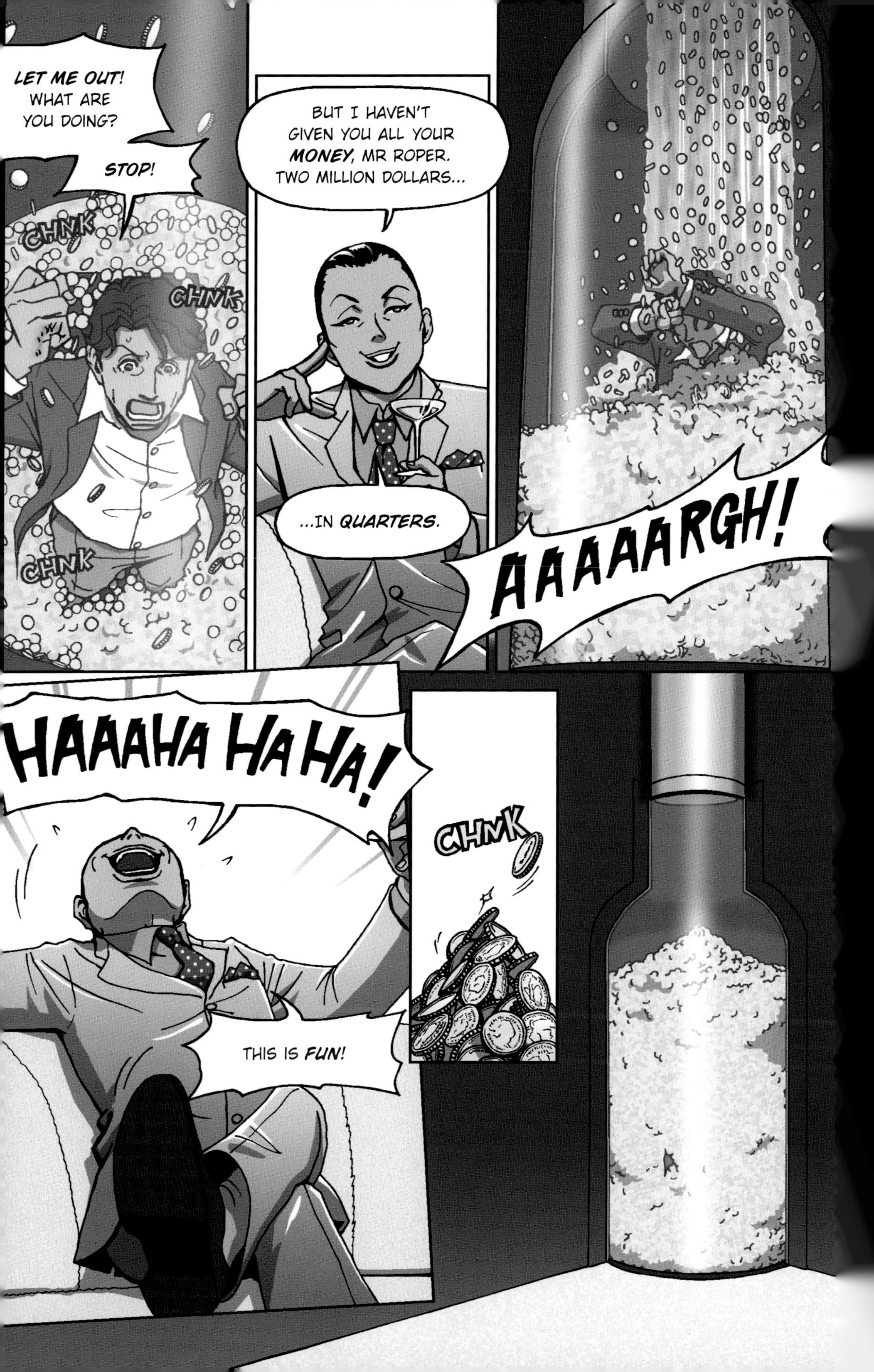
LET ME OUT! WHAT ARE YOU DOING?
STOP!
CHNK
CHNK
CHNK
BUT I HAVEN'T GIVEN YOU ALL YOUR MONEY, MR ROPER. TWO MILLION DOLLARS...
...IN QUARTERS.
AAAAARGH!
HAAAHA HAHA!
THIS IS FUN!
CHNK

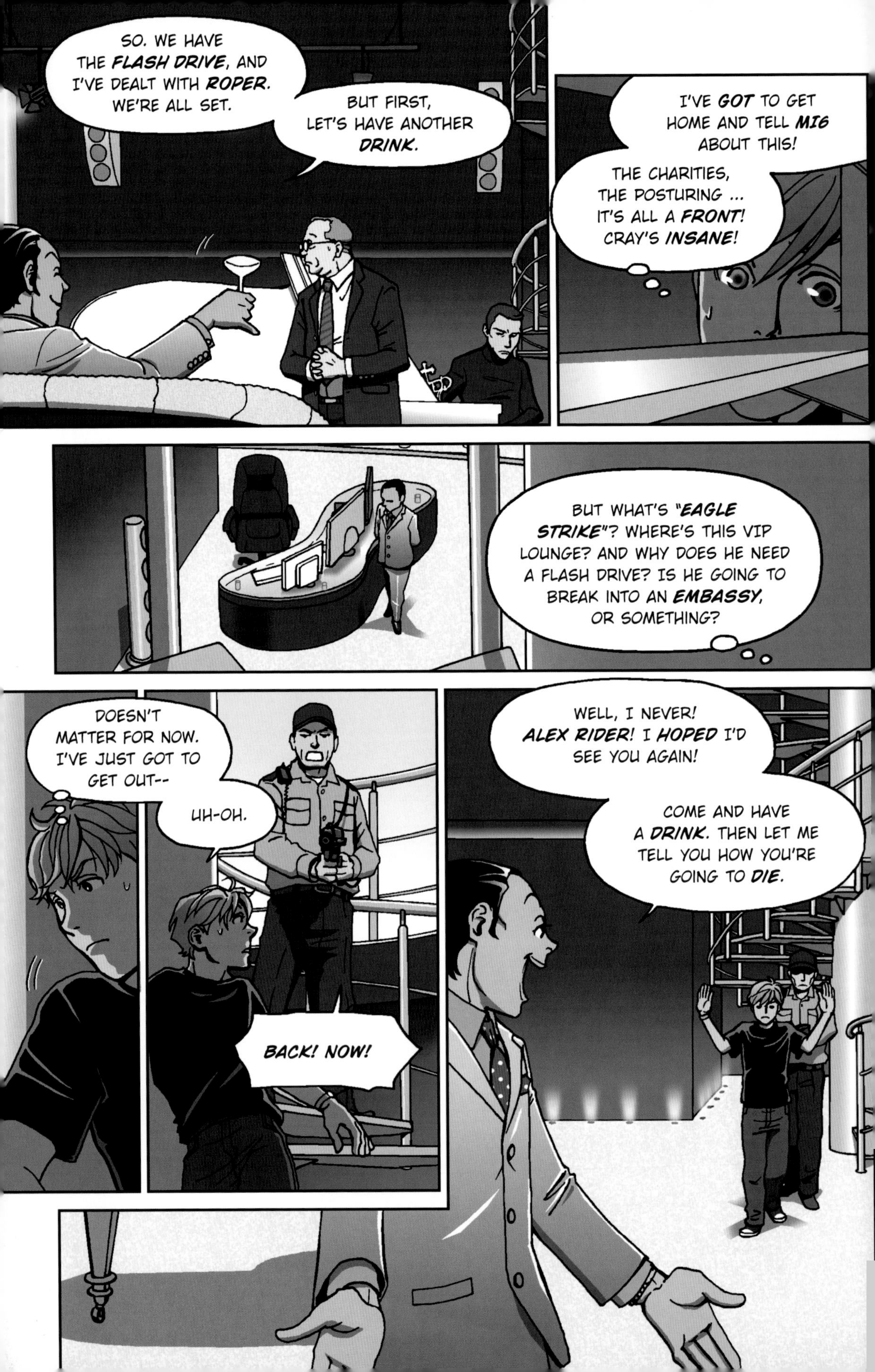
SO. WE HAVE THE FLASH DRIVE, AND I'VE DEALT WITH ROPER. WE'RE ALL SET.
BUT FIRST, LET'S HAVE ANOTHER DRINK.
I'VE GOT TO GET HOME AND TELL MI6 ABOUT THIS!
THE CHARITIES, THE POSTURING ... IT'S ALL A FRONT! CRAY'S INSANE!
BUT WHAT'S "EAGLE STRIKE"? WHERE'S THIS VIP LOUNGE? AND WHY DOES HE NEED A FLASH DRIVE? IS HE GOING TO BREAK INTO AN EMBASSY, OR SOMETHING?
DOESN'T MATTER FOR NOW. I'VE JUST GOT TO GET OUT--
UH-OH.
BACK! NOW!
WELL, I NEVER! ALEX RIDER! I HOPED I'D SEE YOU AGAIN!
COME AND HAVE A DRINK. THEN LET ME TELL YOU HOW YOU'RE GOING TO DIE.

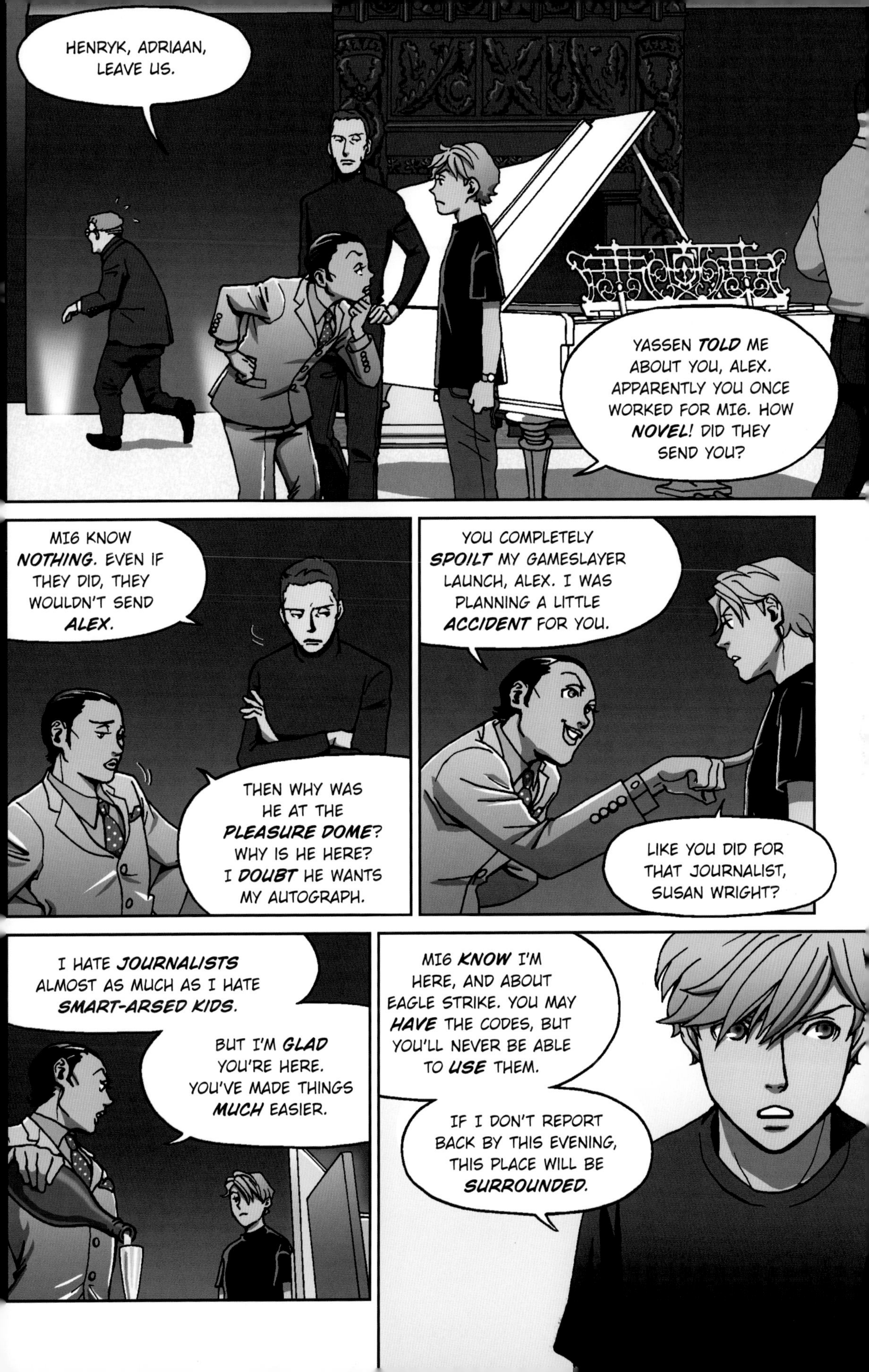
HENRYK, ADRIAAN, LEAVE US.
YASSEN TOLD ME ABOUT YOU, ALEX. APPARENTLY YOU ONCE WORKED FOR MI6. HOW NOVEL! DID THEY SEND YOU?
MI6 KNOW NOTHING. EVEN IF THEY DID, THEY WOULDN'T SEND ALEX.
THEN WHY WAS HE AT THE PLEASURE DOME? WHY IS HE HERE? I DOUBT HE WANTS MY AUTOGRAPH.
YOU COMPLETELY SPOILT MY GAMESLAYER LAUNCH, ALEX. I WAS PLANNING A LITTLE ACCIDENT FOR YOU.
LIKE YOU DID FOR THAT JOURNALIST, SUSAN WRIGHT?
I HATE JOURNALISTS ALMOST AS MUCH AS I HATE SMART-ARSED KIDS.
BUT I'M GLAD YOU'RE HERE. YOU'VE MADE THINGS MUCH EASIER.
MI6 KNOW I'M HERE, AND ABOUT EAGLE STRIKE. YOU MAY HAVE THE CODES, BUT YOU'LL NEVER BE ABLE TO USE THEM.
IF I DON'T REPORT BACK BY THIS EVENING, THIS PLACE WILL BE SURROUNDED.

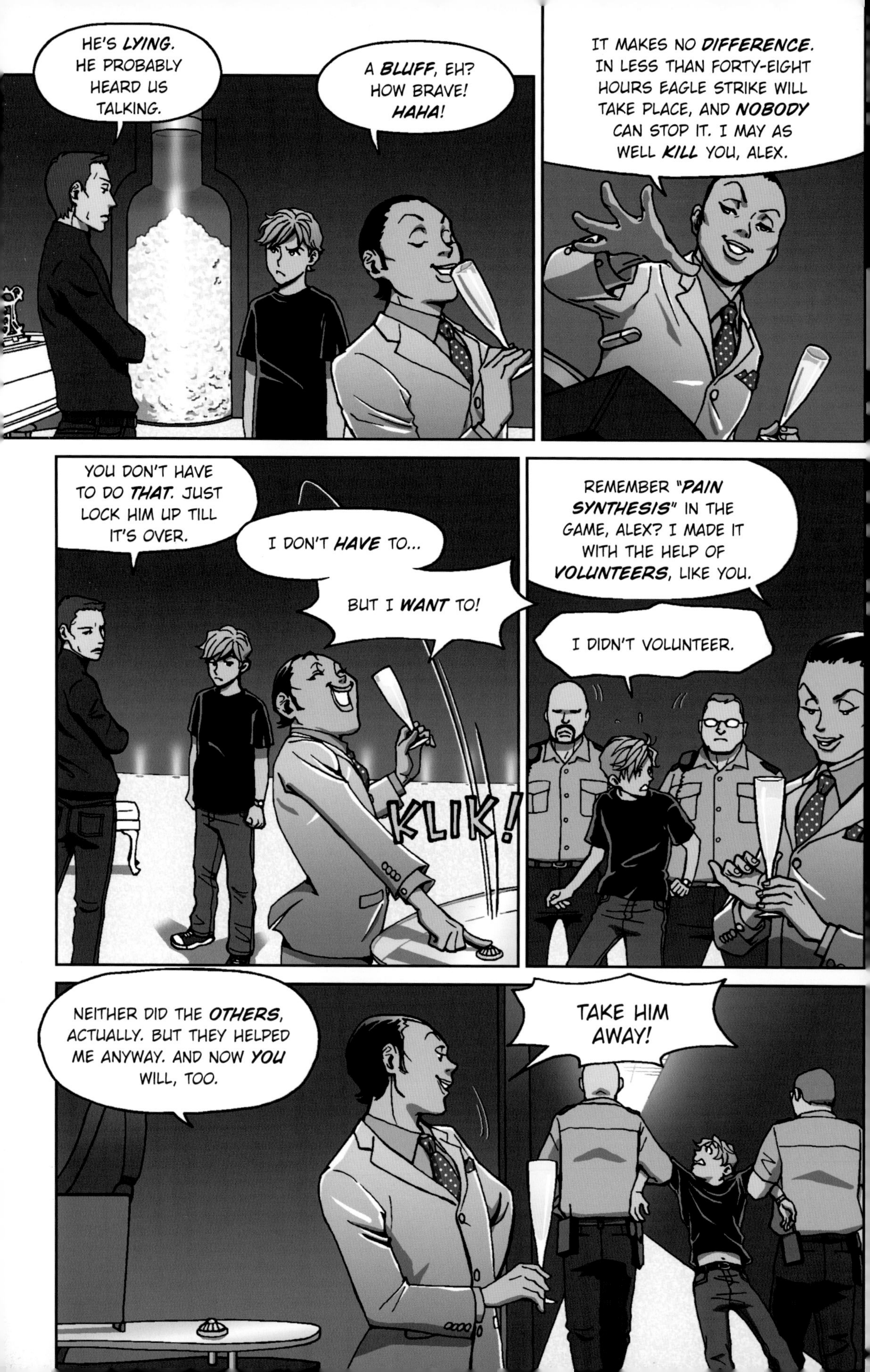
HE'S *LYING*. HE PROBABLY HEARD US TALKING.
A *BLUFF*, EH? HOW BRAVE! *HAHA*!
IT MAKES NO *DIFFERENCE*. IN LESS THAN FORTY-EIGHT HOURS EAGLE STRIKE WILL TAKE PLACE, AND *NOBODY* CAN STOP IT. I MAY AS WELL *KILL* YOU, ALEX.
YOU DON'T HAVE TO DO *THAT*. JUST LOCK HIM UP TILL IT'S OVER.
I DON'T *HAVE* TO...
BUT I *WANT* TO!
KLIK!
REMEMBER "*PAIN SYNTHESIS*" IN THE GAME, ALEX? I MADE IT WITH THE HELP OF *VOLUNTEERS*, LIKE YOU.
I DIDN'T VOLUNTEER.
NEITHER DID THE *OTHERS*, ACTUALLY. BUT THEY HELPED ME ANYWAY. AND NOW *YOU* WILL, TOO.
TAKE HIM AWAY!

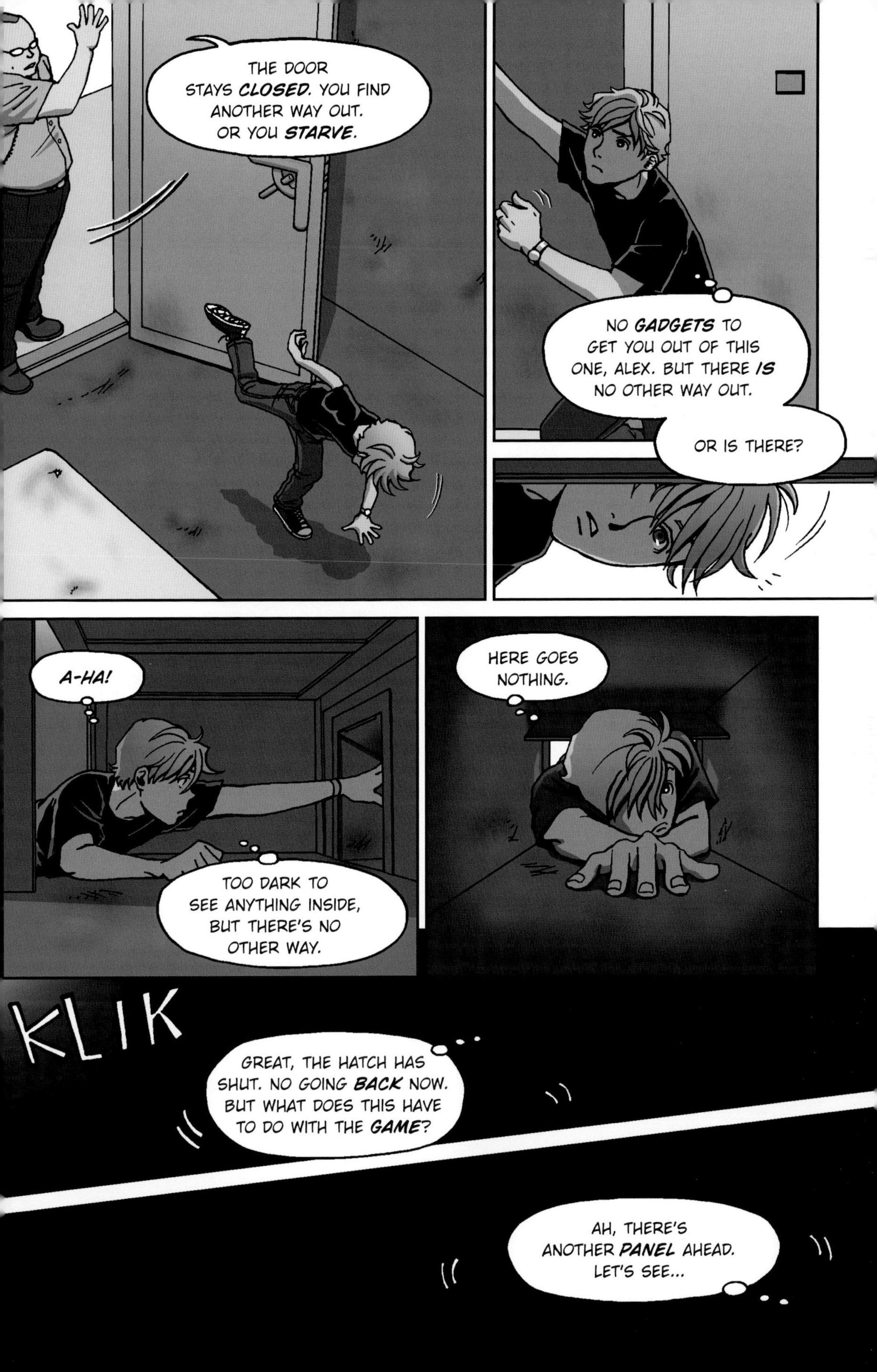
THE DOOR STAYS **CLOSED**. YOU FIND ANOTHER WAY OUT. OR YOU **STARVE**.
NO **GADGETS** TO GET YOU OUT OF THIS ONE, ALEX. BUT THERE **IS** NO OTHER WAY OUT.
OR IS THERE?
A-HA!
TOO DARK TO SEE ANYTHING INSIDE, BUT THERE'S NO OTHER WAY.
HERE GOES NOTHING.
KLIK
GREAT, THE HATCH HAS SHUT. NO GOING **BACK** NOW. BUT WHAT DOES THIS HAVE TO DO WITH THE **GAME**?
AH, THERE'S ANOTHER **PANEL** AHEAD. LET'S SEE...

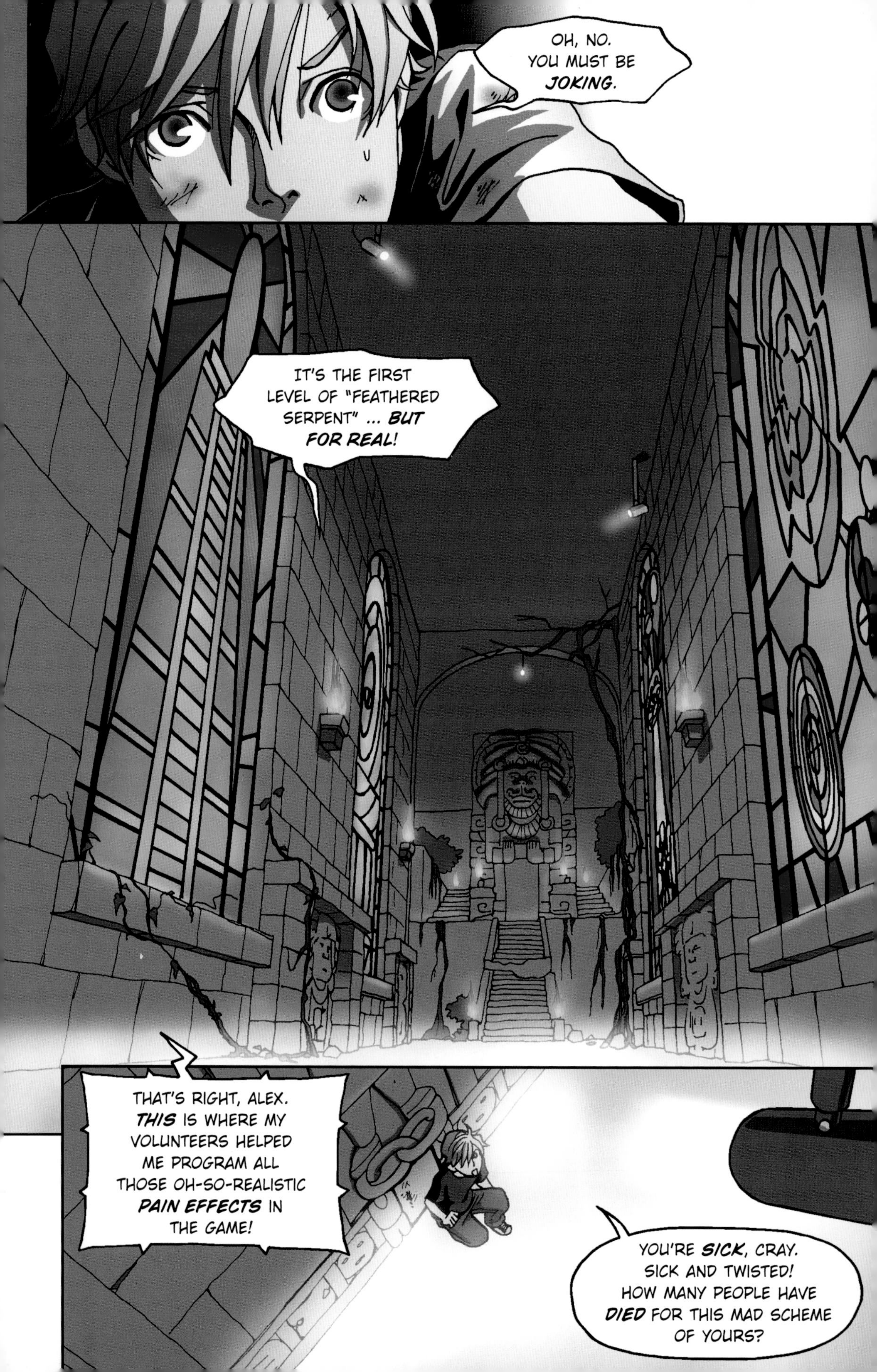
OH, NO. YOU MUST BE JOKING.
IT'S THE FIRST LEVEL OF "FEATHERED SERPENT" ... BUT FOR REAL!
THAT'S RIGHT, ALEX. THIS IS WHERE MY VOLUNTEERS HELPED ME PROGRAM ALL THOSE OH-SO-REALISTIC PAIN EFFECTS IN THE GAME!
YOU'RE SICK, CRAY. SICK AND TWISTED! HOW MANY PEOPLE HAVE DIED FOR THIS MAD SCHEME OF YOURS?

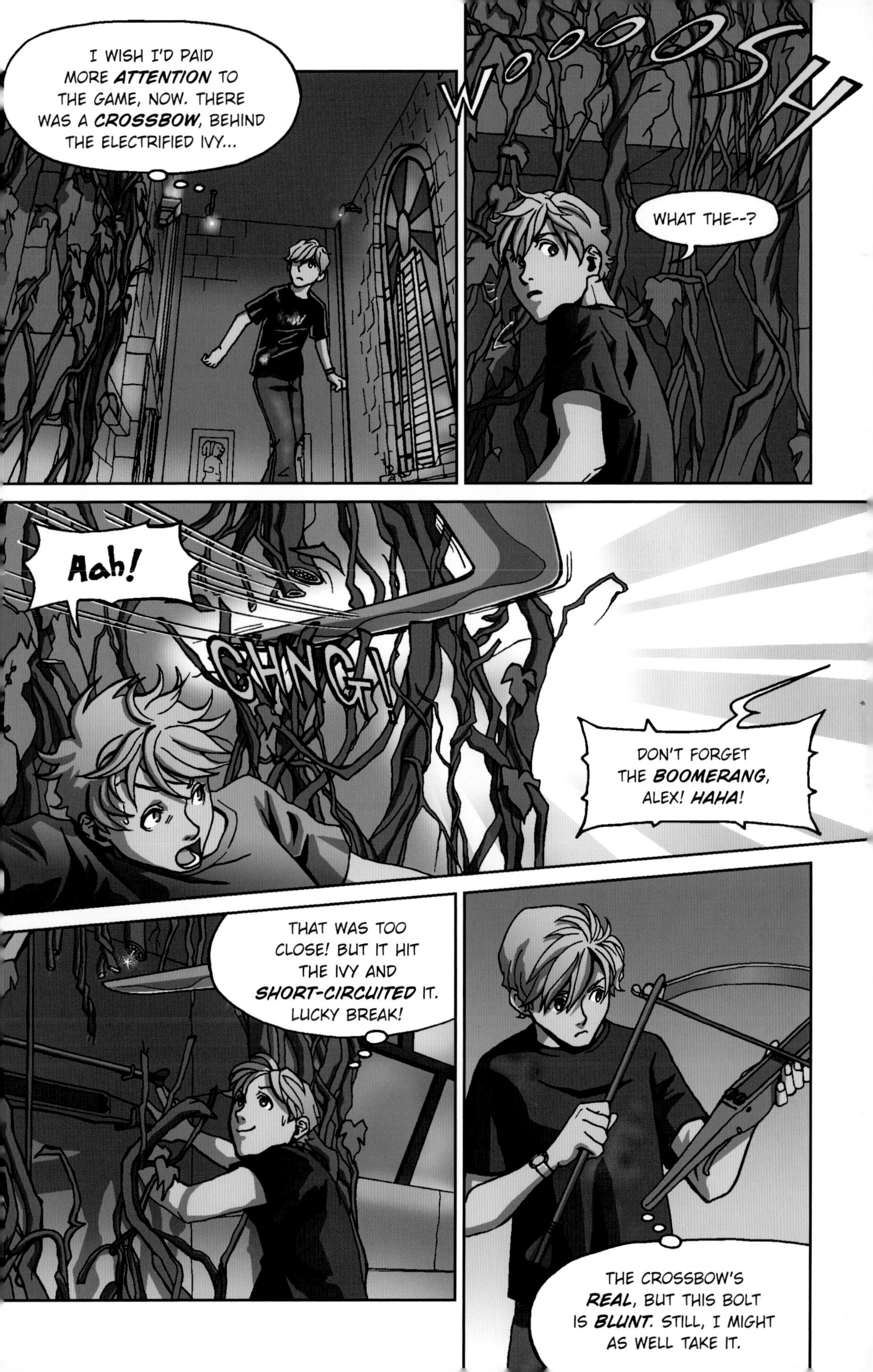
I WISH I'D PAID MORE ATTENTION TO THE GAME, NOW. THERE WAS A CROSSBOW, BEHIND THE ELECTRIFIED IVY...
WOOOOSH
WHAT THE--?
Aah!
CHNG!
DON'T FORGET THE BOOMERANG, ALEX! HAHA!
THAT WAS TOO CLOSE! BUT IT HIT THE IVY AND SHORT-CIRCUITED IT. LUCKY BREAK!
THE CROSSBOW'S REAL, BUT THIS BOLT IS BLUNT. STILL, I MIGHT AS WELL TAKE IT.

NOW FOR THE SWORD... NO, *WAIT!*

THERE WAS ANOTHER *BOOMERANG.*

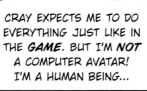

CRAY EXPECTS ME TO DO EVERYTHING JUST LIKE IN THE *GAME.* BUT I'M *NOT* A COMPUTER AVATAR! I'M A HUMAN BEING...

...AND I CAN *CHEAT!*

THIS IS THE CHAMBER WHERE THE *FLYING CREATURE* ATTACKED.

THERE, A *MODEL* UP IN THE RAFTERS! AND IT'S ON A *WIRE,* WAITING TILL I'M HALFWAY ACROSS.

WELL, NOT FOR LONG.

SNAP!

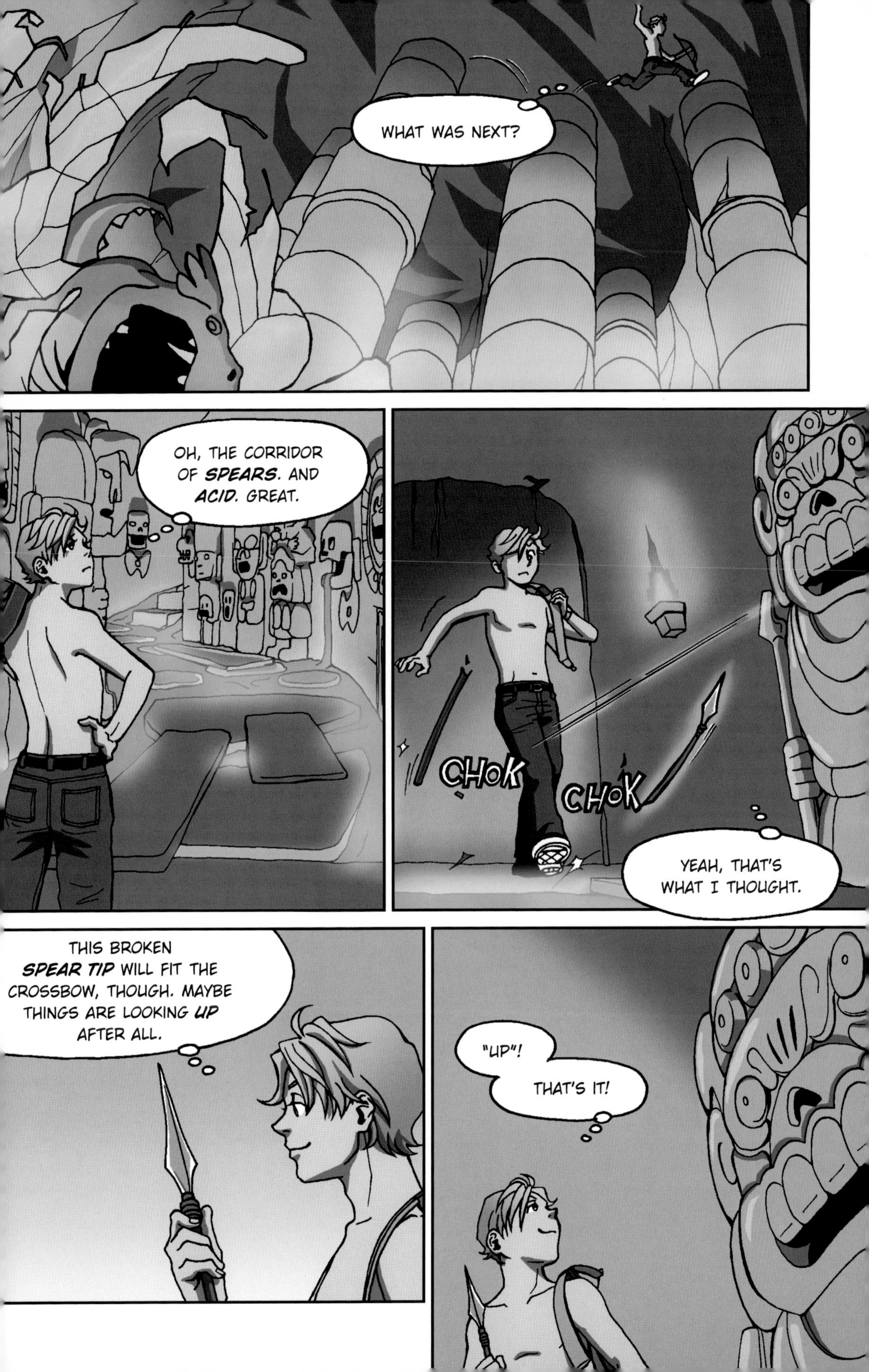
WHAT WAS NEXT?
OH, THE CORRIDOR OF SPEARS. AND ACID. GREAT.
CHOK
CHOK
YEAH, THAT'S WHAT I THOUGHT.
THIS BROKEN SPEAR TIP WILL FIT THE CROSSBOW, THOUGH. MAYBE THINGS ARE LOOKING UP AFTER ALL.
"UP"!
THAT'S IT!

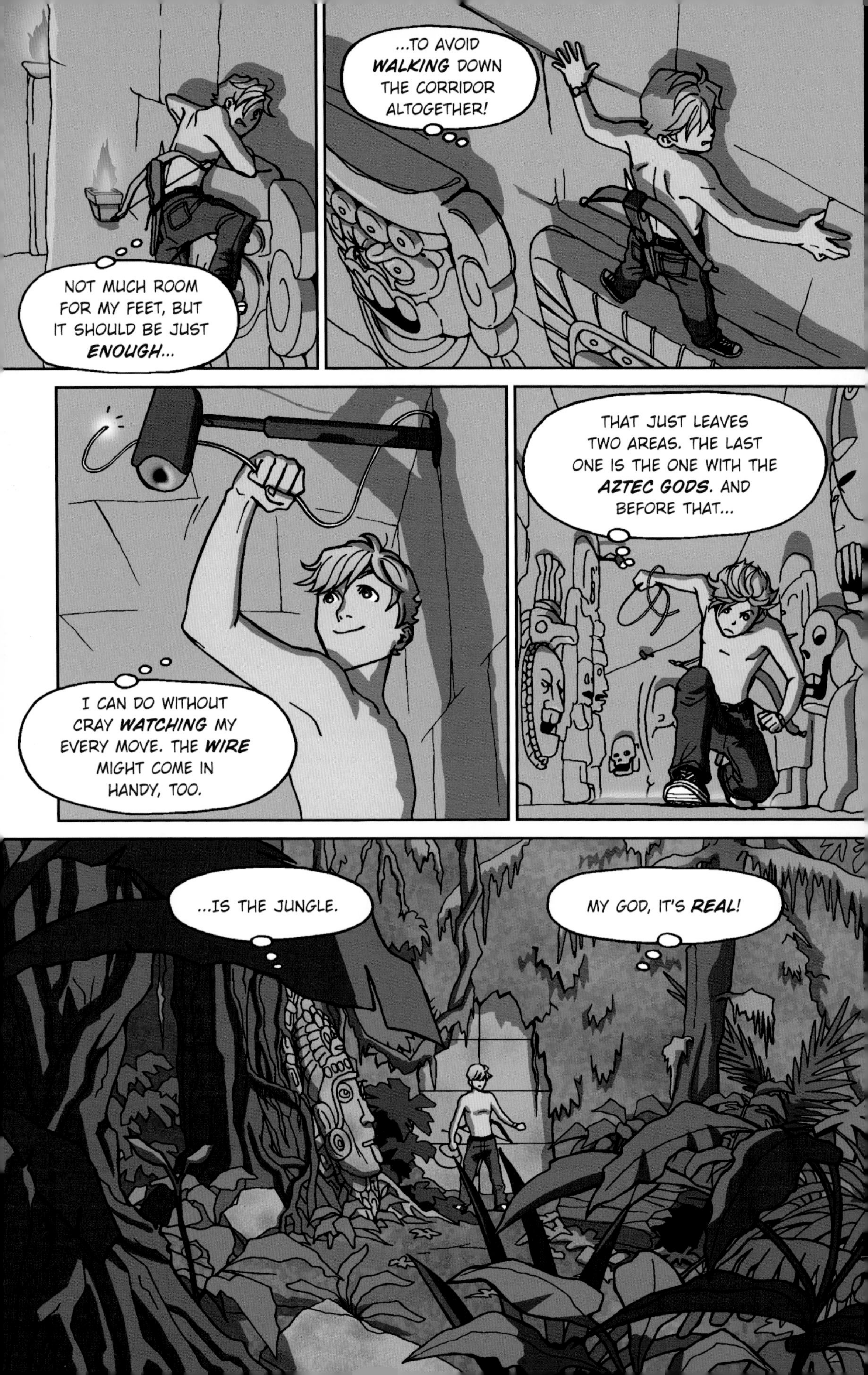
NOT MUCH ROOM FOR MY FEET, BUT IT SHOULD BE JUST *ENOUGH*...
...TO AVOID *WALKING* DOWN THE CORRIDOR ALTOGETHER!
I CAN DO WITHOUT CRAY *WATCHING* MY EVERY MOVE. THE *WIRE* MIGHT COME IN HANDY, TOO.
THAT JUST LEAVES TWO AREAS. THE LAST ONE IS THE ONE WITH THE *AZTEC GODS*. AND BEFORE THAT...
...IS THE JUNGLE.
MY GOD, IT'S *REAL*!

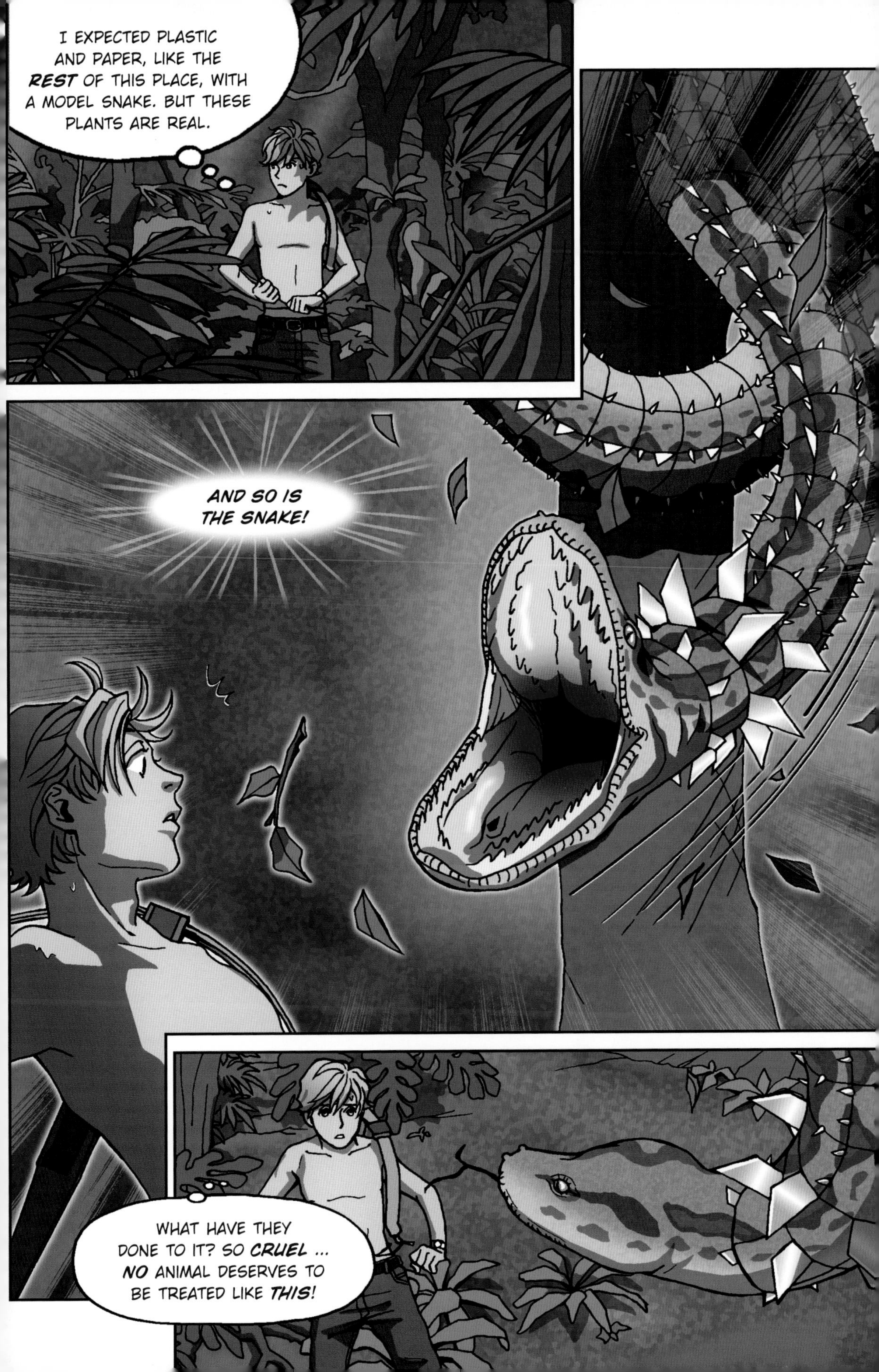
I EXPECTED PLASTIC AND PAPER, LIKE THE REST OF THIS PLACE, WITH A MODEL SNAKE. BUT THESE PLANTS ARE REAL.
AND SO IS THE SNAKE!
WHAT HAVE THEY DONE TO IT? SO CRUEL ... NO ANIMAL DESERVES TO BE TREATED LIKE THIS!

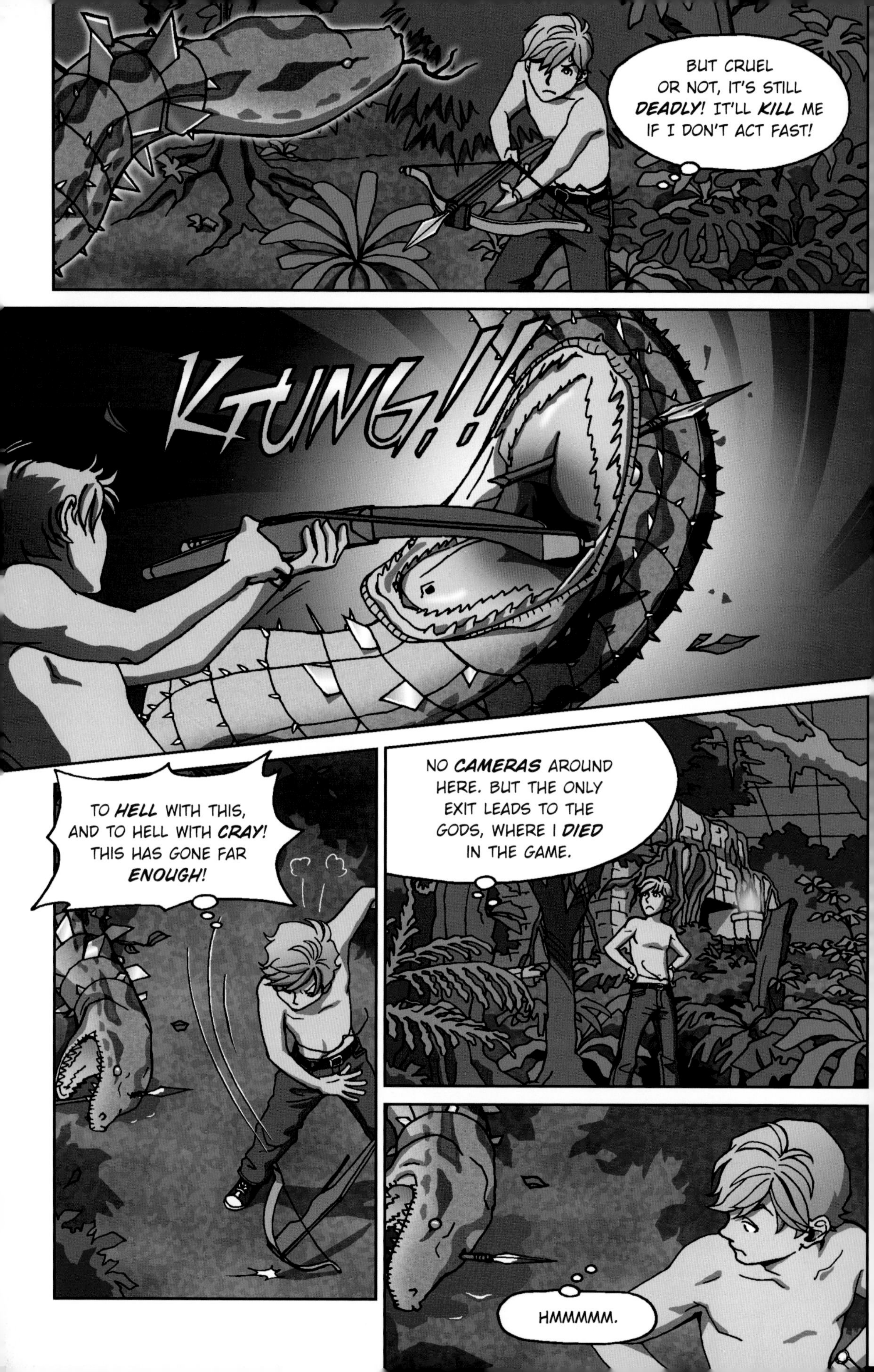
BUT CRUEL OR NOT, IT'S STILL DEADLY! IT'LL KILL ME IF I DON'T ACT FAST!
KTUNG!!
TO HELL WITH THIS, AND TO HELL WITH CRAY! THIS HAS GONE FAR ENOUGH!
NO CAMERAS AROUND HERE. BUT THE ONLY EXIT LEADS TO THE GODS, WHERE I DIED IN THE GAME.
HMMMMM.

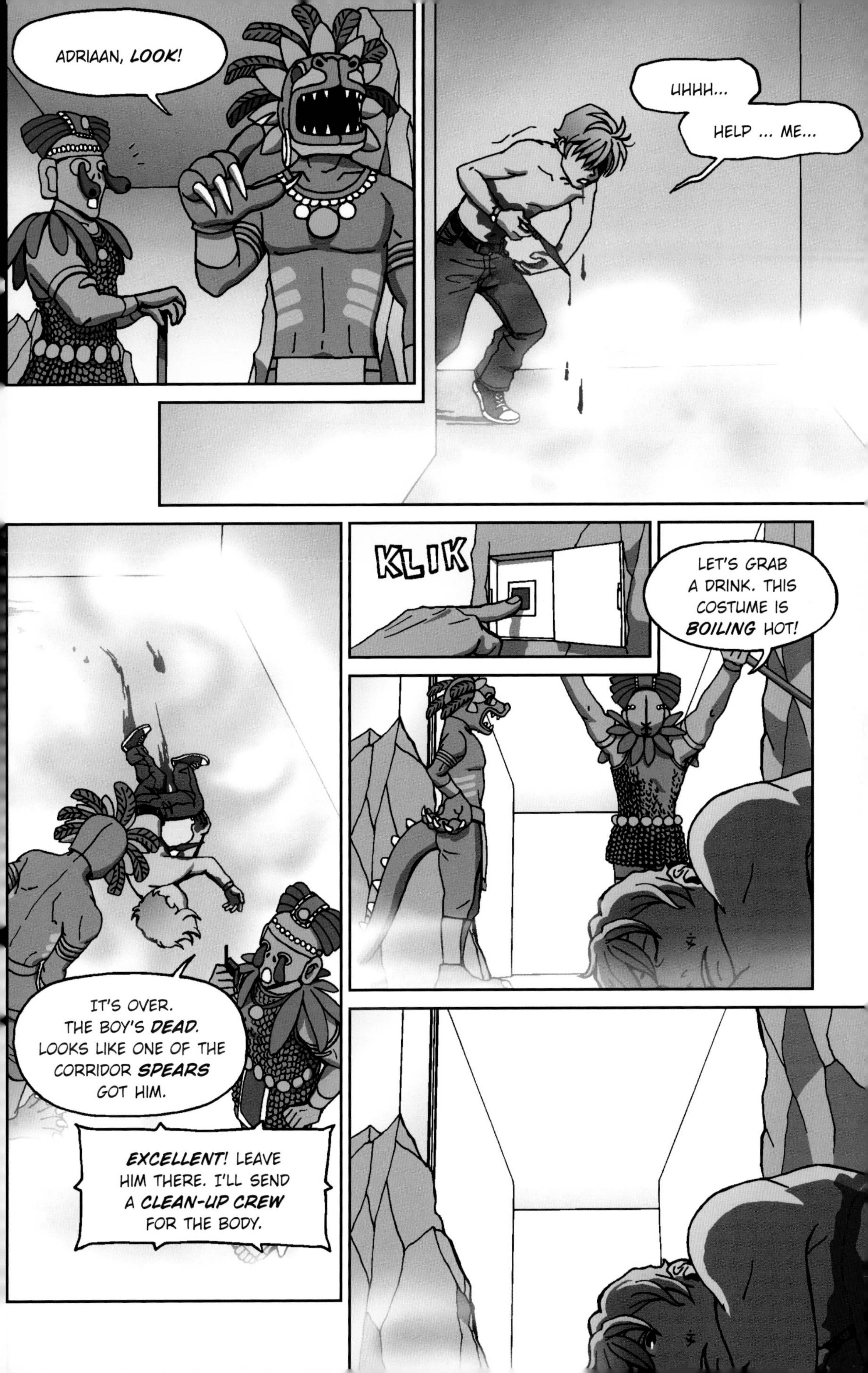
ADRIAAN, LOOK!
UHHH...
HELP ... ME...
KLIK
LET'S GRAB A DRINK. THIS COSTUME IS BOILING HOT!
IT'S OVER. THE BOY'S DEAD. LOOKS LIKE ONE OF THE CORRIDOR SPEARS GOT HIM.
EXCELLENT! LEAVE HIM THERE. I'LL SEND A CLEAN-UP CREW FOR THE BODY.

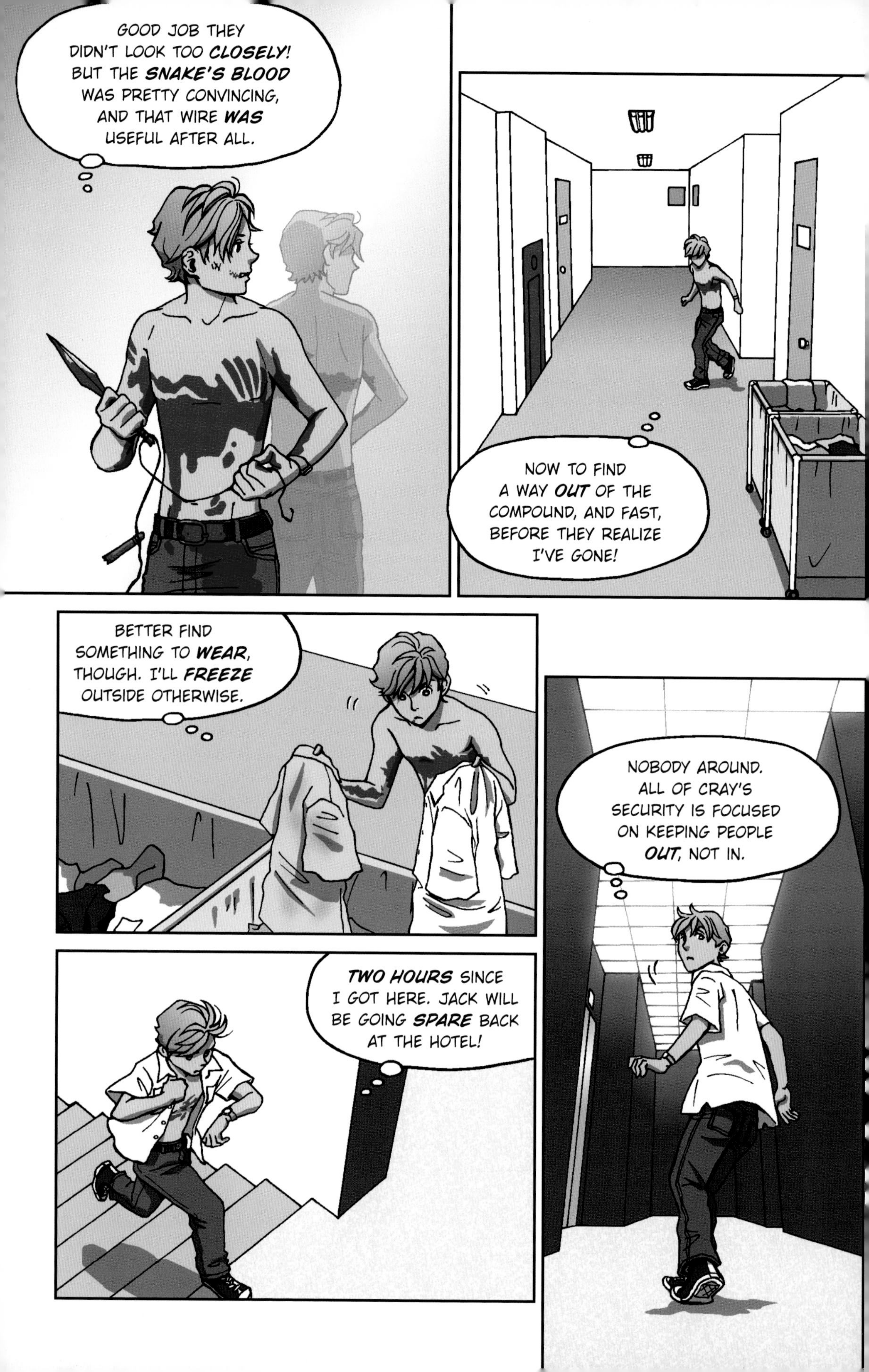
GOOD JOB THEY DIDN'T LOOK TOO **CLOSELY**! BUT THE **SNAKE'S BLOOD** WAS PRETTY CONVINCING, AND THAT WIRE **WAS** USEFUL AFTER ALL.
NOW TO FIND A WAY **OUT** OF THE COMPOUND, AND FAST, BEFORE THEY REALIZE I'VE GONE!
BETTER FIND SOMETHING TO **WEAR**, THOUGH. I'LL **FREEZE** OUTSIDE OTHERWISE.
TWO HOURS SINCE I GOT HERE. JACK WILL BE GOING **SPARE** BACK AT THE HOTEL!
NOBODY AROUND. ALL OF CRAY'S SECURITY IS FOCUSED ON KEEPING PEOPLE **OUT**, NOT IN.

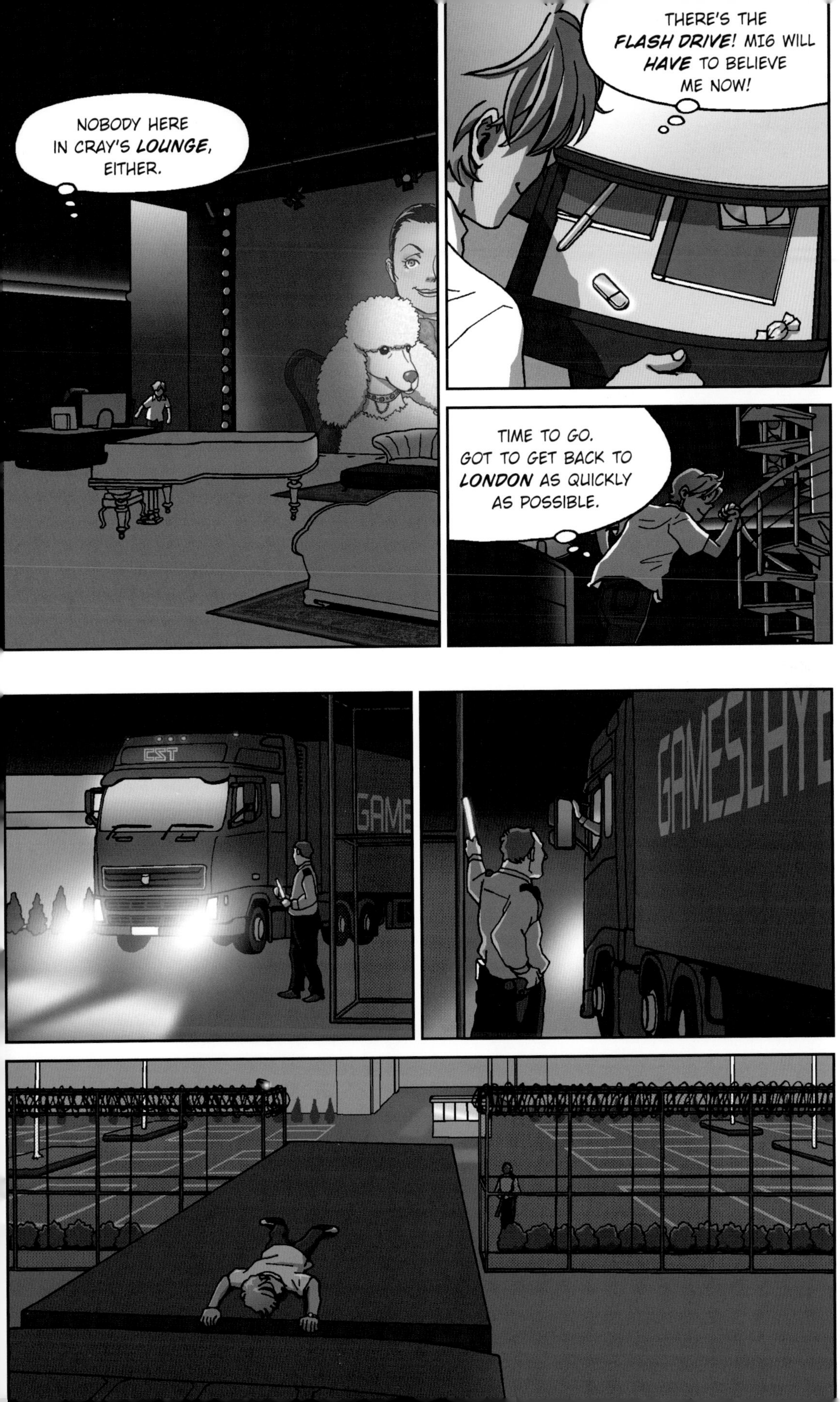
NOBODY HERE IN CRAY'S LOUNGE, EITHER.
THERE'S THE FLASH DRIVE! MI6 WILL HAVE TO BELIEVE ME NOW!
TIME TO GO. GOT TO GET BACK TO LONDON AS QUICKLY AS POSSIBLE.
CST
GAME
GAMESLAYE

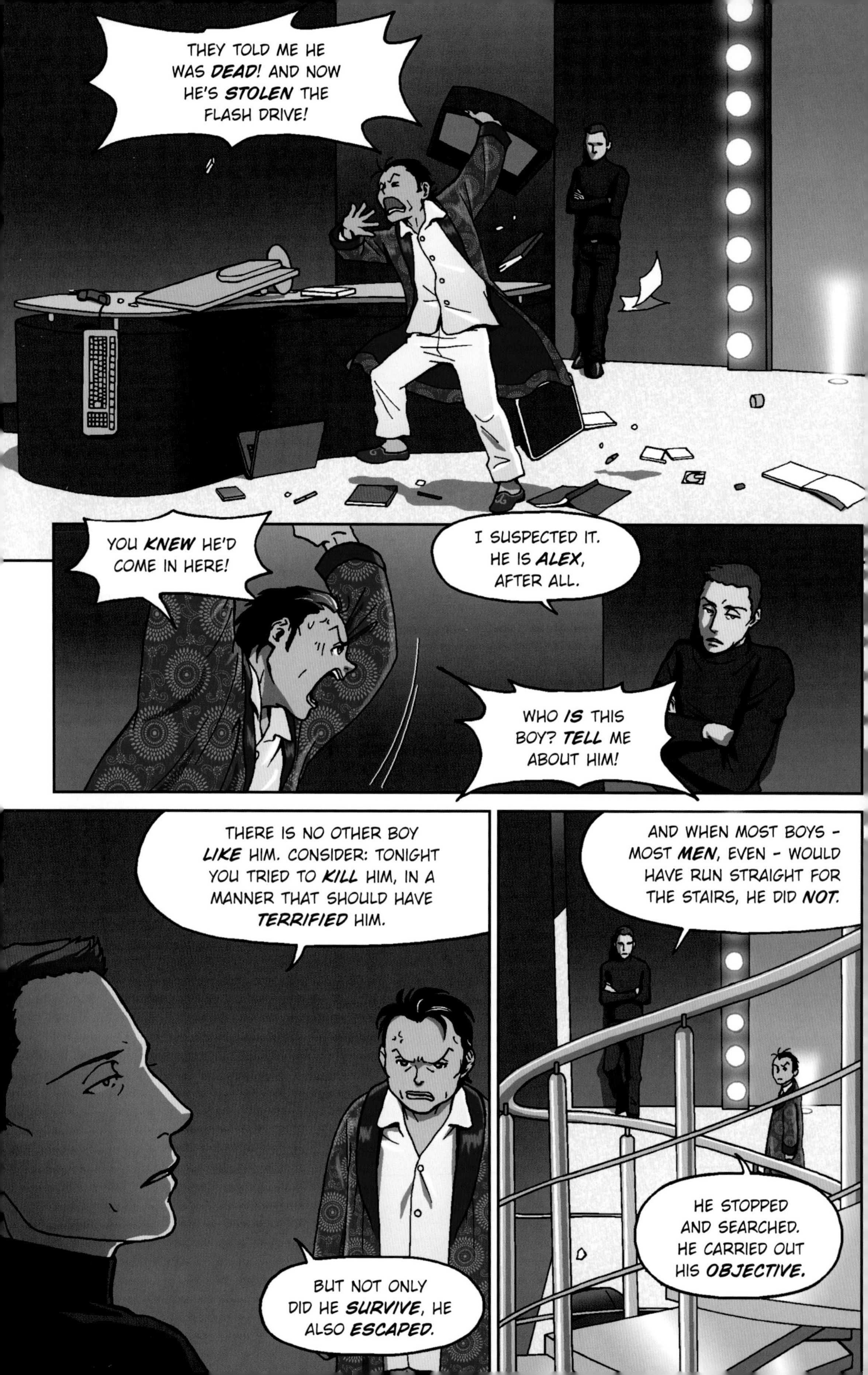
THEY TOLD ME HE WAS DEAD! AND NOW HE'S STOLEN THE FLASH DRIVE!
YOU KNEW HE'D COME IN HERE!
I SUSPECTED IT. HE IS ALEX, AFTER ALL.
WHO IS THIS BOY? TELL ME ABOUT HIM!
THERE IS NO OTHER BOY LIKE HIM. CONSIDER: TONIGHT YOU TRIED TO KILL HIM, IN A MANNER THAT SHOULD HAVE TERRIFIED HIM.
BUT NOT ONLY DID HE SURVIVE, HE ALSO ESCAPED.
AND WHEN MOST BOYS - MOST MEN, EVEN - WOULD HAVE RUN STRAIGHT FOR THE STAIRS, HE DID NOT.
HE STOPPED AND SEARCHED. HE CARRIED OUT HIS OBJECTIVE.

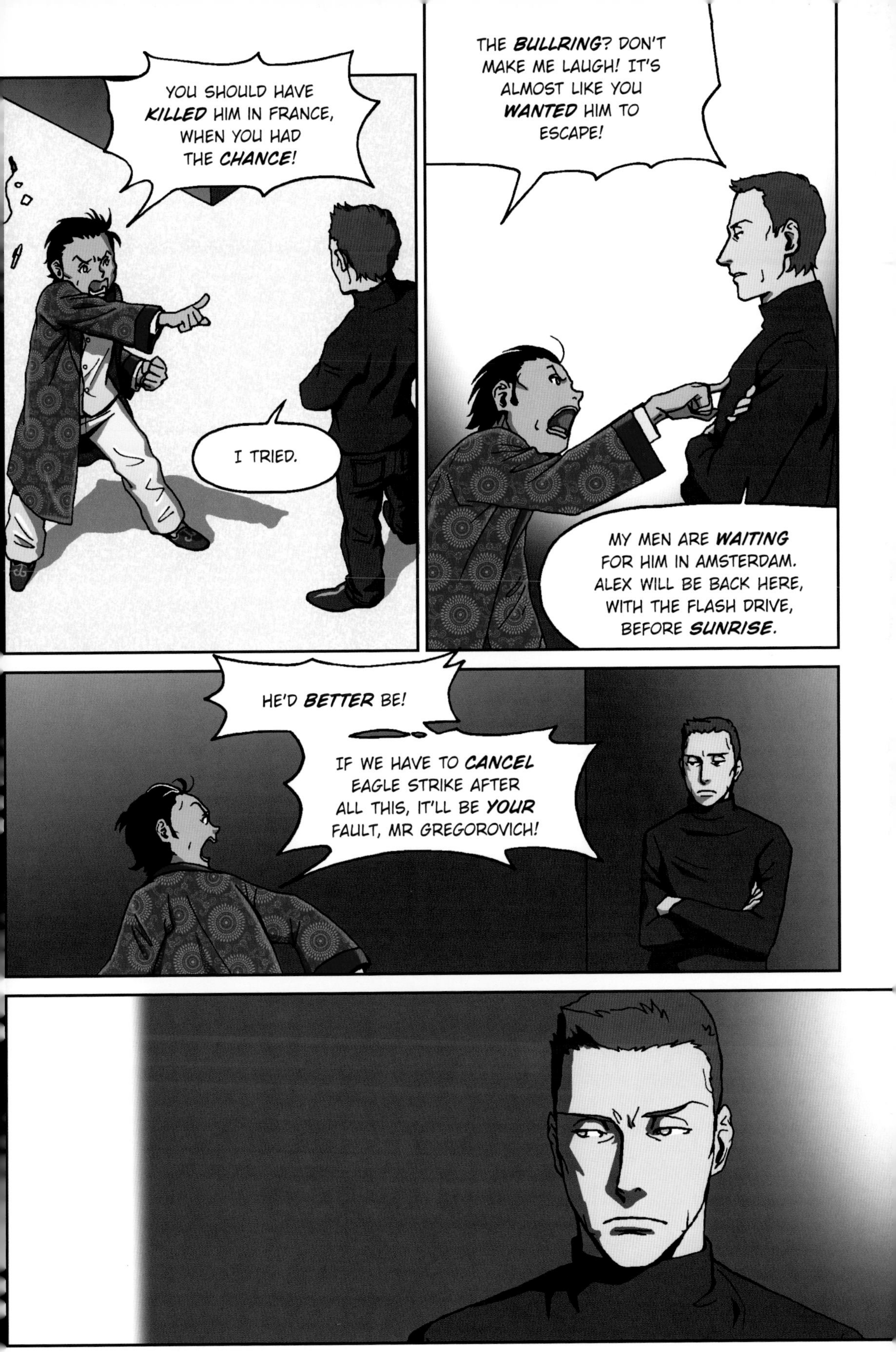
YOU SHOULD HAVE KILLED HIM IN FRANCE, WHEN YOU HAD THE CHANCE!
I TRIED.
THE BULLRING? DON'T MAKE ME LAUGH! IT'S ALMOST LIKE YOU WANTED HIM TO ESCAPE!
MY MEN ARE WAITING FOR HIM IN AMSTERDAM. ALEX WILL BE BACK HERE, WITH THE FLASH DRIVE, BEFORE SUNRISE.
HE'D BETTER BE!
IF WE HAVE TO CANCEL EAGLE STRIKE AFTER ALL THIS, IT'LL BE YOUR FAULT, MR GREGOROVICH!

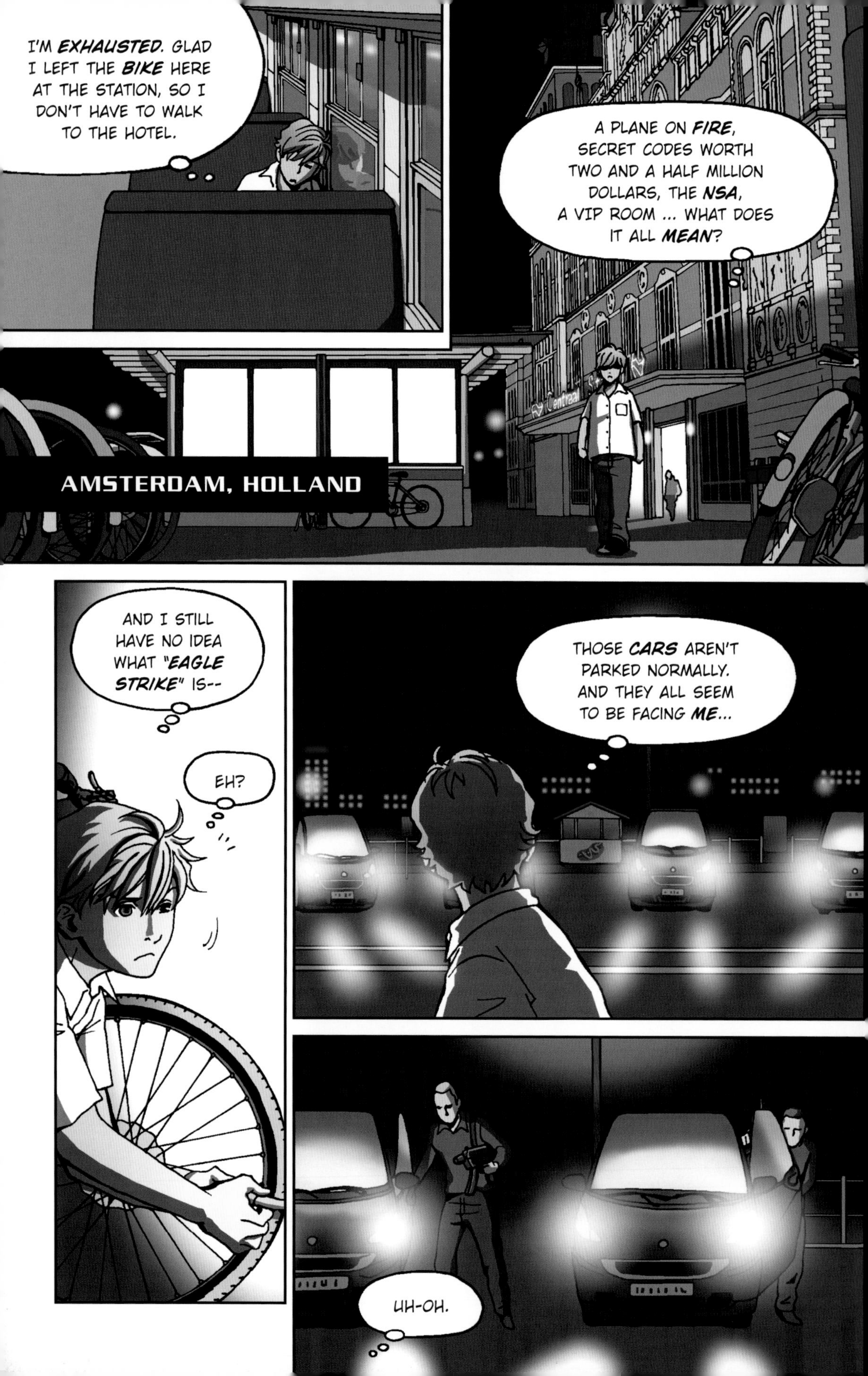
I'M EXHAUSTED. GLAD I LEFT THE BIKE HERE AT THE STATION, SO I DON'T HAVE TO WALK TO THE HOTEL.
A PLANE ON FIRE, SECRET CODES WORTH TWO AND A HALF MILLION DOLLARS, THE NSA, A VIP ROOM ... WHAT DOES IT ALL MEAN?
AMSTERDAM, HOLLAND
AND I STILL HAVE NO IDEA WHAT "EAGLE STRIKE" IS--
EH?
THOSE CARS AREN'T PARKED NORMALLY. AND THEY ALL SEEM TO BE FACING ME...
UH-OH.

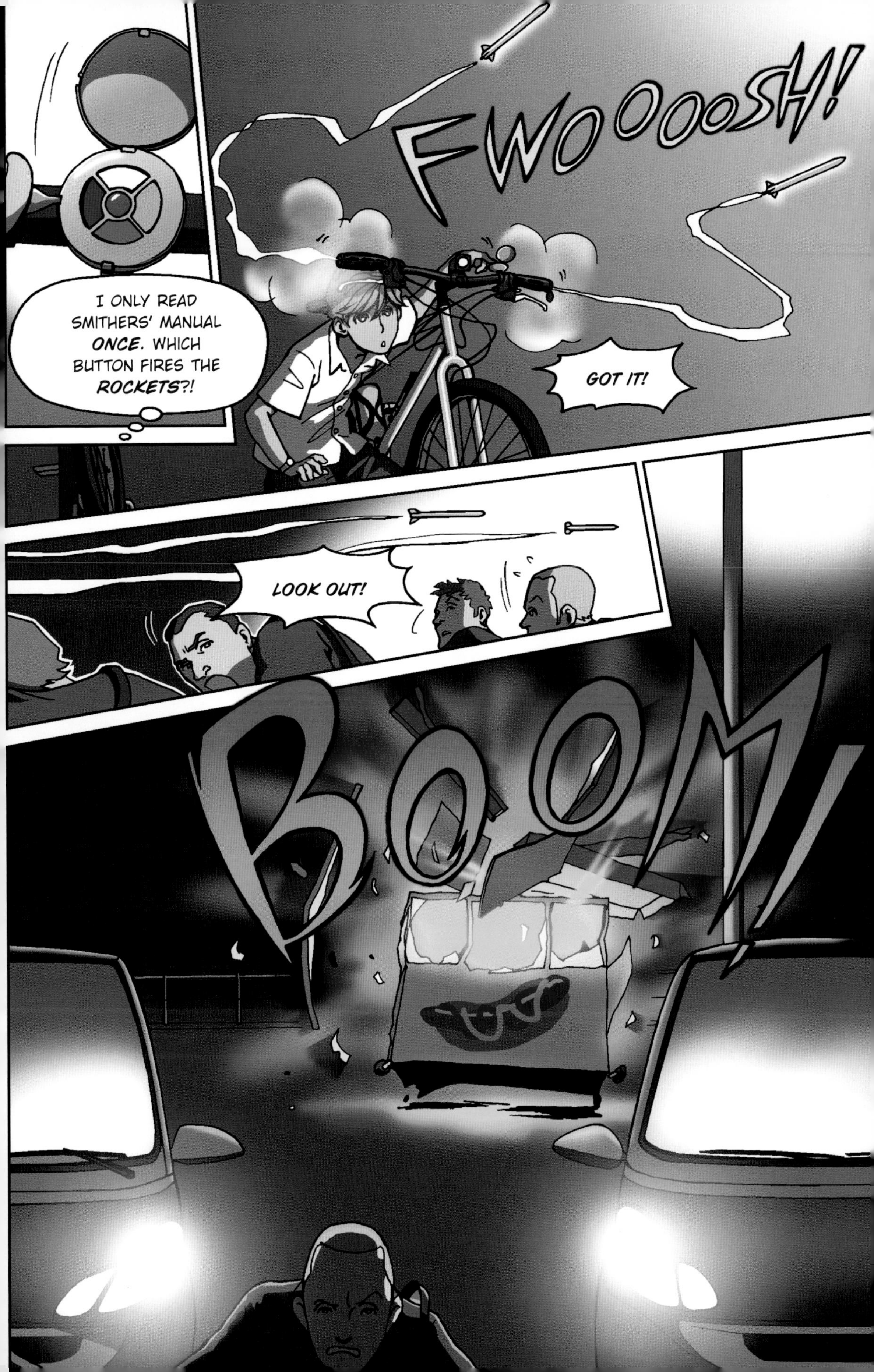
FWOOOOOSH!
I ONLY READ SMITHERS' MANUAL ONCE. WHICH BUTTON FIRES THE ROCKETS?!
GOT IT!
LOOK OUT!
BOOM!

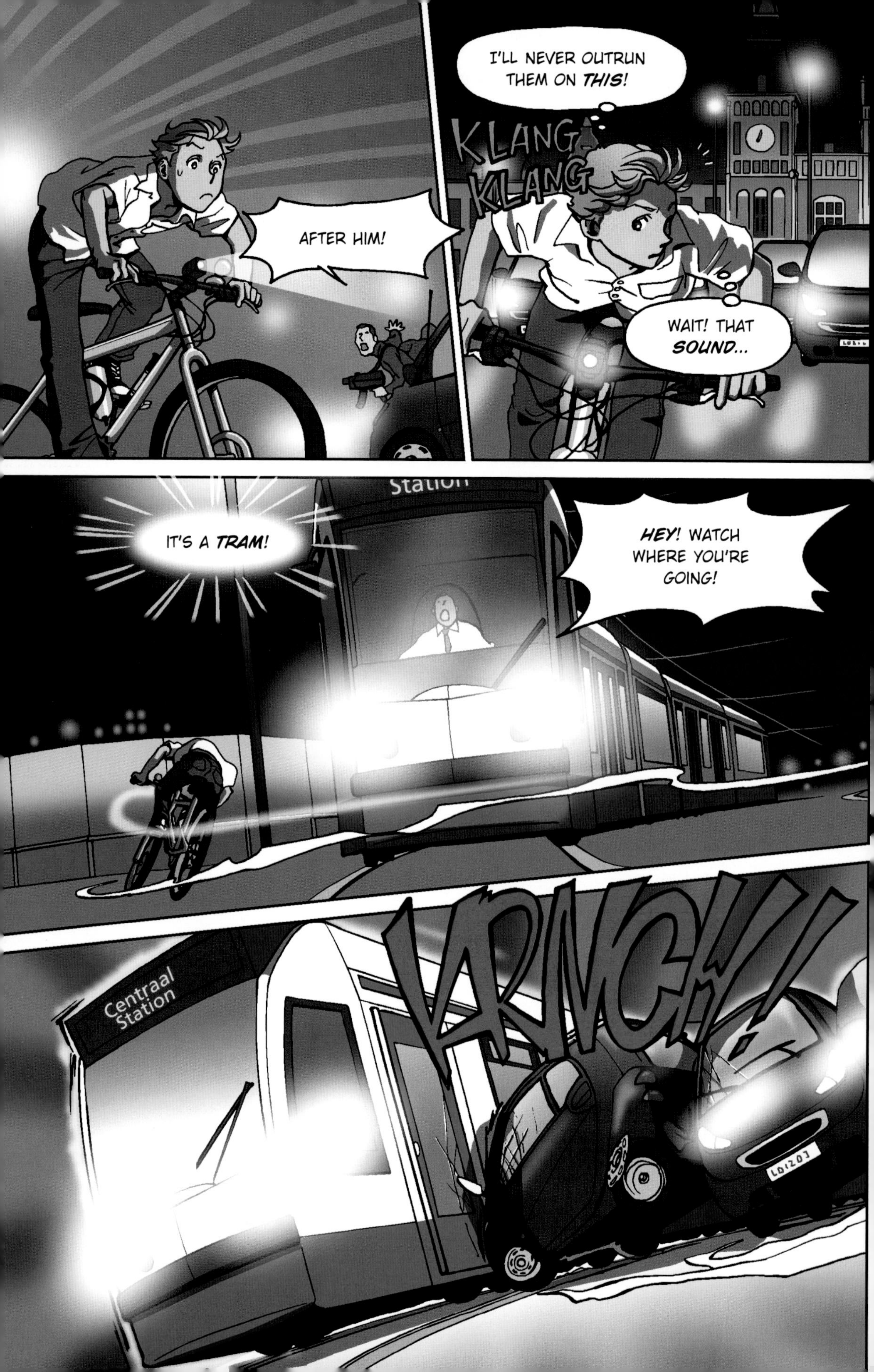
AFTER HIM!
I'LL NEVER OUTRUN THEM ON *THIS*!
KLANG KLANG
WAIT! THAT *SOUND*...
Station
IT'S A *TRAM*!
HEY! WATCH WHERE YOU'RE GOING!
KRUNCH!!
Centraal Station

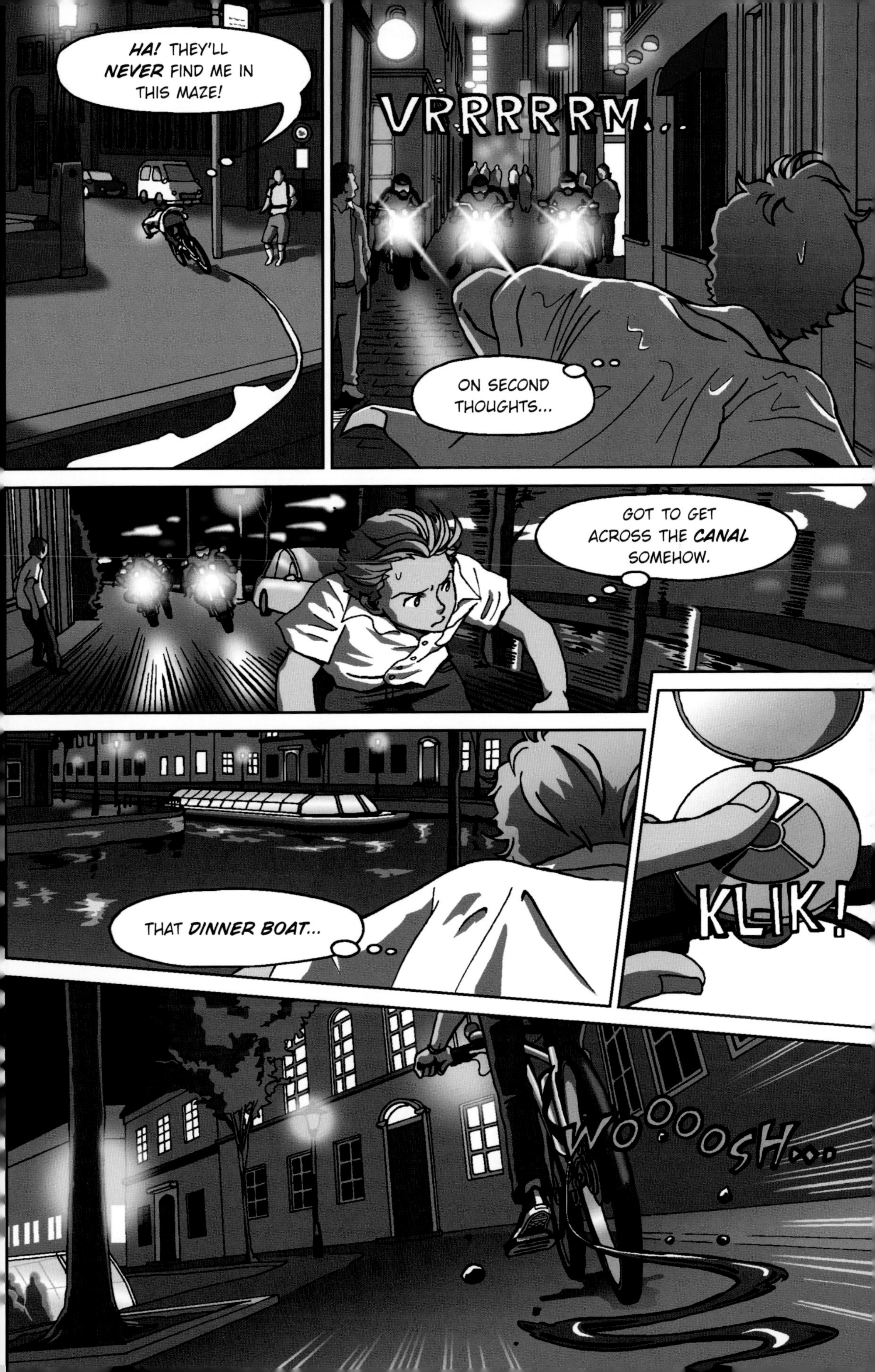
HA! THEY'LL NEVER FIND ME IN THIS MAZE!
VRRRRRRM...
ON SECOND THOUGHTS...
GOT TO GET ACROSS THE CANAL SOMEHOW.
THAT DINNER BOAT...
KLIK!
WOOOOSH...

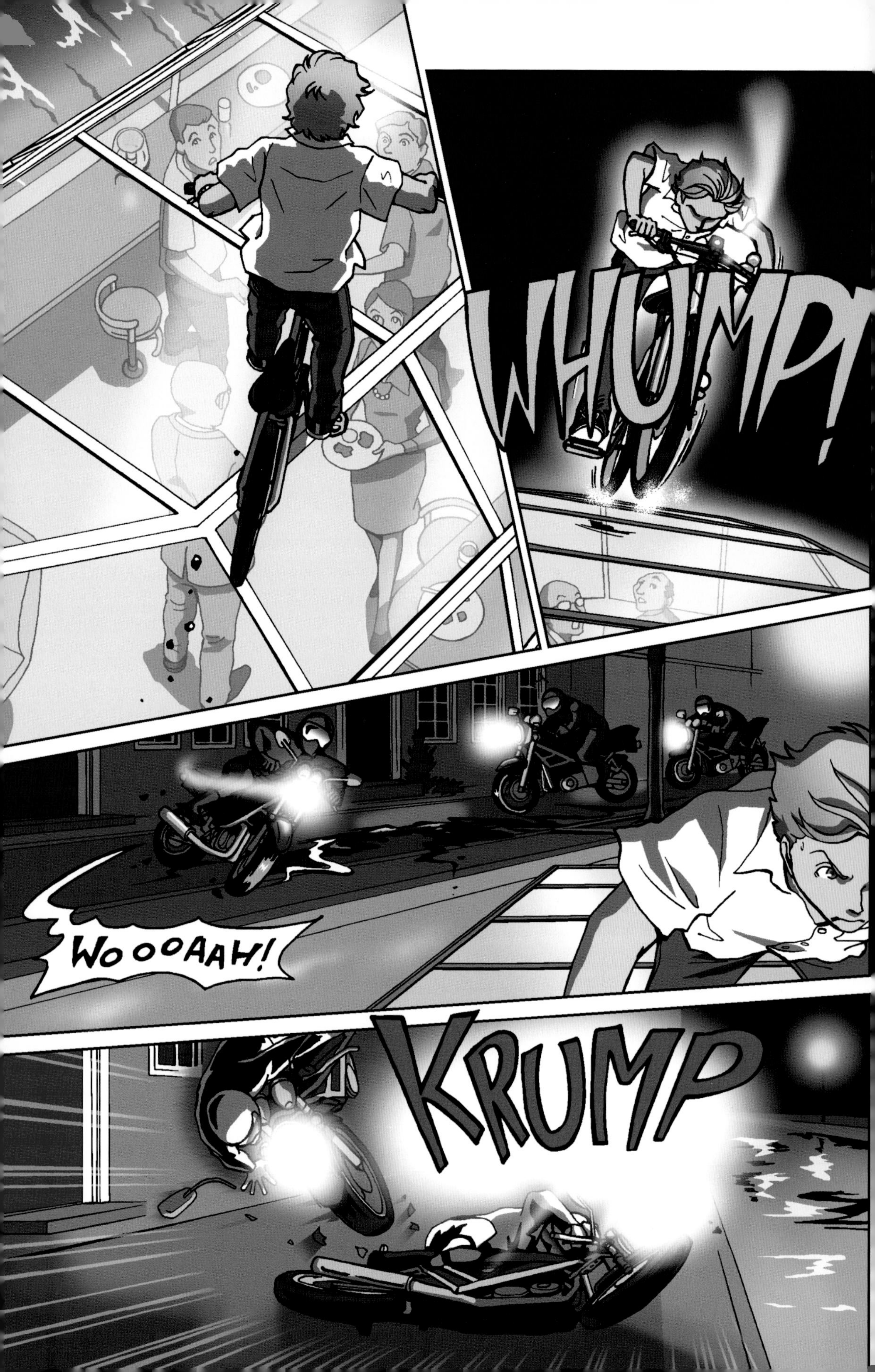
WHUMP!
WOOOAAH!
KRUMP

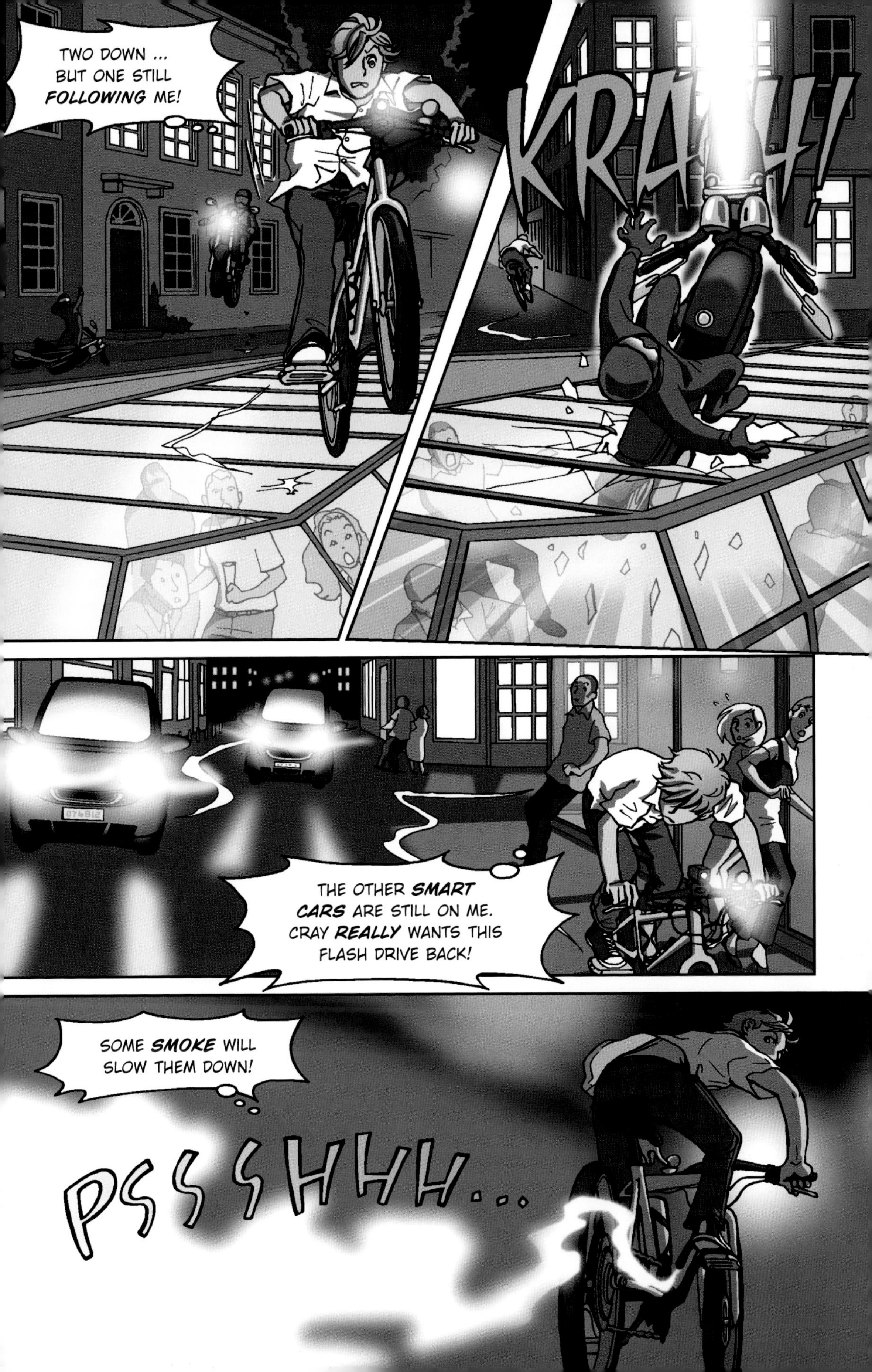
TWO DOWN ... BUT ONE STILL FOLLOWING ME!
KRASH!
THE OTHER SMART CARS ARE STILL ON ME. CRAY REALLY WANTS THIS FLASH DRIVE BACK!
SOME SMOKE WILL SLOW THEM DOWN!
PSSSHHH...

AAAAH!
SPLASH
JUST ONE CAR LEFT! BUT THE BRIDGE IS OPENING...
MMMMF! COME ON, ALEX! FASTER!
NO GOOD ... I'M NOT GOING TO MAKE IT!
JUST ONE CHANCE...
KLIK!

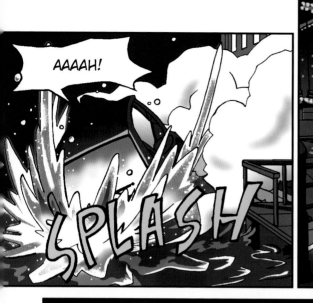

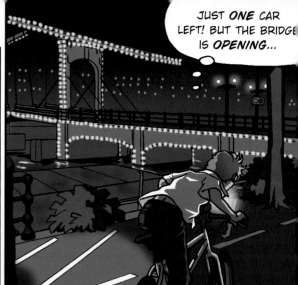

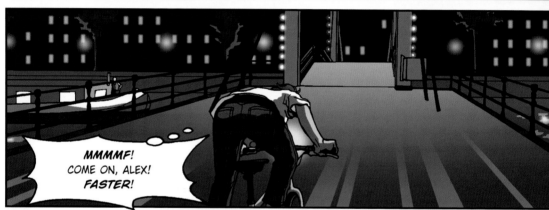

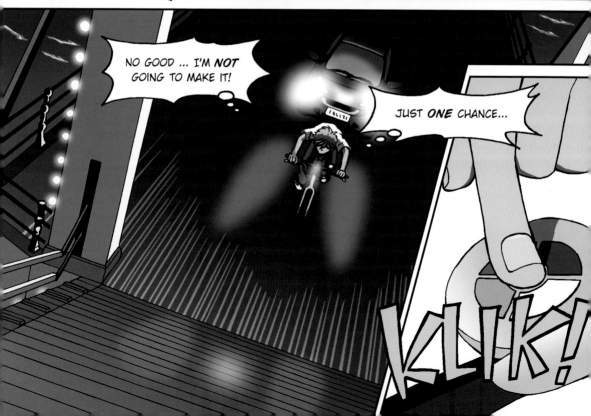

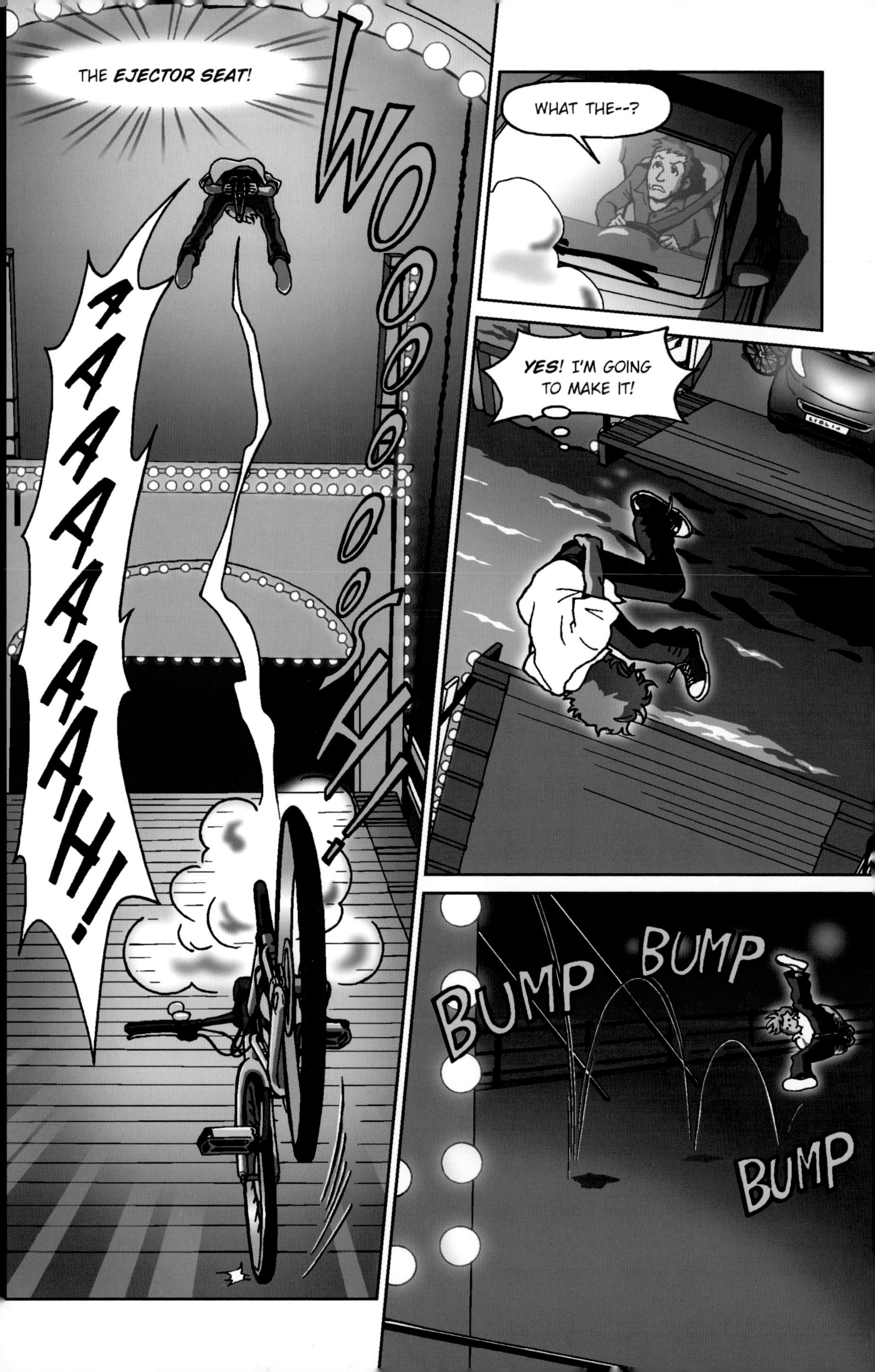
THE EJECTOR SEAT!
WOOOOOOOOOSH!
AAAAAAAAH!
WHAT THE--?
YES! I'M GOING TO MAKE IT!
BUMP
BUMP
BUMP

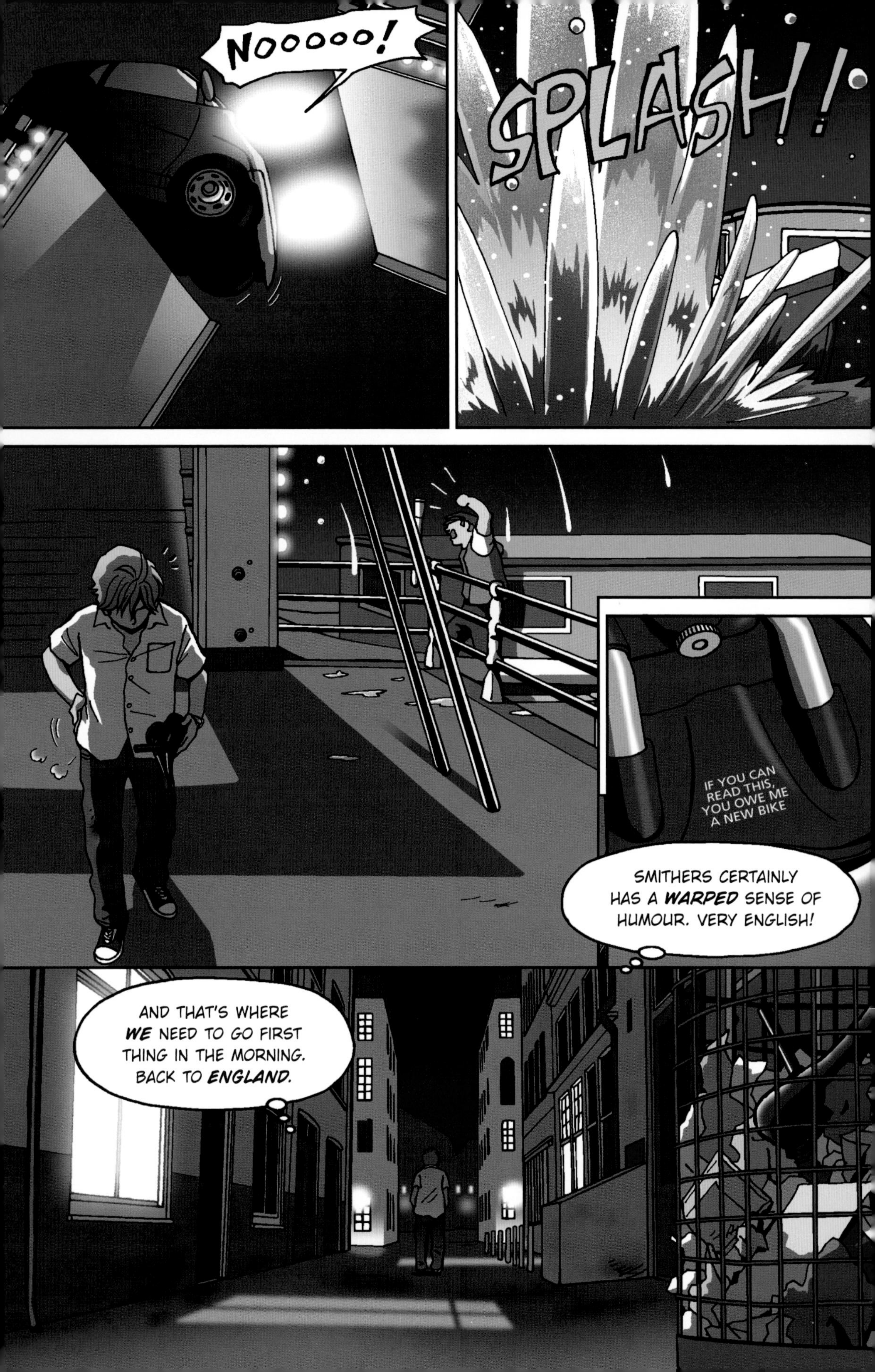
NOOOOO!
SPLASH!
IF YOU CAN READ THIS, YOU OWE ME A NEW BIKE
SMITHERS CERTAINLY HAS A WARPED SENSE OF HUMOUR. VERY ENGLISH!
AND THAT'S WHERE WE NEED TO GO FIRST THING IN THE MORNING. BACK TO ENGLAND.

I HAVE MEN WATCHING *EVERY* STATION AND AIRPORT IN HOLLAND. BUT I THINK ALEX WILL HEAD FOR *PARIS*, OR *BRUSSELS*, AND FROM THERE TO ENGLAND.

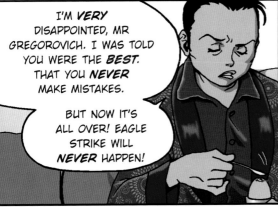

I'M *VERY* DISAPPOINTED, MR GREGOROVICH. I WAS TOLD YOU WERE THE *BEST*. THAT YOU *NEVER* MAKE MISTAKES.

BUT NOW IT'S ALL OVER! EAGLE STRIKE WILL *NEVER* HAPPEN!

IT'S *NOT* OVER. I HAVE PEOPLE IN ENGLAND. WE *WILL* GET THE FLASH DRIVE BACK.

HOW?!

WHY WAS ALEX IN FRANCE? *WHY* DID HE CARE ABOUT THIS JOURNALIST? HE RISKED HIS LIFE FOR THIS MAN.

IT IS BECAUSE OF HIS *DAUGHTER*. *THAT* IS WHO ALEX WAS STAYING WITH.

A *GIRLFRIEND*...

OH, YES. *YES*, THAT SHOULD BE VERY USEFUL *INDEED*.

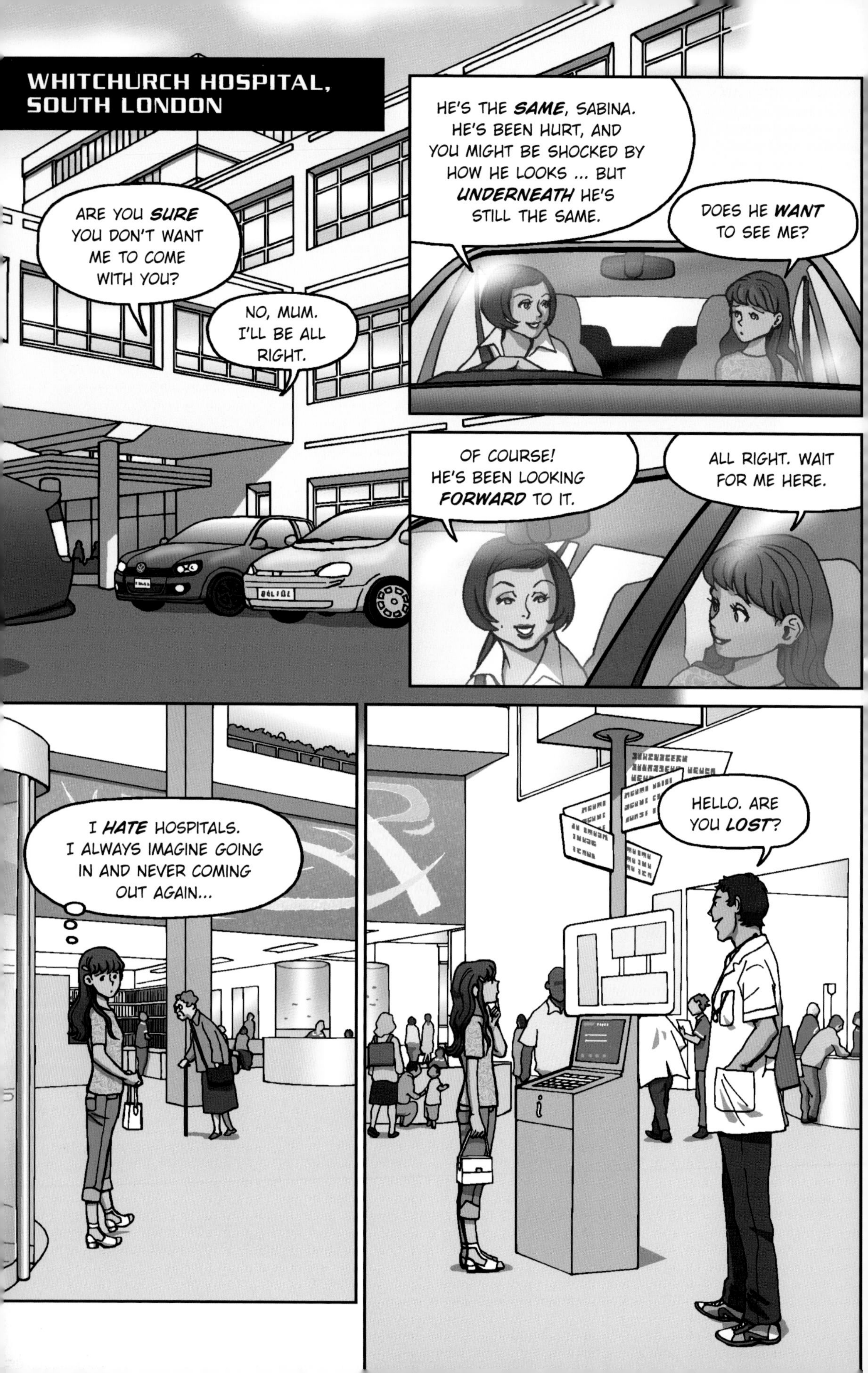
WHITCHURCH HOSPITAL, SOUTH LONDON
ARE YOU SURE YOU DON'T WANT ME TO COME WITH YOU?
NO, MUM. I'LL BE ALL RIGHT.
HE'S THE SAME, SABINA. HE'S BEEN HURT, AND YOU MIGHT BE SHOCKED BY HOW HE LOOKS ... BUT UNDERNEATH HE'S STILL THE SAME.
DOES HE WANT TO SEE ME?
OF COURSE! HE'S BEEN LOOKING FORWARD TO IT.
ALL RIGHT. WAIT FOR ME HERE.
I HATE HOSPITALS. I ALWAYS IMAGINE GOING IN AND NEVER COMING OUT AGAIN...
HELLO. ARE YOU LOST?

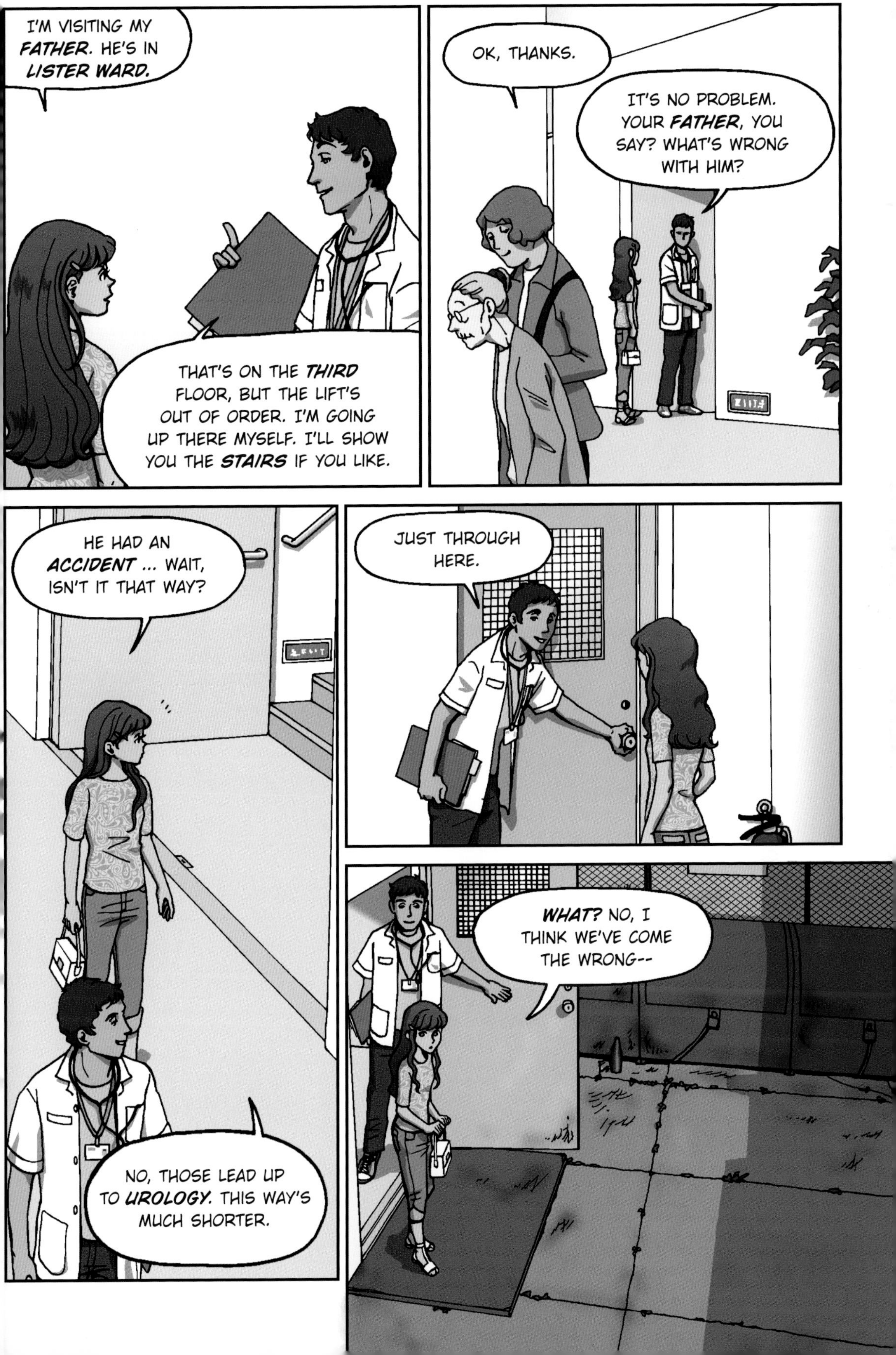
I'M VISITING MY FATHER. HE'S IN LISTER WARD.
THAT'S ON THE THIRD FLOOR, BUT THE LIFT'S OUT OF ORDER. I'M GOING UP THERE MYSELF. I'LL SHOW YOU THE STAIRS IF YOU LIKE.
OK, THANKS.
IT'S NO PROBLEM. YOUR FATHER, YOU SAY? WHAT'S WRONG WITH HIM?
HE HAD AN ACCIDENT ... WAIT, ISN'T IT THAT WAY?
NO, THOSE LEAD UP TO UROLOGY. THIS WAY'S MUCH SHORTER.
JUST THROUGH HERE.
WHAT? NO, I THINK WE'VE COME THE WRONG--

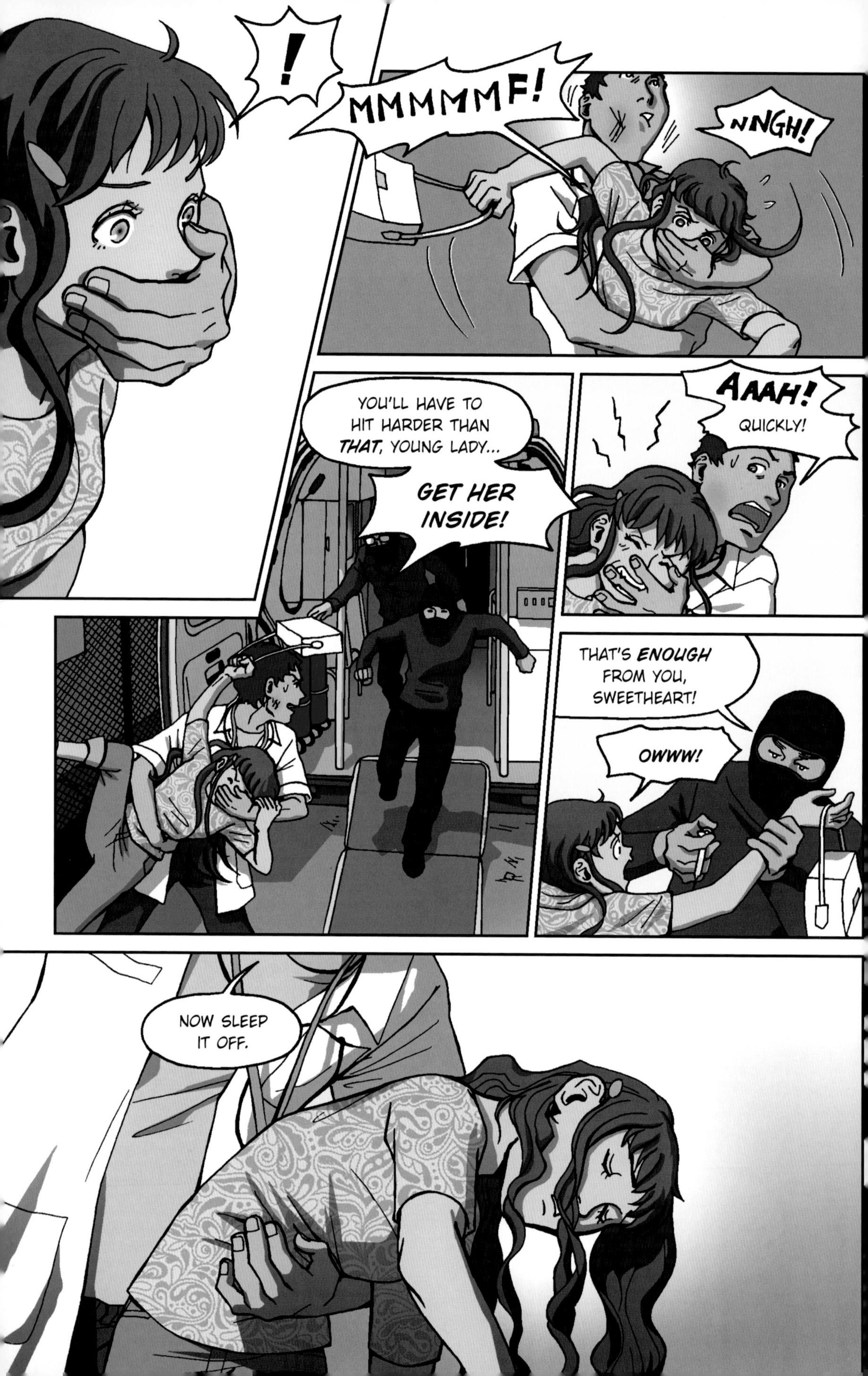
!
MMMMMF!
NNGH!
YOU'LL HAVE TO HIT HARDER THAN *THAT*, YOUNG LADY...
GET HER INSIDE!
AAAH!
QUICKLY!
THAT'S **ENOUGH** FROM YOU, SWEETHEART!
OWWW!
NOW SLEEP IT OFF.

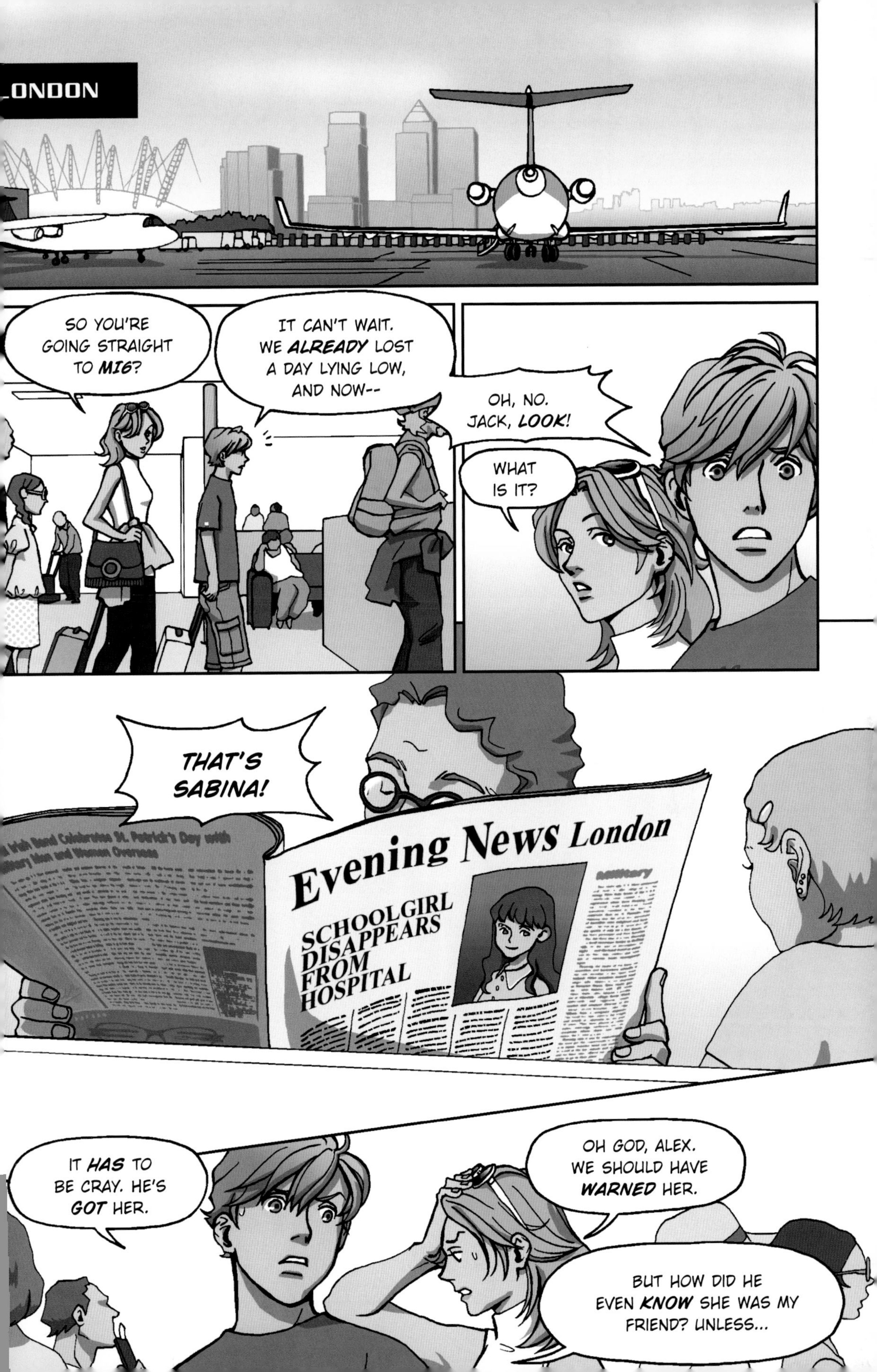
LONDON
SO YOU'RE GOING STRAIGHT TO MI6?
IT CAN'T WAIT. WE ALREADY LOST A DAY LYING LOW, AND NOW--
OH, NO. JACK, LOOK!
WHAT IS IT?
THAT'S SABINA!
Evening News London
SCHOOLGIRL DISAPPEARS FROM HOSPITAL
IT HAS TO BE CRAY. HE'S GOT HER.
OH GOD, ALEX. WE SHOULD HAVE WARNED HER.
BUT HOW DID HE EVEN KNOW SHE WAS MY FRIEND? UNLESS...

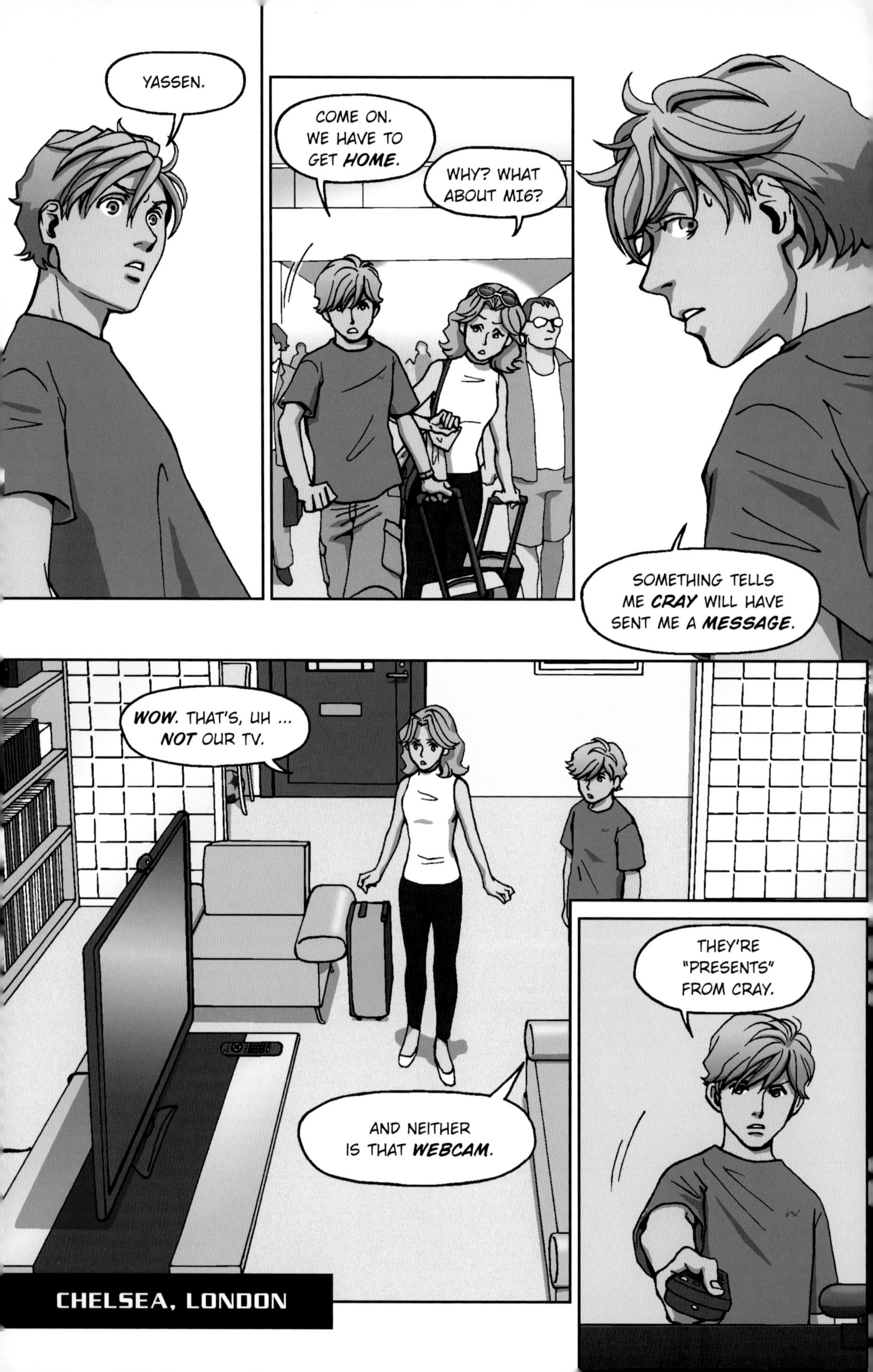
YASSEN.
COME ON. WE HAVE TO GET HOME.
WHY? WHAT ABOUT MI6?
SOMETHING TELLS ME CRAY WILL HAVE SENT ME A MESSAGE.
CHELSEA, LONDON
WOW. THAT'S, UH ... NOT OUR TV.
AND NEITHER IS THAT WEBCAM.
THEY'RE "PRESENTS" FROM CRAY.

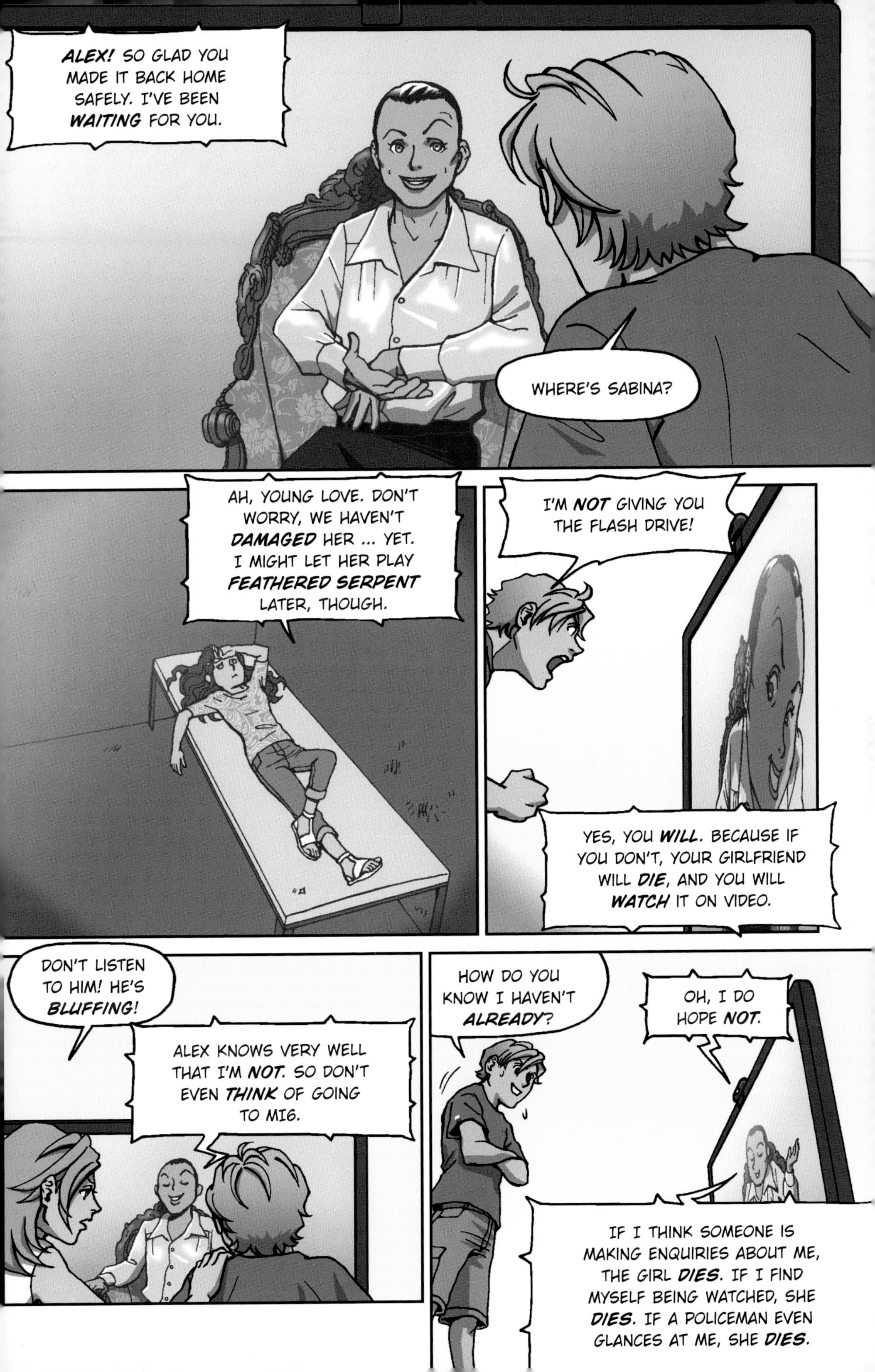
ALEX! SO GLAD YOU MADE IT BACK HOME SAFELY. I'VE BEEN WAITING FOR YOU.
WHERE'S SABINA?
AH, YOUNG LOVE. DON'T WORRY, WE HAVEN'T DAMAGED HER ... YET. I MIGHT LET HER PLAY FEATHERED SERPENT LATER, THOUGH.
I'M NOT GIVING YOU THE FLASH DRIVE!
YES, YOU WILL. BECAUSE IF YOU DON'T, YOUR GIRLFRIEND WILL DIE, AND YOU WILL WATCH IT ON VIDEO.
DON'T LISTEN TO HIM! HE'S BLUFFING!
ALEX KNOWS VERY WELL THAT I'M NOT. SO DON'T EVEN THINK OF GOING TO MI6.
HOW DO YOU KNOW I HAVEN'T ALREADY?
OH, I DO HOPE NOT.
IF I THINK SOMEONE IS MAKING ENQUIRIES ABOUT ME, THE GIRL DIES. IF I FIND MYSELF BEING WATCHED, SHE DIES. IF A POLICEMAN EVEN GLANCES AT ME, SHE DIES.

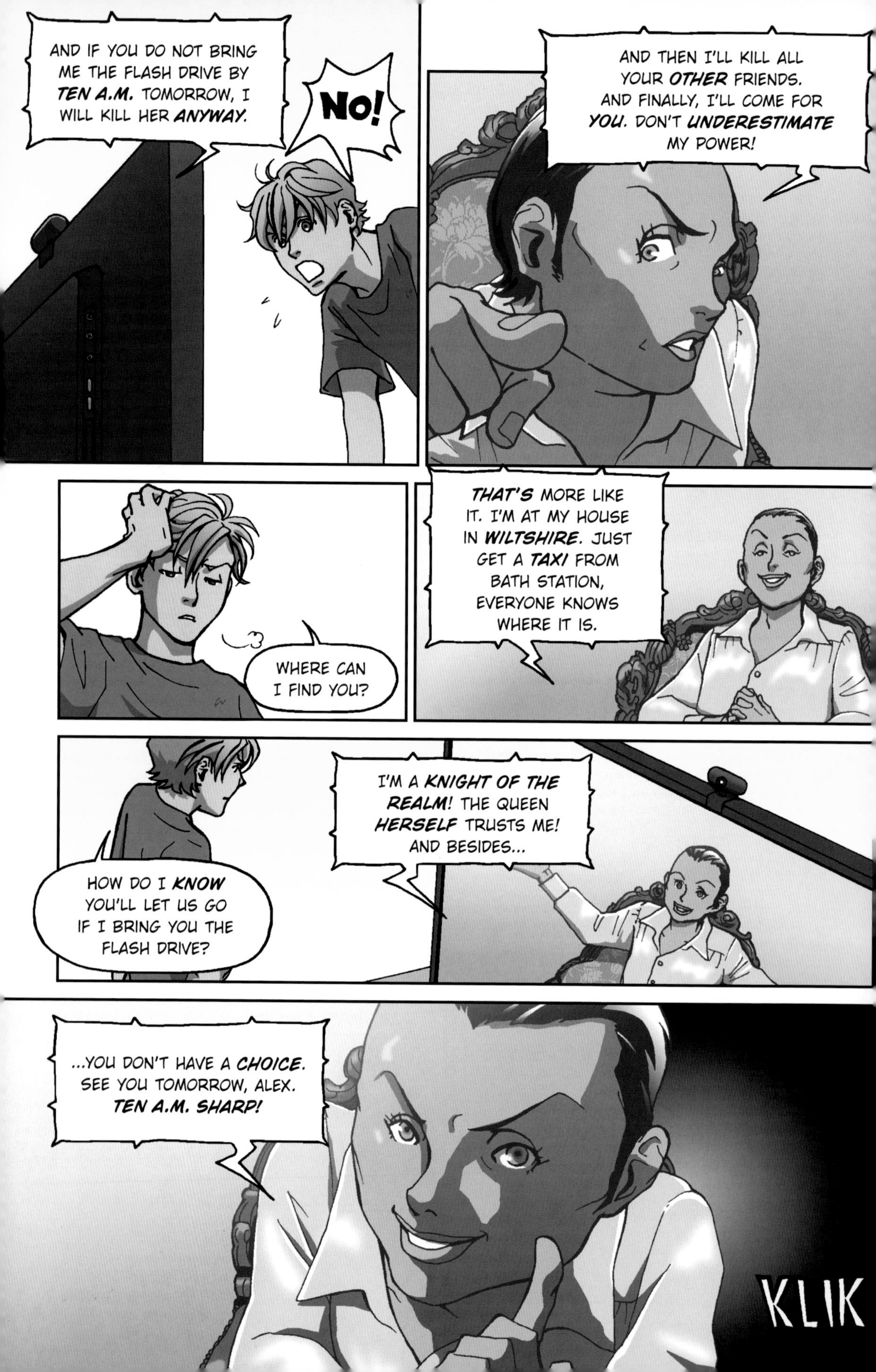
AND IF YOU DO NOT BRING ME THE FLASH DRIVE BY TEN A.M. TOMORROW, I WILL KILL HER ANYWAY.
NO!
AND THEN I'LL KILL ALL YOUR OTHER FRIENDS. AND FINALLY, I'LL COME FOR YOU. DON'T UNDERESTIMATE MY POWER!
WHERE CAN I FIND YOU?
THAT'S MORE LIKE IT. I'M AT MY HOUSE IN WILTSHIRE. JUST GET A TAXI FROM BATH STATION, EVERYONE KNOWS WHERE IT IS.
HOW DO I KNOW YOU'LL LET US GO IF I BRING YOU THE FLASH DRIVE?
I'M A KNIGHT OF THE REALM! THE QUEEN HERSELF TRUSTS ME! AND BESIDES...
...YOU DON'T HAVE A CHOICE. SEE YOU TOMORROW, ALEX. TEN A.M. SHARP!
KLIK

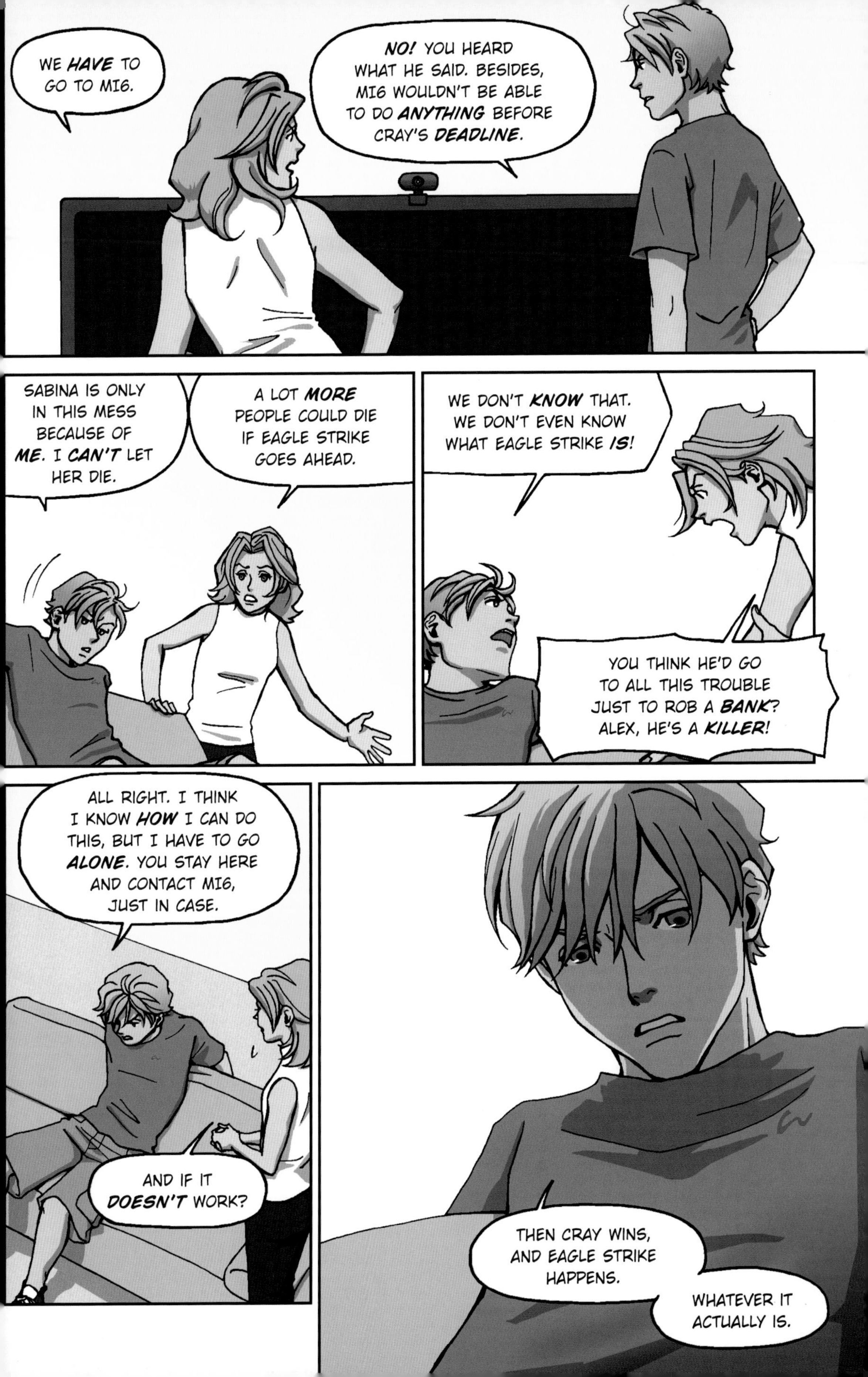
WE HAVE TO GO TO MI6.
NO! YOU HEARD WHAT HE SAID. BESIDES, MI6 WOULDN'T BE ABLE TO DO ANYTHING BEFORE CRAY'S DEADLINE.
SABINA IS ONLY IN THIS MESS BECAUSE OF ME. I CAN'T LET HER DIE.
A LOT MORE PEOPLE COULD DIE IF EAGLE STRIKE GOES AHEAD.
WE DON'T KNOW THAT. WE DON'T EVEN KNOW WHAT EAGLE STRIKE IS!
YOU THINK HE'D GO TO ALL THIS TROUBLE JUST TO ROB A BANK? ALEX, HE'S A KILLER!
ALL RIGHT. I THINK I KNOW HOW I CAN DO THIS, BUT I HAVE TO GO ALONE. YOU STAY HERE AND CONTACT MI6, JUST IN CASE.
AND IF IT DOESN'T WORK?
THEN CRAY WINS, AND EAGLE STRIKE HAPPENS.
WHATEVER IT ACTUALLY IS.

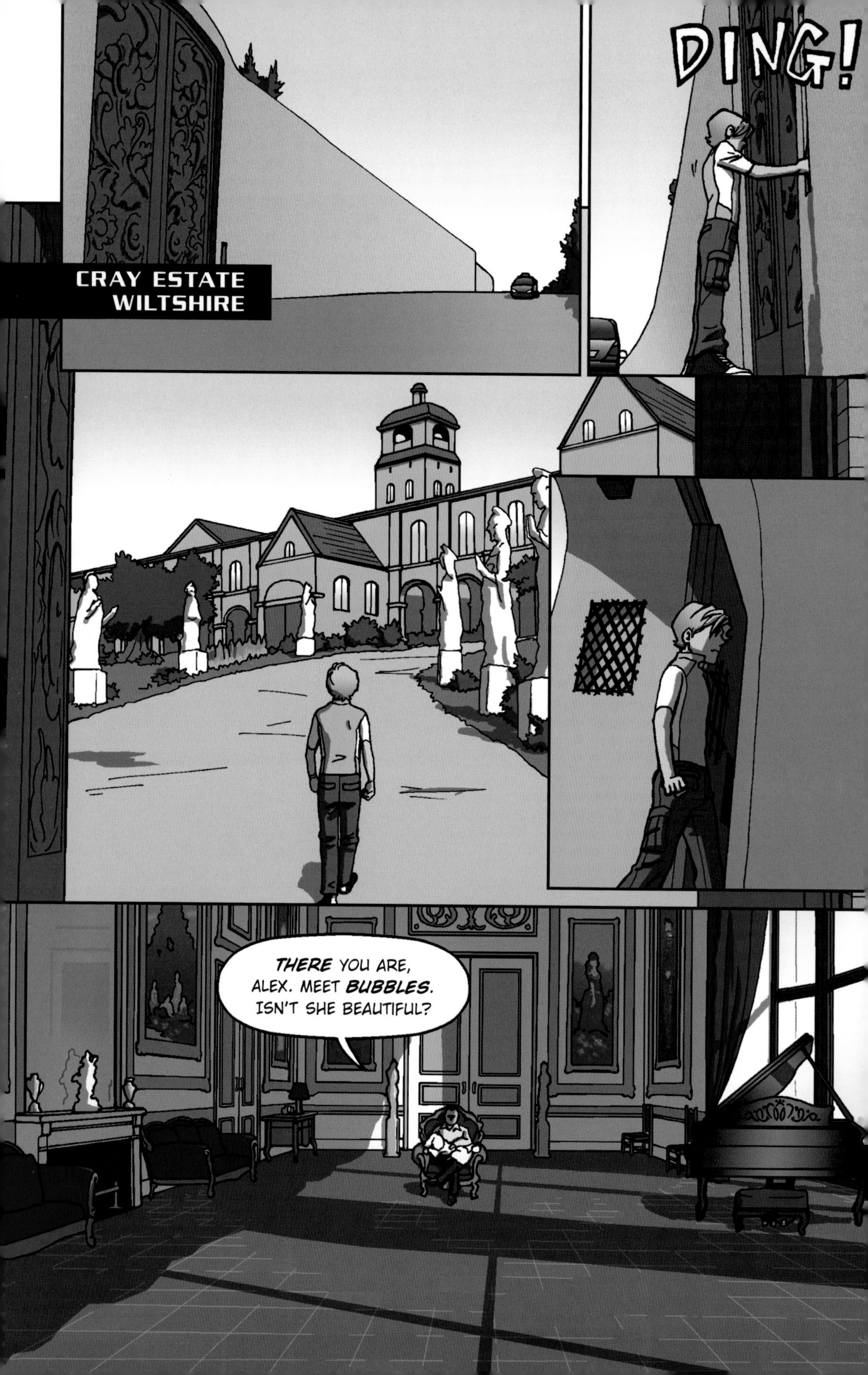
CRAY ESTATE
WILTSHIRE
DING!
THERE YOU ARE, ALEX. MEET BUBBLES. ISN'T SHE BEAUTIFUL?

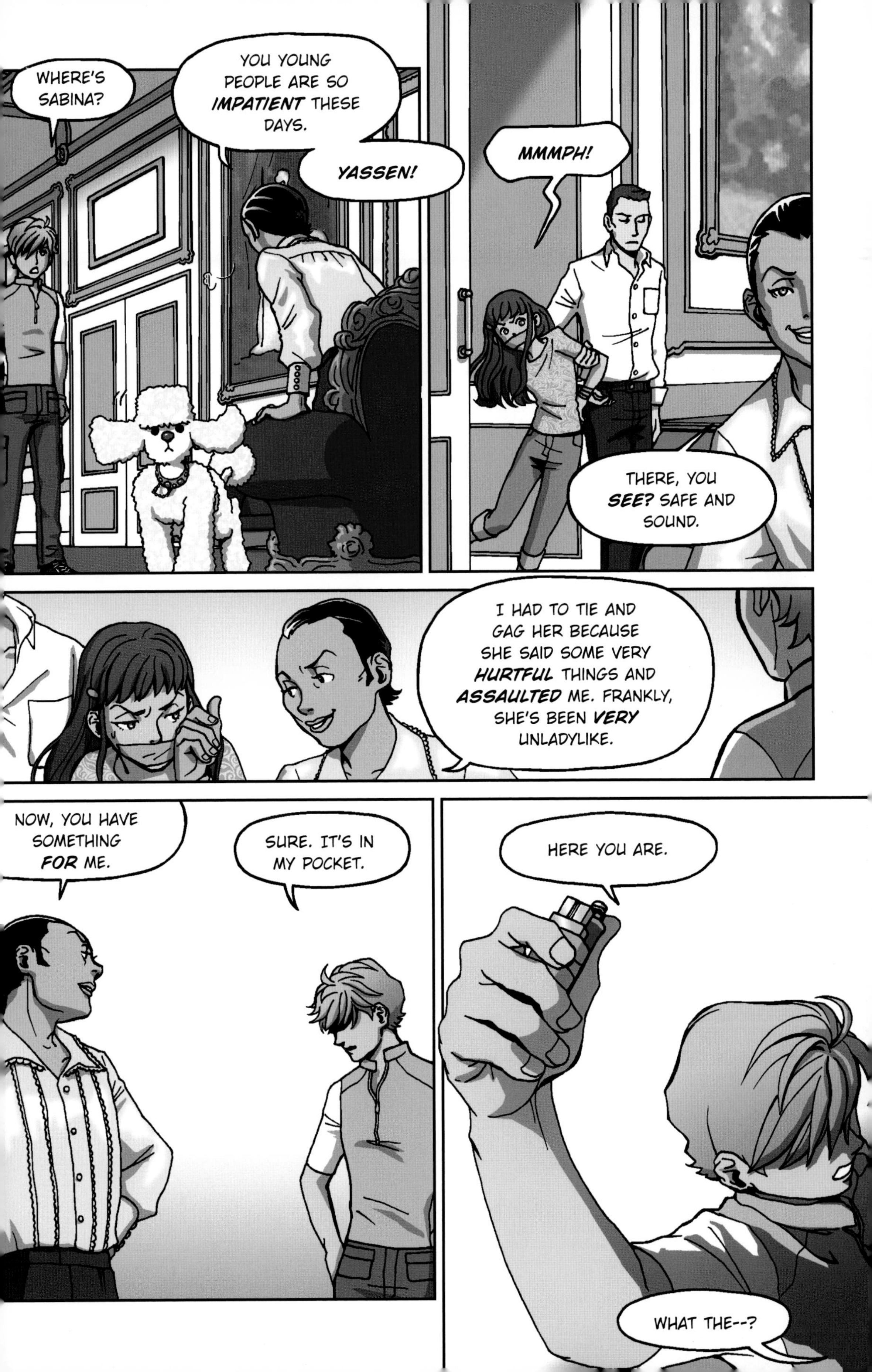
WHERE'S SABINA?
YOU YOUNG PEOPLE ARE SO *IMPATIENT* THESE DAYS.
YASSEN!
MMMPH!
THERE, YOU *SEE?* SAFE AND SOUND.
I HAD TO TIE AND GAG HER BECAUSE SHE SAID SOME VERY *HURTFUL* THINGS AND *ASSAULTED* ME. FRANKLY, SHE'S BEEN *VERY* UNLADYLIKE.
NOW, YOU HAVE SOMETHING *FOR* ME.
SURE. IT'S IN MY POCKET.
HERE YOU ARE.
WHAT THE--?

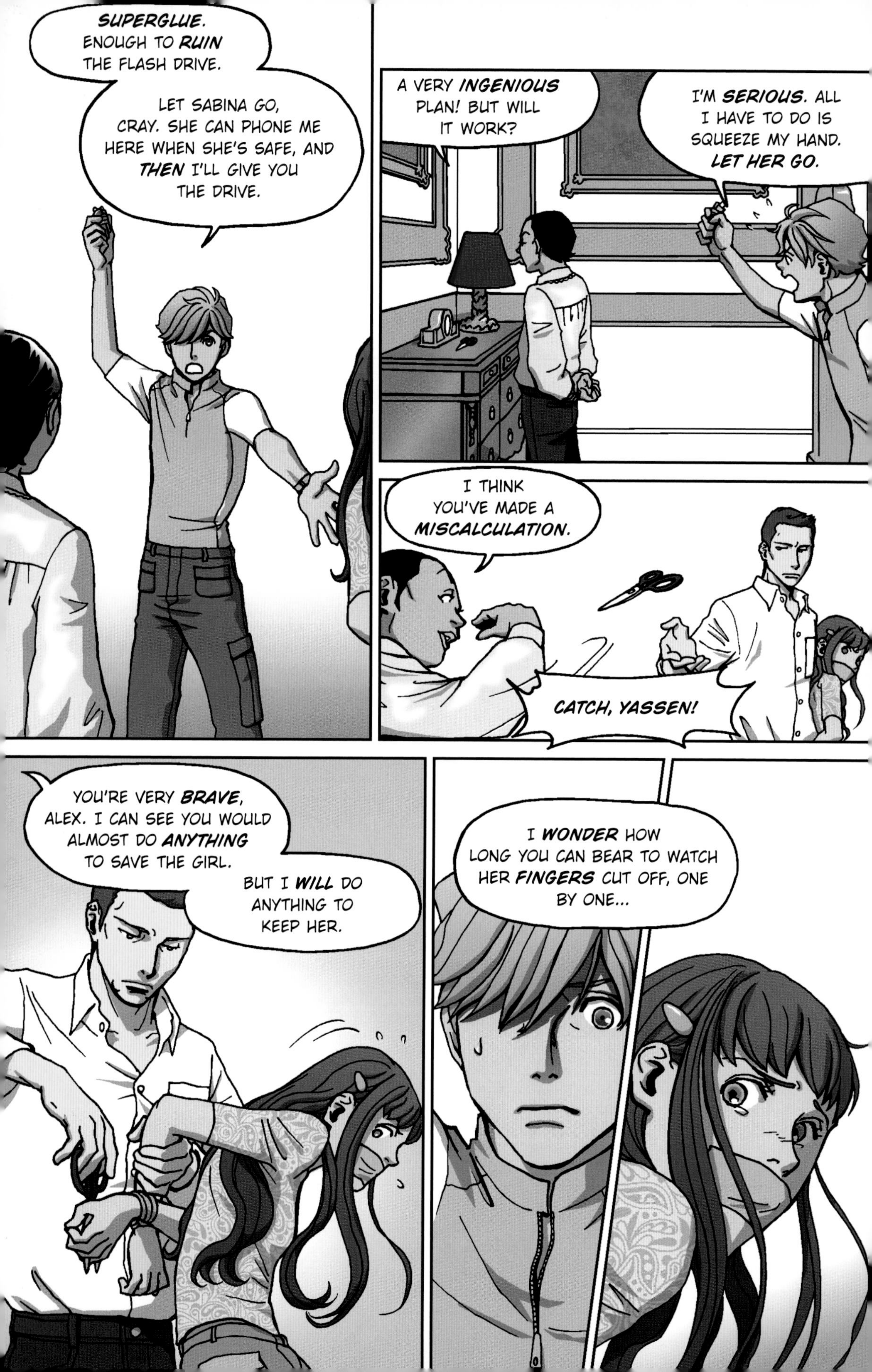

SUPERGLUE. ENOUGH TO RUIN THE FLASH DRIVE.
LET SABINA GO, CRAY. SHE CAN PHONE ME HERE WHEN SHE'S SAFE, AND THEN I'LL GIVE YOU THE DRIVE.
A VERY INGENIOUS PLAN! BUT WILL IT WORK?
I'M SERIOUS. ALL I HAVE TO DO IS SQUEEZE MY HAND. LET HER GO.
I THINK YOU'VE MADE A MISCALCULATION.
CATCH, YASSEN!
YOU'RE VERY BRAVE, ALEX. I CAN SEE YOU WOULD ALMOST DO ANYTHING TO SAVE THE GIRL.
BUT I WILL DO ANYTHING TO KEEP HER.
I WONDER HOW LONG YOU CAN BEAR TO WATCH HER FINGERS CUT OFF, ONE BY ONE...

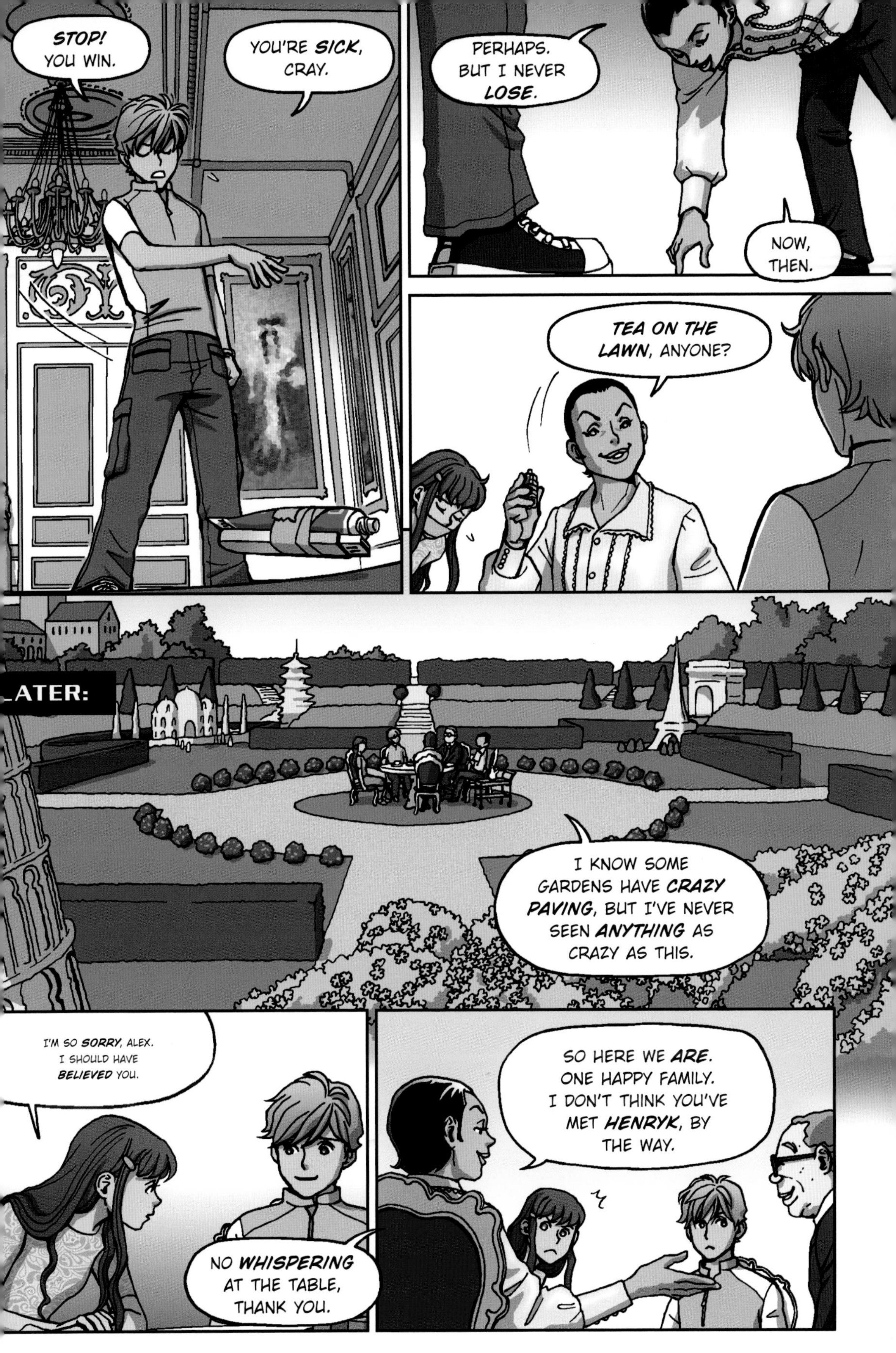
STOP! YOU WIN.
YOU'RE SICK, CRAY.
PERHAPS. BUT I NEVER LOSE.
NOW, THEN.
TEA ON THE LAWN, ANYONE?
LATER:
I KNOW SOME GARDENS HAVE CRAZY PAVING, BUT I'VE NEVER SEEN ANYTHING AS CRAZY AS THIS.
I'M SO SORRY, ALEX. I SHOULD HAVE BELIEVED YOU.
NO WHISPERING AT THE TABLE, THANK YOU.
SO HERE WE ARE. ONE HAPPY FAMILY. I DON'T THINK YOU'VE MET HENRYK, BY THE WAY.

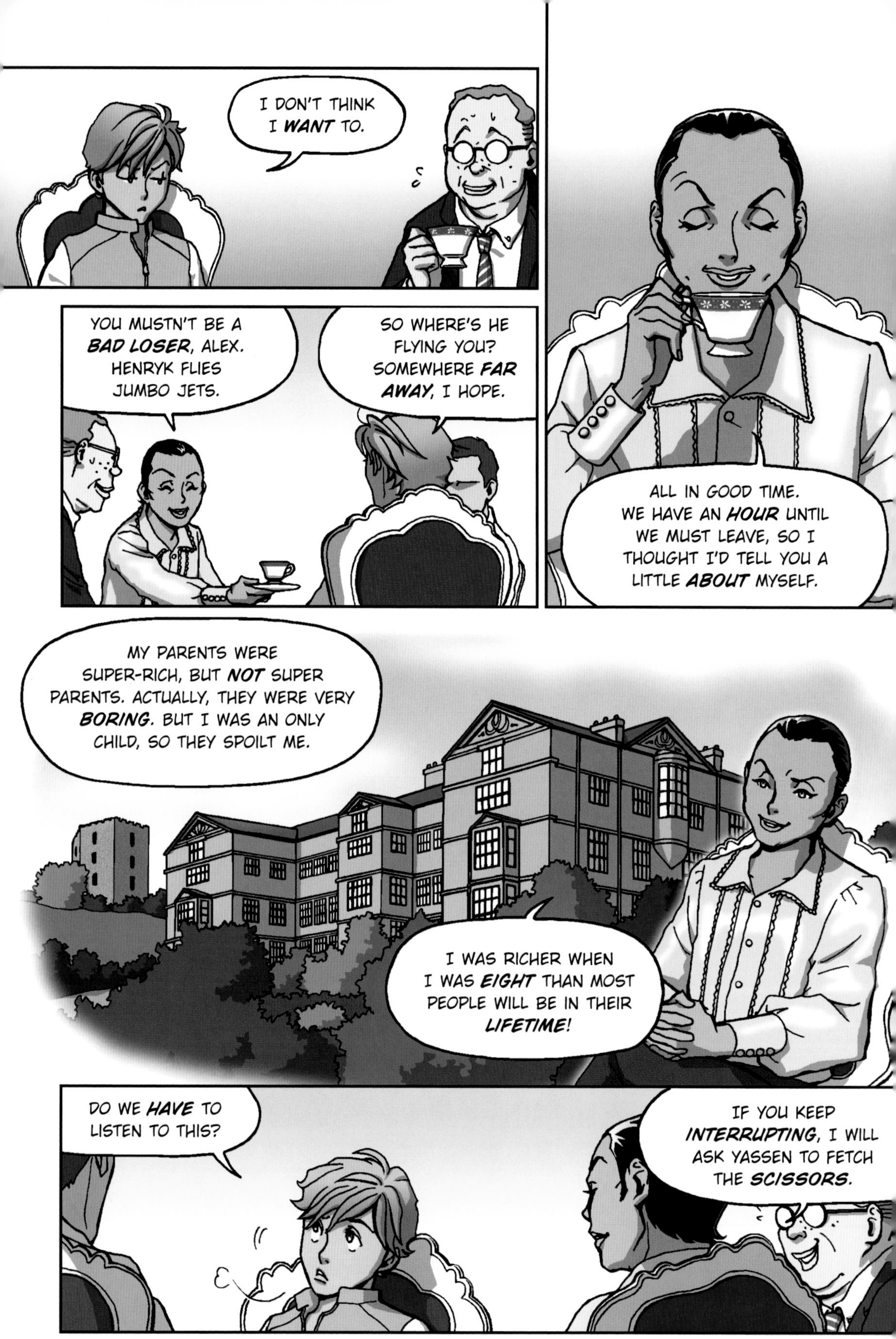
I DON'T THINK I *WANT* TO.
YOU MUSTN'T BE A *BAD LOSER*, ALEX. HENRYK FLIES JUMBO JETS.
SO WHERE'S HE FLYING YOU? SOMEWHERE *FAR AWAY*, I HOPE.
ALL IN GOOD TIME. WE HAVE AN *HOUR* UNTIL WE MUST LEAVE, SO I THOUGHT I'D TELL YOU A LITTLE *ABOUT* MYSELF.
MY PARENTS WERE SUPER-RICH, BUT *NOT* SUPER PARENTS. ACTUALLY, THEY WERE VERY *BORING*. BUT I WAS AN ONLY CHILD, SO THEY SPOILT ME.
I WAS RICHER WHEN I WAS *EIGHT* THAN MOST PEOPLE WILL BE IN THEIR *LIFETIME*!
DO WE *HAVE* TO LISTEN TO THIS?
IF YOU KEEP *INTERRUPTING*, I WILL ASK YASSEN TO FETCH THE *SCISSORS*.

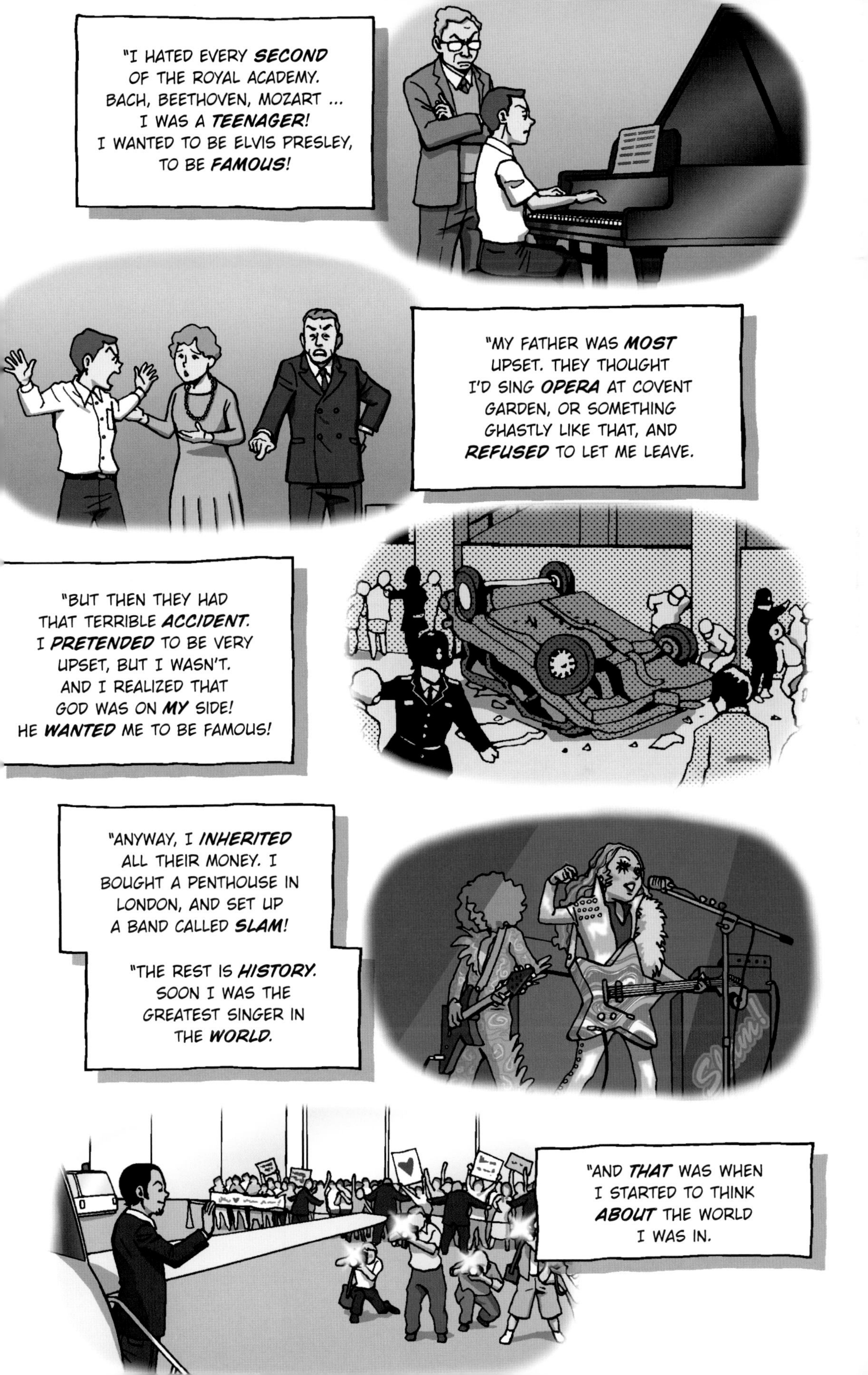
"I HATED EVERY SECOND OF THE ROYAL ACADEMY. BACH, BEETHOVEN, MOZART ... I WAS A TEENAGER! I WANTED TO BE ELVIS PRESLEY, TO BE FAMOUS!
"MY FATHER WAS MOST UPSET. THEY THOUGHT I'D SING OPERA AT COVENT GARDEN, OR SOMETHING GHASTLY LIKE THAT, AND REFUSED TO LET ME LEAVE.
"BUT THEN THEY HAD THAT TERRIBLE ACCIDENT. I PRETENDED TO BE VERY UPSET, BUT I WASN'T. AND I REALIZED THAT GOD WAS ON MY SIDE! HE WANTED ME TO BE FAMOUS!
"ANYWAY, I INHERITED ALL THEIR MONEY. I BOUGHT A PENTHOUSE IN LONDON, AND SET UP A BAND CALLED SLAM!
"THE REST IS HISTORY. SOON I WAS THE GREATEST SINGER IN THE WORLD.
"AND THAT WAS WHEN I STARTED TO THINK ABOUT THE WORLD I WAS IN.

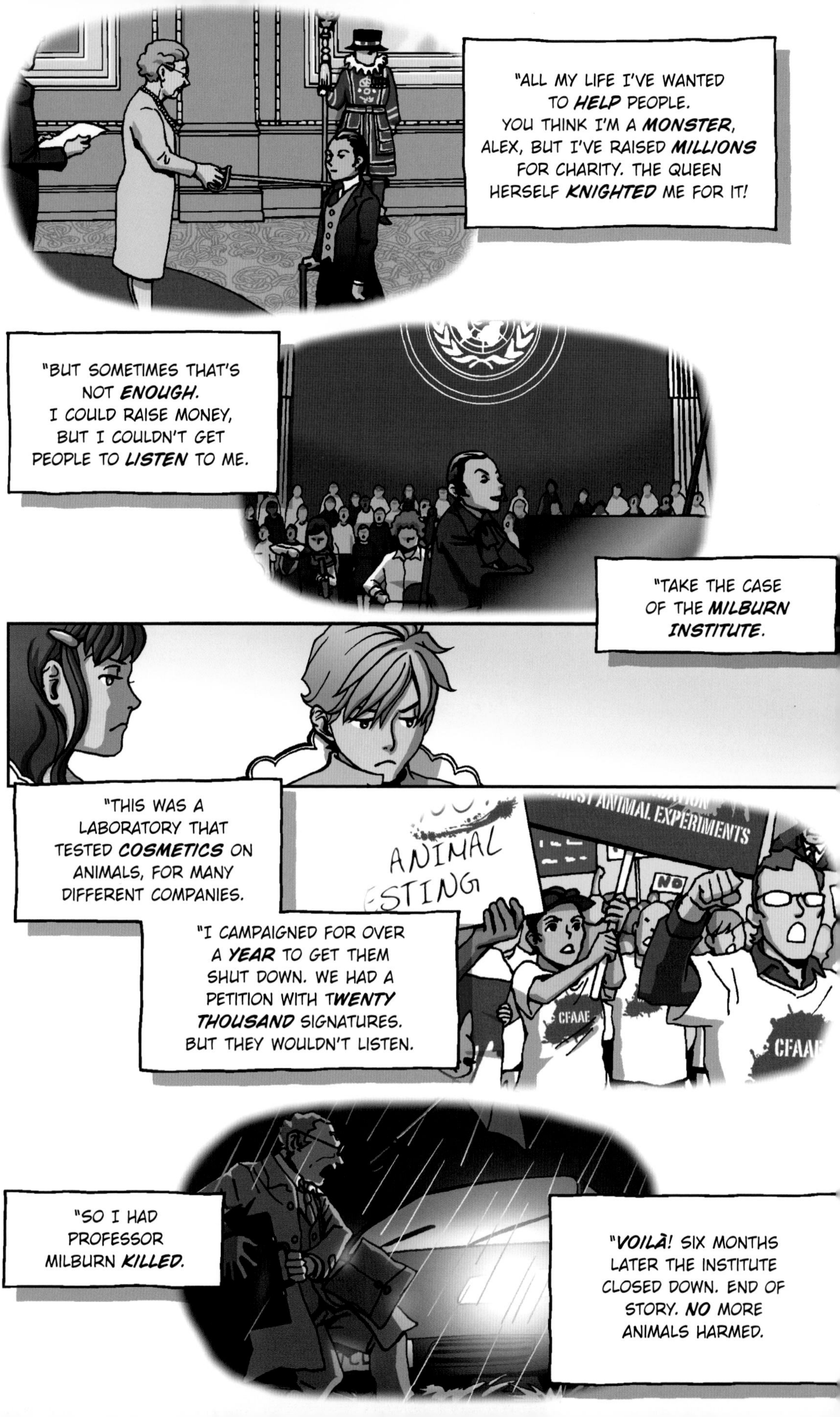
"ALL MY LIFE I'VE WANTED TO HELP PEOPLE. YOU THINK I'M A MONSTER, ALEX, BUT I'VE RAISED MILLIONS FOR CHARITY. THE QUEEN HERSELF KNIGHTED ME FOR IT!
"BUT SOMETIMES THAT'S NOT ENOUGH. I COULD RAISE MONEY, BUT I COULDN'T GET PEOPLE TO LISTEN TO ME.
"TAKE THE CASE OF THE MILBURN INSTITUTE.
"THIS WAS A LABORATORY THAT TESTED COSMETICS ON ANIMALS, FOR MANY DIFFERENT COMPANIES.
ANIMAL EXPERIMENTS
ANIMAL
NO
"I CAMPAIGNED FOR OVER A YEAR TO GET THEM SHUT DOWN. WE HAD A PETITION WITH TWENTY THOUSAND SIGNATURES. BUT THEY WOULDN'T LISTEN.
CFAAE
"SO I HAD PROFESSOR MILBURN KILLED.
"VOILÀ! SIX MONTHS LATER THE INSTITUTE CLOSED DOWN. END OF STORY. NO MORE ANIMALS HARMED.

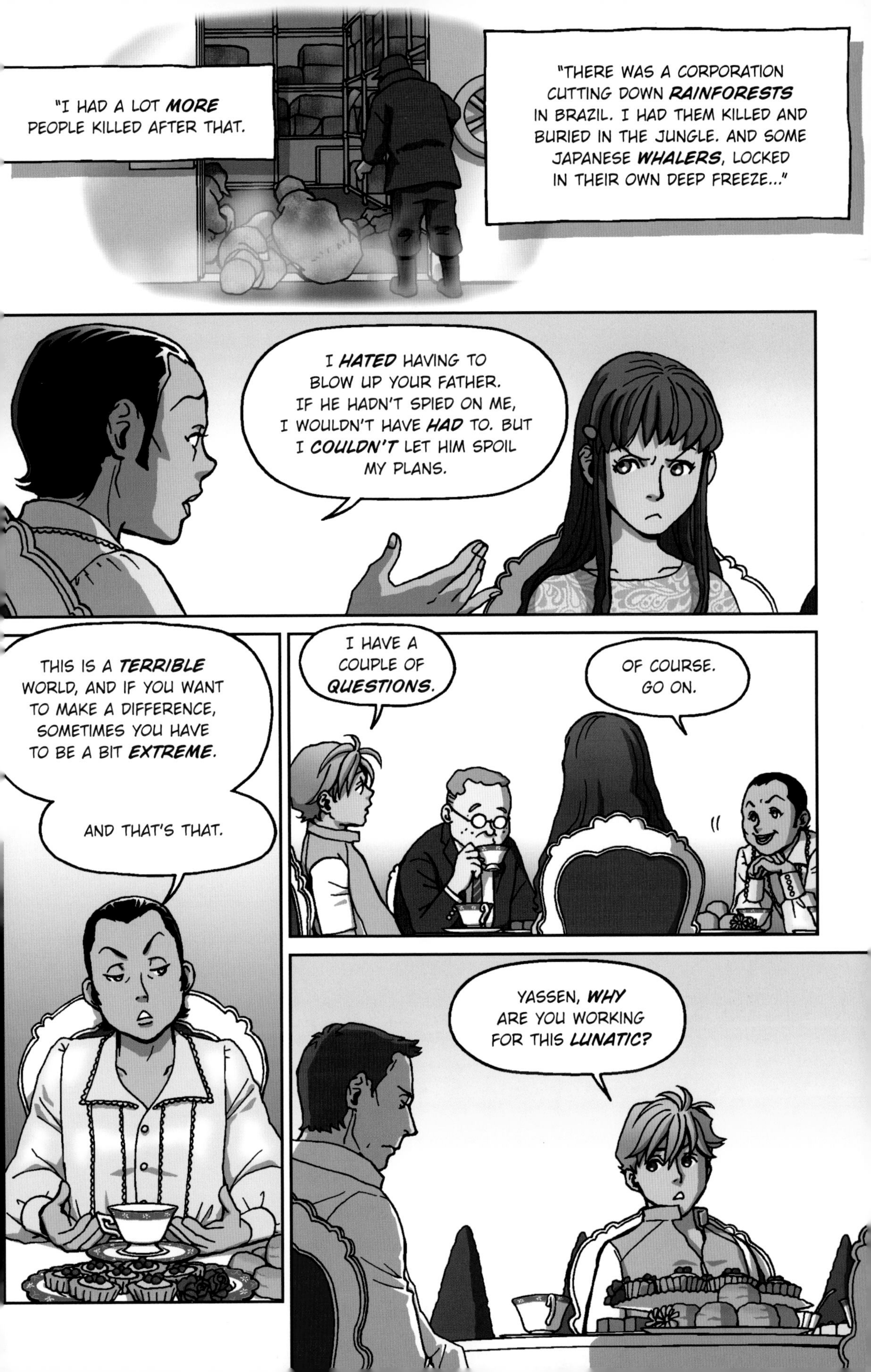
"I HAD A LOT MORE PEOPLE KILLED AFTER THAT.
"THERE WAS A CORPORATION CUTTING DOWN RAINFORESTS IN BRAZIL. I HAD THEM KILLED AND BURIED IN THE JUNGLE. AND SOME JAPANESE WHALERS, LOCKED IN THEIR OWN DEEP FREEZE..."
I HATED HAVING TO BLOW UP YOUR FATHER. IF HE HADN'T SPIED ON ME, I WOULDN'T HAVE HAD TO. BUT I COULDN'T LET HIM SPOIL MY PLANS.
THIS IS A TERRIBLE WORLD, AND IF YOU WANT TO MAKE A DIFFERENCE, SOMETIMES YOU HAVE TO BE A BIT EXTREME.
AND THAT'S THAT.
I HAVE A COUPLE OF QUESTIONS.
OF COURSE. GO ON.
YASSEN, WHY ARE YOU WORKING FOR THIS LUNATIC?

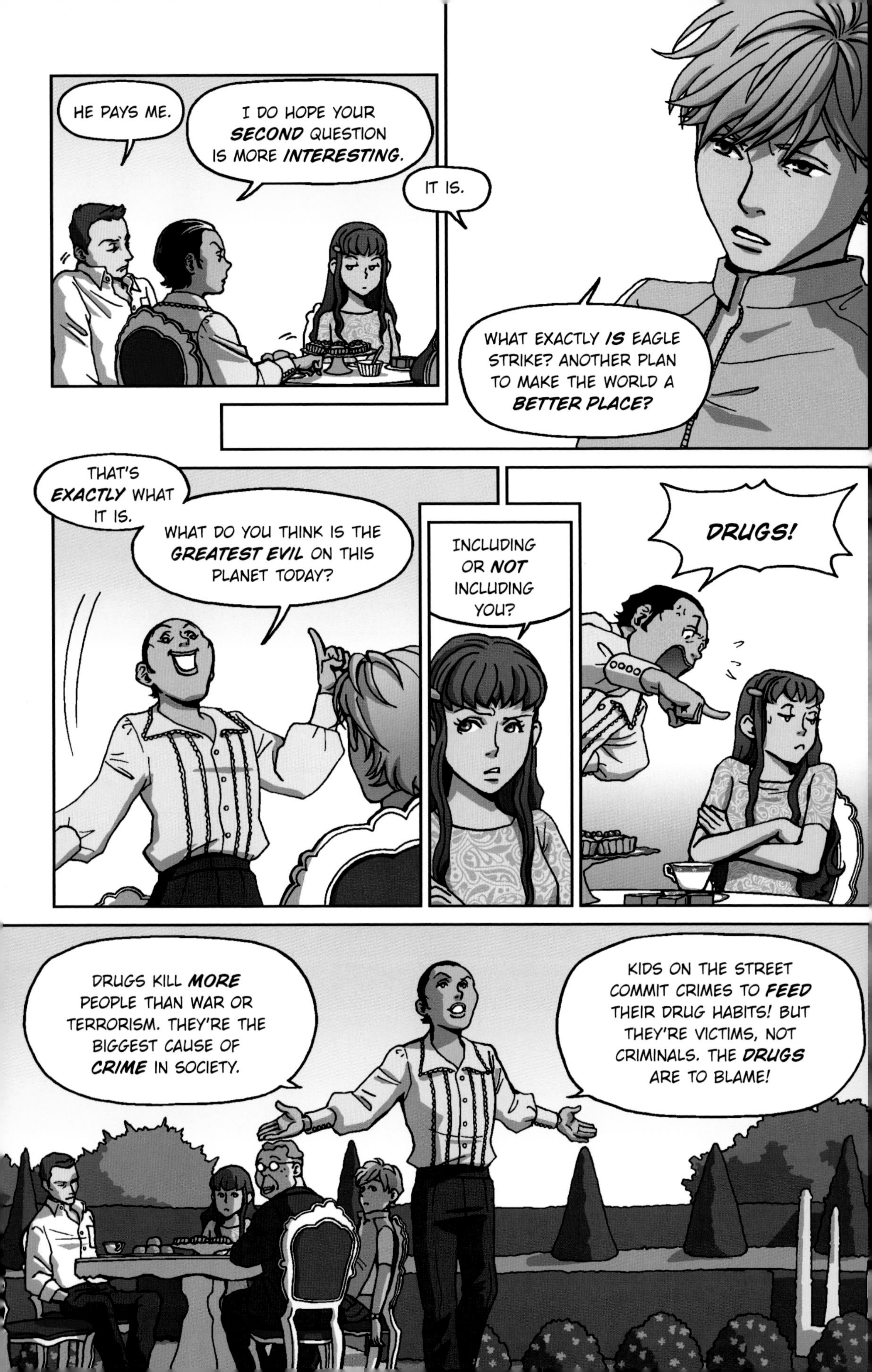
HE PAYS ME.
I DO HOPE YOUR **SECOND** QUESTION IS MORE **INTERESTING.**
IT IS.
WHAT EXACTLY **IS** EAGLE STRIKE? ANOTHER PLAN TO MAKE THE WORLD A **BETTER PLACE?**
THAT'S **EXACTLY** WHAT IT IS.
WHAT DO YOU THINK IS THE **GREATEST EVIL** ON THIS PLANET TODAY?
INCLUDING OR **NOT** INCLUDING YOU?
DRUGS!
DRUGS KILL **MORE** PEOPLE THAN WAR OR TERRORISM. THEY'RE THE BIGGEST CAUSE OF **CRIME** IN SOCIETY.
KIDS ON THE STREET COMMIT CRIMES TO **FEED** THEIR DRUG HABITS! BUT THEY'RE VICTIMS, NOT CRIMINALS. THE **DRUGS** ARE TO BLAME!

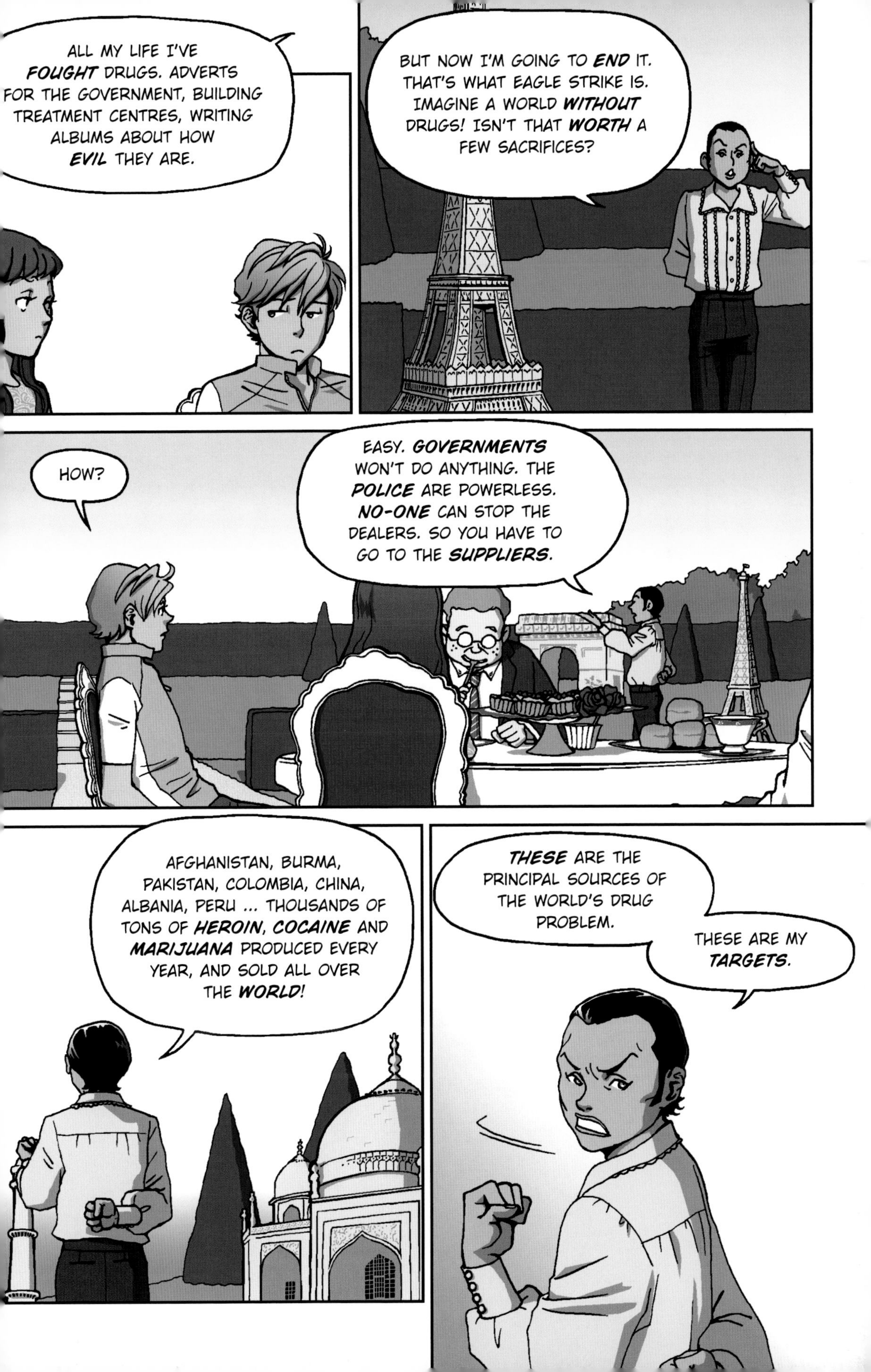
ALL MY LIFE I'VE FOUGHT DRUGS. ADVERTS FOR THE GOVERNMENT, BUILDING TREATMENT CENTRES, WRITING ALBUMS ABOUT HOW EVIL THEY ARE.
BUT NOW I'M GOING TO END IT. THAT'S WHAT EAGLE STRIKE IS. IMAGINE A WORLD WITHOUT DRUGS! ISN'T THAT WORTH A FEW SACRIFICES?
HOW?
EASY. GOVERNMENTS WON'T DO ANYTHING. THE POLICE ARE POWERLESS. NO-ONE CAN STOP THE DEALERS. SO YOU HAVE TO GO TO THE SUPPLIERS.
AFGHANISTAN, BURMA, PAKISTAN, COLOMBIA, CHINA, ALBANIA, PERU ... THOUSANDS OF TONS OF HEROIN, COCAINE AND MARIJUANA PRODUCED EVERY YEAR, AND SOLD ALL OVER THE WORLD!
THESE ARE THE PRINCIPAL SOURCES OF THE WORLD'S DRUG PROBLEM.
THESE ARE MY TARGETS.

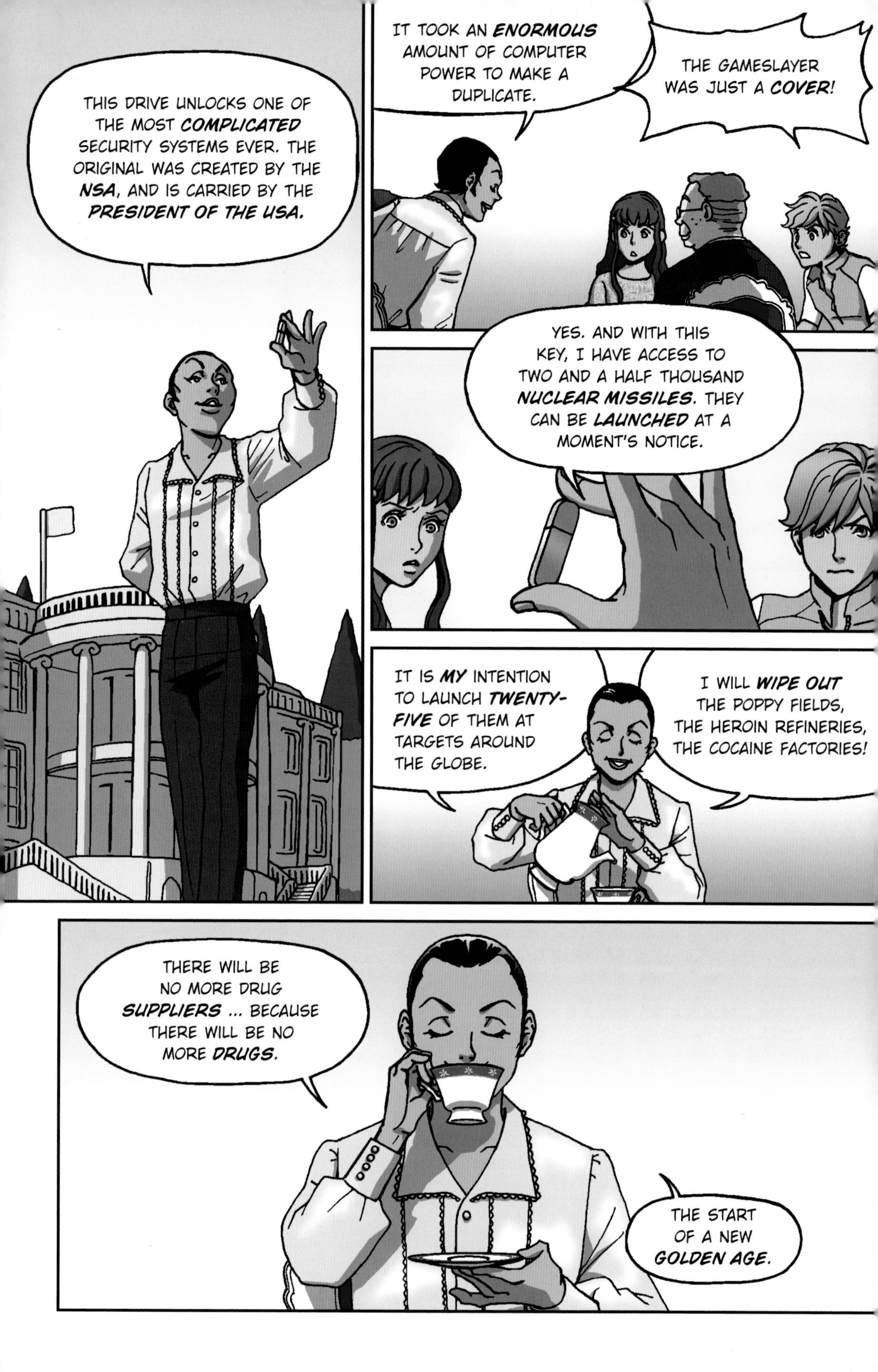
THIS DRIVE UNLOCKS ONE OF THE MOST COMPLICATED SECURITY SYSTEMS EVER. THE ORIGINAL WAS CREATED BY THE NSA, AND IS CARRIED BY THE PRESIDENT OF THE USA.
IT TOOK AN ENORMOUS AMOUNT OF COMPUTER POWER TO MAKE A DUPLICATE.
THE GAMESLAYER WAS JUST A COVER!
YES. AND WITH THIS KEY, I HAVE ACCESS TO TWO AND A HALF THOUSAND NUCLEAR MISSILES. THEY CAN BE LAUNCHED AT A MOMENT'S NOTICE.
IT IS MY INTENTION TO LAUNCH TWENTY-FIVE OF THEM AT TARGETS AROUND THE GLOBE.
I WILL WIPE OUT THE POPPY FIELDS, THE HEROIN REFINERIES, THE COCAINE FACTORIES!
THERE WILL BE NO MORE DRUG SUPPLIERS ... BECAUSE THERE WILL BE NO MORE DRUGS.
THE START OF A NEW GOLDEN AGE.

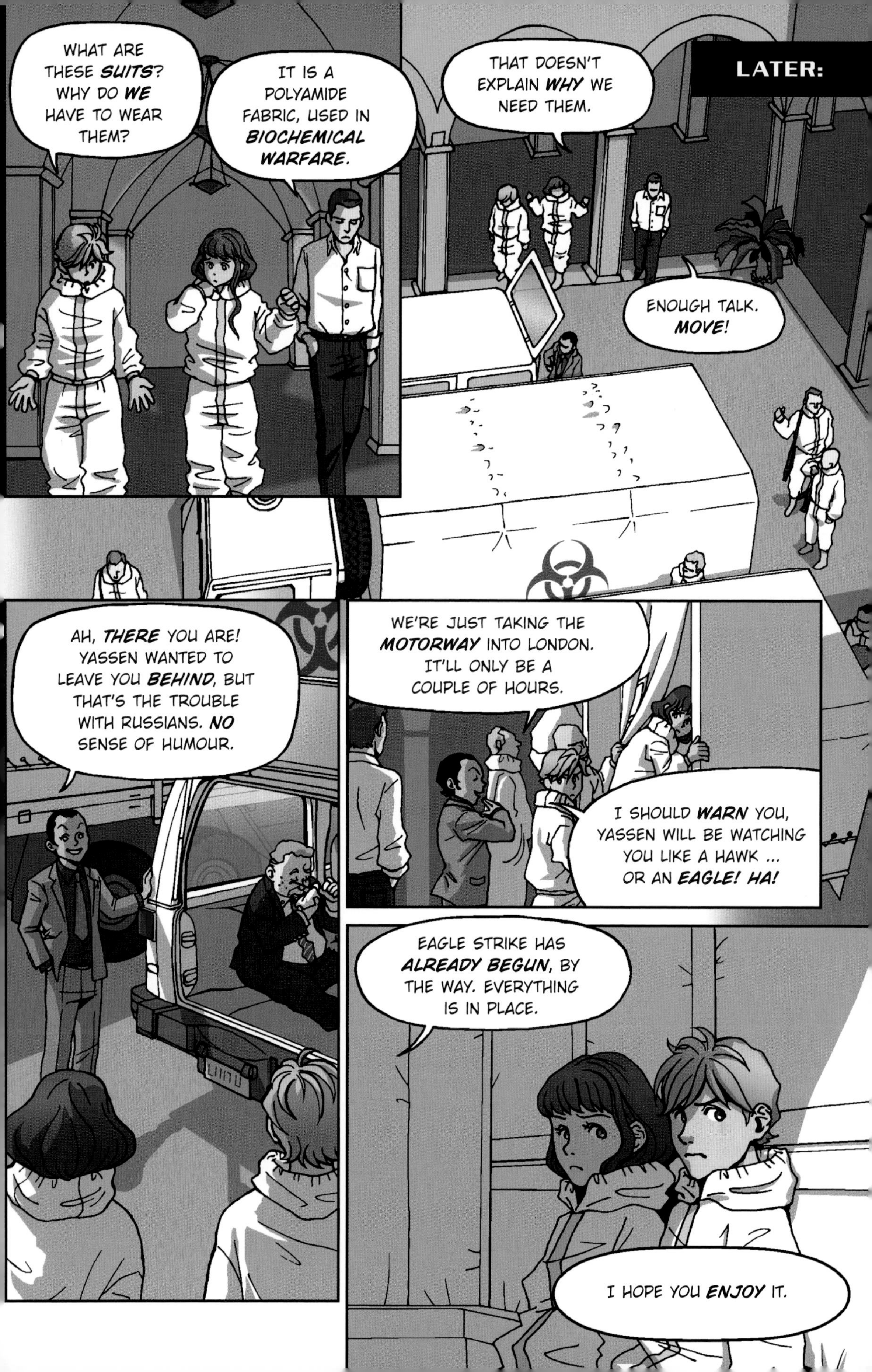
WHAT ARE THESE SUITS? WHY DO WE HAVE TO WEAR THEM?
IT IS A POLYAMIDE FABRIC, USED IN BIOCHEMICAL WARFARE.
LATER:
THAT DOESN'T EXPLAIN WHY WE NEED THEM.
ENOUGH TALK. MOVE!
AH, THERE YOU ARE! YASSEN WANTED TO LEAVE YOU BEHIND, BUT THAT'S THE TROUBLE WITH RUSSIANS. NO SENSE OF HUMOUR.
WE'RE JUST TAKING THE MOTORWAY INTO LONDON. IT'LL ONLY BE A COUPLE OF HOURS.
I SHOULD WARN YOU, YASSEN WILL BE WATCHING YOU LIKE A HAWK ... OR AN EAGLE! HA!
EAGLE STRIKE HAS ALREADY BEGUN, BY THE WAY. EVERYTHING IS IN PLACE.
I HOPE YOU ENJOY IT.

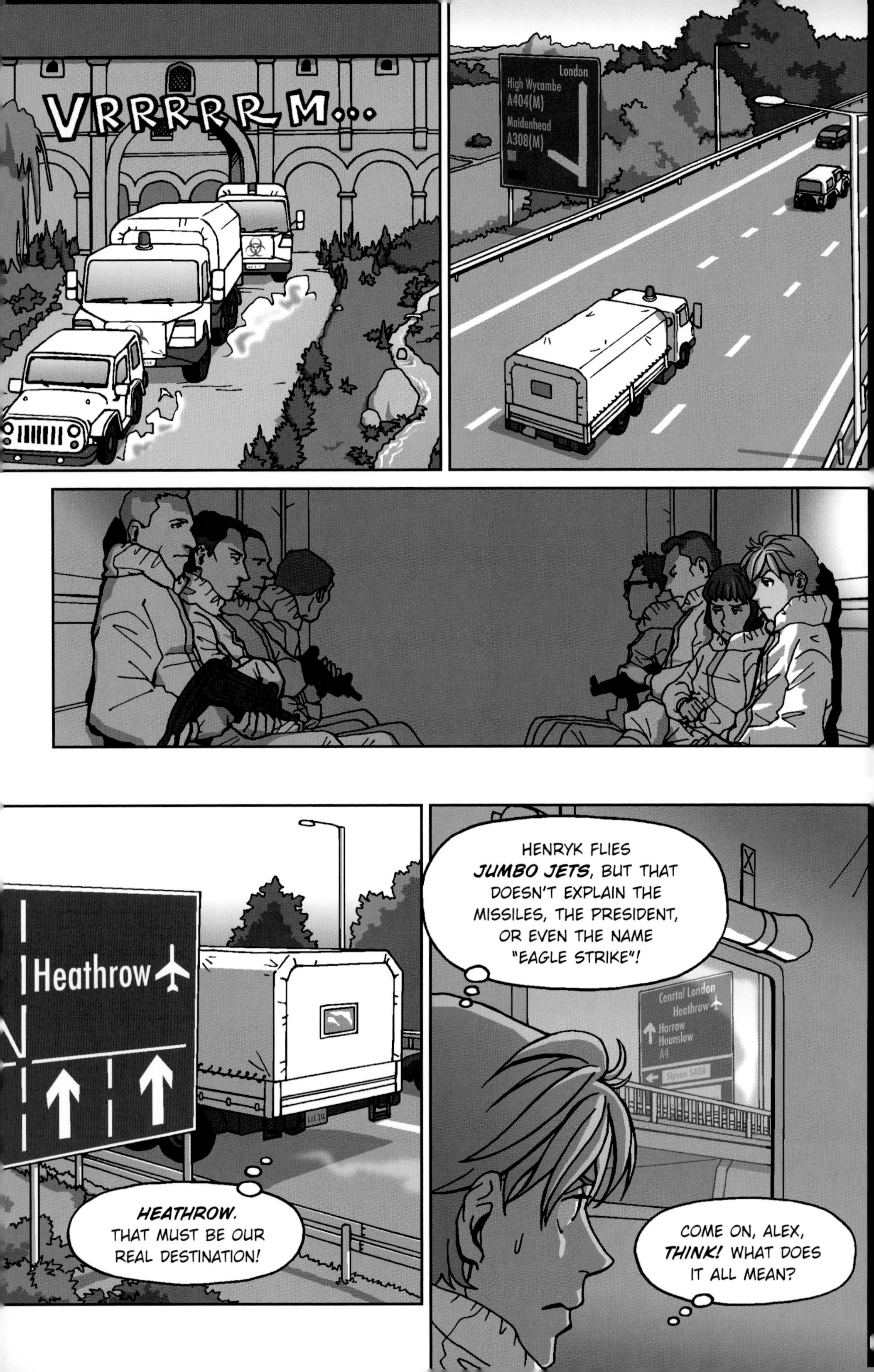
VRRRRRM...
London
High Wycombe
A404(M)
Maidenhead
A308(M)
Heathrow
HEATHROW. THAT MUST BE OUR REAL DESTINATION!
HENRYK FLIES JUMBO JETS, BUT THAT DOESN'T EXPLAIN THE MISSILES, THE PRESIDENT, OR EVEN THE NAME "EAGLE STRIKE"!
Central London
Heathrow
Harrow
Hounslow
A4
COME ON, ALEX, THINK! WHAT DOES IT ALL MEAN?

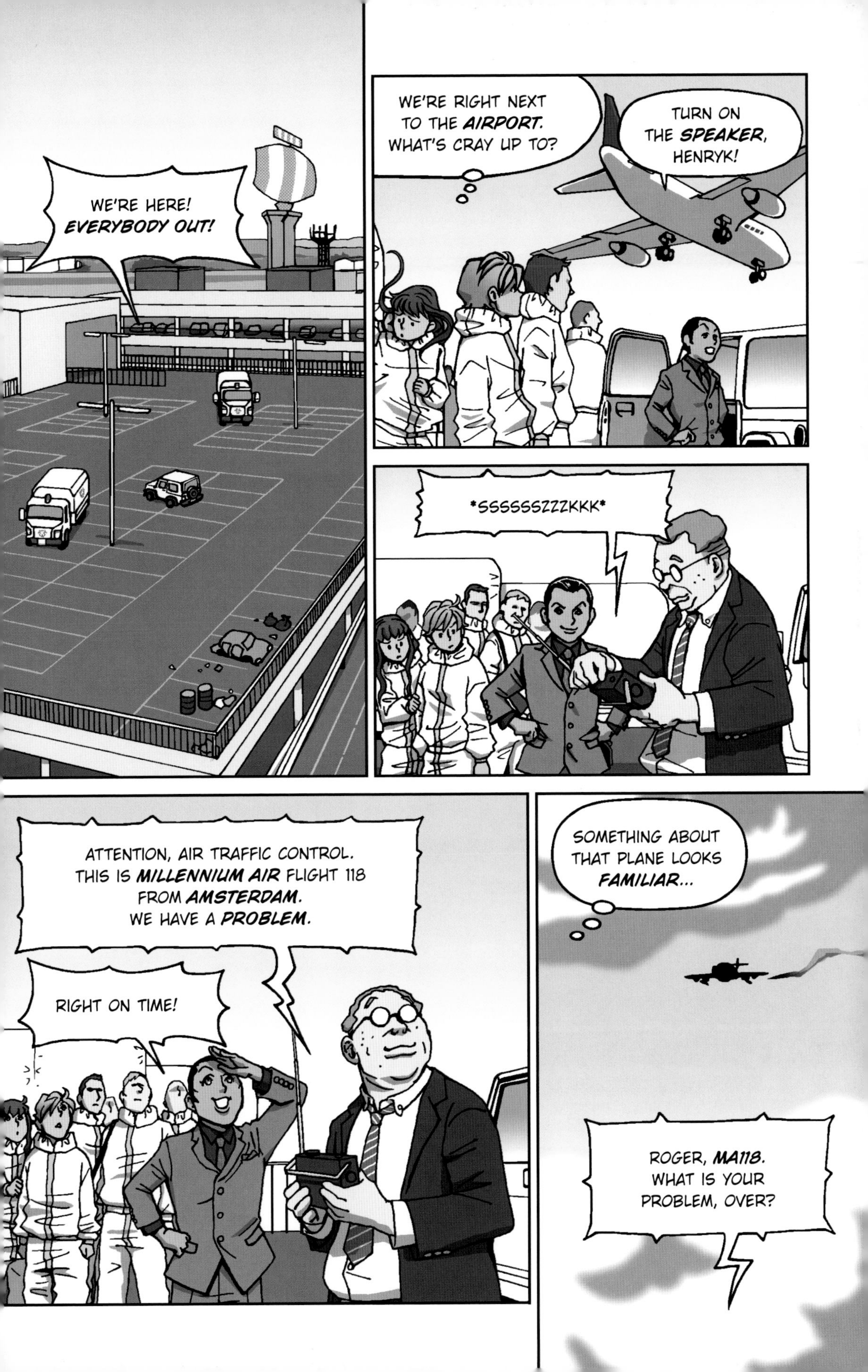
WE'RE HERE! EVERYBODY OUT!
WE'RE RIGHT NEXT TO THE AIRPORT. WHAT'S CRAY UP TO?
TURN ON THE SPEAKER, HENRYK!
SSSSSSZZZKKK
ATTENTION, AIR TRAFFIC CONTROL. THIS IS MILLENNIUM AIR FLIGHT 118 FROM AMSTERDAM. WE HAVE A PROBLEM.
RIGHT ON TIME!
SOMETHING ABOUT THAT PLANE LOOKS FAMILIAR...
ROGER, MA118. WHAT IS YOUR PROBLEM, OVER?

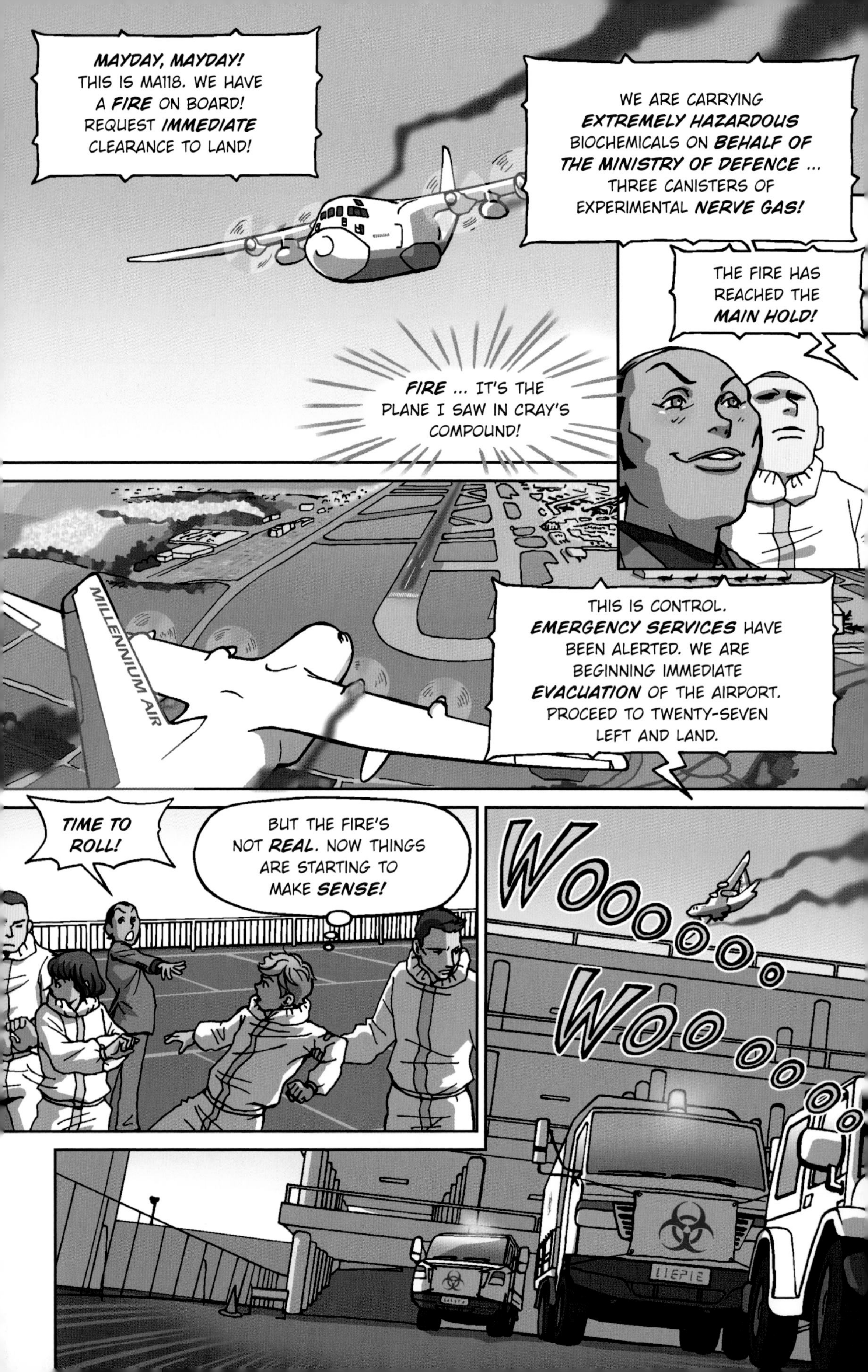

MAYDAY, MAYDAY! THIS IS MA118. WE HAVE A FIRE ON BOARD! REQUEST IMMEDIATE CLEARANCE TO LAND!
WE ARE CARRYING EXTREMELY HAZARDOUS BIOCHEMICALS ON BEHALF OF THE MINISTRY OF DEFENCE ... THREE CANISTERS OF EXPERIMENTAL NERVE GAS!
THE FIRE HAS REACHED THE MAIN HOLD!
FIRE ... IT'S THE PLANE I SAW IN CRAY'S COMPOUND!
MILLENNIUM AIR
THIS IS CONTROL. EMERGENCY SERVICES HAVE BEEN ALERTED. WE ARE BEGINNING IMMEDIATE EVACUATION OF THE AIRPORT. PROCEED TO TWENTY-SEVEN LEFT AND LAND.
TIME TO ROLL!
BUT THE FIRE'S NOT REAL. NOW THINGS ARE STARTING TO MAKE SENSE!
WOOOOOO... WOOOOOO

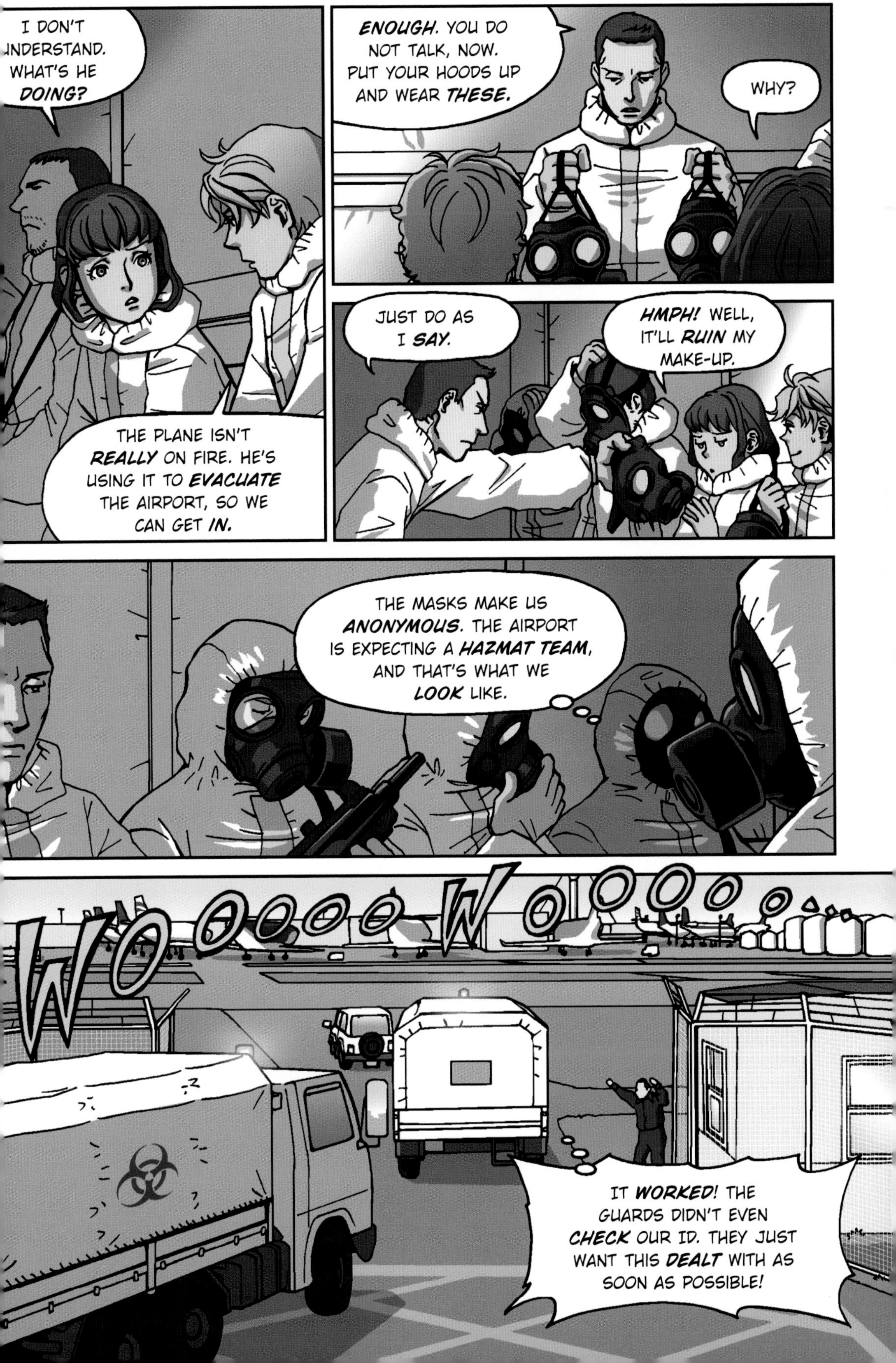
I DON'T UNDERSTAND. WHAT'S HE DOING?
THE PLANE ISN'T REALLY ON FIRE. HE'S USING IT TO EVACUATE THE AIRPORT, SO WE CAN GET IN.
ENOUGH. YOU DO NOT TALK, NOW. PUT YOUR HOODS UP AND WEAR THESE.
WHY?
JUST DO AS I SAY.
HMPH! WELL, IT'LL RUIN MY MAKE-UP.
THE MASKS MAKE US ANONYMOUS. THE AIRPORT IS EXPECTING A HAZMAT TEAM, AND THAT'S WHAT WE LOOK LIKE.
WOOOOOWOOOOO
IT WORKED! THE GUARDS DIDN'T EVEN CHECK OUR ID. THEY JUST WANT THIS DEALT WITH AS SOON AS POSSIBLE!

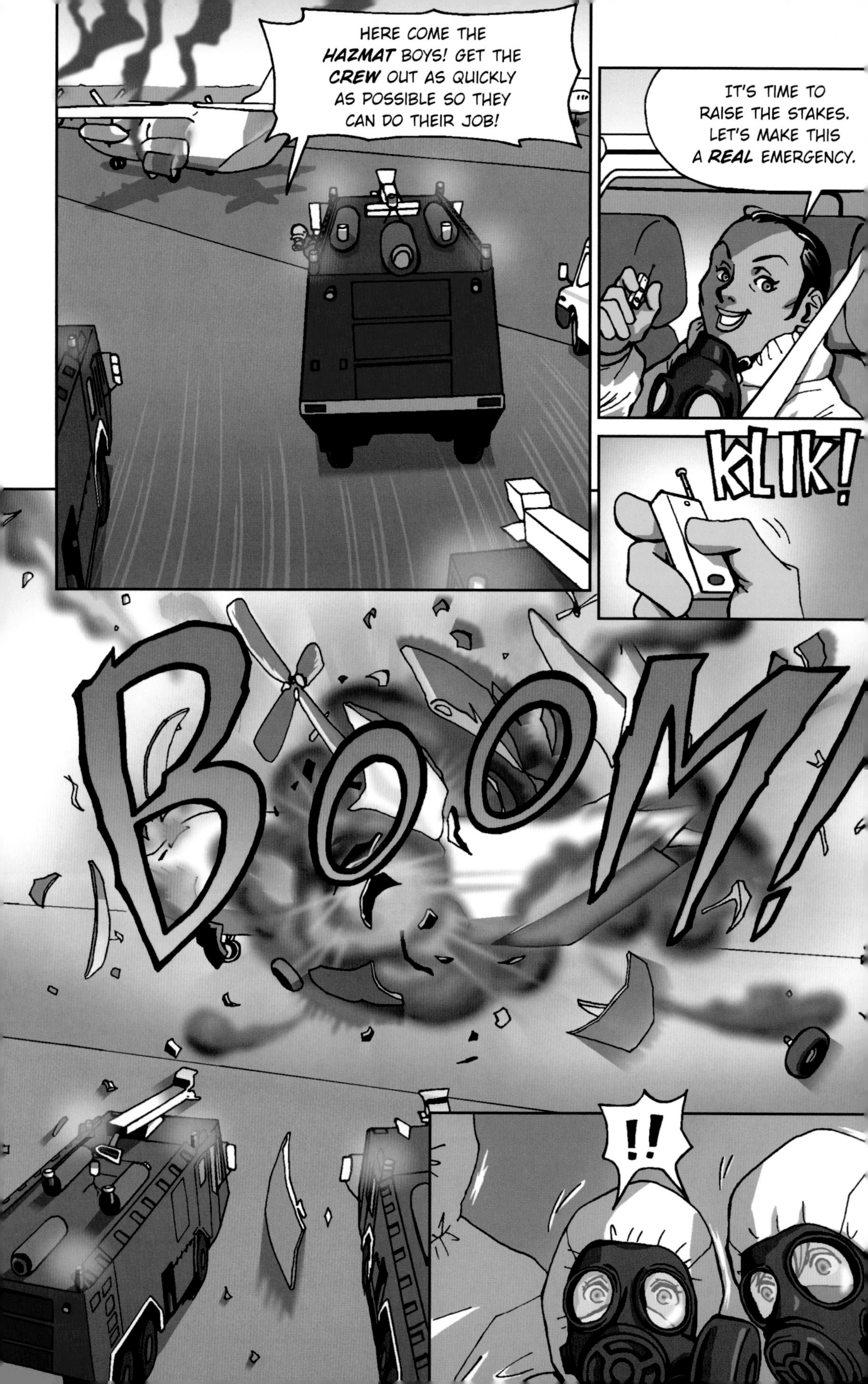
HERE COME THE HAZMAT BOYS! GET THE CREW OUT AS QUICKLY AS POSSIBLE SO THEY CAN DO THEIR JOB!
IT'S TIME TO RAISE THE STAKES. LET'S MAKE THIS A REAL EMERGENCY.
KLIK!
BOOM!
!!

TOO LATE!

EVERYBODY OUT! THERE'S NOTHING WE CAN DO, LEAVE IT FOR THE *BIOCHEM* TEAM!

SO NOW IT'S JUST US AND A WRECKED PLANE. I BET CRAY TRICKED THE *PILOT*, TOO. HE PROBABLY EXPECTED TO GO TO PRISON, NOT *DIE* ON A RUNWAY!

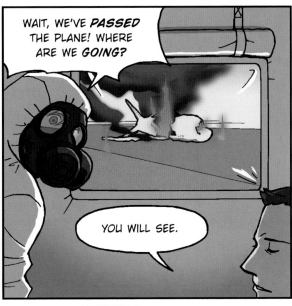

WAIT, WE'VE *PASSED* THE PLANE! WHERE ARE WE *GOING*?

YOU WILL SEE.

WE'RE *IN*, AND THE REST OF THE AIRPORT HAS BEEN *EVACUATED*. BUT I STILL DON'T UNDERSTAND WHAT IT'S ALL *FOR*...

!!

OH, NO.

NOW IT ALL MAKES SENSE!

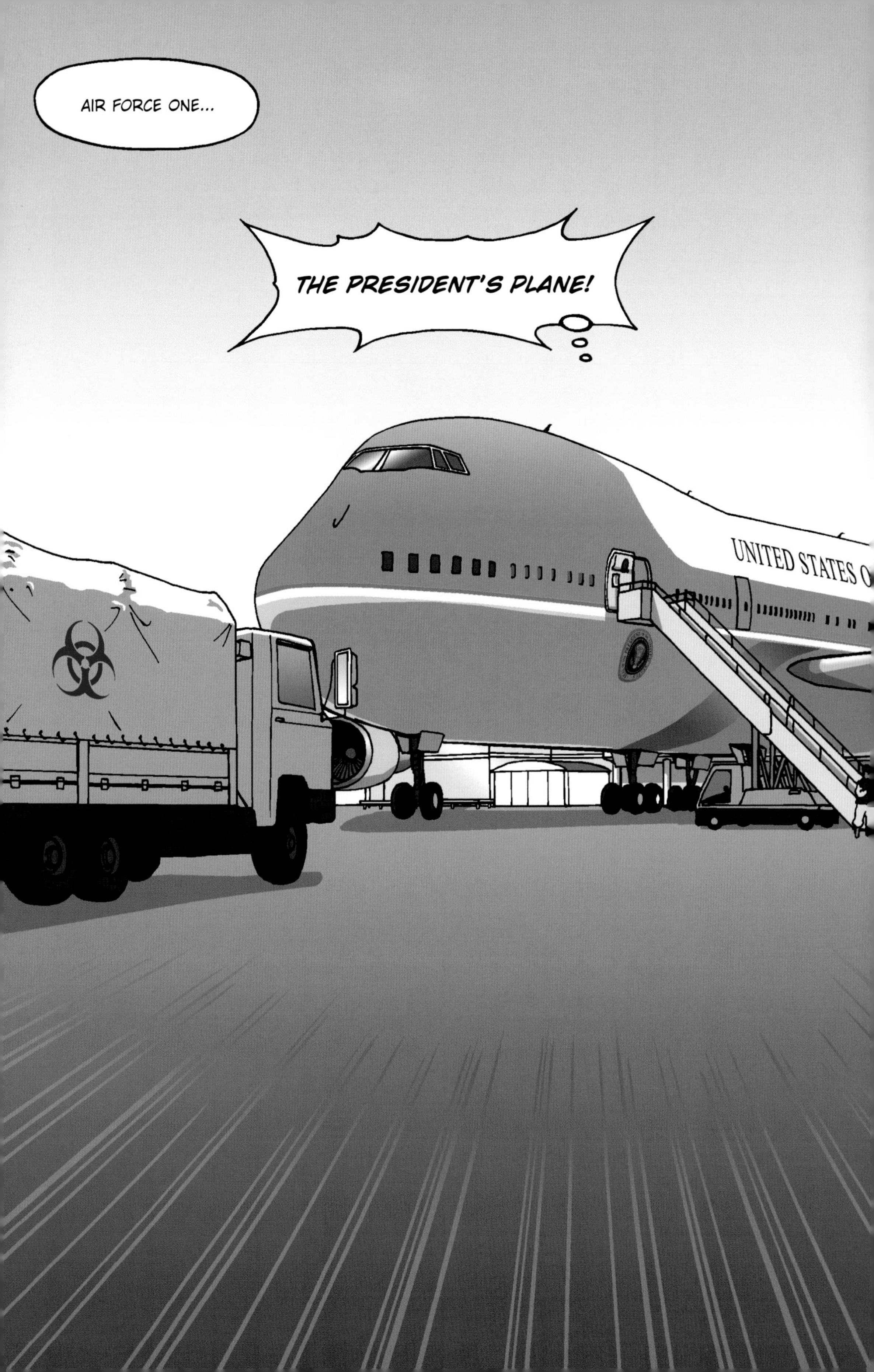
AIR FORCE ONE...
THE PRESIDENT'S PLANE!
UNITED STATES O

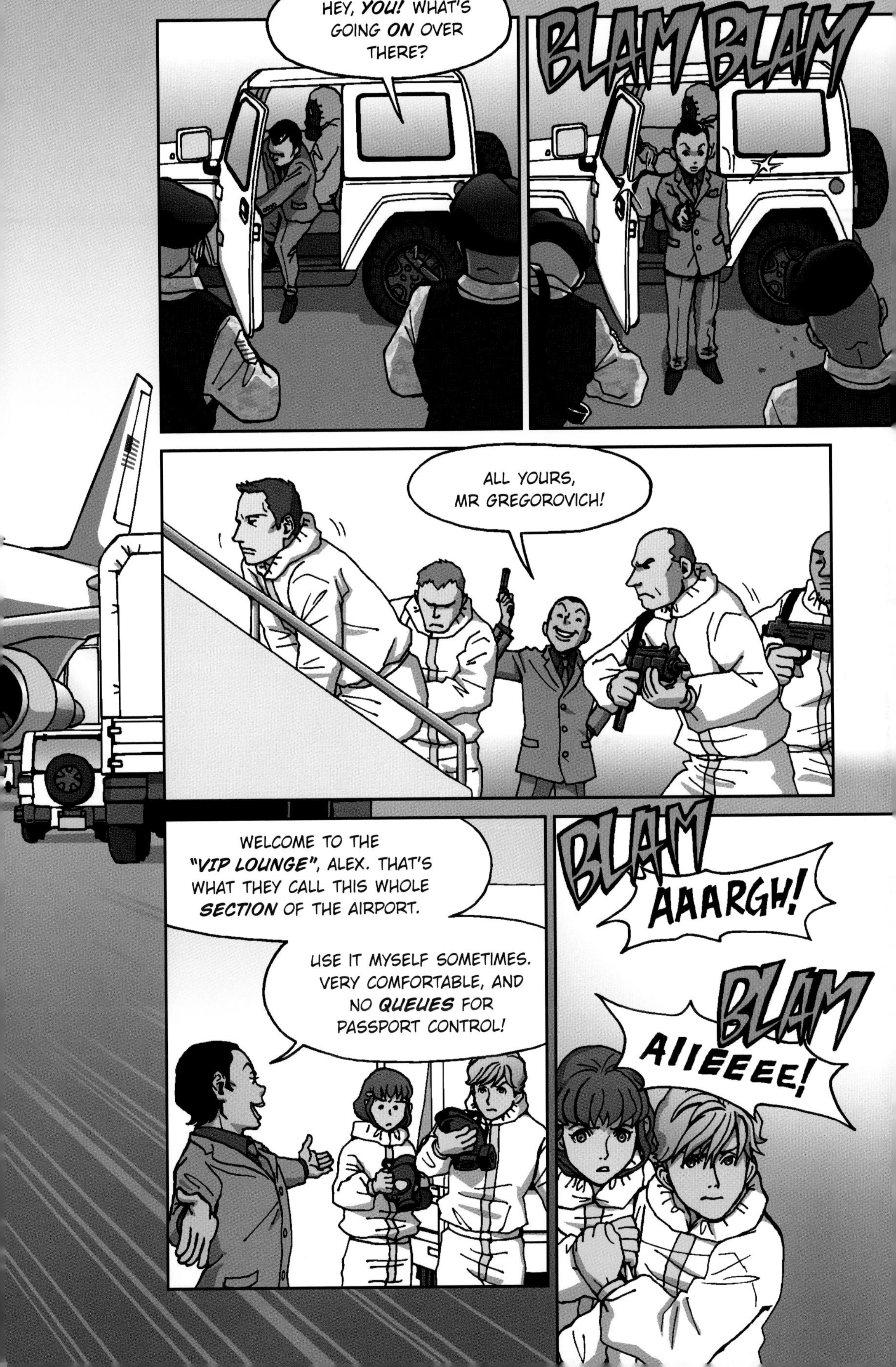
HEY, YOU! WHAT'S GOING ON OVER THERE?
BLAM BLAM
ALL YOURS, MR GREGOROVICH!
WELCOME TO THE "VIP LOUNGE", ALEX. THAT'S WHAT THEY CALL THIS WHOLE SECTION OF THE AIRPORT.
USE IT MYSELF SOMETIMES. VERY COMFORTABLE, AND NO QUEUES FOR PASSPORT CONTROL!
BLAM
AAARGH!
BLAM
AIIEEEEE!

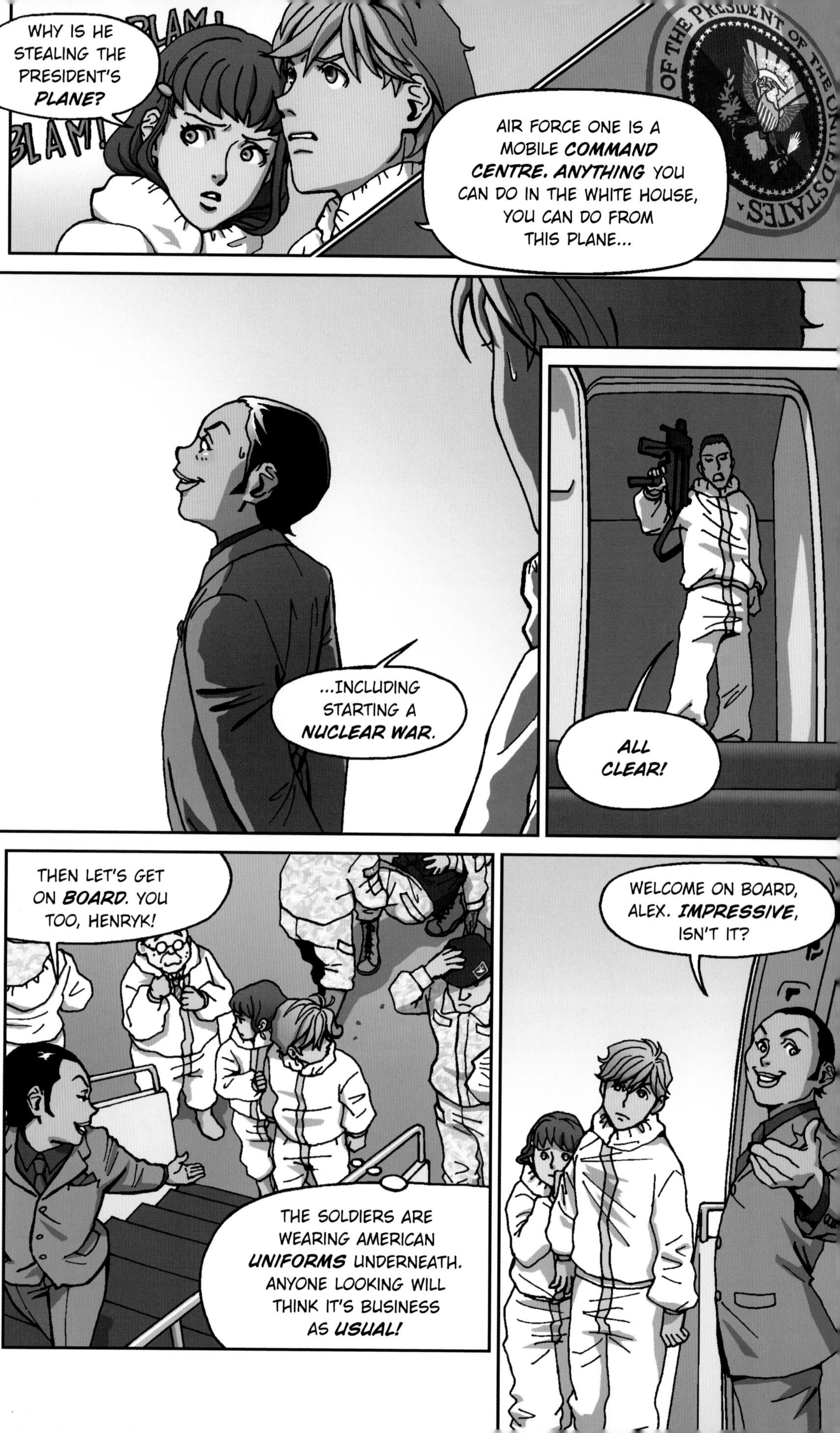
WHY IS HE STEALING THE PRESIDENT'S PLANE?
BLAM! BLAM!
AIR FORCE ONE IS A MOBILE COMMAND CENTRE. ANYTHING YOU CAN DO IN THE WHITE HOUSE, YOU CAN DO FROM THIS PLANE...
...INCLUDING STARTING A NUCLEAR WAR.
ALL CLEAR!
THEN LET'S GET ON BOARD. YOU TOO, HENRYK!
THE SOLDIERS ARE WEARING AMERICAN UNIFORMS UNDERNEATH. ANYONE LOOKING WILL THINK IT'S BUSINESS AS USUAL!
WELCOME ON BOARD, ALEX. IMPRESSIVE, ISN'T IT?

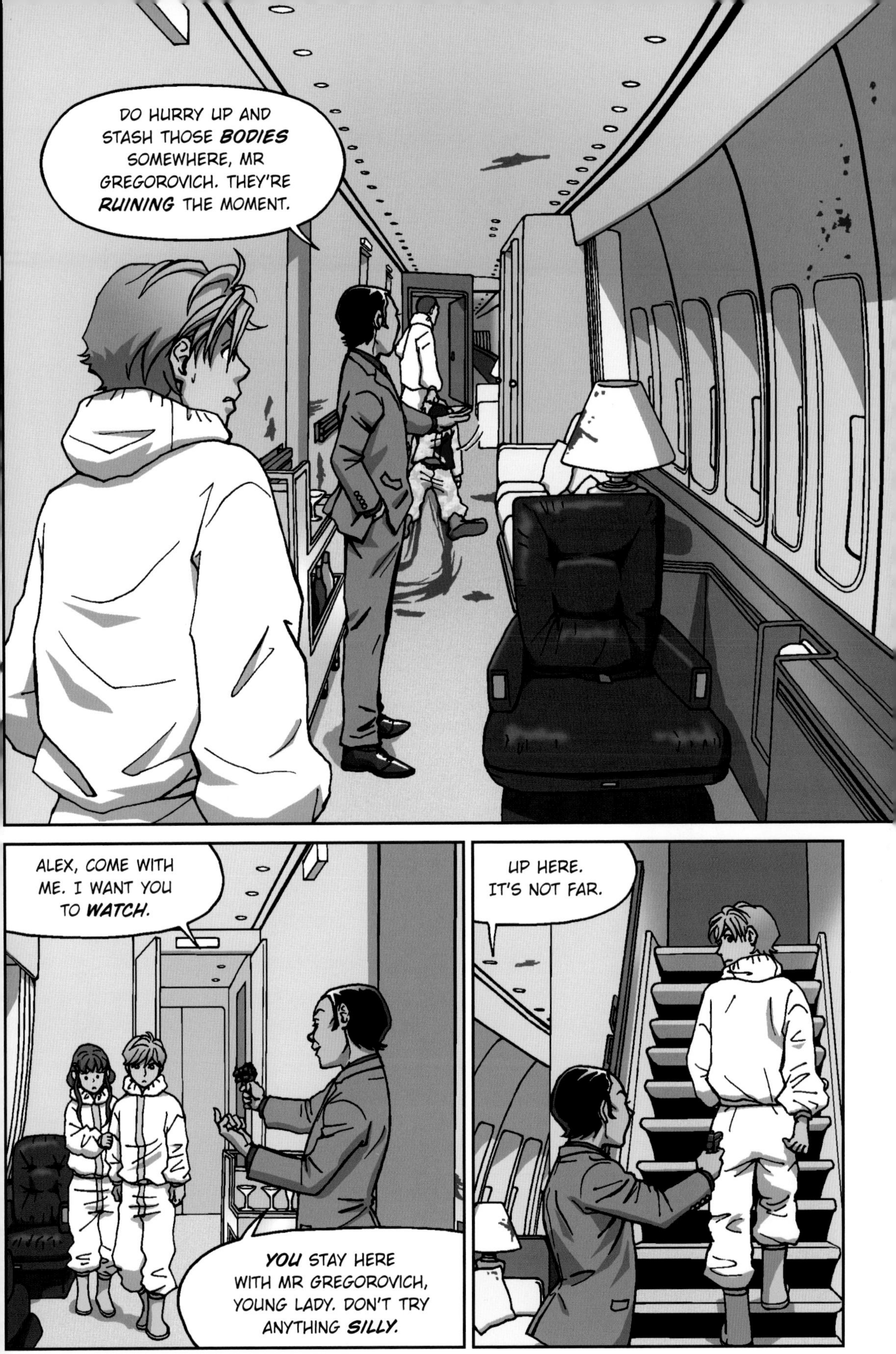
DO HURRY UP AND STASH THOSE BODIES SOMEWHERE, MR GREGOROVICH. THEY'RE RUINING THE MOMENT.
ALEX, COME WITH ME. I WANT YOU TO WATCH.
YOU STAY HERE WITH MR GREGOROVICH, YOUNG LADY. DON'T TRY ANYTHING SILLY.
UP HERE. IT'S NOT FAR.

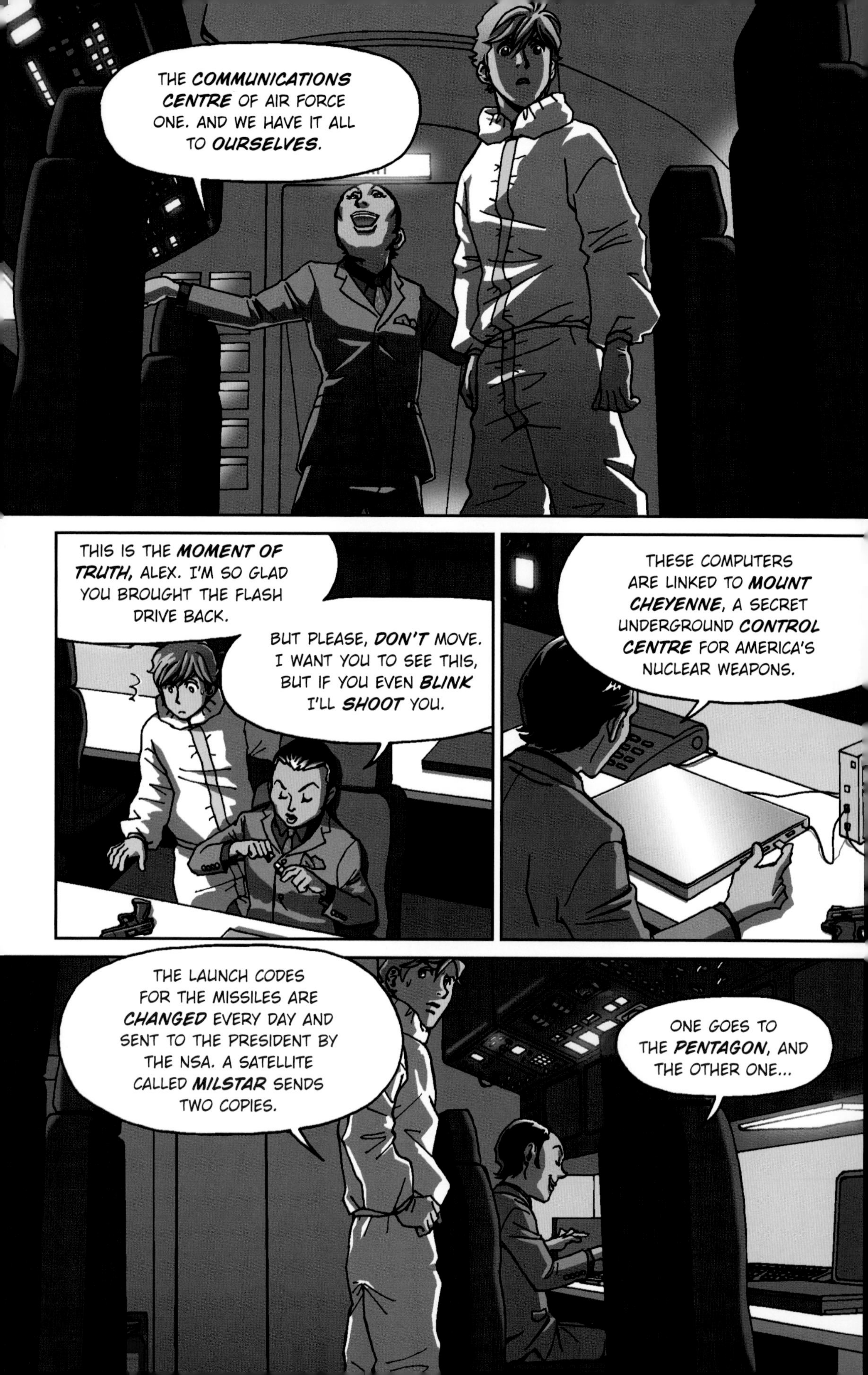
THE COMMUNICATIONS CENTRE OF AIR FORCE ONE. AND WE HAVE IT ALL TO OURSELVES.
THIS IS THE MOMENT OF TRUTH, ALEX. I'M SO GLAD YOU BROUGHT THE FLASH DRIVE BACK.
BUT PLEASE, DON'T MOVE. I WANT YOU TO SEE THIS, BUT IF YOU EVEN BLINK I'LL SHOOT YOU.
THESE COMPUTERS ARE LINKED TO MOUNT CHEYENNE, A SECRET UNDERGROUND CONTROL CENTRE FOR AMERICA'S NUCLEAR WEAPONS.
THE LAUNCH CODES FOR THE MISSILES ARE CHANGED EVERY DAY AND SENT TO THE PRESIDENT BY THE NSA. A SATELLITE CALLED MILSTAR SENDS TWO COPIES.
ONE GOES TO THE PENTAGON, AND THE OTHER ONE...

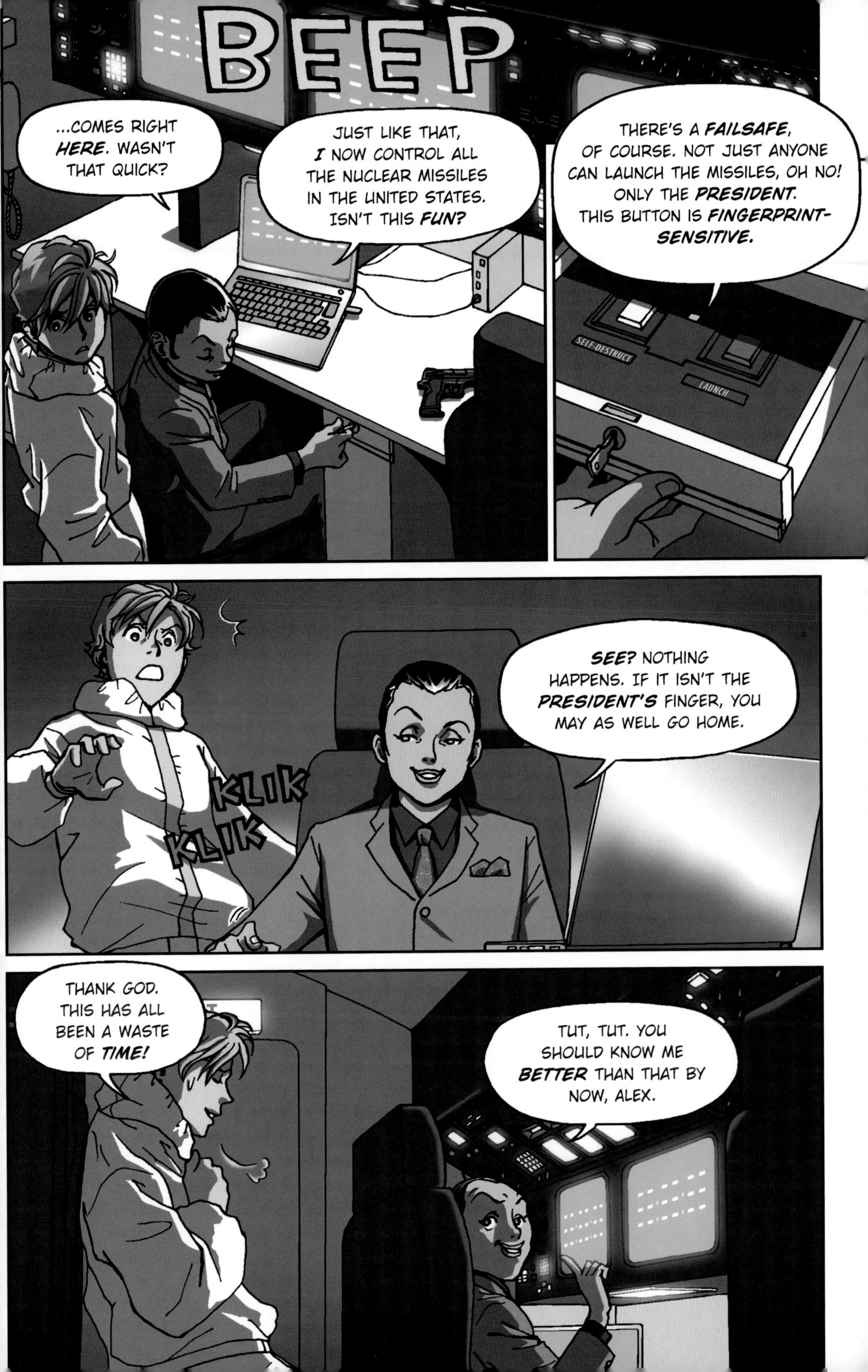
BEEP
...COMES RIGHT HERE. WASN'T THAT QUICK?
JUST LIKE THAT, I NOW CONTROL ALL THE NUCLEAR MISSILES IN THE UNITED STATES. ISN'T THIS FUN?
THERE'S A FAILSAFE, OF COURSE. NOT JUST ANYONE CAN LAUNCH THE MISSILES, OH NO! ONLY THE PRESIDENT. THIS BUTTON IS FINGERPRINT-SENSITIVE.
SELF-DESTRUCT
LAUNCH
SEE? NOTHING HAPPENS. IF IT ISN'T THE PRESIDENT'S FINGER, YOU MAY AS WELL GO HOME.
KLIK
KLIK
THANK GOD. THIS HAS ALL BEEN A WASTE OF TIME!
TUT, TUT. YOU SHOULD KNOW ME BETTER THAN THAT BY NOW, ALEX.

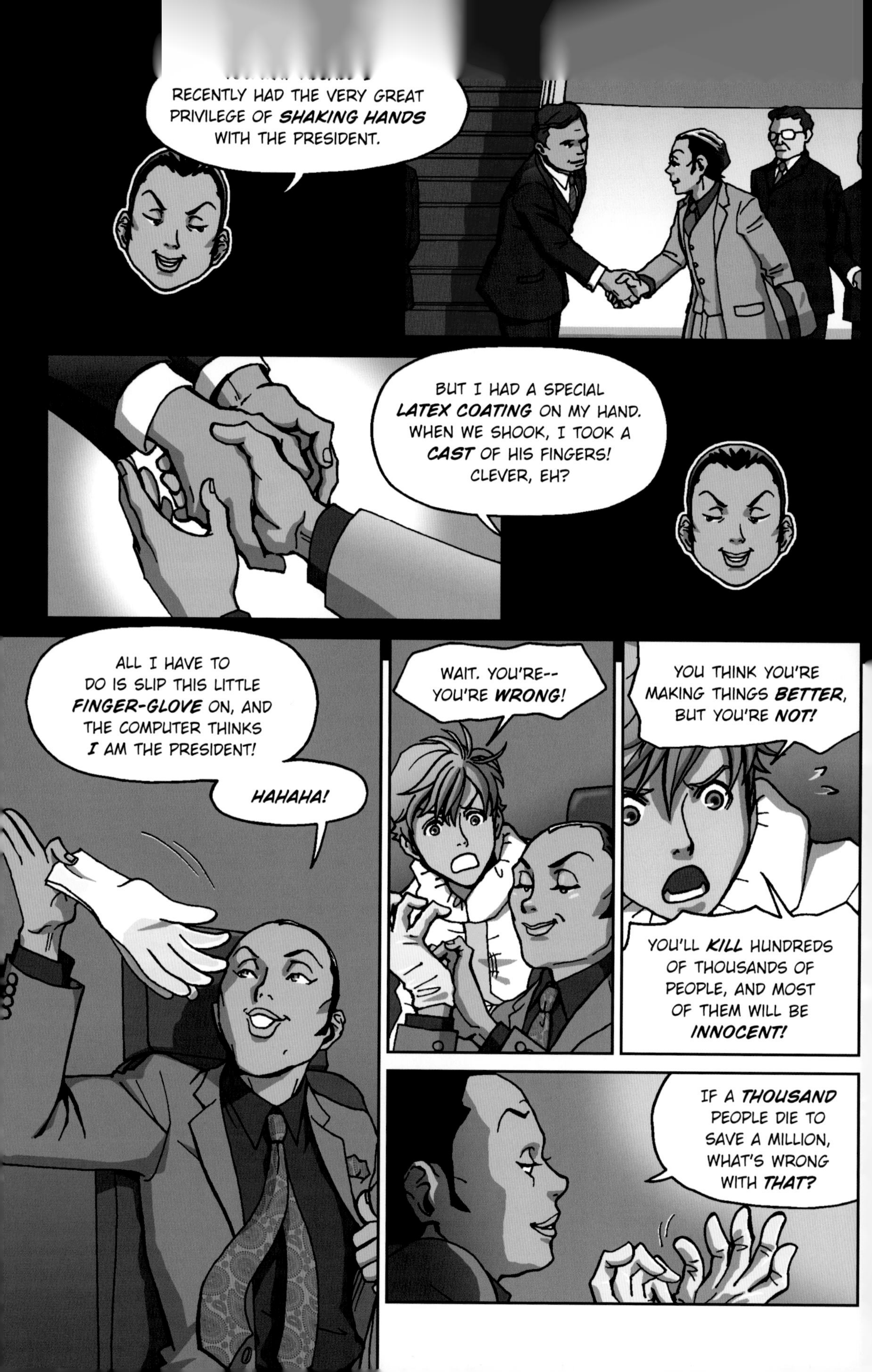
RECENTLY HAD THE VERY GREAT PRIVILEGE OF SHAKING HANDS WITH THE PRESIDENT.
BUT I HAD A SPECIAL LATEX COATING ON MY HAND. WHEN WE SHOOK, I TOOK A CAST OF HIS FINGERS! CLEVER, EH?
ALL I HAVE TO DO IS SLIP THIS LITTLE FINGER-GLOVE ON, AND THE COMPUTER THINKS I AM THE PRESIDENT!
HAHAHA!
WAIT. YOU'RE-- YOU'RE WRONG!
YOU THINK YOU'RE MAKING THINGS BETTER, BUT YOU'RE NOT!
YOU'LL KILL HUNDREDS OF THOUSANDS OF PEOPLE, AND MOST OF THEM WILL BE INNOCENT!
IF A THOUSAND PEOPLE DIE TO SAVE A MILLION, WHAT'S WRONG WITH THAT?

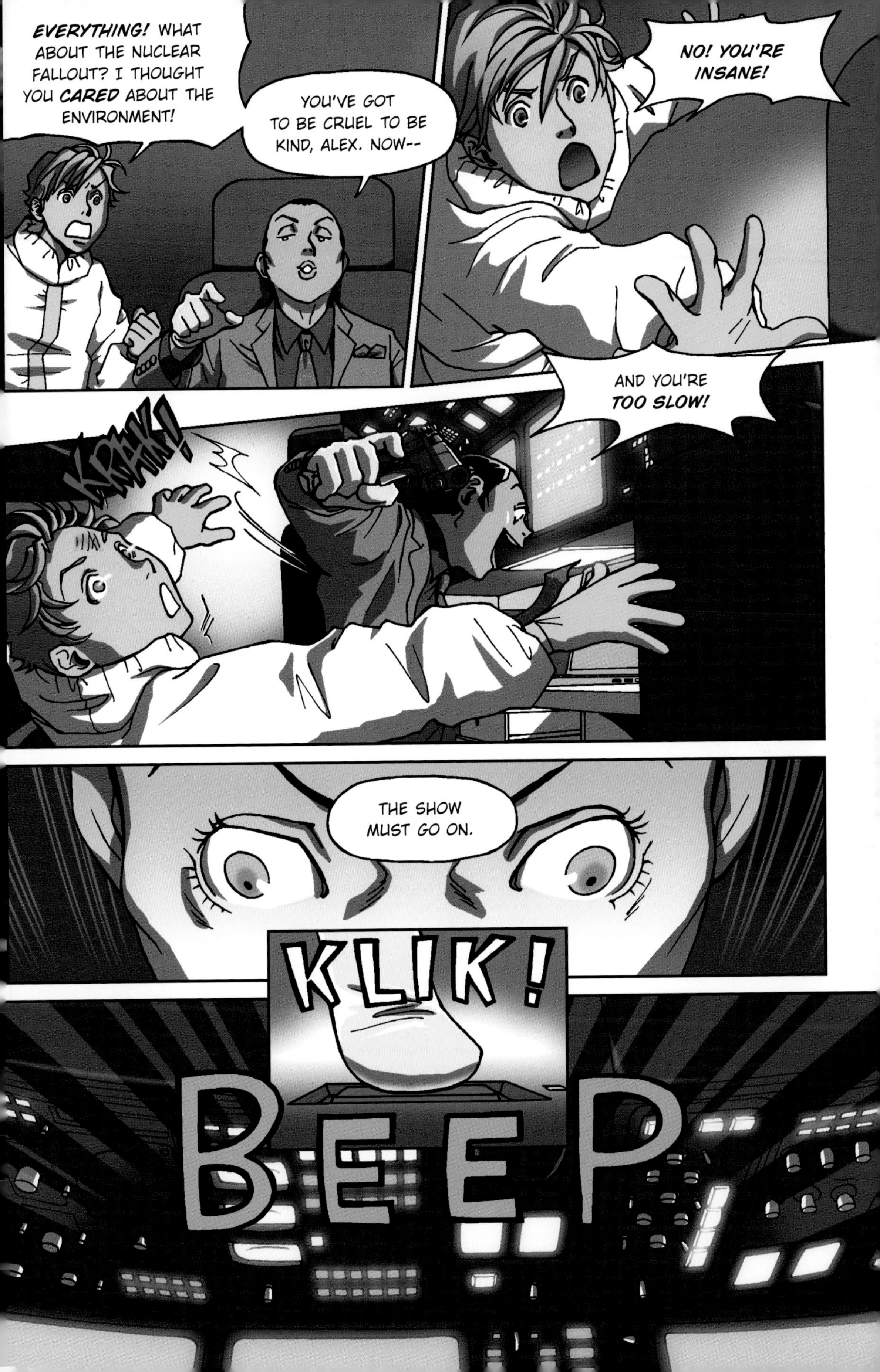
EVERYTHING! WHAT ABOUT THE NUCLEAR FALLOUT? I THOUGHT YOU CARED ABOUT THE ENVIRONMENT!
YOU'VE GOT TO BE CRUEL TO BE KIND, ALEX. NOW--
NO! YOU'RE INSANE!
AND YOU'RE TOO SLOW!
KRAAK!
THE SHOW MUST GO ON.
KLIK!
BEEP!

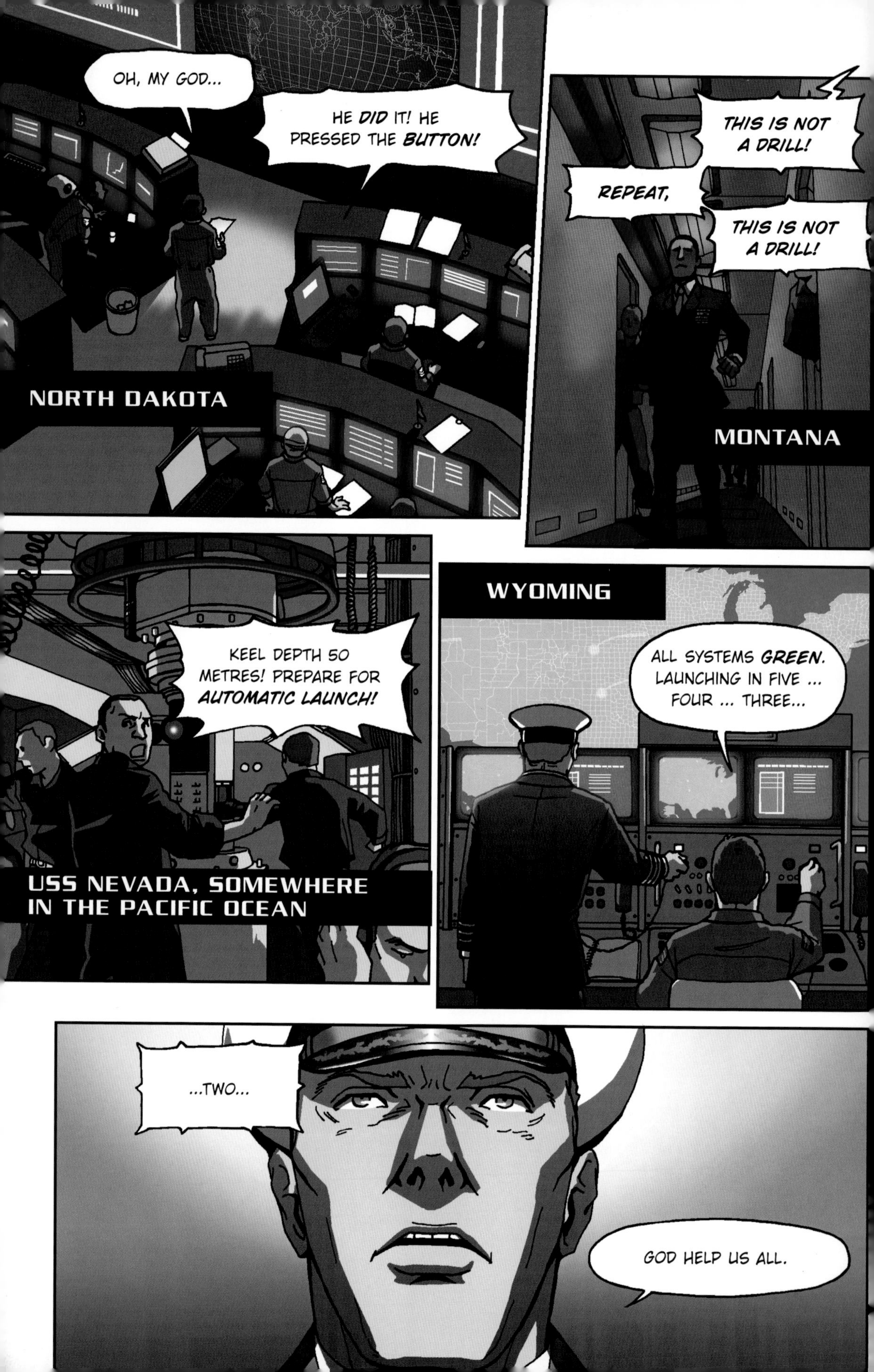
OH, MY GOD...
HE DID IT! HE PRESSED THE BUTTON!
NORTH DAKOTA
THIS IS NOT A DRILL!
REPEAT,
THIS IS NOT A DRILL!
MONTANA
KEEL DEPTH 50 METRES! PREPARE FOR AUTOMATIC LAUNCH!
USS NEVADA, SOMEWHERE IN THE PACIFIC OCEAN
WYOMING
ALL SYSTEMS GREEN. LAUNCHING IN FIVE ... FOUR ... THREE...
...TWO...
GOD HELP US ALL.

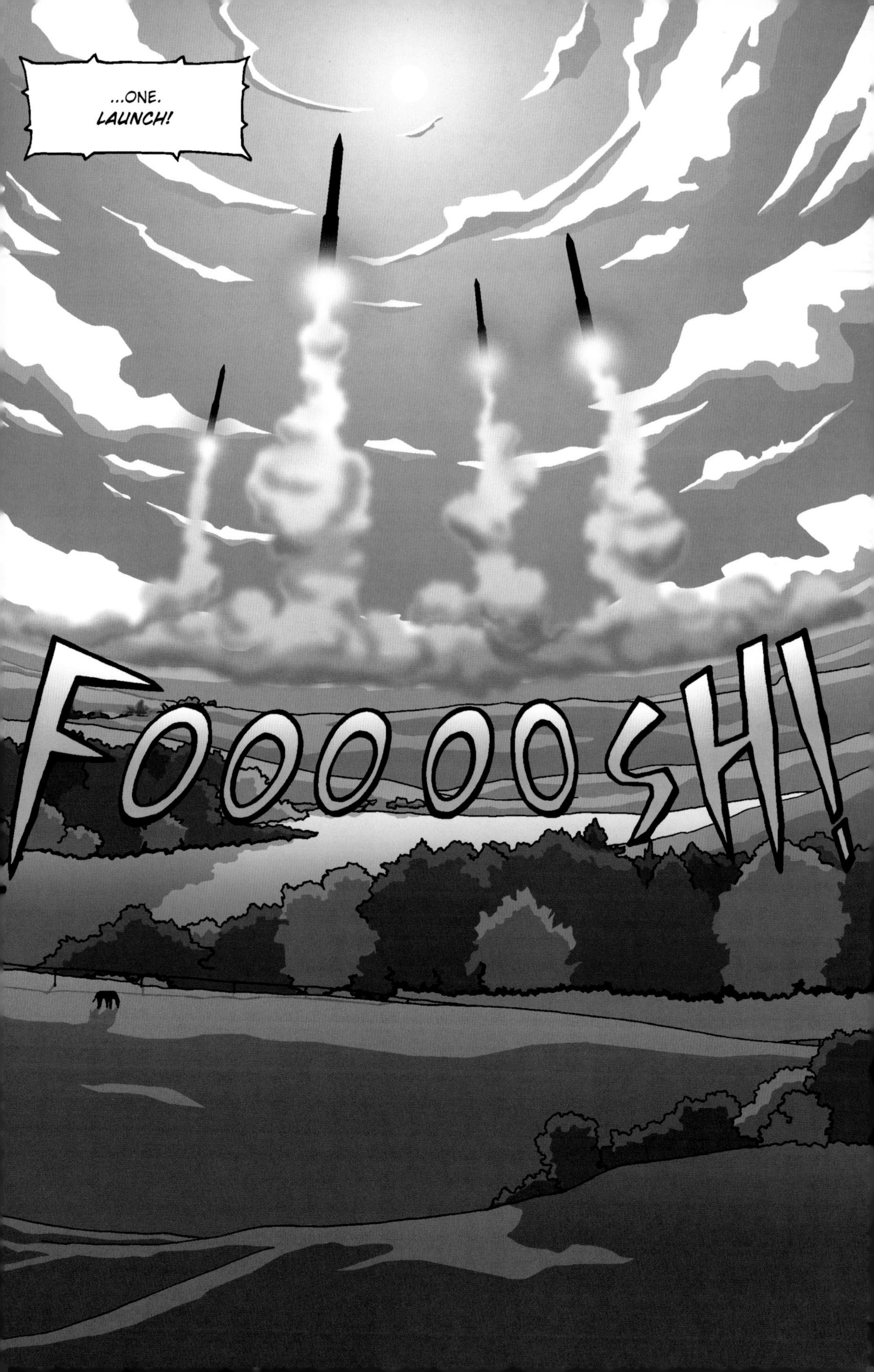
...ONE.
LAUNCH!
FOOOOOSH!

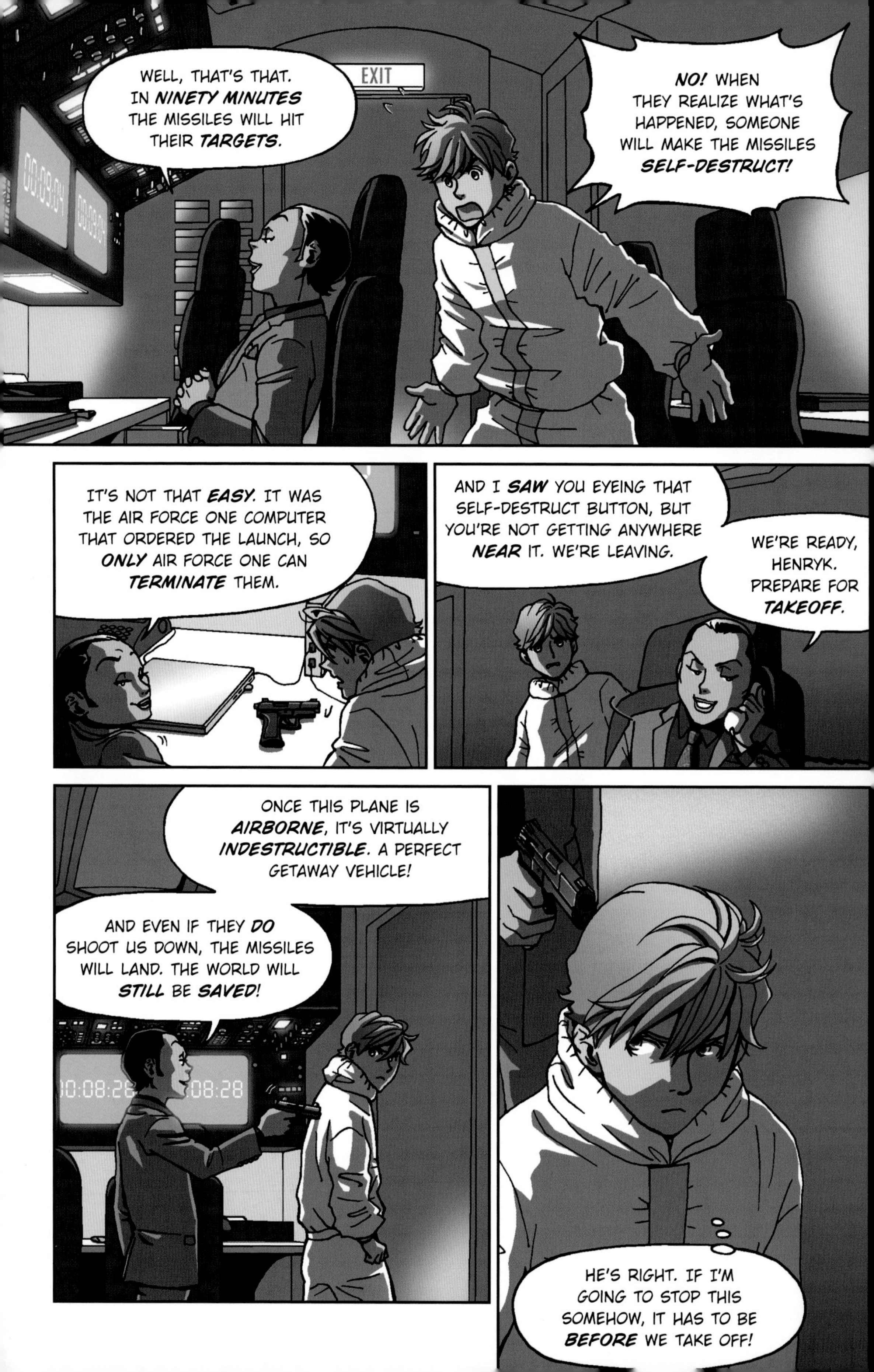
WELL, THAT'S THAT. IN NINETY MINUTES THE MISSILES WILL HIT THEIR TARGETS.
EXIT
NO! WHEN THEY REALIZE WHAT'S HAPPENED, SOMEONE WILL MAKE THE MISSILES SELF-DESTRUCT!
IT'S NOT THAT EASY. IT WAS THE AIR FORCE ONE COMPUTER THAT ORDERED THE LAUNCH, SO ONLY AIR FORCE ONE CAN TERMINATE THEM.
AND I SAW YOU EYEING THAT SELF-DESTRUCT BUTTON, BUT YOU'RE NOT GETTING ANYWHERE NEAR IT. WE'RE LEAVING.
WE'RE READY, HENRYK. PREPARE FOR TAKEOFF.
ONCE THIS PLANE IS AIRBORNE, IT'S VIRTUALLY INDESTRUCTIBLE. A PERFECT GETAWAY VEHICLE!
AND EVEN IF THEY DO SHOOT US DOWN, THE MISSILES WILL LAND. THE WORLD WILL STILL BE SAVED!
00:08:28
00:08:28
HE'S RIGHT. IF I'M GOING TO STOP THIS SOMEHOW, IT HAS TO BE BEFORE WE TAKE OFF!

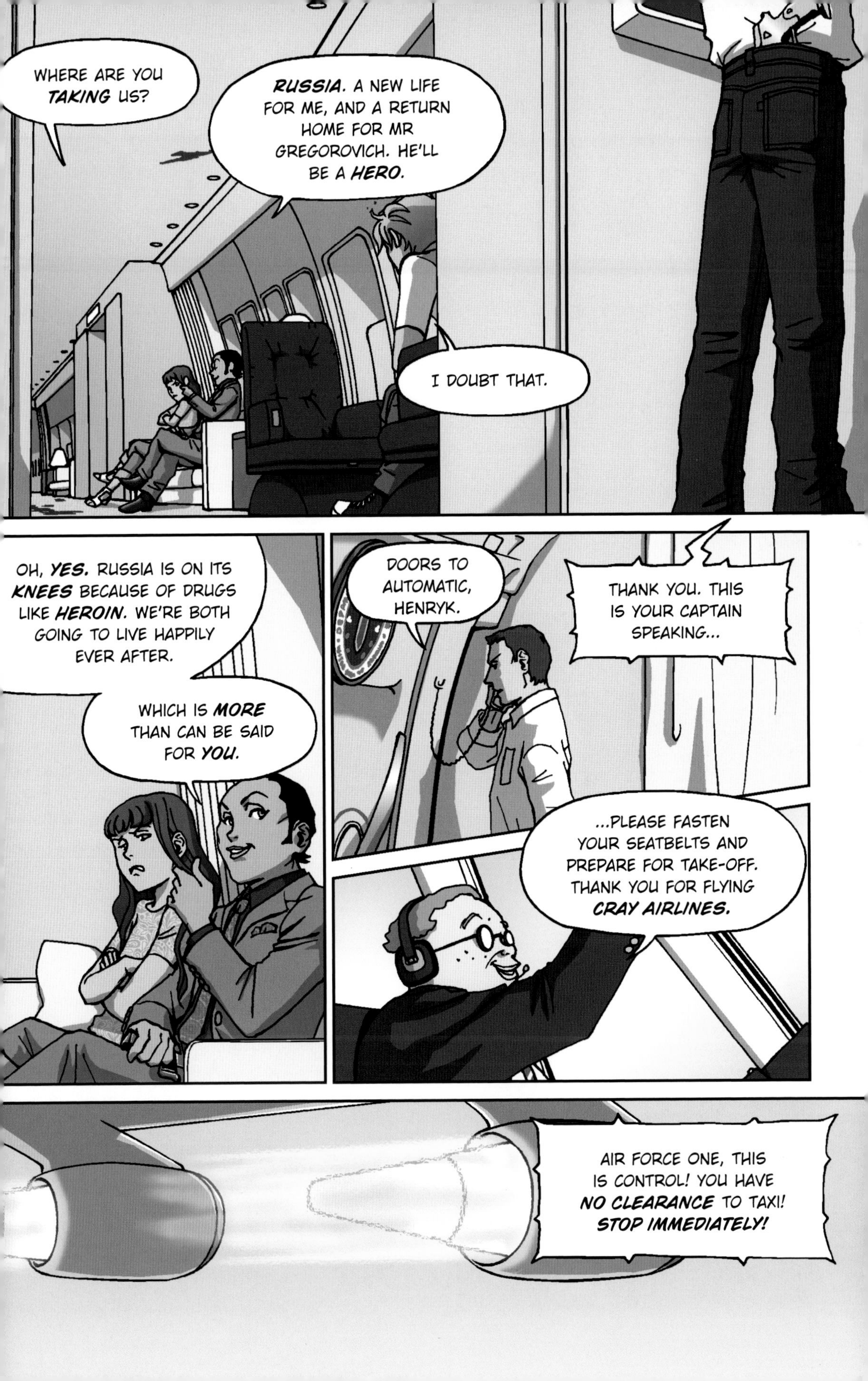
WHERE ARE YOU TAKING US?
RUSSIA. A NEW LIFE FOR ME, AND A RETURN HOME FOR MR GREGOROVICH. HE'LL BE A HERO.
I DOUBT THAT.
OH, YES. RUSSIA IS ON ITS KNEES BECAUSE OF DRUGS LIKE HEROIN. WE'RE BOTH GOING TO LIVE HAPPILY EVER AFTER.
WHICH IS MORE THAN CAN BE SAID FOR YOU.
DOORS TO AUTOMATIC, HENRYK.
THANK YOU. THIS IS YOUR CAPTAIN SPEAKING...
...PLEASE FASTEN YOUR SEATBELTS AND PREPARE FOR TAKE-OFF. THANK YOU FOR FLYING CRAY AIRLINES.
AIR FORCE ONE, THIS IS CONTROL! YOU HAVE NO CLEARANCE TO TAXI! STOP IMMEDIATELY!

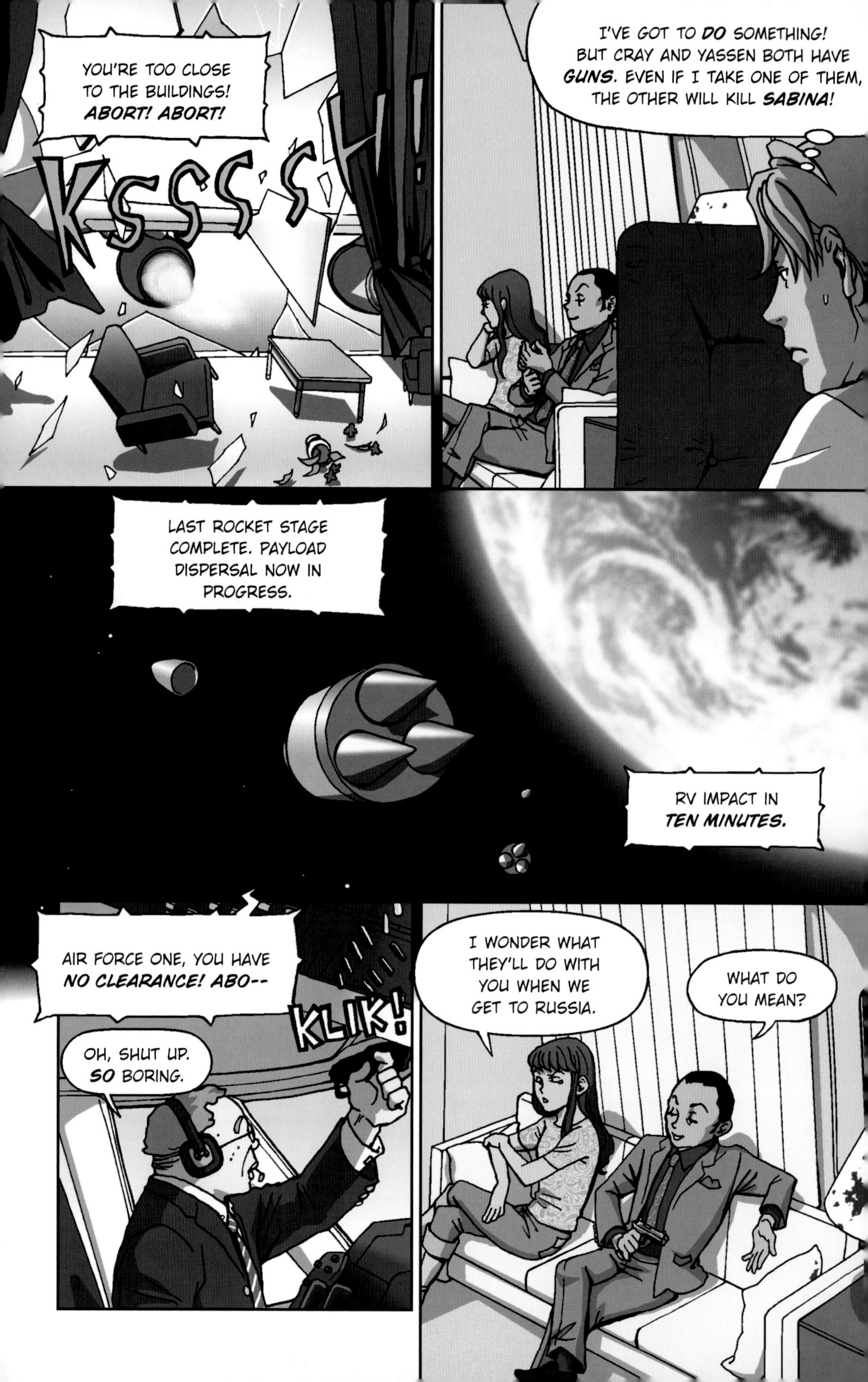
YOU'RE TOO CLOSE TO THE BUILDINGS! ABORT! ABORT!
KSSSSH!
I'VE GOT TO DO SOMETHING! BUT CRAY AND YASSEN BOTH HAVE GUNS. EVEN IF I TAKE ONE OF THEM, THE OTHER WILL KILL SABINA!
LAST ROCKET STAGE COMPLETE. PAYLOAD DISPERSAL NOW IN PROGRESS.
RV IMPACT IN TEN MINUTES.
AIR FORCE ONE, YOU HAVE NO CLEARANCE! ABO--
KLIK!
OH, SHUT UP. SO BORING.
I WONDER WHAT THEY'LL DO WITH YOU WHEN WE GET TO RUSSIA.
WHAT DO YOU MEAN?

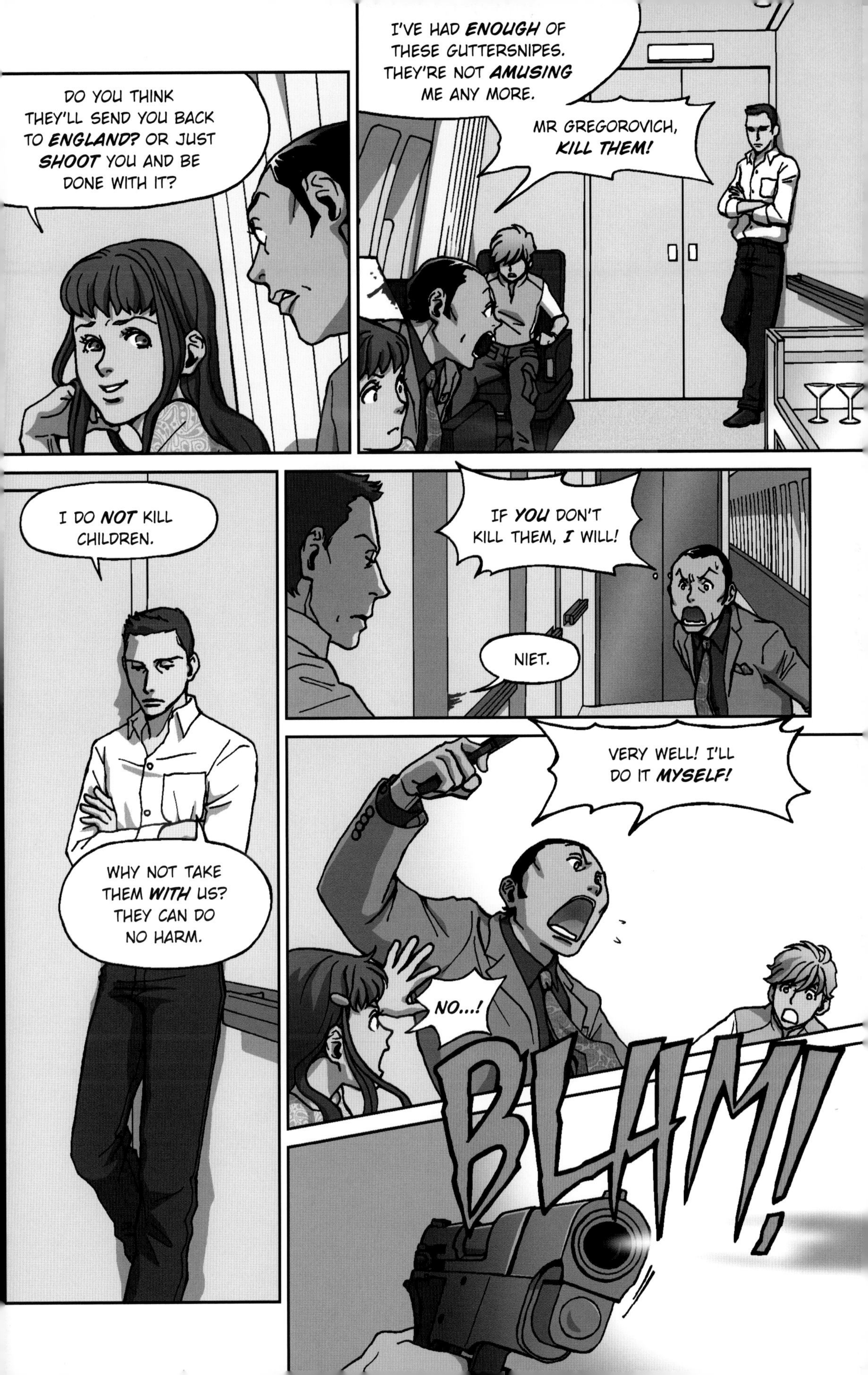

DO YOU THINK THEY'LL SEND YOU BACK TO ENGLAND? OR JUST SHOOT YOU AND BE DONE WITH IT?
I'VE HAD ENOUGH OF THESE GUTTERSNIPES. THEY'RE NOT AMUSING ME ANY MORE.
MR GREGOROVICH, KILL THEM!
I DO NOT KILL CHILDREN.
WHY NOT TAKE THEM WITH US? THEY CAN DO NO HARM.
IF YOU DON'T KILL THEM, I WILL!
NIET.
VERY WELL! I'LL DO IT MYSELF!
NO...!
BLAM!

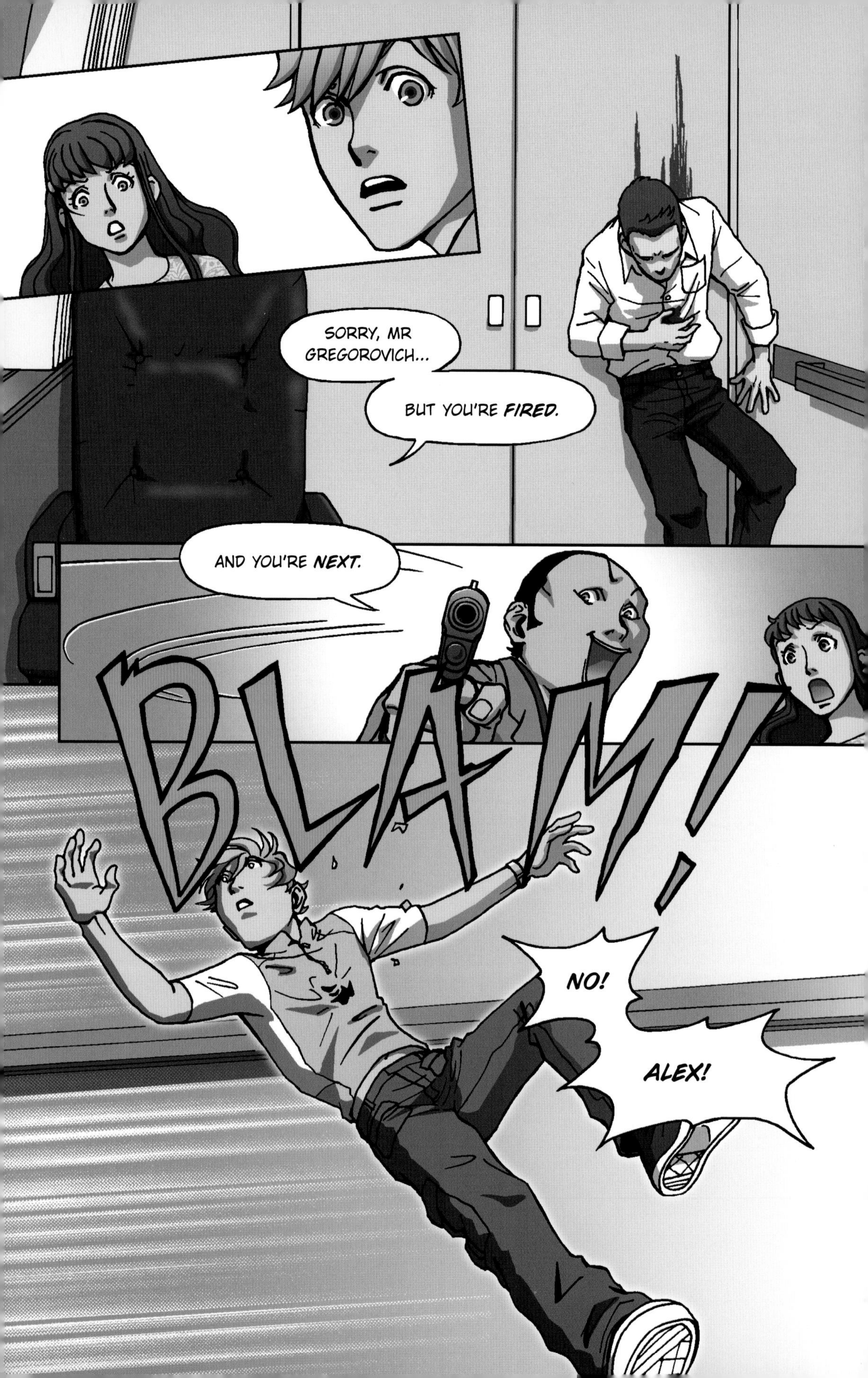
SORRY, MR GREGOROVICH...
BUT YOU'RE FIRED.
AND YOU'RE NEXT.
BLAM!
NO!
ALEX!

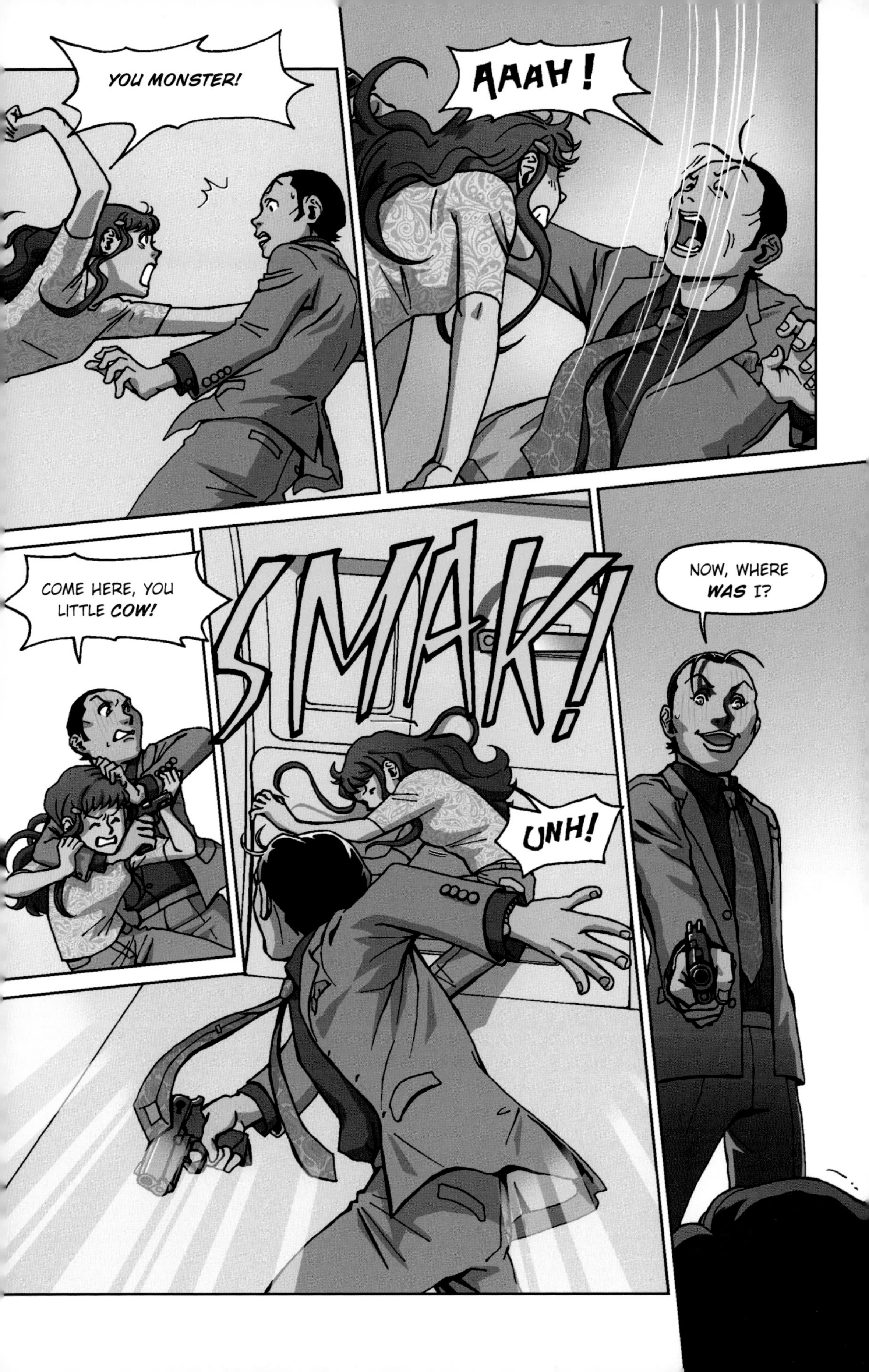
YOU MONSTER!
AAAH!
COME HERE, YOU LITTLE COW!
SMAK!
UNH!
NOW, WHERE WAS I?

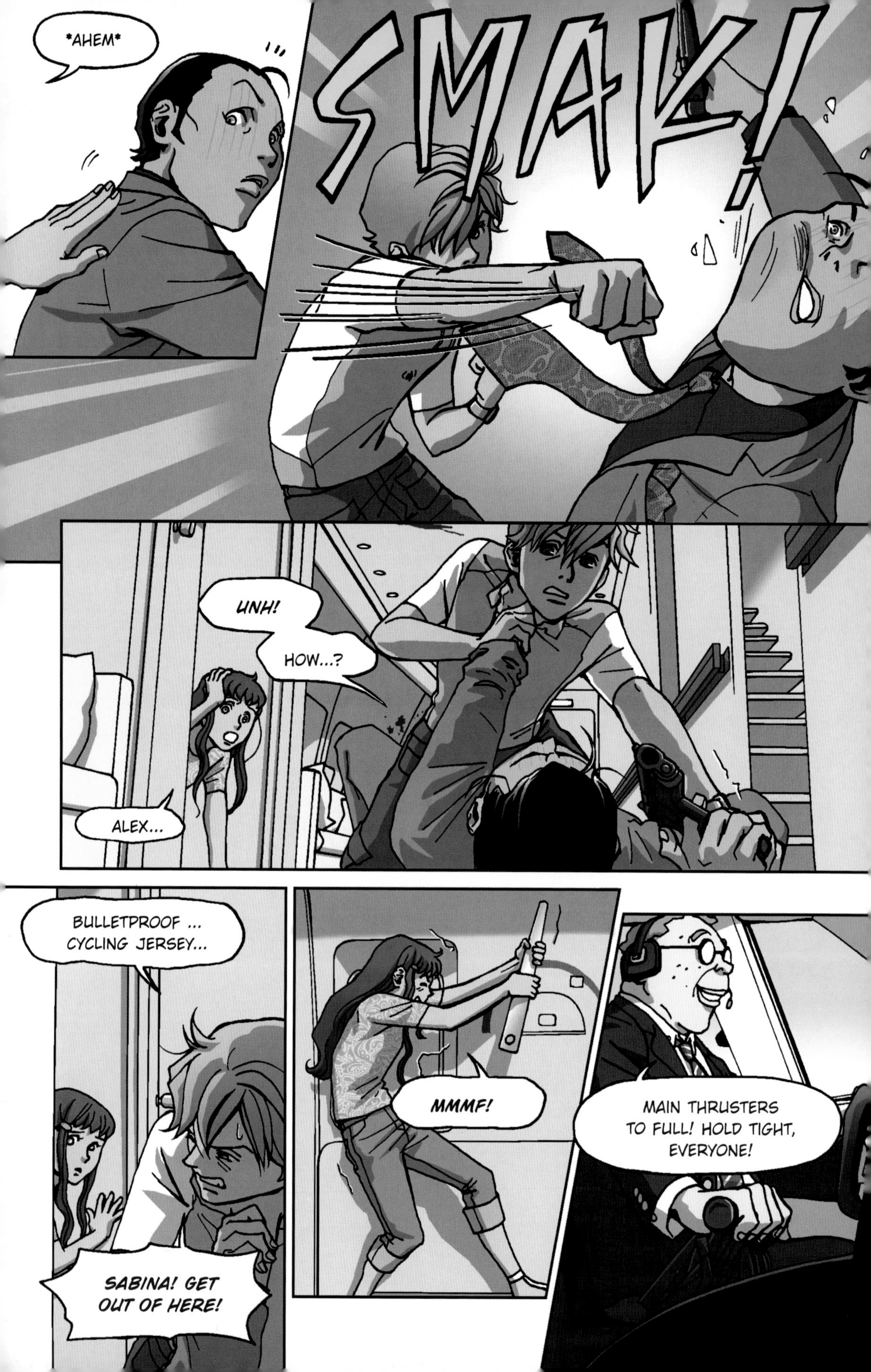
AHEM
SMAK!
UNH!
HOW...?
ALEX...
BULLETPROOF ... CYCLING JERSEY...
SABINA! GET OUT OF HERE!
MMMF!
MAIN THRUSTERS TO FULL! HOLD TIGHT, EVERYONE!

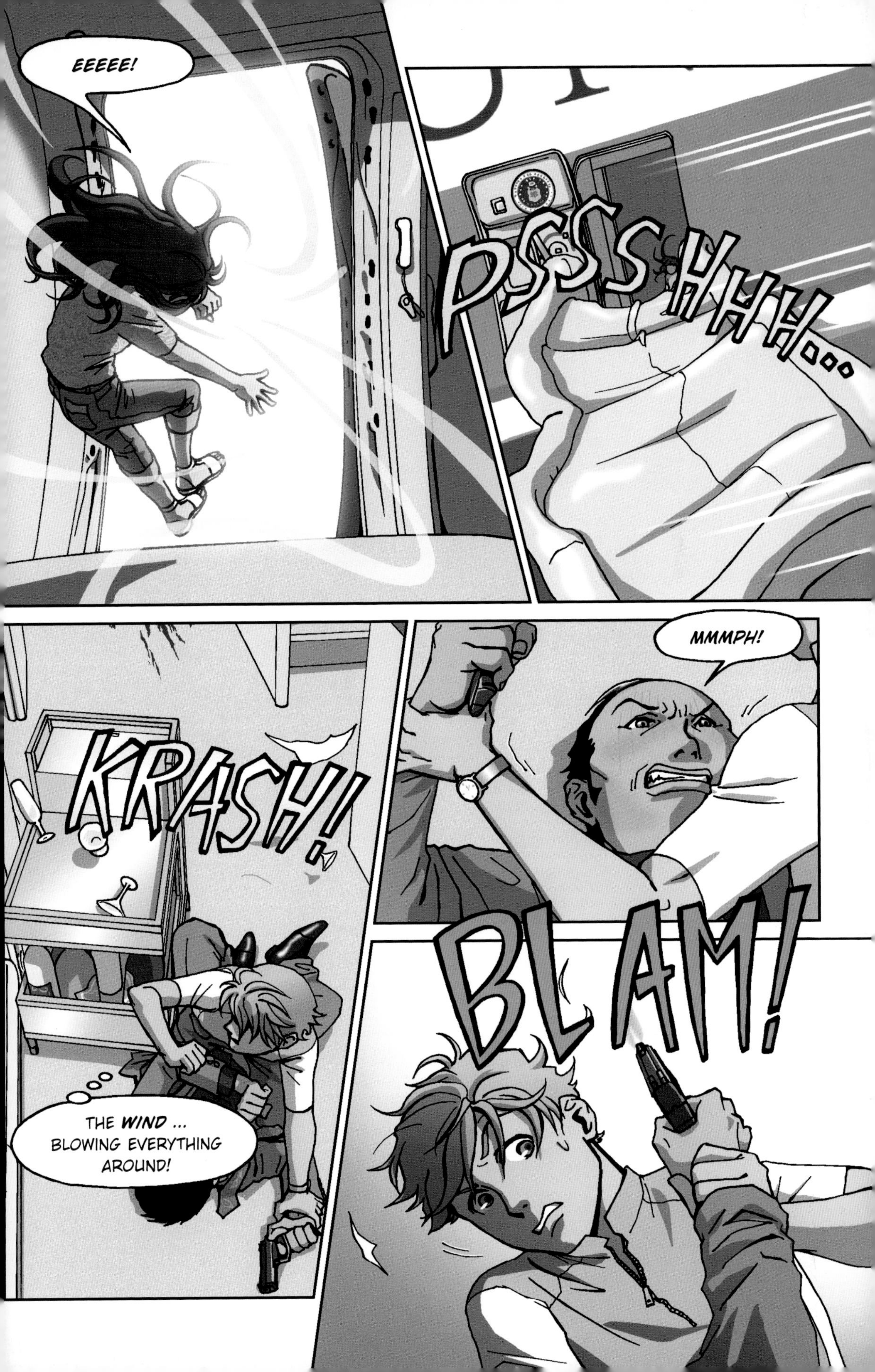
EEEEE!
PSSSHHH...
KRASH!
THE WIND ... BLOWING EVERYTHING AROUND!
MMMPH!
BLAM!

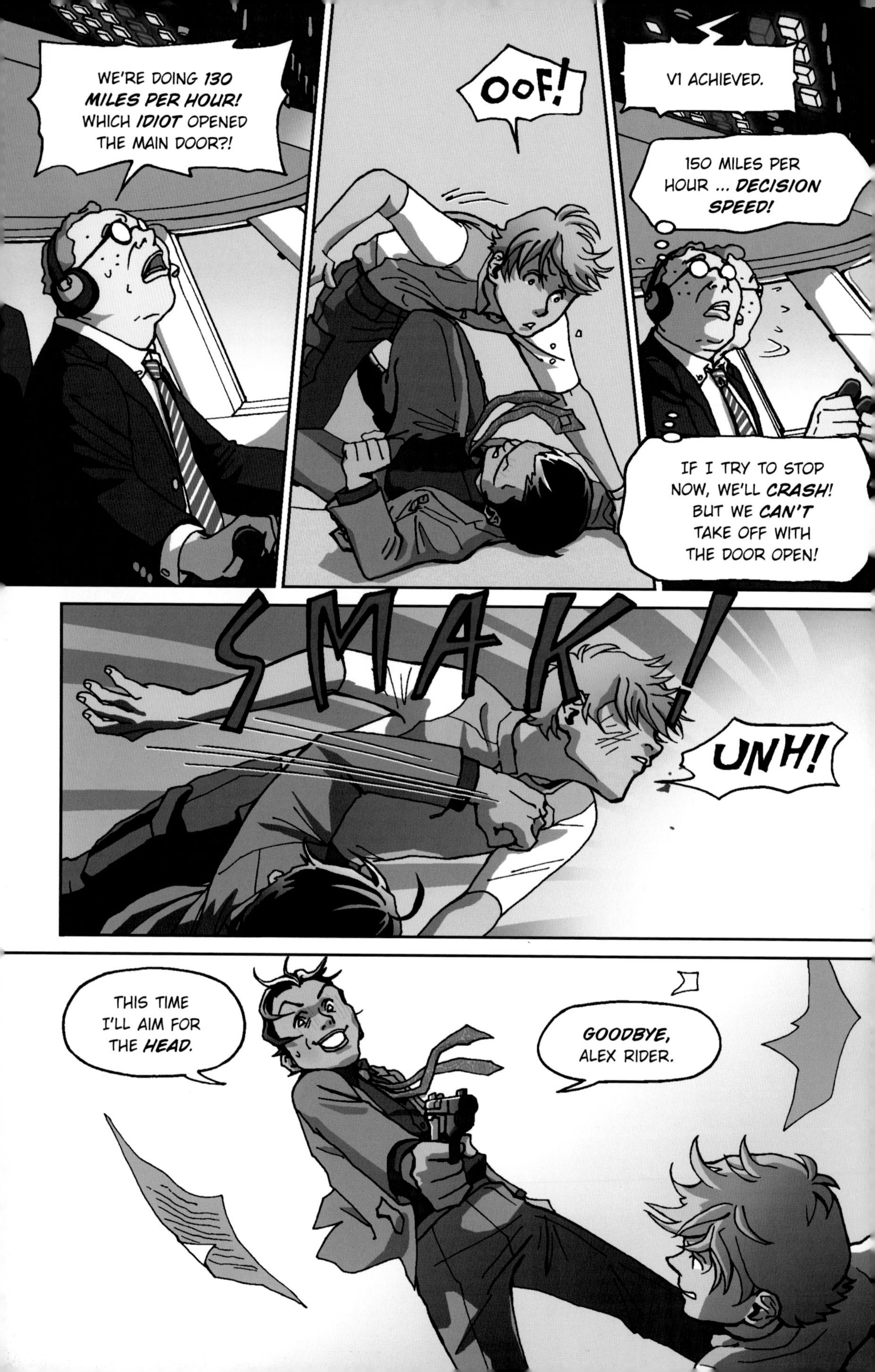
WE'RE DOING 130 MILES PER HOUR! WHICH IDIOT OPENED THE MAIN DOOR?!
OOF!
V1 ACHIEVED.
150 MILES PER HOUR ... DECISION SPEED!
IF I TRY TO STOP NOW, WE'LL CRASH! BUT WE CAN'T TAKE OFF WITH THE DOOR OPEN!
SMAK!
UNH!
THIS TIME I'LL AIM FOR THE HEAD.
GOODBYE, ALEX RIDER.

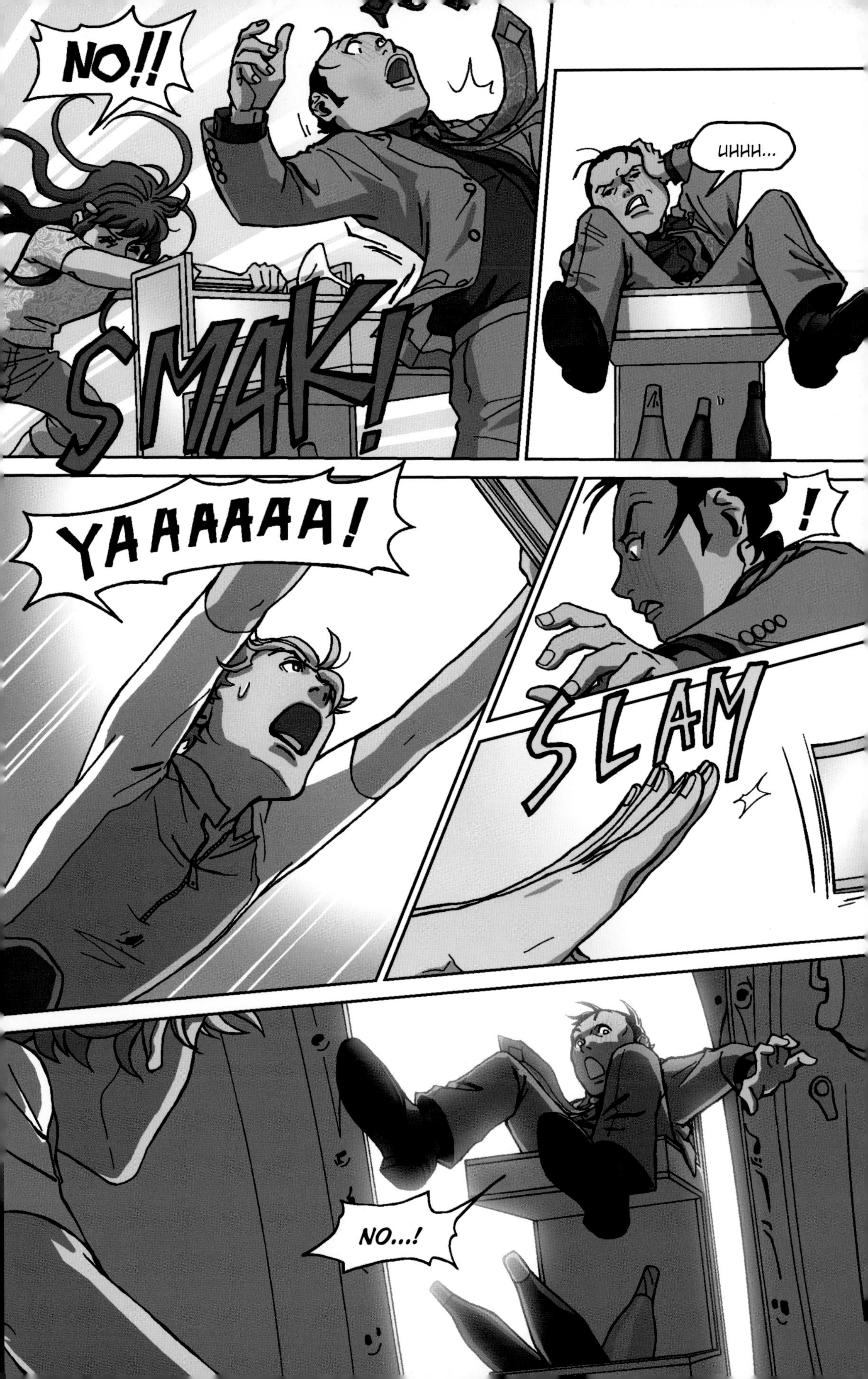
NO!!
SMAK!
UHHH...
YAAAAAA!
!
SLAM
NO...!

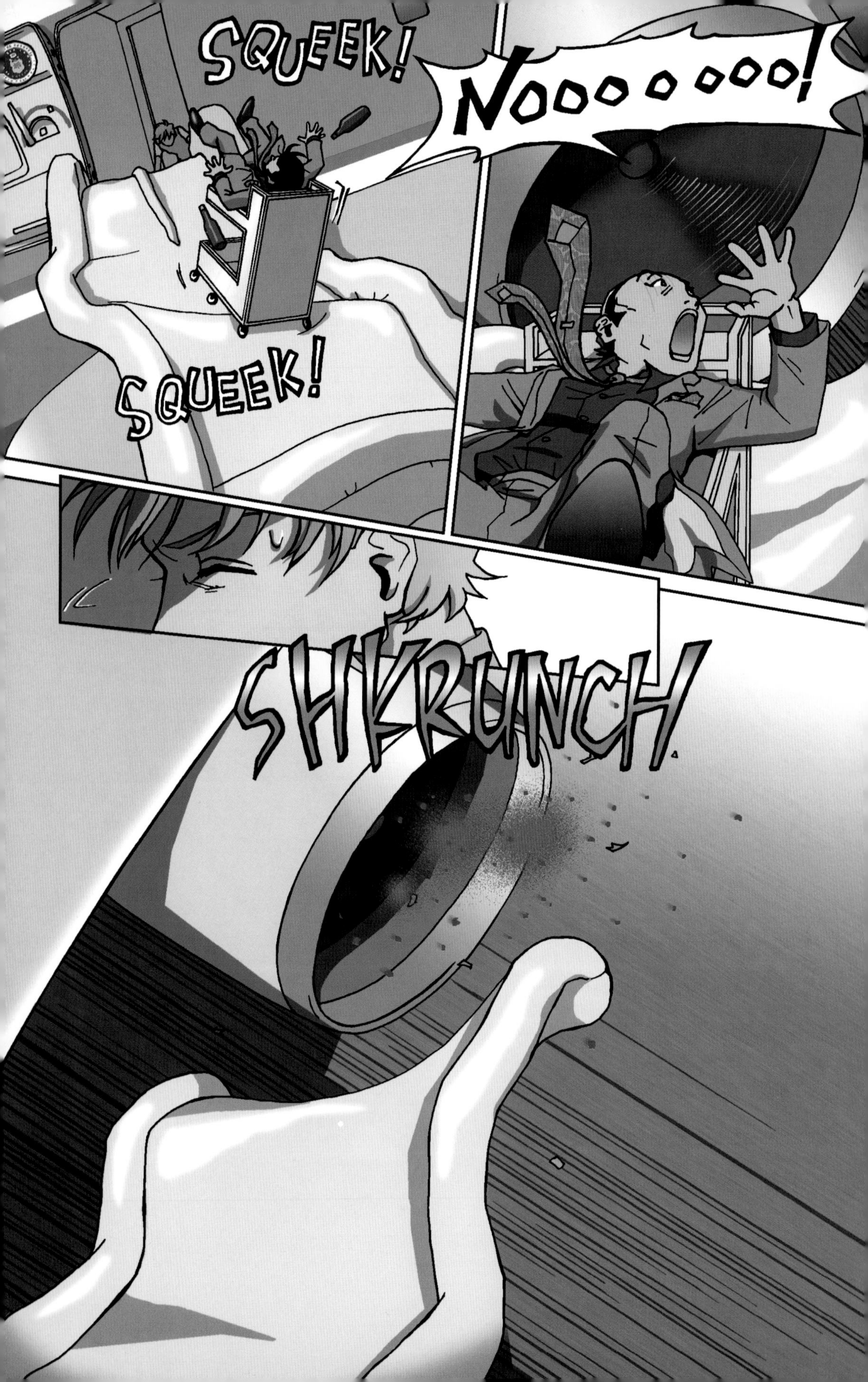
SQUEEK!
SQUEEK!
NOOOOOOO!
SHKRUNCH

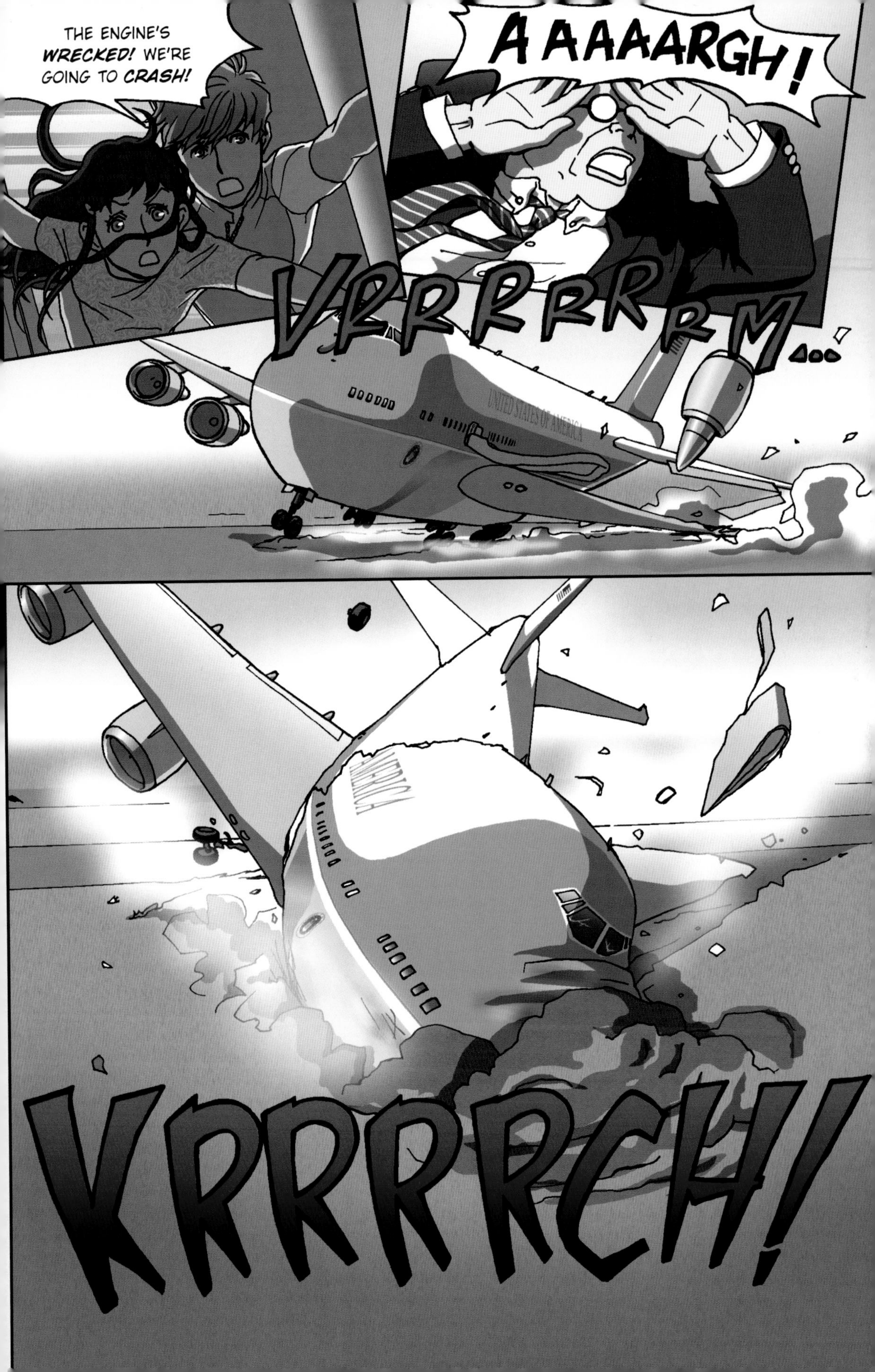
THE ENGINE'S WRECKED! WE'RE GOING TO CRASH!
AAAAARGH!
VRRRRRRRM
UNITED STATES OF AMERICA
AMERICA
KRRRRCH!

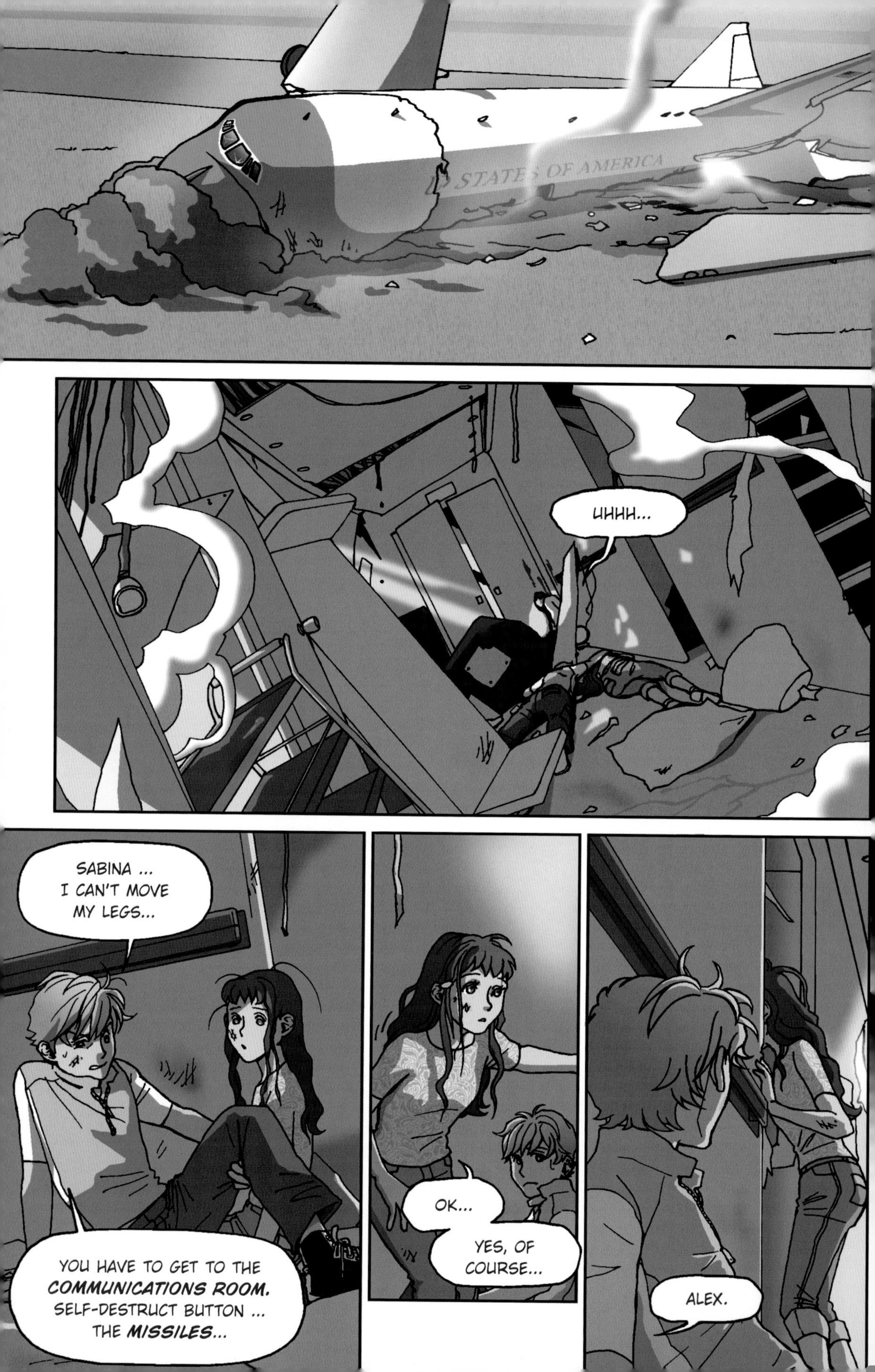

STATES OF AMERICA
UHHH...
SABINA ... I CAN'T MOVE MY LEGS...
YOU HAVE TO GET TO THE **COMMUNICATIONS ROOM.** SELF-DESTRUCT BUTTON ... THE **MISSILES**...
OK...
YES, OF COURSE...
ALEX.

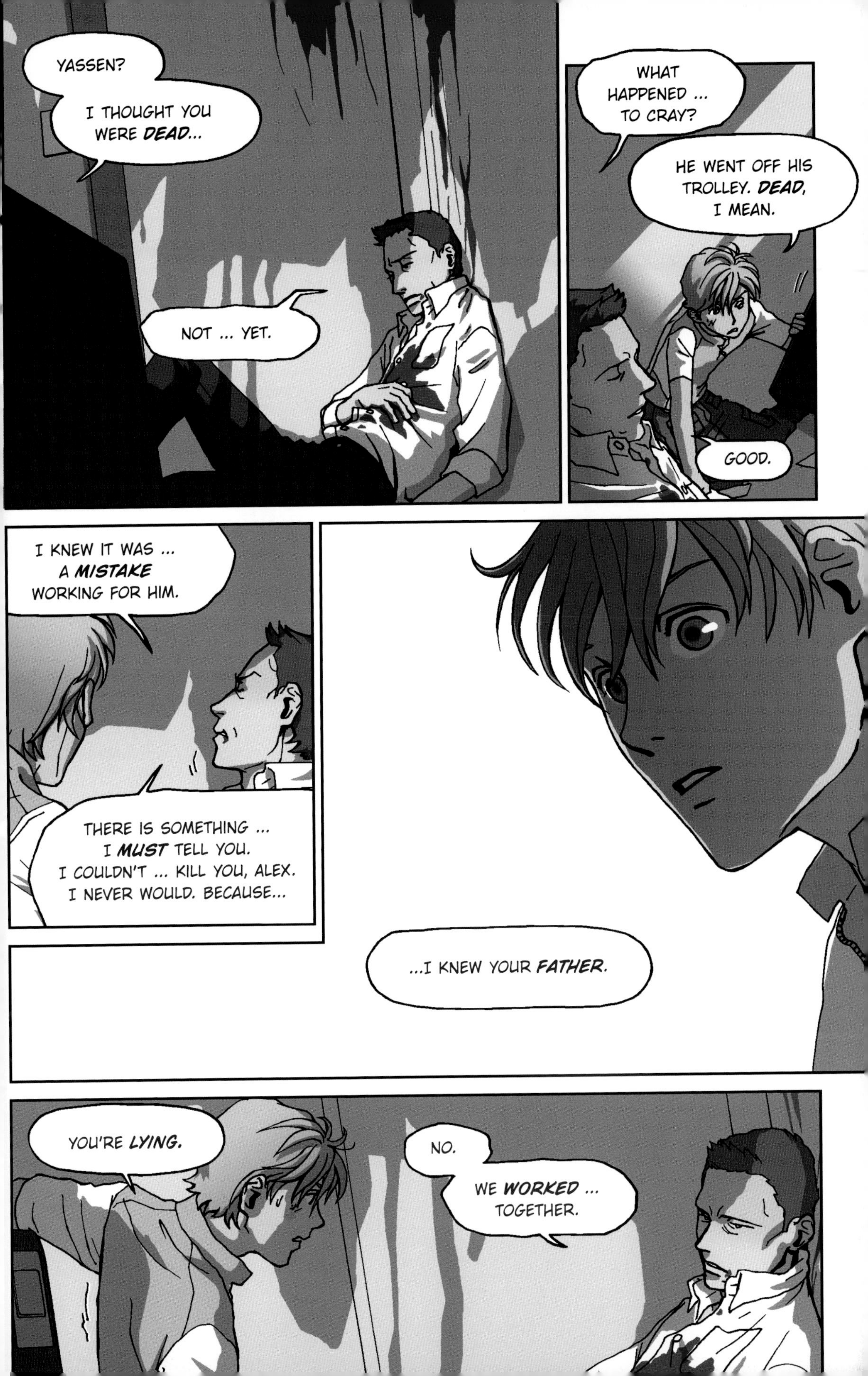
YASSEN?
I THOUGHT YOU WERE DEAD...
NOT ... YET.
WHAT HAPPENED ... TO CRAY?
HE WENT OFF HIS TROLLEY. DEAD, I MEAN.
GOOD.
I KNEW IT WAS ... A MISTAKE WORKING FOR HIM.
THERE IS SOMETHING ... I MUST TELL YOU. I COULDN'T ... KILL YOU, ALEX. I NEVER WOULD. BECAUSE...
...I KNEW YOUR FATHER.
YOU'RE LYING.
NO.
WE WORKED ... TOGETHER.

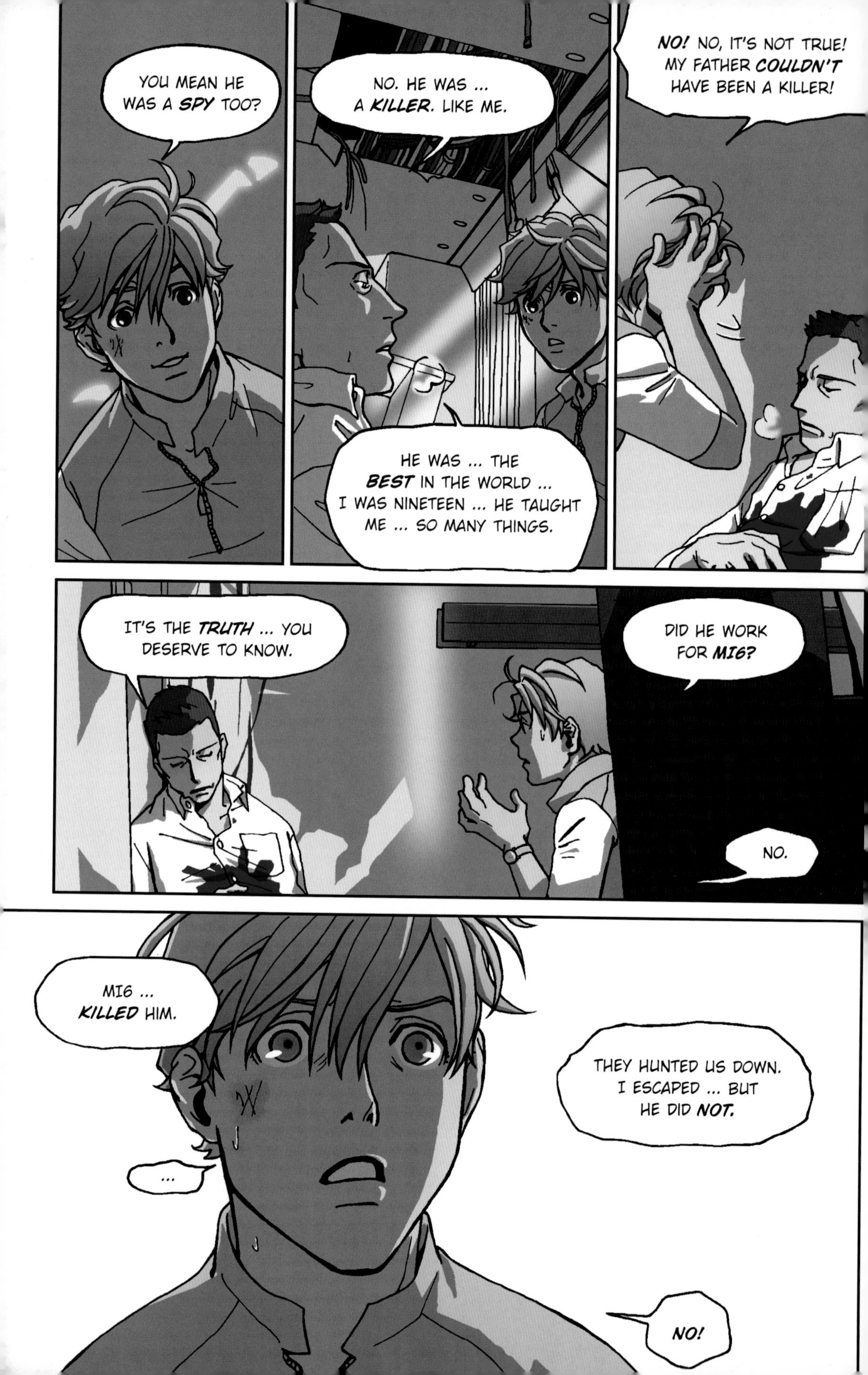
YOU MEAN HE WAS A *SPY* TOO?
NO. HE WAS ... A *KILLER*. LIKE ME.
HE WAS ... THE *BEST* IN THE WORLD ... I WAS NINETEEN ... HE TAUGHT ME ... SO MANY THINGS.
NO! NO, IT'S NOT TRUE! MY FATHER *COULDN'T* HAVE BEEN A KILLER!
IT'S THE *TRUTH* ... YOU DESERVE TO KNOW.
DID HE WORK FOR *MI6?*
NO.
MI6 ... *KILLED* HIM.
THEY HUNTED US DOWN. I ESCAPED ... BUT HE DID *NOT.*
...
NO!

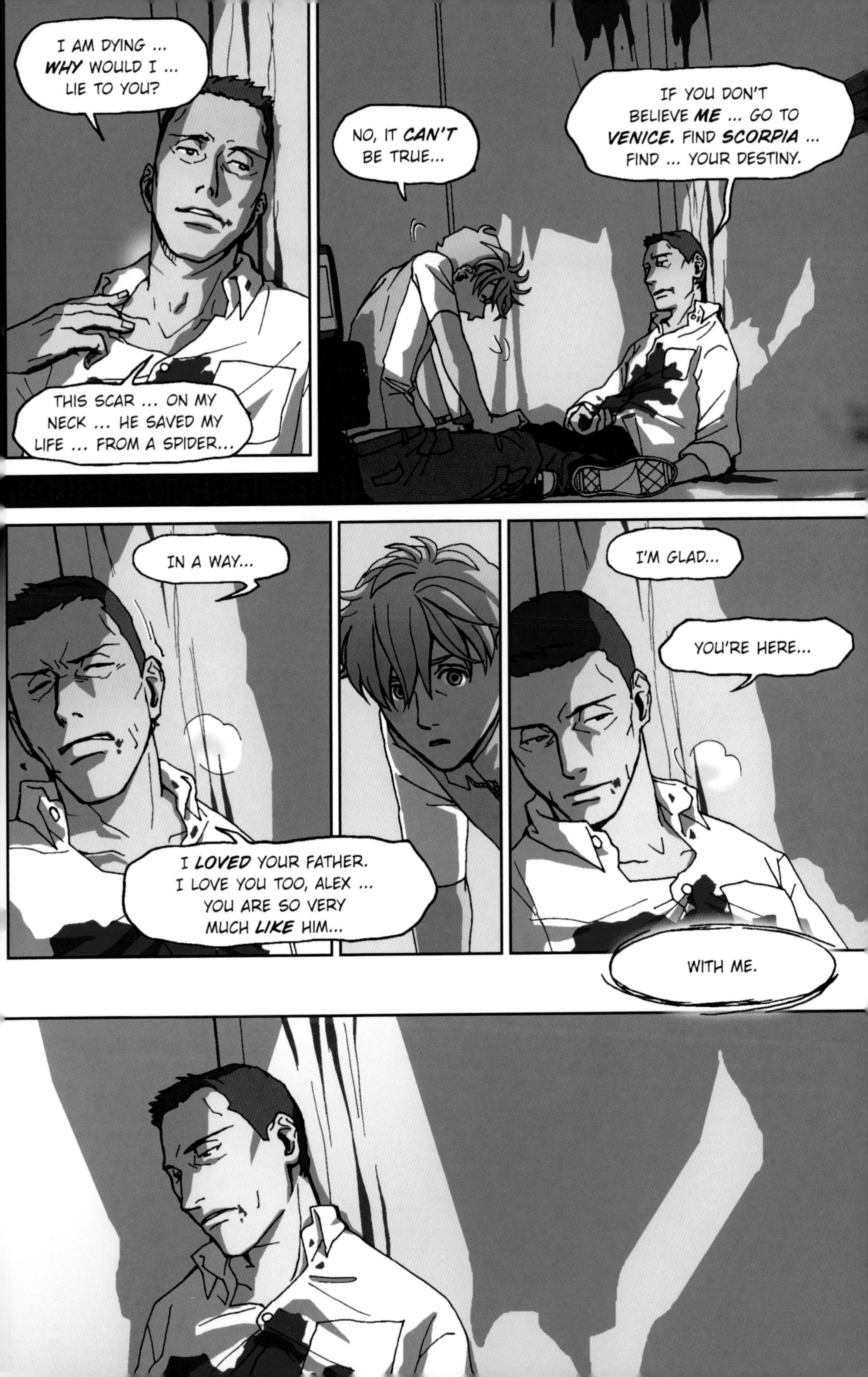
I AM DYING ... WHY WOULD I ... LIE TO YOU?
THIS SCAR ... ON MY NECK ... HE SAVED MY LIFE ... FROM A SPIDER...
NO, IT CAN'T BE TRUE...
IF YOU DON'T BELIEVE ME ... GO TO VENICE. FIND SCORPIA ... FIND ... YOUR DESTINY.
IN A WAY...
I LOVED YOUR FATHER. I LOVE YOU TOO, ALEX ... YOU ARE SO VERY MUCH LIKE HIM...
I'M GLAD...
YOU'RE HERE...
WITH ME.

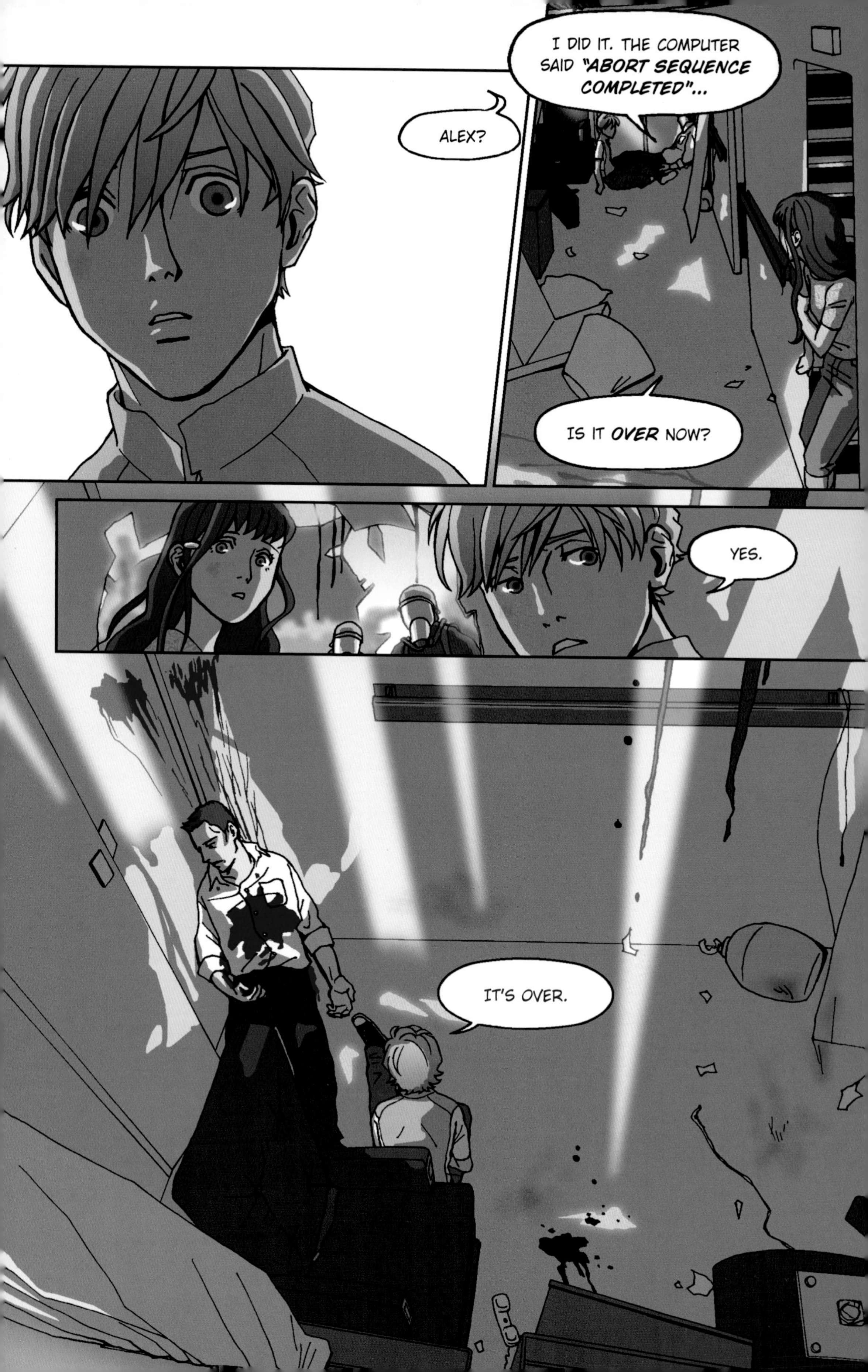
ALEX?
I DID IT. THE COMPUTER SAID "ABORT SEQUENCE COMPLETED"...
IS IT OVER NOW?
YES.
IT'S OVER.

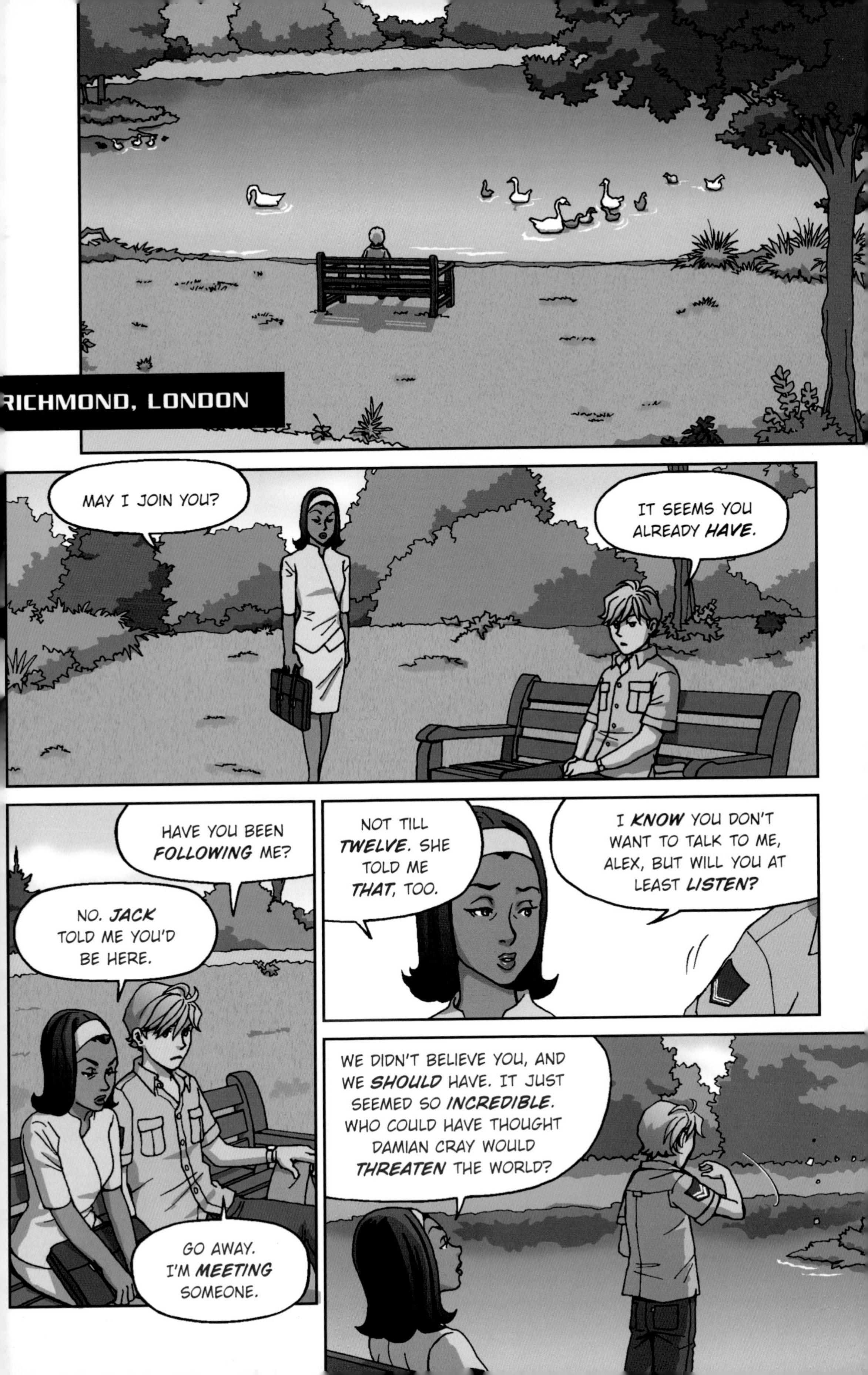
RICHMOND, LONDON
MAY I JOIN YOU?
IT SEEMS YOU ALREADY HAVE.
HAVE YOU BEEN FOLLOWING ME?
NO. JACK TOLD ME YOU'D BE HERE.
GO AWAY. I'M MEETING SOMEONE.
NOT TILL TWELVE. SHE TOLD ME THAT, TOO.
I KNOW YOU DON'T WANT TO TALK TO ME, ALEX, BUT WILL YOU AT LEAST LISTEN?
WE DIDN'T BELIEVE YOU, AND WE SHOULD HAVE. IT JUST SEEMED SO INCREDIBLE. WHO COULD HAVE THOUGHT DAMIAN CRAY WOULD THREATEN THE WORLD?

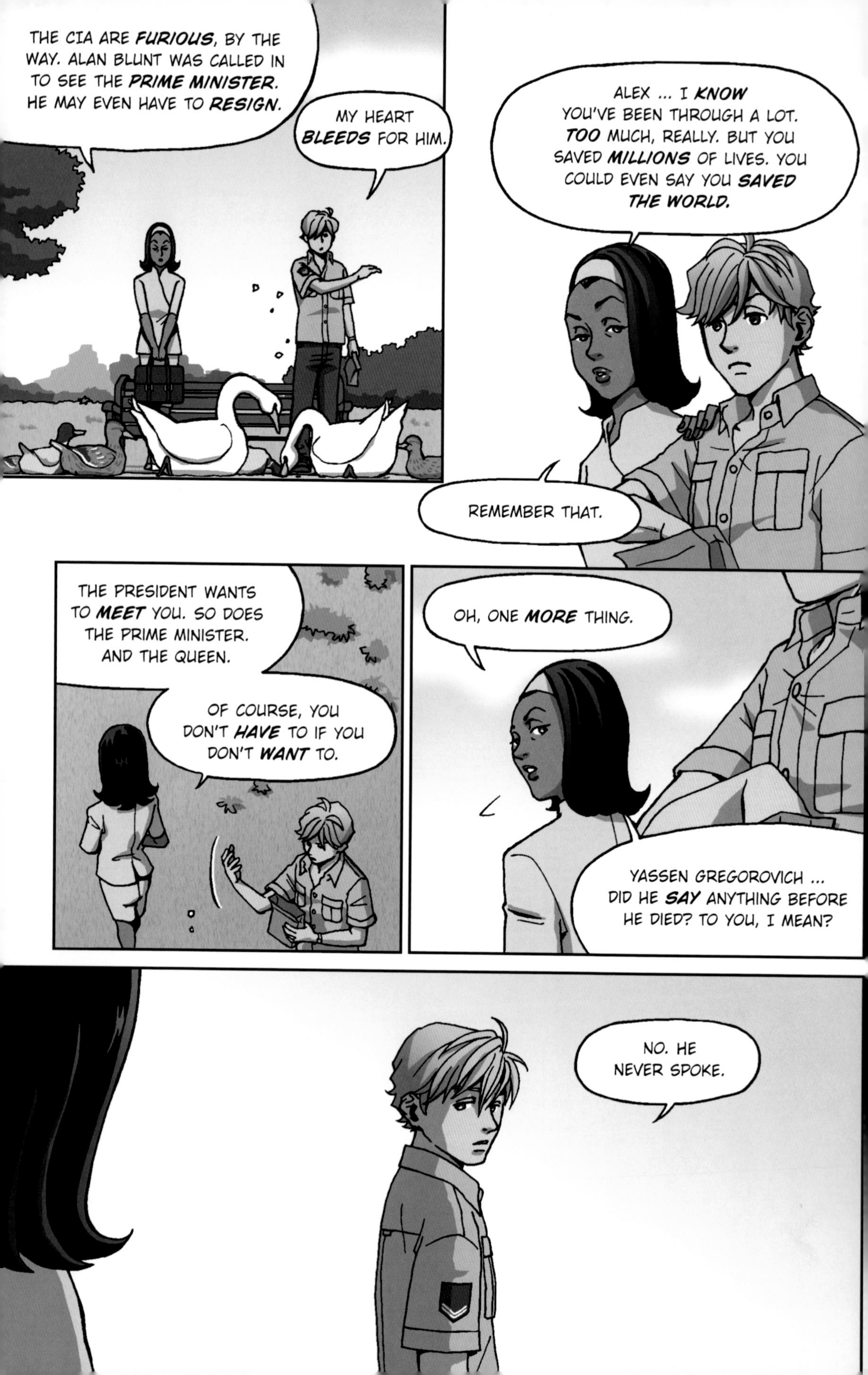
THE CIA ARE FURIOUS, BY THE WAY. ALAN BLUNT WAS CALLED IN TO SEE THE PRIME MINISTER. HE MAY EVEN HAVE TO RESIGN.
MY HEART BLEEDS FOR HIM.
ALEX ... I KNOW YOU'VE BEEN THROUGH A LOT. TOO MUCH, REALLY. BUT YOU SAVED MILLIONS OF LIVES. YOU COULD EVEN SAY YOU SAVED THE WORLD.
REMEMBER THAT.
THE PRESIDENT WANTS TO MEET YOU. SO DOES THE PRIME MINISTER. AND THE QUEEN.
OF COURSE, YOU DON'T HAVE TO IF YOU DON'T WANT TO.
OH, ONE MORE THING.
YASSEN GREGOROVICH ... DID HE SAY ANYTHING BEFORE HE DIED? TO YOU, I MEAN?
NO. HE NEVER SPOKE.

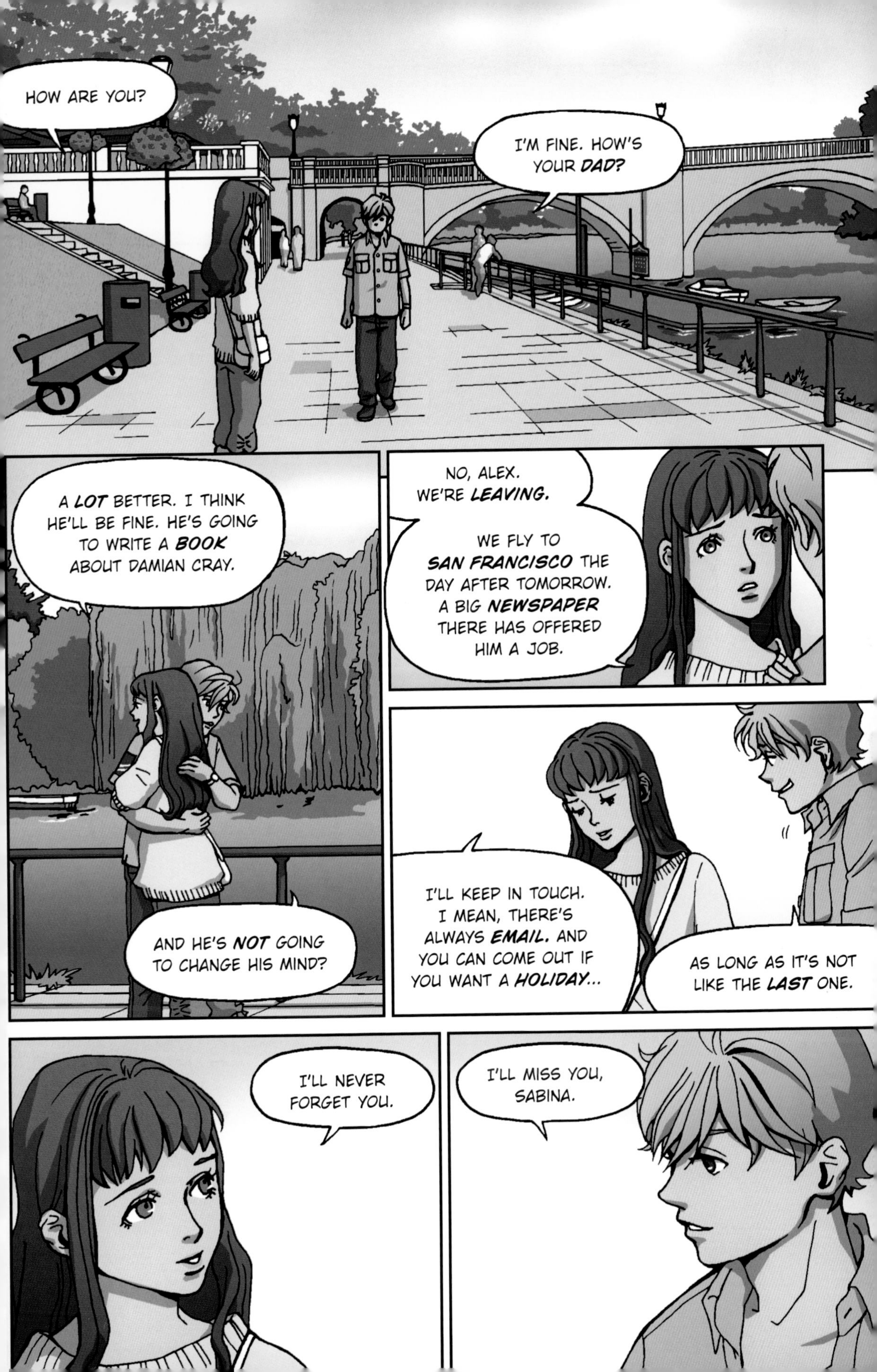
HOW ARE YOU?
I'M FINE. HOW'S YOUR **DAD?**
A **LOT** BETTER. I THINK HE'LL BE FINE. HE'S GOING TO WRITE A **BOOK** ABOUT DAMIAN CRAY.
NO, ALEX. WE'RE **LEAVING.**
WE FLY TO **SAN FRANCISCO** THE DAY AFTER TOMORROW. A BIG **NEWSPAPER** THERE HAS OFFERED HIM A JOB.
AND HE'S **NOT** GOING TO CHANGE HIS MIND?
I'LL KEEP IN TOUCH. I MEAN, THERE'S ALWAYS **EMAIL.** AND YOU CAN COME OUT IF YOU WANT A **HOLIDAY...**
AS LONG AS IT'S NOT LIKE THE **LAST** ONE.
I'LL NEVER FORGET YOU.
I'LL MISS YOU, SABINA.

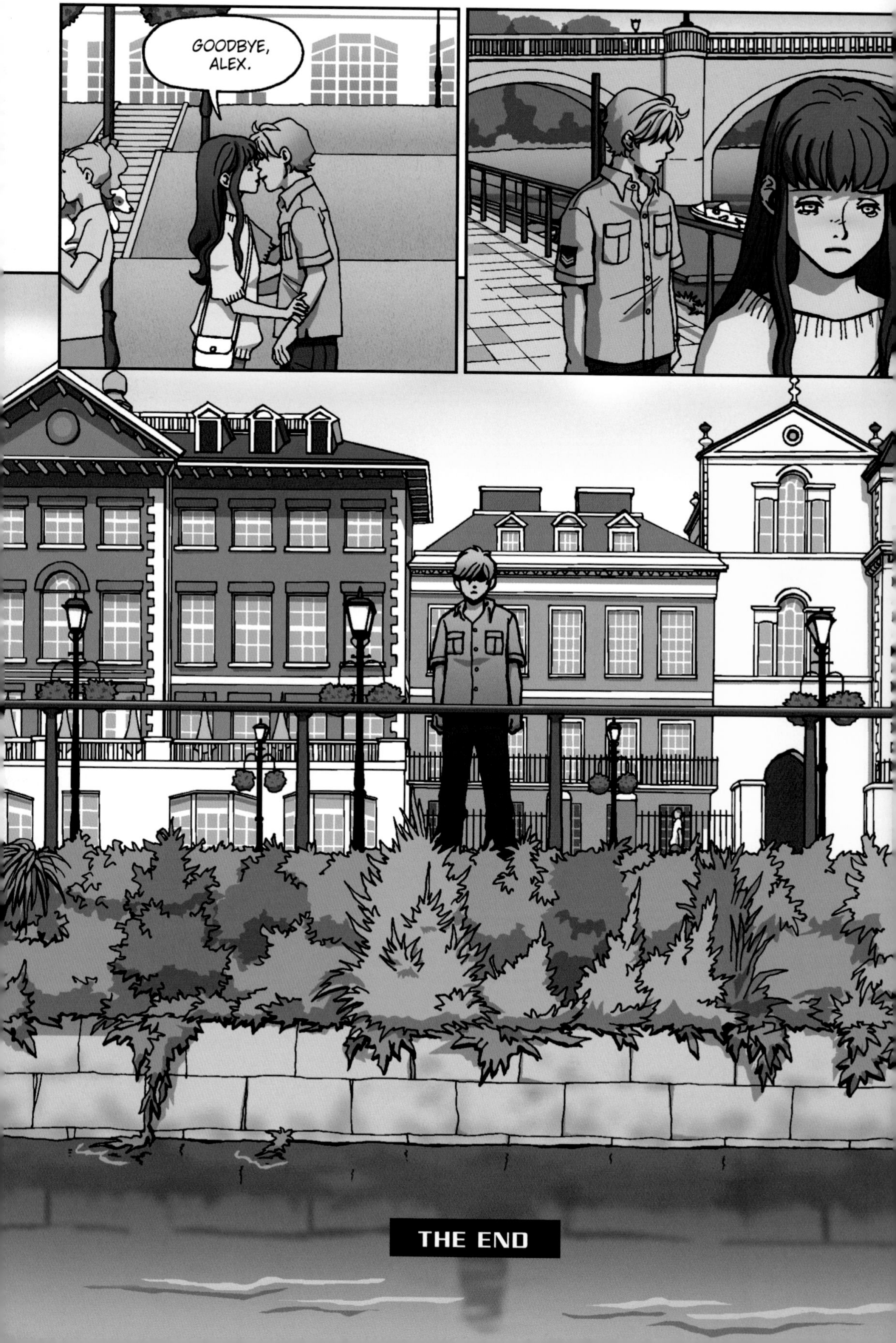
GOODBYE, ALEX.
THE END

ANTHONY HOROWITZ (BA/Nielsen Author of the Year) is one of the most popular children's writers working today. His hugely successful Alex Rider series has sold over ten million copies worldwide and won numerous awards, including the Children's Book of the Year Award for ARK ANGEL at the British Book Awards and the Red House Children's Book Award for SKELETON KEY. He scripted the blockbuster movie STORMBREAKER from his own novel, and also writes extensively for TV, with programmes including MIDSOMER MURDERS, COLLISION, INJUSTICE and FOYLE'S WAR. Anthony Horowitz is the author of THE HOUSE OF SILK: THE NEW SHERLOCK HOLMES NOVEL. He is married to television producer Jill Green and lives in Clerkenwell with his two sons, Nicholas and Cassian, and the ghost of their dog, Lucky.

www.anthonyhorowitz.com

ANTONY JOHNSTON, who wrote the script for this book, is a veteran author of comics and graphic novels, from superheroes such as DAREDEVIL and WOLVERINE, to science-fiction adventures like WASTELAND and DEAD SPACE, and even thrillers such as THE COLDEST CITY and JULIUS. He also writes videogames, including many of the DEAD SPACE series, and other games like BINARY DOMAIN and XCOM. His debut fiction novel FRIGHTENING CURVES won an IPPY award for Best Horror. Antony lives in North-West England with his partner Marcia, his dogs Connor and Rosie, and far too many gadgets with apples printed on them.

www.antonyjohnston.com

The artwork in this graphic novel is the work of two artists, **KANAKO DAMERUM** and **YUZURU TAKASAKI**, who collaborate on every illustration. Although living on opposite sides of the globe, these Japanese sisters work seamlessly together via the Internet.

Living and working in Tokyo, **YUZURU** produced all the line work for these illustrations using traditional means. The quality of her draughtsmanship comes from years of honing her skills in the highly competitive world of manga.

KANAKO lives and works out of her studio in London. She managed and directed the project as well as colouring and rendering the artwork digitally using her wealth of knowledge in graphic design.

www.manga-media.com
www.thorogood.net

Collect all the Alex Rider books

ALEX RIDER MISSION 1 : STORMBREAKER
ANTHONY HOROWITZ

ALEX RIDER MISSION 2 : POINT BLANC
ANTHONY HOROWITZ

ALEX RIDER MISSION 3 : SKELETON KEY
ANTHONY HOROWITZ

ALEX RIDER MISSION 4 : EAGLE STRIKE
ANTHONY HOROWITZ

ALEX RIDER MISSION 5 : SCORPIA
ANTHONY HOROWITZ

ALEX RIDER MISSION 6 : ARK ANGEL
ANTHONY HOROWITZ

ALEX RIDER MISSION 7 : SNAKEHEAD
ANTHONY HOROWITZ

ALEX RIDER MISSION 8 : CROCODILE TEARS
ANTHONY HOROWITZ

ALEX RIDER MISSION 9 : SCORPIA RISING
ANTHONY HOROWITZ

and the graphic novels

ALEX RIDER
ANTHONY HOROWITZ
ANTONY JOHNSTON
KANAKO AND YUZURU
THE GRAPHIC NOVEL
STORMBREAKER

ALEX RIDER
ANTHONY HOROWITZ
ANTONY JOHNSTON
KANAKO AND YUZURU
THE GRAPHIC NOVEL
POINT BLANC

ALEX RIDER
ANTHONY HOROWITZ
ANTONY JOHNSTON
KANAKO AND YUZURU
THE GRAPHIC NOVEL
SKELETON KEY

alexrider.com